Between Life and Death

Sabine Berking
Magdalena Zolkos
(eds.)

Between Life and Death

Governing Populations in the Era of Human Rights

PETER LANG
Frankfurt am Main · Berlin · Bern · Bruxelles · New York · Oxford · Wien

Bibliographic Information published by the Deutsche Nationalbibliothek
The Deutsche Nationalbibliothek lists this publication in the Deutsche Nationalbibliografie; detailed bibliographic data is available in the internet at <http://www.d-nb.de>.

Layout:
www.kumpernatz-bromann.de

ISBN 978-3-631-58733-9

Printed in Germany 1 2 3 4 5 7

www.peterlang.de

Table of Contents

Acknowledgments

This collection originated in the Sixth Berlin Roundtable on Transnationality titled "Population Politics and Human Rights", which took place from 14-20 February 2007 in Berlin and was organized by the Irmgard Coninx Foundation in cooperation with the Social Science Research Center Berlin (WZB) and Humboldt University.

The editors would like to acknowledge the assistance and support of Prof. Dr. Susanne Baer, Prof. Michael Bommes, Dr. Leopold von Carlowitz, Prof. Dr. Ingo Richter, Ms. Sabine Richter-Ellermann, and Prof. Chiara Saraceno, as well as Paul Knowlton, who translated chapters 1 and 7 from the German original. The assistance of Dr. Benjamin Kloss, editor at Peter Lang, and Lora Anne Viola and Jan Henrik von Dallwitz as proof readers, is also gratefully acknowledged.

Some of the contributions first appeared in the following sources, from which permission to reprint is gratefully acknowledged.

Mookherjee, Nayanika. "Available Motherhood: Legal Technologies, 'State of Exception' and the Dekinning of 'War-babies' in Bangladesh", appeared in 2007 under the same title in *Childhood: a Journal of Global Child Research* 14 (3), August, Special issue: The State and Children's Fate: Reproduction in Traumatic Times, pp. 339-354.

Caroline Bledsoe's chapter is a revised version of Bledsoe, Caroline H. 2004. "Reproduction at the Margins: Reproduction, Migration and Legitimacy in the New Europe." In Gunnar Andersson and Gerda Neyer, eds. *Demographic Research, Special Collection* 3, pp. 87-116. Available at: www.demographic-research.org.

The chapter written by Shalini Randeria is a translation from the German original that first appeared as: "Bevölkerungspolitik, Gender und Kultur aus ethnologischer Perspektive", in *Historische Anthropologie*, 1/2006, Cologne: Böhlau Verlag, pp. 30-48.

Introduction

–

Human Rights, Human Populations, and the Controversies of Natality

Sabine Berking and Magdalena Zolkos

Population Governance and Human Rights

How does the focus on human rights change the study of population governance? What, if any, new insights, perspectives and challenges do human rights bring to population studies and the politics of population governance? Is the protection of and respect for human rights in conflict with policies that manage and control the organization of populations, or is there a possibility for their compatibility, or even reciprocal facilitation? These questions are the point of departure for this volume, which brings into conversation contributions from different academic disciplines on the topic of human rights and their relevance for population governance. This volume builds upon the assumption that thinking in terms of human rights necessitates a critical re-consideration and re-evaluation of any politics that equates "population" with the efficient management of statistics. As such, the contributions to this volume might be classified as representative of the anthropocentric approach to population governance. While this labeling might be justified due to its overall human rights focus, it does not mean that the contributions to this volume are unsympathetic to, or unfamiliar with, the so-called eco-centric or bio-centric perspectives on population growth and management.

From the human rights perspective, "population" instead needs to be seen as an aggregation of individual persons who have certain needs and entitlements. Here, the notion of "individual" does not have the classical liberal implication of persons being fundamentally "separate" from their communities. Rather, it is based on recognition of the social relationality of people. Furthermore, the significant impact of human rights discourse on population politics is already evident in the vocabulary of "governing populations", which cannot be equated with top-down management and control. Rather, population governance needs to account for, and facilitate, the exercise of its targets' agency and subjectivity. In doing so, the discourse of human rights complicates the goals of population governance by "trumping" the considerations of effectiveness and utility with a set of principles based on the dignity and integrity of a person. Human rights thus have the potential to shed a critical light onto the existing modalities of contemporary population governance and to initiate better social practices (cf. Cook et al. 2003).

For definitional clarity, this volume understands human rights in accordance with their existing conceptualization in international law, namely as a set of entitlements and freedoms that ensure dignified life of every person (see e.g. the *Universal Declaration of Human Rights,* articles 1 and 2). In turn, "population politics" is an umbrella term that links demographic dynamics with the idea of governance and includes such diverse issues as family planning, reproductive health, contraception, population control, and migration. A major challenge in the juxtaposition of population politics and human rights is of a practical-methodological nature. While human rights constitute a complex international discourse that has developed diverse institutional, juridical and political components, until very recently population politics have remained almost entirely within the domain of state competences (with the exception of those violent practices such as purges, forced migration or war-time rape, which have been prohibited by international law and which, as in the case of the Balkan wars, have only very recently been brought to the attention of international criminal and human rights courts).

It is important to recognize the emerging international consensus, and a sense of urgency, in the area of governing the world's population. In 1994, the International Conference on Population and Development in Cairo (hereafter ICPD) for the first time made a link between global population politics, sustainable development and human rights. Its 20-year *Programme of Action* became one of the key documents of the United Nations Population Fund. The *Programme of Action* pays particular attention to issues of gender equality, empowerment of women and elimination of violence against women, protection of indigenous people, children and the elderly, reproductive health and education, reduction of mortality in infants, children and mothers, to problems linked to the accelerated urbanization ,and migratory movements. One result of the ICPD and its *Programme of Action* has been the so-called "Cairo consensus", an agreement among the participating states that the steps suggested by the *Programme of Action* need to be actively pursued. It builds on the international cooperation and awareness developed in connection with two earlier conferences on world population, in Bucharest in 1974 and in Mexico City in 1984. It is also important to acknowledge mixed opinions about the "Cairo consensus." For some, it signifies an undeniable achievement in bringing together reproductive and sexual health services with the post-Cold War discourse on women and human rights (Cohen and Richards 1994). For others, however, its pursuit of a common platform for actors that have not only different but often antagonistic interests and identities turned the "Cairo consensus" into a "Cairo compromise", and allowed the strengthening of neo-liberal economic influence on global population politics, resulting in numerous "drawbacks and contradictions" of the *Programme of Action* (Hartmann 1995). Following up on the 1994 conference in Cairo were (a) the ICPD +5 (a special session held by the United Nations General Assembly in 1999 on the achievements of and challenges to the ICPD with a particular focus on reproductive health and education) and (b) the ICPD at 10, which resulted in detailed country-based analyses of the national implementation of the *Programme of Action* agenda. Despite the often justified critiques, the "Cairo consensus" greatly influenced the contents of the Millennium Development Goals formulated at the UN Millennium Summit in 2000.

This volume acknowledges that in practice the relationship between population politics and human rights is often complex, ambiguous and multi-leveled. It includes concerns about the way in which attempts to control national and global demographics can interfere with the rights of individuals, such as the rights to life, health, and the dignity of the human person; the rights of women and children; the freedom from gender discrimination; the freedom of movement; the right to reproductive freedom and to bodily self-determination. At the same time, it also includes concerns about the attempts to instrumentalize and de-contextualize human rights in order to pursue policies of population control guided by a patriarchic or colonial mentality, or motivated by racist and/or sexist intent.

The claim that the juxtaposition of human rights and population politics problematizes the focus of the latter on "numbers and statistics", and instead brings into population governance considerations of individual entitlements and human subjectivity, could be considered a problematic move. This is because, as Curtis (2005, p. 510) reminds us, the conceptual architecture of the notion of "population" points to a "statistical artifact." As he further argues, this means that "population is connected to the law of large numbers, which causes individual variation to disappear in favor of regularity" (2005, p. 510). In other words, there is a potential conflict between the political-statistical matrix of the population discourse and the legal-ethical concept of human rights, which could make this volume's juxtaposition of populations and individuals paradoxical and non-operative. However, rather than think of the discursive categories of "populations" and "individuals" as incompatible, this volume assumes that there is a productive tension between the population and individual rights discourses, and the contributions of this volume point to and attempt to bridge this chasm in a variety of ways.

The complexity and diversity of situations addressed by the texts in this volume demonstrate both the possibilities and limitations of human rights as a heuristic and critical instrument. They also make clear that, normatively, it is not possible to find *one universal solution* that would embody a perfect union of population governance and individual rights. Rather, a focus on human rights makes us alert to the complexity, changeability and unpredictability of social life, and, with it, the necessity for flexibility in legal and political policies. In the context of population governance, the importance of the human rights perspective is that it provides a language to name the vulnerability of people vis-à-vis population laws and societal regulations, which, even if they are formally egalitarian, often produce results that deepen the privation and dependence of those who have *already* been economically underprivileged and/or socially marginalized. It is therefore important to understand the insights of human rights for population governance not (or at least not primarily) through the liberal notions of formal equality and universality of the human condition, but in terms of the *particularities* of human vulnerability in regard to the categories of race, ethnicity, gender, age, class, sexual orientation, and so on.

Governing Populations / Producing Desirable Citizens

In addition to the emphasis on the international dimensions of the human rights/population governance nexus, one needs to recognize its national importance or, more specifically, the historical interconnections between the idea of the population and the state- and nation-building projects. In his 1977-1978 lectures on security, territory and population, Michel Foucault (2007) sketches a conceptual history of "population", its political-cultural use, and its centrality for the modern state project. For Foucault (2007, pp.72 and 79), it is crucial to understand population in terms of "the axis of sovereign and subject, […] the correlate of power and the object of knowledge." Accordingly, the concept of population emerges in close temporal proximity to the idea of governmentality, a systemic organization of national/state subjects, or governing for the purpose of improving "the condition of the population, to increase its wealth, its longevity, and its health" (Foucault 2007, p. 105).

Many of the contributions to this volume suggest, sometimes implicitly, that both the notions "population" and "governance" have potentially misleading connotations. This is, first, because the concept of a "population" has an unspecified and generalized, possibly even euphemistic, quality as if its perspective was offering a holistic and indiscriminate view on society without making any intra-societal distinctions (Bandarage 1997). It is thus viewed as "a set of processes to be managed at the level and on the basis of what [appears to be] natural in these processes, […] a set of elements in which we can note constants and regularities even in accidents, in which we can identify the universal of desire regularly producing the benefit of all, and with regard to which we can identify a number of modifiable variables on which it depends" (Foucault 2007, pp.72 and 76). The point is, however, that in social, political and cultural practices of governance, "population" is not a value-neutral term. In fact, the contributions to this volume demonstrate that the framework of population governance operates with the categories of "desirable" and "less desirable" (or "undesirable") people. Elaine Scarry (1988) has famously argued that population discourse (or what she metaphorically termed the modern project of "body count") spills into historical narratives of the nation and into symbolic-cultural productions of national literature. An example here is the practice of social sex selection in such countries as India or China where male offspring are often preferred for cultural and economic reasons. The "undesirability" of female offspring leads not only to the use of different pre-implantation methods, but it can also result in sex selective abortion, abandonment of female babies, and infanticide. From a larger societal perspective, it has further deleterious consequences related to gender imbalance. This example does not mean, however, that the distinction between the desirable and undesirable populations pertains only to "exceptional" situations and/or is restricted to the contexts of developing countries. The discourses of desirability and undesirability can also be identified in, for example, political debates in some European countries on managing the birth rates of their ethnic minorities or immigrant populations. In 2003 the Center for Reproductive Rights documented the discrimination and forced sterilization of Slovak Roma women. In Germany a new parental allowance favors younger academics and professionals with relatively high incomes over poor families who often have an immigrant background (see Bothfeld 2006). Another example are the regulations introduced in Europe, Canada, the USA and Australia, which aim to attract a *particular type* of immigrant group according to their education, profession, country of origin or age.

Related to the claim that the notion of "population" implies the desirability of some and undesirability of others, is the observation that the notion of "governance" also exceeds its conventional meaning of management, control or supervision of people whose existence (allegedly) precedes implementation of the governing rules. Rather, in accordance with the foucauldian governmentality approach to population studies, to "govern" a population is an act of exercising authority that is creative and formative, and which *brings the (national) people into being* or *produces (desirable) citizens* (Ransom 1997). The importance of drawing a conceptual link between "governance" and "creation" reflects the rapid change in population patterns in the late 20th and the early 21st centuries, and thus the recognition that populations are capable of being radically transformed by policy interventions, supported by recent medical and technological innovations (Petersen 2003; Tobin 2004). The suggestion that the governance of populations invokes the creation of (desirable) people is probably nowhere more visible than in anti-abortion rhetoric, which identifies the life of the fetus with its national, ethnic and racial belongings, and consequently constructs the decision of fetal removal as subversive for the functioning of the national collective body to which the woman and the fetus belong.

Another example of the nexus between population governance and the project of creating desirable citizens for a nation is the issue of indigenous populations in the settlement history of the Americas and Oceania. Patterns of autochthonous reproduction, fertility and territorial placement became a central "problem" to be managed in the history of colonization, and led to such atrocious experiments as the separation of children of the Aboriginal Australian or the Torres Strait Islander descent from their families (the so-called "Stolen Generation"), or the Canadian residential school system with its violent methods of assimilation.

Biopolitics and Natality

Population governance concerns a particular area of human existence, namely that of *natality,* or the event of "birth." As such, it brings into the heart of public debates and decision-making processes issues that originate in a private, even intimate, sphere of life that relates to family, fertility and sexuality. This paradoxical placement of population politics at the core of both public discourses of governmentality and private discourses of the human body situates this volume's themes vis-à-vis Michel Foucault's observations on biopolitics. In *History of Sexuality, Volume 1* (1990, p. 140), Foucault suggests that modernity witnessed the development of technologies of power for the purpose of "subjugations of bodies and the control of populations." This means that the modern state has not only developed a systemic interest in classifying, regulating and disciplining biological aspects of human life, but also that it derives its power and reconfirms its sovereignty through biopolitics. The importance of the foucauldian perspective for this volume is that population governance as an expression of biopower does not necessarily have negative connotations, i.e. does not imply the repression of those who are its subjects. Rather, it describes a certain mode of human existence that becomes subject to "organized practices (mentalities, rationalities, and techniques)", in regard to questions of family, fertility and sexuality (Mayhew 2004).

The use of the notions of biopolitics and governmentality in population studies further elucidates this approach. For instance, Greenhalgh (2005) emphasizes that the usefulness of the notion of governmentality in the study of populations is that it opens up a more complex understanding of power than the conventional system of state-society regulations. Governmentality, therefore, includes the "disciplinary conduct by nonstate social institutions", as well as "the cultivation by individuals themselves of the capacity to regulate their own behavior" (Greenhalgh 2005, p. 4). Similarly, Curtis (2002, p. 506) has argued that for Foucault, the biopolitics of population is "the pivot [..] which turned the transition from rule based on sovereign authority to a 'governmentalized' rule which decenters the state under liberalism." The point here is not to suggest that all contributions to this volume follow critical and/or foucauldian approaches in examining the relationship between "governing populations" and "human rights." However, all of them recognize the contemporary complexity (factual, conceptual, methodological) of, and the tensions involved in, studying population politics. They therefore agree that one needs to go beyond the analysis of state-society regulatory relationships to understand the intricacy of the juxtaposition of the two modes of human existence that are central to this volume: on the one hand, population and statistical-political life and, on the other, subjective life defined through principles of rights and dignity. Consequently, the contributions to this volume not only explore the dynamics and effects of biopower (the collective administration, control of and intervention into biological and subjective life), but also ask questions about the individual accommodation of that biopower through complex processes of meaning-making, creative and flexible adaptation, and, at least potentially, practices of critique and resistance. This latter point suggests, of course, that the disciplinary and regulatory workings of population discourses are not modes of *determination*, but that they simultaneously structure and facilitate human agency and meaning-making.

Natality, Fertility and Hope

In 2006 Mexican director Alfonso Cuarón made a futuristic movie *Children of Men* about a world in which there are no children. One of the challenges of the film is precisely that it re-contextualizes for its viewers questions of natality and fertility. It problematizes the conceptualization of "birth" in the dominant modern population discourse by which the occurrence of birth is entirely predictable and taken for granted, and as such functions as a problem of effective management and organization at least potentially under human control. In other words, in the modern discourse on population governmentality the occurrence of "birth" appears to be a manageable, measurable and predictable event. In *Children of Men*, however, the concept of "birth" is stripped of that modernist certainty and exists only as a non-occurrence; as an absent object of the global desire for the preservation, renewal and continuity of life.

The film depicts a world in the not too distant future, which is surprisingly like our own. We can recognize in it elements that constitute our current socio-political reality (like the securitization of immigration, quasi-democratic technocracy, ecological devastation or refugee camps), only in a somewhat advanced, or intensified, form. The result is ambiguity of reception: the dystoptian image of the world in 2027 as being, at the same time, recognized as the *same* and the *other*. The only element of that world which marks its radical difference to our own is its global condition of infertility. In the movie, infertility not only becomes the driving-force behind the individual plot of Theo and Kee's adventure, but is emblematic of the all-pervasive hopelessness of that futuristic reality. The synopsis of the movie encapsulates that reality in a simple chain of equivalence: "No children. No future. No hope", which not only suggests that the factual preservation of humanity depends entirely on the occurrence of "birth", but also that it is not possible to think of "hope" and "future" in separation from the idea of natality. In his commentary on *Children of Men*, the philosopher Slavoj Žižek suggests on the website of the movie that the meaning of the condition of infertility in the late-modern world interplays with its predicament of a "lack of meaningful historical experience." Thus, in Cuarón's movie infertility is not primarily a "biological problem", but an epitome of the Nietschean Last Man, a dark and ironic realization of Fukuyama's notion of the end of history.

The question is, of course, whether one could try to take the point of departure in Cuarón's provocative image to reverse its logic of negation and suggest the imbrication of the event of "birth" (natality), the possibility of a population politics that centers upon the recognition of human dignity and individual subjectivity, and a hopeful future. In this context, it is important to mention the name of Hannah Arendt, who in her book *The Human Condition* (1998 [1958]) theorized the nexus between (a) natality as making a new and radically different intervention into the world; (b) the dignity of the human condition; and (c) the secular notion of hope as the *possibility* of a meaningful change and formation of the world (see also Birmingham 2006). Her words are thus epigraphic for this volume's acknowledgement of the urgency of the issues of population governance and the significance of human rights:

> The miracle that saves the world, the realm of human affairs, from its normal, "natural" ruin is ultimately the fact of natality, in which the faculty of action is ontologically rooted. It is [...] the birth of new men and the new beginning, the action they are capable of by the virtue of being born (Arendt 1998 [1958], p. 247).

Thematic Division and Overview of the Contributions

This volume is divided into four major sections, (1) global perspectives; (2) paradoxes of social engineering; (3) reproductive politics as religious and national icons; and (4) population politics and minorities.

The first section offers introductory and comprehensive presentations of the complexity involved in bringing together population governance and human rights. Shalini Randeria's contribution introduces the problematic of population control and human rights with a particular emphasis on the issues of gender, culture and ethnological research. It is a critical confrontation of the low fertility population discourse in the North with the overpopulation discourse in the South. She outlines the paradigmatic difference between the approach to population control developed by Thomas Robert Malthus and the approach developed by the Marquis de Condorcet. Her particular focus is on the Indian state of Kerala, which, according to 1999 data, had one of the lowest total fertility rates in the country. Randeria's contribution offers a detailed ethnographic and comparative investigation of the Indian case, especially in relation to the African population problematique.

Maja K. Eriksson's contribution introduces the international legal perspective on reproductive rights and freedoms. It gives a detailed overview of relevant conceptual and legal issues, documents, institutionalizations and international events. In particular, it focuses on the legality of abortion and the availability of health services for women, as well as the controversial practice of medical personnel declaring "conscientious objection" in the provision of abortion services to women. Finally, it also provides information about the existing reproductive case law at global, regional and national levels.

In her contribution Susan Greenhalgh argues that the notion of population should be considered in relation to the manifestations and complexities of modern power. The discourse on population, she shows, has its own distinctive rules, imaginaries, vocabularies, institutionalizations and social effects. This contribution is based on an ethnographic study of "birth planning" in China. Greenhalgh traces China's distinctive approach to population control to its Marxist, Leninist and Maoist influences, and shows how its historical, political and bureaucratic development is closely connected to the development of the modern Chinese state. She argues that the implementation of policies that control and create a particular and desirable population has coincided with new dynamics of social and political exclusion. This is because one of its effects has been the emergence of people that are "unwanted", "unplanned" and peripheral to Chinese society because of, inter alia, their lack of citizenship rights.

In her contribution, Caroline Bledsoe asks how immigrants' (perceptions of) security are threatened by changes to their reproductive life trajectories caused by their displacement. On the basis of recent sources from demography, anthropology, and the media this text suggests that while demographers tend to see immigrant fertility as a potential source of support for Europe's subfertile, aging populations, for immigrant families the most pressing fertility question is not numbers of children. Rather, it is the legitimacy that children may confer on family efforts to gain work, social security, and rights to settle. This is an important contribution both for classical anthropology and contemporary human rights debates. This text points out the increasing demands placed on immigrants to orient reproduction, like everything else in their lives, to securing legitimacy in the host country. It concludes that, first, the fertility issues in Europe need to be linked to the discussion of European immigration, and that, second, the levels of fertility among immigrants are unlikely to assimilate to the national norms until their status becomes more secure.

The second section, on paradoxes of social engineering, focuses on situations and cases that capture the element of perplexity, ambiguity and unpredictability in how population politics and human rights function in practice. Khadija R. Turay's chapter probes human rights and population politics in India by focusing in particular on the period of the State of Emergency from 1975 until 1977, when the National Population Policy was implemented. Turay argues that it was the end of the Emergency that signalled an ideological transition which informs the population and public health politics of contemporary India. This contribution offers a detailed historical analysis of the context of the emergence and implementation of the National Population Policy. Drawing on human rights and women's rights perspectives, this text critiques the sterilization campaign and its accompanying violence. It concludes that political intervention in family planning can be reconciled with human rights only when political will creates a climate that includes multidisciplinary public policies, as well as programs that promote informed reproductive decision making that is free from unjust coercion.

Lisa Ann Richey's text examines the HIV/Aids pandemic and global health interventions in Africa. In particular, it focuses on the post-Cairo population policies and their integration of the objective to promote women's reproductive health. Drawing upon fieldwork in Tanzania and Uganda, Richey examines some of the challenges that remain at the interface between population policy and HIV/AIDS prevention in Africa. She thus offers a critique of the paradigm shift away from population control and toward promoting reproductive health, in particular as regards the dominant discourses of African "exceptionalism." While the reproductive health agenda seems to be caught between family planning programs that are based on population-control ideologies and the depth of the challenge of the HIV/AIDS pandemic, human rights should provide the foundation for a new generation of integrated policies that promote healthy sexuality, informed and consensual reproductive choices, and the development of the individual and her or his society.

Rachel Sullivan Robinson argues that in the geo-political space of Sub-Saharan Africa there has been a positive correlation between population policies aimed at reducing population growth, and the protection of human rights. Focusing in particular on Nigeria, the author argues that the implementation of population policies in Sub-Saharan Africa has been relatively free of the human rights tensions and violations witnessed for instance in China and India. Instead, in Sub-Saharan Africa the population policies have been harmonized with, as well as generally supportive of, human rights on four distinctive grounds: (i) increased opportunity to address unequal gender rights; (ii) increased potential to solve poverty-related problems; (iii) increased capacity to carry out reproductive decisions; and, finally, (iv) improved survival rates of women and children.

Steffen Kröhnert and Reiner Klingholz analyse recent changes in family policies in Germany in a comparative (Western) European perspective. This study is based on a quantitative analysis of different fertility rates and the various underlying social conditions that affect these rates. The main argument proposed by Kröhnert and Klingholz is that the traditionally negative correlation between wealth and social development on the one hand and fertility on the other no longer holds once a society has reached a certain level of development. The data indicates that today more children are born in the countries with the most advanced social systems in regard to gender equality. This chapter concludes that the problem of low-fertility in selected Western European countries cannot be solved simply by means of (increased) child benefits or other sources of financial aid. Rather, in these countries increased fertility correlates strongly with the societal level of equality among men and women and their opportunities to participate in the labor market.

Julie Y. Chu in her contribution on identification papers and burial rights in the capital of the Fujian province, Fuzhou, offers an examination of the pursuit of U.S. Green Cards among the city's older population. She argues that rather than being valued as an entitlement to working mobility and residence, for the elders in Fuzhou the Green Card has meant a possibility to avoid a new local policy of mandatory cremation. This contribution highlights the challenges raised by the Fuzhounese case over ID's claims on bodies in relation to questions of personhood and entitlement, economy and value, and the biopolitics of family, population and social reproduction. It suggests how the pursuit of immigration papers can reframe the very terms of "persons" and their "rights" beyond the conventional domains of nation, market and life itself. In turn, it raises questions about the limits of the "human" in human rights discourses and claims.

The third section, on reproductive rights as icons of national and religious politics, focuses on the problems of reproductive health, education, and freedom vis-à-vis the prerogatives of collective nation-building projects. Homa Hoodfar's contribution focuses on population politics in the Islamic Republic of Iran. Drawing upon anthropological fieldwork in Iran, she offers an in-depth analysis of the recent history of Iranian family planning programs following the 1979 revolution. This contribution maps the various phases of Iran's family planning project in the contentious context of Islamic family values, anti-Western politics, and societal modernization.

In her contribution Elise Andaya analyzes Cuba's low fertility rate over the last 30 years, which has given rise to the Cuban government's intervention in fertility behavior. The policies designed to respond to the low fertility problem need to be considered vis-à-vis human rights. Drawing on her ethnographic fieldwork, Andaya argues that Cuba's fertility decline reveals the confluence of social, cultural, and structural changes associated with "modernity" and the difficulties of combining work and motherhood in an economically underdeveloped country. She suggests in conclusion that political intervention should not attempt to influence fertility *per se*, bur rather Cubans' sense of familial well-being.

The contribution by Magdalena Zolkos discusses the concepts of (reproductive) human rights in the so-called "pro-life" and "pro-choice" discourses in the Polish abortion debates. These debates testify to the dangerous development of contemporary human rights into a highly politicized, abstract and all-inclusive discourse that gives legitimacy to various (often adversary) political positions, but that consequently forfeits its transformative and critical power. This contribution suggests that reproductive rights need to be positioned within the pursuits of civic politics and radicalized democracy.

Nayanika Mookherjee in her contribution on Bangladesh provides an ethnographic exploration of the "state of exception." Through the perspective of exception legal technologies of abortion and adoption of "war-babies" (children born as a result of war-time rapes) enabled, on the one hand, the "dekinning" and elimination of certain childhoods and, on the other hand, the "rekinning" of raped women within legitimate heterosexual motherhoods. The role of the law in guaranteeing an erasure of blood relations ensured the regulation and availability of women's reproductive capacity and the categorization of the child by the state. Through this process and in the context of bilateral foreign aid, the Bangladeshi family planning program was institutionalized.

The fourth section, on population politics and minorities, brings the perspective of minority rights and the rights of indigenous populations into discussion of populational governance. Steven Rousso-Schindler focuses on the impact of Israeli population politics on the human rights of Palestinians. He argues that demographic preoccupations have been highly important for the Israeli government ever since the establishment of the state of Israel. Israel enacted a number of demographic policies and strategies the goals of which were to minimize the birthrate of Palestinian citizens of Israel while simultaneously raising the birthrates of Jewish-Israelis. In addition, a complicated discriminatory system of child allowances evolved beginning in the 1960s that provided Jewish-Israeli families with economic incentives for having many children, but no such incentives for Palestinian citizens of Israel.

Finally, Ricardo M. Pereira's contribution investigates whether a right to reproductive autonomy can be derived from the right to self-determination under international law. Coercive sterilization programs have been held to be contrary to the objectives of both the 1994 International Conference on Population Development and the 1995 Beijing World Conference on Women Declaration. Pereira argues that the right to internal self-determination, of which the most prominent forms are the right to self-government and autonomy, must also include the indigenous right to reject government policies that force communities to yield to birth control programs.

References

Arendt, Hannah. 1998 [1958]. *The Human Condition.* Chicago : University of Chicago Press.

Bandarage, Asoka. 1997. *Women, Population and Global Crisis. A Political-Economic Analysis*. London: Zed Books.

Birmingham, Peg. 2006. *Hannah Arendt and Human Rights. The Predicament of Common Responsibility*. Bloomington, IN.: Indiana University Press.

Bothfeld, Silke. 2006. "Das Elterngeld – Einige Anmerkungen zum Unbehagen mit der Neuregelung." femina politica, 2.

Center for Reproductive Rights. 2003. *Body and Soul: Forced Sterilization and Other Assaults on Roma Reproductive Freedom in Slovakia*. New York.

Cohen, Susan A. and Cory L. Richards. 1994. "The Cairo Consensus: Population, Development and Women", *Family Planning Perspectives* 26.6, pp. 272-277.

Cook, Rebecca J., Bernard M. Dickens and Mahmoud F. Fathalla. 2003. *Reproductive Health and Human Rights. Integrating Medicine, Ethics, and Law*. Oxford: Oxford University Press.

Curtis, Bruce. 2002. "Foucault on Governmentality and Population: The Impossible Discovery", *Canadian Journal of Sociology* 27.4, pp. 505-533;

Foucault, Michel. 2007. *Security, Territory, Population. Lectures at the Collège de France 1977-1978*. New York: Macmillan Palgrave.

Greenhalgh, Susan and Edwin A. Winckler. 2005. *Governing China's Population: From Leninist to Neoliberal Biopolitics*. Stanford, Calif.: Stanford University Press.

Hartman, Betsy. 1995. *Reproductive Rights and Wrongs: The Global Politics of Population Control and Contraceptive Choice*. New York: Harper and Row.

Mayhew, Susan. 2004. "Governmentality", in Susan Mayhew, ed. *A Dictionary of Geography*. Oxford: OUP.

Peterson, William. 2003. *From Persons to People: Further Studies in the Politics of Population*. New Brunswick, N.J.: Transaction Publishers.

Ransom, John. 1997. *Foucault's Discipline: Politics of Subjectivity*. Durham: Duke University Press..

Scarry, Elaine. 1988. "Introduction", in Elaine Scarry, ed. *Literature and the Body. Essays on Populations and Persons*. Baltimore: the John Hopkins University Press, pp. vii-xxvii.

Tobin, Kathleen. 2004. *Politics and Population Control: A Documentary History*. Westport, Conn.: Greenwood Press.

Universal Declaration of Human Rights. http://www.un.org/Overview/rights.html [accessed on March 14, 2008].

Žižek, Slavoj. "Commentary on *Children of Men*." *Children of Men* official website, http://www.childrenofmen.net/ [accessed on March 14, 2008].

[illegible]

Part 1

Global Perspectives

Chapter 1

Malthus versus Condorcet – Population Policy, Gender and Culture from an Ethnological Perspective

Shalini Randeria

In dealing with the issue of population policy I often have a sense of living in a schizophrenic world. Whereas in Europe public discussion is dominated by concern over declining fertility, in India it is precisely high fertility that is viewed as one of the most important problems facing the country. In view of our global village's simultaneous adherence to two contradictory sets of ideas and objectives on population policy, Hans Magnus Enzensberger has aptly spoken of "demographic bulimia" (Enzensberger 1993). While both experts and the general public believe that the boat is full, they are at the same time convinced that there are too few Germans or Europeans. While I was attending school in New Delhi in the 1970s, the Indian government propagated, on huge billboards, the message: "A small family is a happy family" or "Wait before you have your first child, delay the second birth, prevent the third." To my surprise, ten years later, while I was working on my Ph.D. in Heidelberg, the government of the German state of Baden-Württemberg announced, on billboards just as large, "Children bring more joy into your life." And when in 1986 I took up my first job at the Free University of Berlin, I spotted a number of state-government-sponsored billboards reading, "Children are more grateful than any boss" and "Children make you happier than money"-messages with which I was very well acquainted from my field research in Indian villages.

Konrad Adenauer, Germany's first post-war chancellor, was right when he said that people will always have children, though he could not yet know that it would soon prove difficult for the governments of industrialized countries to ensure that these children also have the right nationality. By 1992 Countess Dönhoff, Edzard Reuter, Helmut Schmidt, Wolfgang Thierse, et al. published a manifesto containing a chapter entitled "Saving the Germans from Extinction", which warned that migration could lead to a "depacification of community life, including an at least partial marginalization of the German population in individual schools, urban districts, or rural areas" if nothing were done to induce "the population to raise, within the foreseeable future, its fertility to a rate once again in excess of the replacement level"(Dönhoff et al. 1992, p. 27). When the world is perceived at the same time as both "overpopulated" and "underpopulated", depending on what country and what ethnic groups or classes figure as the focus of concern, it is invariably the "others" that are too many.[1]

While the Indian government once paid premiums for sterilization, and in some Indian states couples with more than two children are not eligible to run for local political office, Germany in contrast has sought to stimulate the population's interest in having children by threatening to raise taxes for childless couples or by offering what is known as a "welcome allowance" for newborn children. While a new anti-pregnancy serum is being tested in India (Richter 1994), and some Indian states are conditioning new school construction and the funding of government rural development programs on the rate of contraceptive use, German health insurance providers are willing to pay for up to three attempts at artificial insemination. Examples like these are good illustrations of the opposing population-policy strategies targeted to different segments of the population in our "One World" – a world in which four out of five people are born in the South, but four fifths of total world resources are consumed in the North.

How is it possible, under the condition of inequality between and within nations, to import, through the modern means of contraception, the ideal of the two-child family to the countries of the South? How much coercion should the state be allowed to use in the name of the common good; and can we already speak of coercion when the state offers monetary incentives for birth control, or only when actual physical force is brought to bear? How do sociostructural framework conditions and cultural contexts influence population growth? As early as 1741 a German clergyman, Johan Peter Süssmilch, calculated the Earth's carrying capacity to be seven billion people. He based his calculations on two factors known to him: the development potential of agriculture and the rations issued to Brandenburg soldiers (Weber 1988). Since then, though, the discussion on population has been defined not by Süssmilch's optimistic calculations but by the darker forecasts made by Thomas Malthus.

The first edition of Malthus' "Essay on the Principle of Population", was published anonymously in 1798. It was directed explicitly against Condorcet's optimistic treatise, which had appeared in English translation in the same year. Malthus borrowed from Condorcet the thesis of a growing disequilibrium be-

---

1 That holds as well for the propaganda of leading Hindu nationalist politicians. They have repeatedly called on India's Hindus to counteract the official government population-policy targets by having at least three children per family in order not to lose the demographic race with the countries Muslim population. Otherwise, they claim, India will soon be faced with the risk of Hindus becoming a minority in their own country. For a highly differentiated, state-level analysis of the somewhat higher fertility rate of Muslims compared with Hindus in India, see Jeffery et al. (1997). According to the authors, these disparities are due more to economic and political interests of the religious groups and the positions they hold in the local context than to religious affiliation or disparities in the status of women and in gender relations.

tween population growth and food supply. In 1795 Condorcet had pointed out, for the first time, that an "increase of the number of men surpassing their means of subsistence" must necessarily lead to "a continual diminution of happiness" (Condorcet 1968, p. 123 f.). For Condorcet, however, this was not an alarming conclusion; in his eyes the use of scientific means to boost productivity growth in agriculture was the key to solving the problem. Condorcet also made explicit mention of the possibility that sexuality might be treated separately from reproduction in order to avert the risk of overpopulation. Quite in the spirit of the Enlightenment, Condorcet hoped that ultimately reason would prevail and that targeted and voluntary change in reproductive behavior, in particular through the education of women, would set in motion a transition leading to smaller family sizes. This implied a belief on his part in the effectiveness of public debate and rational decisions at both the individual and the collective level as a means of initiating reform of social institutions.

Malthus, on the other hand, was convinced that population growth could be curbed only by constraint and necessity, such as through later marriage ages, restriction of marriage to persons with property, or on the basis of a "moral restraint" rooted in poverty and economic deprivation (Malthus 1830, p. 243). Convinced of the inevitability of periodic famines and increasing mortality rates due to natural disasters (Malthus 1798, pp. 206, 209), he rejected contraception as unnatural, and was at the same time against any kind of public support for the poor. The latter, he claimed, would do no more than encourage the poor to marry early, bringing even more children into the world (Malthus 1830, p. 243). The only effect of the English Poor Laws, he asserted, was to artificially increase population growth. Malthus' primary concern here was less to reduce fertility than to absolve owners of private property of any social duty to alleviate poverty. In his eyes, without material need the poor would have no incentive to engage in strenuous work. Condorcet, on the other hand, who represented Paris in the new post-Revolution French National Assembly, was of the opinion that governments had the duty to ensure that the people were not "exposed to misery, to humiliation, to oppression", "that all members of society should have an assured subsistence each season, each year, and wherever they live; that those who live on their wages, above all, should be able to buy the subsistence they need" (Rothschild 1996, p. 341).

While Condorcet's insights on the key role played by reason and women's rights in reducing fertility rates and his belief in social policy as a means of alleviating poverty were soon to be forgotten, Malthus' pessimism is still as topical as ever. Both thinkers were among the first to recognize the long-term impact and the social implications of demographic processes, and to address the issue in both political and theoretical terms. It is thanks to their discourses that fertility and population growth have come to be regarded as social problems, not as natural phenomena. It was the dispute between them that created the conditions for governments to make use of specialized knowledge and technical means to intervene in and regulate population development. It is since then that the relations between married couples have been subject to official scrutiny, control, and planning, with sexuality and the desire for children coming to be seen as a matter of national welfare.

One of the objects of this paper is to show that even today this historical controversy continues to mark the boundaries of discourses on an assumed compatibility and complex interrelationship between state population policy and the reproductive rights of individuals. In part one I will discuss the continuing effects of the opposition between constraint and free will and between economic need and social policy in the debates of the 18th century, as reflected in present-day approaches to population policy. In part two I will discuss a number of studies on the regional variance in fertility and the status of women in India with a view to casting a critical light on some of the central assumptions of modernization theory regarding the process of demographic change. Based on ethnological material from Africa, in part three I will discuss the cultural logic guiding reproductive decisions as well as the social context in which contraceptive methods are used. The paper's conclusions suggest the need for a postcolonial approach to the issue, one that places the ongoing transnational interventions in development policy in the context of colonial population policy.

Coercion versus Insight

Neo-Malthusians continue to share the diagnosis of their mentor – large families are at the root of poverty – and they therefore reject approaches to poverty reduction based on social policy. But unlike Malthus, neo-Malthusians reject the notion of divine dispensation, and are instead in favor of state intervention – coercive if need be – in the reproductive sphere as a means of reaching demographic objectives. An example from the US may serve to illustrate this state of affairs. Shortly after Norplant, a hormone implant contraceptive, was approved for use in 1991, a California court ordered a 27-year-old Black woman, a mother of four children who had been charged with child abuse, to use this contraceptive device for a period of at least three years (Spiller 1994). In 1993 the governor of Maryland even went so far as to propose that welfare payments be made conditional on the use of Norplant. It is remarkable to note that even today neoconservatives, otherwise strictly against the use of sterilization and abortion in connection with population programs in developing countries, continue to advocate the use of coercive measures against the poor in their own country. The characteristics of today's neo-Malthusian position include the interpretation of lower fertility trends as successes of direct state intervention in the reproductive sphere, and the continued insistence on a general Malthus-inspired rejection of any and all social policy.

Criticism of the neo-Malthusian position has come from several different quarters. An alliance of critics, stemming for the most part from Catholic, Islamic fundamentalist, and neoconservative circles, has agitated against any state promotion of family planning programs in Asia, Africa, and Latin America. At the same time, though, these critics reject Condorcet's Enlightenment-inspired insight that reproductive decisions are best left to the individuals concerned. A second group opposed to the neo-Malthusian position brings together, surprisingly, neoliberal economists with advocates of a human capital approach. Both groups agree that what is crucial to establishing the small, nuclear family as the norm is not a state-provided supply of contraceptives and compulsion to use them, but a fundamental change in values. In Europe, they point out the demographic transition was not achieved with modern contraceptive methods or through interventionist population policies. Neoliberal economists for this reason recommend that the state withdraw from population policy with a view to redressing the market-distorting effects of government action in this area. Proponents of the human capital approach to population policy, on the other hand, propose that the state should invest in programs such as poverty reduction, health, education, employment for women, and should provide voluntary family planning programs. It is thanks to the efforts of Indian Nobel laureate Amartya Sen, a proponent of this approach, that we can now speak of a new reception of Condorcet's ideas (Sen 1997).

The reception of the neo-Malthusian study by Robey, Rutstein, and Morris on the worldwide decline in fertility may serve as an illustration of the ongoing debates as well as of the persistence of the antinomies that mark the positions held by Malthus and Condorcet (Robey et al. 1993). The authors of the study attribute 90% of the variance in fertility rates of different countries to national differences in the use of modern contraception. An increase of 15% in contraceptive use, they claim, serves to prevent, on average, the birth of one child per woman. If, the authors further assert, the worldwide need for contraceptives were met, the result would be a decline in population growth in developing countries from 2.3% to 1.6%, and this would take no more than an investment of 2 billion euros in contraceptives. As an example, the authors point to Bangladesh, where a massive rise in contraceptive use from 3% to 40% between 1970 and 1990 led to a decline in the total fertility rate from 7 to 5.5 children per woman. This development took place even though poverty and child mortality levels remained high and no change was reported for the social status of women. The authors conclude that neither economic development nor the welfare state provides the conditions needed to contain population growth in the South. Following the logic of this study, preference would have to be given to efforts to increase the publicly available supply of contraceptives as a cheaper and quicker alternative to international development assistance or public social policy.

The international women's health movement has pointed critically to the reductionist concept of humanity implied by one-dimensional and technocratic approaches of this kind. It has also pointed out that scholarly studies of this kind tend to benefit the pharmaceutical industry by neglecting to report the harmful side- and after-effects of many long-term contraceptives (Wichterich 1994; Correa 1994).

The neoliberal camp has also categorically rejected such approaches. To cite an example, in his critique of Robey et al. (1993), World Bank economist Lant Pritchett (Pritchett 1994) furnished evidence that, as a rule, families throughout the world have as many children as they desire. The high fertility rates in the developing countries, he notes, are due to the desire for a large family, not to a lack of contraceptives or knowledge concerning the means available to regulate fertility. There is no simple correlation between number of children and use of contraceptives. In Costa Rica, Pritchett points out, more contraceptives are used than in Japan, and yet, on average, 1.5 more children are born per women in Costa Rica than in Japan. Put differently: the problem, if there is a problem in the first place, must be sought in a large demand for children and not in an insufficient supply of contraceptives. World Fertility Survey data for the 1990s on the number of children desired in countries of the South indicate the following average figures: Cameroon 8, Ghana 6, Pakistan and Bangladesh 4.1, Mexico 4.4. The actual total fertility rates in these countries were accordingly high: Cameroon 6.4, Ghana and Pakistan 6, Bangladesh 5.4, Mexico 5.7. Pritchett thus concludes that desired family size accounts for 90% of the differences noted between the fertility levels of various countries. What is needed to restrain population growth, he argues, is to reduce the "demand" for children, not to boost the supply of contraceptives.

Contraceptives distributed, in part free of cost, by the state have little effect, as leftist critics of population programs have long argued (Mamdani 1985). This has been conceded in the meantime even by USAID, the US development agency and one of the leading advocates of an interventionist population policy in the so-called developing countries. While I was engaged in archival work in Washington, D.C., I came across an interesting evaluation report for Population Services International concerned with the so-called condom gap: "the puzzling gap between condom sales/distribution and condom use" in Bangladesh (Williamson 1982, p. 4). The report advances twelve hypotheses to explain why the fertility rate there has not been influenced by the distribution of growing quantities of condoms by government agencies and international programs. Among other issues, the report looks into whether the condoms provided by the US are smuggled across the border to India or Burma, and whether they are used in Bangladesh more to produce toys for children and to improve mobility than to reduce fertility, since, as was noted, the excellent quality of these condoms recommend them for use in repairing bicycle tires in rural Bangladesh, where roads tend to be quite bumpy. World Bank economists see in the provision of contraceptives by the state and by international development agencies evidence of the market-distorting effects of goods distributed free of charge. After all, writes William Easterly in his devastating critique of the failures of the World Bank's policies (Easterly 2001), neither the US government nor the World Bank subsidizes Coca Cola in developing countries in order to enable poor families to consume another good for which there may well be unsatisfied demand – a highly entertaining read that cost Easterly his job as senior economist with the World Bank.

Would it not, in view of the negative experiences of population policy, be preferable for the state to withdraw from the reproduction arena, as neoliberal critics of state population policy have been demanding? These critics point, for example, to the success achieved by Brazil, where between 1960 and 1984 fertility declined as rapidly as it did in India – without any state program designed to control population growth. As Georgia Kaufmann and Elza Berquo have shown in their studies (Berquo 1998; Kaufmann 1998), however, the decline in the fertility rate in Brazil, as in many other developing countries, was achieved without any improvement of women's health (Dalsgaard 2003).[2] The success statistics on reduced fertility rates conceal a high level of illegal and unsafe abortions as well as a female sterilization rate of 45%. In obstructing the free choice of fertility regulation methods and in marginalizing individual health-related family planning measures, both uncontrolled market mechanisms and state programs designed to achieve demographic objectives serve to prevent the realization of reproductive rights. This is why advocates of a human capital approach like Amartya Sen propose that state population programs be linked with social measures in the field of education (Sen 1999). They have come to share Condorcet's insight that if we "have a duty towards those who are not yet born, that duty is not to give them existence but to give them happiness" (Condorcet 1955, pp. 188-9).

Social Policy as Contraception – Kerala's Experience in the Indian Context

Condorcet's conception of the effects of social progress, and in particular of women's education, on fertility is one of the keys to understanding the marked demographic discrepancies to be observed in India. However, the spirit of neo-Malthusianism continues to dominate the Indian government's population-policy discourses and programs (Rao 2005). Malthus, a clergyman, held the first professorship in political economy at the East India Company College in Haileybury, England for more than thirty years. It was in this function that he shaped England's official policy, both on the British Isles and in Britain's colonial territories. Not only did the college train British colonial officials, in the

---

2 For an ethnography that embeds acceptance of sterilization in the context of gender asymmetry and women's autonomy under conditions of a substantial measure of structural discrimination, see Dalsgaard (2003).

early 19th century over 100 members of the East India Company also served as members of the House of Commons. The history of the globalization of Malthusian ideas on the correlation between poverty, overpopulation, and hunger is fascinating (see Ross 1998; Heim et al. 1996).[3] Here, I can only point out that its enduring effect has been to veil the important role played by unequal land distribution and unequal access to food as a cause of rural poverty, and instead to hypostasize demographic factors in seeking to explain the phenomenon.[4]

In 1951 India was the world's first country to adopt an official population policy. Apart from a short phase in which an estimated five million or more men were sterilized under a set of emergency measures imposed under Indira Gandhi in the mid-1970s (see Turay in this volume), the government program focused on sterilization of women as well as on what was known as the "cafeteria approach", which gave couples an option to choose their own contraceptives from a range of methods provided by the government. However, these free pills, condoms, spirals, and sterilization techniques were used in very different ways in India's various regions, as the variance in the following table illustrates.

Contraceptive Use, Couple Protection Rate (CPR), and Total Fertility Rate (1999)

INDIAN STATE	CPR in %	Total Fertility Rate
Andhra Pradesh	50.3	2.5
Gujarat	54.5	3.0
Haryana	49.5	3.4
Karnataka	55.4	2.5
Kerala	40.5	1.8
Madhya Pradesh	46.5	4.0
Maharashtra	50.1	2.7
Orissa	39.0	3.0
Punjab	66.0	2.7
Tamil Nadu	50.4	2.0
Uttar Pradesh	38.2	4.8

Source: Department of Family Welfare, Registrar General of India
SRS estimate – Sample Registration Survey, Registrar General of India.

The CPR is an expression of the percentage of married couples of child-bearing age (i.e. between 15-45 years) that use modern contraceptives. The higher the rate,

3 On this issue, see Ross (1998); on the role played post-1945 by private US foundations and the US government in the global diffusion and ultimate hegemony of neo-Malthusian thinking, see Heim/Schatz (1996).

4 Deepa Dhanraj's Film The Legacy of Malthus (1994) points impressively to these connections with regard both to the historical past of the Scottish Highlands and present-day India.

the lower fertility should be. But as the table shows, there is no simple correlation between contraceptive use and number of children actually born. While Kerala has the lowest fertility rate (1.8) in all of India, its CPR is no higher than 40.5%. Punjab, on the other hand, has a far higher fertility rate (2.7), even though statistics indicate that many more couples (66.0%) there have embraced contraceptive use.

How are we to explain a discrepancy of this kind? Sterilization, the most frequently used (90%) method of birth control in India, has little influence on reducing fertility rates. The reason is that most women have themselves sterilized only when they are 35 years of age and older, i.e. when they already have the number of children, or sons, they desire. According to a proverb in my mother tongue, "The wish for a son is the father of many daughters." And this is the reason why the Indian government has in recent years focused more on pills and condoms than on sterilization as a means of slowing population growth. But the figures can also be read differently. Numbers are used to simplify a complex social reality for the purpose of technical intervention, but they also serve to legitimize certain population strategies and at the same time to evaluate the successes reached using them. The field research I conducted in 1999 in Gujarat, Uttar Pradesh, and Washington, D.C. was devoted to an ethnography of these figures, the aim being to investigate the transnational networks in which they are generated, utilized, and circulated. The research centered on the social and political life led by these figures, which constitute one of the most important techniques of modern government (Rose 1999), a development that Condorcet, with his belief in social mathematics, had already foreseen in the 18th century.

I pursued the ways in which these figures are generated by government health centers in the villages of Uttar Pradesh, India's most populous state, move to the health ministry in Lucknow, the state capital, and then further on to Washington, D.C., to USAID and the World Bank, in order then to return to the day-to-day life of rural women. It turned out that what is meant by family planning in India is not the planning by married couples of the size of their own families, but the use of bureaucratic measures to plan births (Randeria 1995). The Indian central government sets target figures for each of the federal states. Each state government then, on this basis, decides how many and which contraceptive methods must be used per year in each administrative district in order to meet the population-growth target levels set by the central government under pressure from international organizations. The healthcare personnel working on the ground is under massive pressure to meet these targets. The peak sterilization season extends from January to March, because at the beginning of April the figures assembled are expected to tally – at least on paper – with the previously set targets.

As compensation, women who had been sterilized were given money or payment in kind, while the responsible staff members of state health centers were given bonuses if they met their targets or penalized by having their salaries docked if they failed to do so. In 1996 both the official quotas for different contraceptives and the annual district fertility targets were abolished with a view to bringing India's official population policy in line with the international Plan of Action adopted in 1994 at the UN International Conference on Population and Development in Cairo. Indian women's rights activists had pointed out repeatedly that the old bureaucratic practice inevitably led to human rights violations, corruption, and the use of coercive methods (Nair 1992). But it also led to falsified statistics, in particular on the use of reversible methods of contraception – including lists containing fictitious names (Visaria et al. 1995). In the course of the field research I conducted at the family planning ministry in New Delhi, I had the opportunity to attend the first official visit by a Chinese delegation. Once the speechifying and formalities were over, the first questions the Chinese officials asked their Indian counterparts were concerned with the production of the desired statistical figures, with both sides engaging in an exchange on how and in what areas statistics were faked in the two countries. While the official Indian statistics merely reflect the number of contraceptives distributed free of charge, they provide little reliable information on the ways in which these contraceptives are actually used. In villages in the state of Gujarat I often observed that while women accepted the free pills offered to them, they did not actually take them. In order to prevent bothersome officials from coming for their monthly visits, they were politely thanked for the presents; the condoms were used as toys on the occasion of children's birthday parties and the pills were fed to the chickens or given to husbands as a headache remedy.

Demographic transition theory, extrapolated from the historical experience of Western Europe and based on assumptions from modernization theory, sees links between decline in fertility rates and a given country's level of economic and social development. It postulates that Western-style economic growth and social modernization led to changes in fertility (Heim et al. 1996).[5] But variation in India's fertility rate constitutes a demographic paradox that cannot be explained on the basis of this theory. India's western, industrialized states of Gujarat and Maharashtra and the wealthy northern states of Punjab and Haryana have higher fertility rates than the far poorer southern states of Kerala and Tamil Nadu.

---

5 After the Second World War, this originally postulated causality between high economic growth and low birth rates was reversed by – among others – Frank Notstein, a leading US demographer. With a view to making population policy a key instrument of US foreign policy during the Cold War, he modified the existing eugenic and Malthusian positions. From now on decline in population growth was seen as a necessary precondition for high economic growth, not as one of its consequences. In the wake of the decolonization of Asia and Africa, this reinterpretation of the theory of demographic transition served to legitimize an interventionist state population policy, one geared to effecting changes in both values and individual behavior patterns in the so-called developing countries. See Heim/Schaz (1996).

Several studies even argue that poverty is the driving force behind the low fertility observed in southern India (Basu 1986; Kishor 1994), i.e. they come to conclusions diametrically opposed to the underlying assumptions of modernization theory. But there are also studies, like those by Dyson and Moore (Dyson et al. 1983) or Caldwell and Caldwell (Calwell at al. 1991), that give consideration to cultural dimensions such as marriage norms, marriage age, rules governing inheritance, and family structures with a view to explaining the difference between the two "demographic regimes" encountered on the subcontinent. The norms regarding village exogamy and hypergamy in northern India are seen as closely associated with a lack of autonomy for women and restrictions on their freedom of choice and movement. The generally low status enjoyed by women in northern India is reflected in lower results on demographic indicators, including far higher rates of fertility and infant and maternal mortality and a higher ratio of men to women in the total population ("sex ratio"). The disparities are significant, and they have widened in the course of the past 30 years. To cite an example, today the infant mortality rate in the northern state of Uttar Pradesh is six times higher than that reported for Kerala, while the total fertility rate in Uttar Pradesh is 5.1 as opposed to 1.3 for Kerala. The ratio of women to men in Uttar Pradesh, 880 to 1000, is among the world's lowest. Kerala, on the other hand, is the only Indian state for which no female deficit is reported (Sen 1990). Interestingly, nearly 70% of the variance in fertility between India's northern and southern states can be explained with sociocultural factors, whereas only 10% can be traced back to state population policy and a further 10% is due to economic factors (Bhat 1998).

Kerala's success story shows that economic development is not a necessary condition for low fertility. Given the political will, relatively low economic growth does not constitute an obstacle to a progressive social policy. In Kerala a high literacy rate, low rates of infant and maternal mortality, later marriage ages, good state health services, and social security have worked in favor of a desire for small families. In the 1980s the Communist government of Kerala, the state with the highest population density in all of India, resolutely carried out agricultural reforms and spent close to 60% of its budget on the social sector. It must, however, also be noted that a variety of contingent and historical factors, including the traditionally high status enjoyed by women in Kerala, a matrilineal right of inheritance, and high levels of male migration to other parts of the country, later also to the Gulf states, are part and parcel of this demographic success story. While these factors do not make Kerala a unique case, they are highly resistant to influence by government measures, and they would be more than difficult to replicate elsewhere – an aspect to which Amartya Sen's otherwise highly convincing analysis fails to do sufficient justice (Randeria 1989; 1994).

Kerala's fertility rate has in the meantime declined to the level typical for Central Europe, just as it has in China (though in China the effect was reached by entirely different means) (Sen et al. 2002)[6]. Today Kerala's total fertility rate has stabilized at 1.3, while the equivalent figure for China, which continues to use coercive measures to reach its fertility targets and control mechanisms to monitor them, is 1.9 (Winckler 2002). Susan Greenhalgh's analysis of China's one-child policy highlights the mix of neo-Malthusian arguments, Stalinist bureaucratic control, nationalist slogans, and eugenic models that typify the country's official population program, "Controlling population growth and raising population quality" (Greenhalgh et al. 2005; Greenhalgh 2003). Based on a so-called "principle of voluntary action", in 1983 the responsible Chinese ministry ordered that all women with one child would be obliged to be fitted with an inter-uterine device, that all impermissible pregnancies must be terminated, and that one of the two parents of families with two children would have to be sterilized. The outcome, for that same year, was, among other things, a total of 14 million abortions and 58 million compulsory sterilizations, measures which reduced the fertility rate to 2.1, known as the population stabilization level. These compulsory reproduction measures were a central component of the socialist dream of a rapid modernization of the poor backward rural population, and they paved the way for the success story of China's economic miracle (Greenhalgh 2005).

In Kerala, on the other hand, a progressive social policy served to reach the same result on a voluntary basis. Not only was the reproductive freedom of individual couples respected, the decline in fertility achieved in Kerala was also accompanied by a higher life expectancy and a higher literacy rate for women and a lower infant mortality rate than in China. Unlike China, Kerala has no female deficit. Condorcet was evidently far ahead of his times in recognizing several important circumstances that Malthus overlooked, including the importance of education and women's rights, which are underlined today by advocates of the human capital approach. The widely acclaimed study by Murthi, Guo, and Freze, likewise in this research tradition, shows that variations in the fertility rates of 300 Indian administrative districts correlate more closely with differences in women's formal education level and employment than with degree of urbanization, income level, or density of health services (Murthi et al. 1995). Policy advisors therefore rely on the trick of pedagogical reason to effect demographic change, even though we know little about the contextuality, the causality, or the interactions between education and fertility (Jejeebhoy 1995; Jeffrey et al. 1996). Consider, for example, that the fertility rate of Thai women without any formal education is two thirds lower than the corresponding figure for women with secondary school education in Uganda. We also do not understand exactly how length of school attendance influences the fertility rate, and we cannot explain

6 For a highly differentiated comparison of economic and demographic developments as well as of social indicators, with a focus on gender, in China and India (with Kerala), see Sen/Dreze (2002), esp. 112-142.

these differences across countries. For this reason, in demographic studies culture is left as a residual when all other variables have been played through.

There is something disturbing about promoting secondary education for girls with a view to the instrumental aspect of its positive demographic effect, because education is generally seen as a value on its own merit. But Condorcet was far ahead of his time when he recognized the connection between women's education and fertility, a correlation that has since proven to be universal and independent of context. This, though, has not induced the Indian government to follow Kerala's example. The countrywide National Population Policy 2000 is keyed to a mix of positive and negative monetary incentives, and it thus follows the approach subscribed to by several other northern Indian states. While official national and regional documents have adopted the language of the politically correct international discourse on "reproductive rights" and "empowerment of women", the states of Rajasthan, Haryana, Uttar Pradesh, and Madhya Pradesh have decided to curtail the political rights of couples with more than two children, and the parents are now banned from running for political office at the local level (Rao 2001; 2003). In 2003 India's Supreme Court ruled that this arrangement was in line with the Constitution, using neo-Malthusian arguments in its judgment to underline the need to restrict reproductive freedom in the interest of national welfare (Bhat 2003).

Africa: Fosterage, or Social Parenthood, as a Strategy for Upward Social Mobility

Modernization theorists and advocates of neo-Malthusian lines of argument would be well advised not to conclude, or to assume, that the worldwide acceptance of modern means of family planning indicates any general convergence toward Western rationality and values, or indeed their wholesale adoption. As the cultural logic at work in the field of reproduction in Africa clearly indicates, biological fertility is only one aspect of social reproduction. And family planning may therefore also serve ends other than reduction of birth rates. If the use of modern contraceptive technologies is viewed exclusively in terms of the theory of demographic transition and its fertility decline premise, which are implicitly Euro-centric in nature and rooted in modernization theory, the result may very well be a temptation to attribute to contraception everywhere the same function and significance it has in the Western industrialized countries. However, research on the role played by contraceptives in shaping people's lifestyle choices in different cultures is a challenge that has been posed for social demography by recent ethnological studies on gender and reproduction. There is little doubt that Condorcet was right in assigning the faculty of reason a larger influence on the demographic future than did Malthus, who regarded African societies as barbaric and therefore incapable of "moral restraint." Not only does reason not appear universally in the form of a uniform human rationality. The ethnological studies on fertility change in Africa discussed in the present paper make it clear that reduction of biological fertility is by no means the only approach available to influence family size.

In view of growing economic and legal insecurity, increasing levels of violence, and contracting national economies, prosperity and security cannot be said to depend only on a family's money and property, indeed they also depend in important ways on the multifarious relationships that each new generation creates with various influential social networks. Demographic theories of a linear stamp, like Caldwell's theory of intergenerational transfer, which underline the long-term economic benefit that a large number of children may create for their parents, are based on the Euro-American model of the nuclear family (Caldwell 1976). By way of contrast, most West African societies separate the various functions of parenthood, assigning them to the children's biological and social parents in whose care most children grown up. As Esther Goody has noted, fosterage, a widespread phenomenon in West Africa, fulfills just this task (Goody 1982). Unlike adoption, the institution of fosterage serves more to cultivate social relationships than to stunt them. Depending on their individual aptitudes, children may be placed with differently situated foster families, where they contribute to establishing and maintaining a dense network of mutual obligations. Fosterage is a gradualist strategy of upward social mobility for the whole of a child's biological family, and for this reason children without social parents are seen as disadvantaged (Alber 2003).

A rural family with five children in Ghana or Benin would, for example, send its first or most talented son to the capital to live with his paternal uncle and to learn a trade; the oldest daughter might be placed, until she married, with her grandmother in a neighboring village, where she would help out with household and farm work; the second son might be sent to his childless aunt in a provincial town to enable him to attend school; and the two youngest children might remain with their biological parents until the eldest son is on his own and able to assume responsibility for one of his siblings. The social parents are responsible for assuming the costs of the schooling, training, and bride price of their foster children, although this also gives them a claim to the future solidarity and income of these children. It would be wrong to interpret the social institution of fosterage as a response to excessively large numbers of children and to conclude that this situation implies the existence of an unsatisfied demand for contraceptive technologies. For in creating links to a number of different networks with resources of their own, fosterage strategies pave the way for upward social mobility and access to a variety of different occupations. In societies with an institution of social parenthood as widespread as it is in Africa, it is more important to increase the intervals between births than to reduce the number of children born. Following Bledsoe, we could view fosterage as a kind of fertility portfolio strategy, since the selective placement of children with foster parents is a practice that serves to diversify the costs of fertility and at the same time to spread risk under conditions of uncertainty (Bledsoe 1990).

It is here that we clearly see the limits of cost-benefit analyses that, like Gary Becker's model of the household economy (Becker 1991), are conceived to explain fertility decisions and have found their way into sociological theories of demographic change. The problem is that these analyses are unable to capture the dynamic of those systems in which neither costs nor benefits are concentrated solely with a child's biological parents. In African societies, what children owe to adults is a matter that is not regulated by law but negotiated throughout the course of a person's life. While children may have an uncertain future, this is due not – as many social demographers think – to high rates of child mortality but to the fact that the economic potential children have for their family unfolds gradually in the course of their biography. Since the birth of a child is seen not as an event promising security once and for all but as the commencement of a relationship with various social networks, one that is continuously renegotiated and, above all, unpredictable, the European-style nuclear family does not appear particularly attractive here. Compared to Western industrialized societies, where contraceptives are used to reduce fertility and limit the size of families to a certain number of children, contraceptives have an entirely different significance in societies with widespread fosterage practices. Many of the parents that Bledsoe interviewed in Sierra Leone and Gambia were convinced that it is the selective (postnatal) allocation of resources to especially promising children that makes it possible for families to effectively exploit the potentials this arrangement offers them to improve their status (Bledsoe 1994). Families in societies in which the development potential of children is determined by the fate of the family tend to prefer contraceptive methods that enable them to keep open their option to have children as long as they possible can. In Bledsoe's opinion, this strategy explains the popularity among young African women of traditional contraceptive methods and contraceptives that can be discontinued on short notice, whereas older women tend to prefer modern long-term contraceptives. The fact that both men and women in Africa strictly reject sterilization as a means of contraception is likewise due to this specific cultural context, in which reproductive decisions are taken under conditions of uncertainty.

Unlike the case in Africa, in India, the country in which sterilization is used most frequently as an instrument of family planning, couples seek to have the number of sons and daughters they desire as soon as possible after they have married. The ways in which fertility has been reduced in Kenya, Zimbabwe, or Botswana may serve to corroborate Bledsoe's thesis that in many African countries modern contraceptive technologies are used not primarily as a means of reducing the number of children born but as a strategic instrument for planning the point of time of a pregnancy and the circumstances accompanying it in the mother's biography (Bledsoe et al. 1994). This decline in fertility was associated with the economic progress and political stability experienced by these countries in the 1980s. But interestingly, it was reached more through prolongation of the interval between births than by attempts to prevent later births in the course of women's reproductive lives. The function of contraceptives also changes for African women in the course of their biographies. As is shown by the data of the World Fertility Surveys from the 1980s and 1990s, younger women in nearly all of Africa prefer to use traditional birth-control methods, or if need be the pill, to prolong the intervals between pregnancies. The reason is that it is more important to them to safeguard their own reproductive future by using "pause strategies" in case they should later desire to have children with another partner. Women over 35 years of age tend to opt for the technologically more advanced three-month injection with a view to reducing the risk entailed by repeated pregnancies and births at a more advanced age. The traditional methods of birth control widely encountered in all of Africa, including a phase of abstinence during the nursing period, which may range from six months to two years, contribute to prolonging the interval between pregnancies. In cultural terms, long nursing periods are seen as just as important as fertility, a point to which we will return below. Family planning should not be equated with a desire for a Western-style nuclear family. A prudent planning of reproduction may therefore serve to pursue a number of different goals, none of which can be equated with the desire for a small family.

Concluding Remarks, from a Postcolonial Perspective

As I have noted in connection with my discussion of India, recent studies on demographic change in developing countries not only pay increasing heed to cultural variables – in particular from the field of kinship ethnology – they also make growing use of qualitative methods borrowed from the field of microdemography (Kerzer et al. 1997). Social-anthropology approaches that might, in allusion to Clifford Geertz, be termed "dense demography" tend to make use of hermeneutic methods with a view to questioning Euro-centric concepts and universalist models, to identifying local discourses and patterns of interpretation, and to understanding culturally-specific logics of action, which are then integrated into micro-structural contexts. Even though quantitative methods continue to be used, ethnological research on population policy indicates a need to abandon attempts to formulate context-independent generalizations, even if such attempts no longer lay claim to the universality of Malthus' population laws. Postcolonial, postmodern, and poststructuralist perspectives, which have recently found their way into demography (Riley et al. 2003)[7], offer an alternative to

[7] For a critique of positivism in demography and a discussion of some more recent hermeneutic approaches, see Riley/McCarthy (2003).

the positivist epistemology and universalist theories that typify Malthusian and Condorcetian views on the population question, despite the antagonisms that mark them. Research on fertility change based on this paradigm shift also contributes to modifying the idea of universally uniform human rationality and linear progress so typical of Condorcet's thinking.

Nancy Rose Hunt's presentation of colonial population policy in the Congo may serve as an example to illustrate this point (Hunt 1996; 2005). Since the country is today regarded as severely overpopulated, it has become an attractive object for countless national and international population-control programs. To this end, the women concerned are advised to use both modern contraceptives and traditional practices such as protracted nursing periods and postnatal abstinence. Viewed from a postcolonial perspective, these attempts are not without a certain irony. For as Hunt shows, what led to the abandonment of traditional practices, including protracted abstinence both following a birth and in the course of the two-to-three year nursing period was the intervention – in the face of fierce resistance by the Congolese population – of the Belgian colonial authorities and the persistent missionary activities of the European League for the Protection of the Black Child. The extent of the demographic panic in the early 20th century in Belgium's African colonies becomes clear when we look at the desperate attempts undertaken by colonial officials, missionaries, and owners of copper mines and factories to raise the fertility of the Congolese population. It was, for instance, argued that reducing the intervals between births served to increase women's fertility and had no negative impacts on women's health.

> "The present situation is certainly irrational. In the course of the approximately thirty years during which women are susceptible of becoming mothers, to place periods of three-four years of breast feeding during which they can have only a single child, while nature would certainly permit them to support more frequent pregnancies without harm" (Hunt 1996, p. 293).

Concerned over low birth rates, the Belgian colonial authorities were unsure whether polygamy was the cause or the effect of the two-to-three-year abstinence period observed following a birth. Missionaries therefore advised couples who had converted to Christianity not only to adhere to monogamy but also "to resume conjugal commerce" (Hunt 1996, p.291) as soon as possible after a child was born and not to persist with unnatural practices. With a view to abbreviating the traditionally long postnatal nursing periods, steps were taken to provide baby food in newly set-up factory day nurseries and to force parents to place their children in these institutions; at the same time, cattle-raising programs were initiated with a view to having children drink cow's milk instead of being nursed by their own mothers. In the 1920s and 1930s the pronatalist interventions undertaken by mining companies, colonial governments, missionaries, and European women's organizations led to changes in the private sphere, in marital sexuality, in nursing times, and in childrearing practices in many African societies.

But it was not only the Belgian government that did its best to raise birth rates by introducing new childrearing practices. Large numbers of children were desirable in the colonies; these children provided sufficient labor for mines, and plantations, and farming and at the same time created demand for European manufactured goods and increased tax revenues by producing more agricultural goods (Ram et al. 1998). The German government was just as concerned about unduly low birth rates in what is today Tanzania as their British counterparts were in India. For the latter, the problem before 1870 was not the subcontinent's "overpopulation" but an acute shortage of labor. Sir Richard Temple, the British governor of Bombay (1877-79), gave assurances that he would do everything in his power "to increase the number of his Majesty's subjects" (Chandrasekhar 1961, p. 93). We do not know how he intended to achieve this. In any case, though, the efforts to increase population growth in the colonies date back to an age when the colonies neither represented a source of immigration to Europe nor offered Europe any economic competition in the form of cheap jobs.

References

Alber, Erdmute. 2003. "Denying Biological Parenthood: Fosterage in Northern Benin." *Ethnos* 68(4), pp. 487-506.

Basu, Alaka. 1986. "Birth Control by Assetless Workers in Kerala: the Possibility of a Population Induced Population Transition." *Development and Change* 17(2), pp. 265-282.

Becker, Gary. 1991. *Treatise on the Family*. Enlarged Edition. Cambridge: Harvard University Press.

Berquo, Elza. 1998. "The Reproductive Health of Brazilian Women During the 'Lost Decade'." In George Martine, et al., eds. *Reproductive Change in India and Brazil: Implications for Understanding Fertility Decline*, pp. 389-404. Delhi: Oxford University Press.

Bhat, P.N. Mari. 1998. "Emerging Regional Differences in Fertility in India: Causes and Correlations." In George Martine, et al., eds. *Reproductive Change in India and Brazil: Implications for Understanding Fertility Decline*, pp. 131-166. Delhi: Oxford University Press.

– 2003. "Two Child Norm: In Defence of the Supreme Court Judgement." *Economic and Political Weekly*, pp. 4714-4716.

Bledsoe, Caroline. 1990. "The Politics of Children: Fosterage and the Social Management of Fertility Among the Mende of Sierra Leone." In Handwerker, W. Penn, ed. *Births and Power: the Politics of Reproduction*, Boulder, Colo., pp. 81-100.

– 1994. "'Children are like young bamboo trees': Potentiality and Reproduction in Subsaharan Africa." In Kerstin Lindahl-Kiessling and Hans Landberg, eds. *Population, Economic Development, and the Environment*, pp. 105-140. Oxford: Oxford University Press.

Bledsoe, Caroline, et al. 1994. "Constructing Natural Fertility: The Use of Western Contraceptive Technologies in Rural Gambia." *Population and Develpment Review* 20(2), pp. 81-103.

Caldwell, John. 1976. "Toward a Restatement of Demographic Transition Theory." *Population and Development Review* 2(3/4), pp. 321-366.

Caldwell, John, P.H. Reddy, and Pat Caldwell. 1982. "The Causes of Demographic Change in Rural South India: A Micro Approach." *Population and Development Review* 8(4), pp. 689-727.

Chandrasekhar, Sripati. 1961. *Population and Planned Parenthood in India*, 2nd edition. London: George, Allen and Unwin.

Condorcet, Marquis de. 1955. *Sketch for a Historical Picture of the Progress of the Human Mind.* Trans. J. Barraclough. London: Weidenfeld and Nicholson.

– 1968. *Esquisse d'un tableau historique des Progrès de l'Esprit Humain* (1795). In *Œuvres de Condorcet*, vi, pp. 256-7.

Correa, Sonia. 1994. *Population and Reproductive Rights: Feminist Perspectives from the South.* New Delhi: Palgrave Macmillan.

Dalsgaard, Anne Line. 2004. *Matters of Life and Longing: Female Sterilization in Northeast Brazil.* Copenhagen.: Museum Tusculanum.

Dönhoff, Marion, et al. 1992. *Ein Manifest: Weil sich das Land ändern muss.* Reinbek b. Hamburg.

Dyson, Tim and Mick Moore. 1983. "On Kinship Structure, Female Autonomy and Demographic Behaviour in India." *Population and Development Review* 9:1 pp. 35-60.

Easterly, William. 2001. *The Elusive Quest for Growth: Economists' Adventures and Misadventures in the Tropics.* Cambridge: MIT.

Enzensberger, Hans-Magnus. 1993. *Die Grosse Wanderung. Essays*. Frankfurt a.M.

Goody, Esther. 1982. *Parenthood and Social Reproduction: Fostering and Occupational Roles in West Africa.* Cambridge: Cambridge University Press.

Greenhalgh, Susan. 2004. "Globalisation and Population Governance in China." In Aihwa Ong and Stephen J. Collier, eds. *Global Assemblages: Technology, Politics and Ethics as Anthropological Problems.* Oxford: Blackwell Publishing.

Greenhalgh, Susan and Edwin Winckler. 2003. "Science, Modernity, and the Making of China's One Child Policy." *Population and Development Review* 29(2), pp. 163-196.

– 2005. *Governing China's Population: From Leninist to Neoliberal Biopolitics in China.* Stanford: Stanford University Press.

Heim, Susanne and Ulrike Schatz. 1996. *Beschwörung und Berechnung, Überbevölkerung – Kritik einer Debatte.* Berlin: Schwarze Risse.

Hunt, Nancy Rose. 1996. "'Le bébé en brousse': European Women, African Birth Spacing and Colonial Intervention in Breast Feeding in the Belgian Congo." In Frederick Cooper and Ann Laura Stoler, eds. *Tensions of Empire: Colonial Cultures in a Bourgeois World.* Berkeley: University of California Press.

– 2005. "Colonial Medical Anthropology and the Making of the Central African Infertility Belt." In Helen Tilley and Robert Gordon, eds. *Anthropology, Imperialism, and the Ordering of Africa.* Manchester: Manchester University Press.

Jeffery, Roger and Patricia Jeffrey. 1997. *Population, Gender and Politics: Demographic Change in Rural North India.* Cambridge: Cambridge University Press.

Jeffrey, Roger and Alaka M. Basu, eds. 1996. *Girl's Schooling, Women's Autonomy and Fertility Change in South Asia.* Delhi: Sage.

Jejeebhoy, Shireen. 1995. *Women's Education, Autonomy and Reproductive Behaviour: Experience from Developing Countries.* Oxford: Clarendon Press.

Kaufmann, Georgia. 1998. "Gender and Reproductive Decision Making: The Contraceptive Choice of Women in a Brazilian *Favela.*" In George Martine, et al., eds. *Reproductive Change in India and Brazil: Implications for Understanding Fertility Decline*, pp. 243-273. Delhi: Oxford University Press.

Kertzer, David I. and Tom Fricke, eds. 1997. *Anthropological Demography: Toward a New Synthesis*. Chicago: University of Chicago Press.

Kishor, Sunita. 1994. "Fertilty Decline in Tamil Nadu India." In Bertil Egero and Mikael Hammarskjold, eds. *Understanding Reproductive Change: Kenya, Tamil Nadu, Punjab, Costa Rica.* Lund: Lund University Press.

Malthus, Thomas Robert. 1798. *An Essay on the Pinciple of Population*. London.

– 1830. *A Summary View of the Principle of Population*. London.

Mamdani, Mahmood. 1985. *The Myth of Population Control: Family, Caste and Class in an Indian Village.* New York: Monthly Review Press.

Murthi, Mamta, Anne-Catherine Guio, and Jean Dreze. 1995. "Mortality, Fertility and Gender Bias in India: A district level analysis." *Population and Development Review* 21(4), pp. 745–782.

Nair, Sumati. 1992. "Population Policies and the Ideology of Population Control in India." *Issues in Reproductive and Genetic Engineering in India* 5, pp. 237-253.

Pritchett, Lant. 1994. "Desired Fertility and the Impact of Population Policies." *Population and Development Review* 20(1), pp. 1–56.

Ram, Kalpana and Margaret Jolly, eds. 1998. *Maternities and Modernities: Colonial and Postcolonial Experiences in Asia and the Pacific*. Cambridge: Cambridge University Press.

Randeria, Shalini. 1989. "Amartya Sen, Indian Development: Lessons and Non-Lessons." *Daedalus* 118, pp. 369-392.

– 1994. "Das Wunder Kerala – eine Erfolgsgeschichte indischer Bevölkerungspolitik?" In Christa Wichterich, ed. *Menschen nach Mass – Bevölkerungspolitik in Nord und Süd, pp.* 239-262. Göttingen: Lamuv.

– 1995. "Die sozio-ökonomische Einbettung reproduktiver Rechte: Frauen und Bevölkerungspolitik in Indien." *Feministische Studien* 1, pp. 119-132.

Rao, Mohan. 2001/2003. "Population Policies: States Approve Coercive Measures." *Economic and Political Weekly* 21.7.2001 and 16.8.2003.

– 2005. *From Population Control to Reproductive Health. Malthusian Arithmetic*. New Delhi: Sage.

Richter, Judith. 1994. "Anti-Schwangerschafts-'Impfstoffe', 'Schwangerschaftsepidemien' und Missbrauch." In Christa Wichterich, ed. *Menschen nach Mass – Bevölkerungspolitik in Nord und Süd*, pp. 163-180, Göttingen: Lamuv.

Riley, Nancy and James McCarthy. 2003. *Demography in the Age of the Postmodern*. Cambridge: Cambridge University Press.

Robey, Bryant, Lea Morris, and Shea O. Rutstein. 1993. "The Fertility Decline in Developing Countries." *Scientific American* 269(6), pp. 60-67.

Rose, Nikolas. 1999. *Powers of Freedom: Reframing Political Thought*. Cambridge: Cambridge University Press.

Ross, Eric B. 1998. *The Malthus Factor, Factor: Poverty, Politics and Population in Capitalist Development*. London/New York: Zed Books.

Rothschild, Emma. 1996. "The Debate on Ecomomic and Social Securty in the Late Eighteenth Century: Lessons of a Road Not Taken." *Development and Change* 27 2, p. 341.

Sen, Amartya. 1990. "More than 100 Million Women Are Missing." *The New York Review of Books* 37(20).

– 1997. "Population Policy: Authoritarianism vs. Cooperation." *Journal of Development Economics*, 10(1), pp. 3-22.

Sen, Amartya and Jean Dreze. 2002. *India: Development and Participation*. New Delhi: Oxford University Press.

Spiller, Ingrid. 1994. "Objekt 'Frau' in Familienplanungsprogrammen." In Christa Wichterich, ed. *Menschen nach Mass – Bevölkerungspolitik in Nord und Süd*, pp. 163-180, Göttingen: Lamuv.

Visaria, Pravin, et al., eds. 1995. *Contraceptive Use and Fertility in India*, New Delhi: Sage.

Weber, Adolf. 1988. "Die agrare Tragfähigkeit der Erde." In Gunter Steinmann, et al., eds. *Probleme und Chancen demographischer Entwicklung in der Dritten Welt*, pp. 76-96. Berlin: Springer Verlag.

Wichterich, Christa, ed. 1994. *Menschen nach Mass – Bevölkerungspolitik in Nord und Süd.* Göttingen: Lamuv.

Williamson, Nancy. 1982. *Evaluation Needs of the Bangladesh Family Planning Social Marketing Project.* New York: Report prepared for Population Services International.

Winckler, Edwin A. 2002. "Chinese Reproductive Policy at the Turn of the Millennium: Dynamic Stability." *Population and Development Review* 28(3), pp. 379-418.

Chapter 2

Reproductive Rights – The Challenge of Reconciling Ethics and Law

Maja Kirilova Eriksson

1. Why this Topic?

Procreation is fundamental to the very existence and survival of mankind. It is "the means by which each society perpetuates itself and its traditions" (Cook, Dickens and Fathalla 2003, p. 3). Because of its impact on demography and environment, among other things, questions related to human reproduction are of vital importance and involve the individual/s, the family unit and society as a whole. It could thus be argued that governments have a legitimate interest in regulating this domain of life through, for example, family planning programmes. Governments may, however, approach family planning from two at times contradicting points of view, especially when individuals' decisions on fertility matters are in conflict with the interests of the society they live in:

1. The demographic and economic aspect, i.e. emphasis is put on population control by governments as the decisive factor in national development, and
2. A human rights aspect (reproductive rights), i.e. priority concern is given to the dignity of the individual and the spouses.

It is apparent that there is inter-connectedness between ethics and laws since the domestic laws/governmental policies relating to human reproduction are not neutral but rather reflect certain ideologies conditioned by, e.g., values and culture.[1] Furthermore, Article 3(3) of the 2004 Arab Charter on Human Rights,

---

1 Other aspects of human procreation which will be excluded from this essay for the simple reason of the space limit but which deserve to be mentioned since they have been currently intensively debated in the Western world is firstly the issue of procreation and parenting by lesbian women and gay men (See, for example, Principle 24 of the Yogyakarta Principles/Principles on the application of international human rights law in relation to sexual orientation and gender identity which have been adopted in March 2007) and secondly the issue dealing with the use of embryos without the consent of the prospective father (ECtHR, *Evans v the UK*, Appl. No. 25389/05, Judgment of 26 April 2007). The European Court has also dealt with a case concerning public authorities' refusal to allow a request for artificial insemination treatment by a prisoner whose wife was at liberty (ECtHR, *Dickinson v the UK*, Appl. No. 44362/04, Judgment of 4 December 2007). The European Court held in both cases that Art. 8 of the European Con-

which stipulates that "Men and women are equal in respect of human dignity, rights and obligations (e)stablished by the Islamic Shari'ah, other divine laws and by applicable laws", provides an example of conditioning the interpretation of human rights through the lens of religious belief systems.[2]

Nevertheless, the first approach, exclusively focused on demographic considerations, raises important issues of the compatibility of certain pro-natalist and anti-natalist policies – such as coercive sterilizations and abortions of certain segments of population,[3] the endorsement of sanctions to families disobeying policies on desired numbers of children, and so on – with international human rights standards which have been created to protect the individual from coercion.

While several of the contributions to this volume will touch upon various features of the first approach to family planning, this essay will focus mainly on one somewhat limited aspect of reproductive rights (*i.e.* reproductive health in the human rights context[4]), including the significance of having guaranteed access to safe abortion services for women's health and life in addition to the overall aim of achieving gender equality (parts 2 and 4). This author will also try to cover some aspects of the practice of conscientious objection on the domestic level (part 4(2)).[5] It goes without saying that the refusal to respond to a request

---

vention protects the right to respect for the decisions to have as well as not to have a child (§ 71 in the first and § 66 of the second judgment).

2 In connection with the entering into force of the Arab Charter in January 2008, the UNOHCHR Mrs. Arbour expressed concern about the provisions in the Charter that do not meet international norms and standards, including the treatment of women. See www.un.org/news/dh/latest , 30 January 2008.

3 For example, in recent years the practice of coercive sterilization of Romani women by medical professionals in Slovakia and in the Czech Republic has been reported on several occasions. See E.R.R.C. (2004), OMCT (2004, p. 41) and Cahn (2004, p. 103 ff.). See the 2006 CEDAW decision in the case *A.S. v Hungary*, Communication No. 4/2004 UN Doc. CEDAW/C/36/D/2004 dealing with the involuntary sterilization of a woman of Roma origin. The *María Mestanza Chávez v Peru* case is also illustrative of a situation when a woman belonging to an indigenous community was affected by a massive, compulsory and systematic governmental policy as a means to influence the reproductive behavior of the population, especially the poor, Indian and rural women. IACtHR, Case 12.191 (friendly settlement), 22 October 2003.

4 Notwithstanding that men also have their reproductive health needs, women have "more at stake" in this regards since they were too often considered as targets in the fertility control (means of reproduction) and they are even risking their lives in situations of unplanned and undesired pregnancies (Cook, Dickens and Fathalla 2003, p. 45). Recently, the UN Secretary – General Mr Ban Ki – Moon expressed his concern about the fact that "too many women die during pregnancy and childbirth because their right to sexual and reproductive health is denied." UNNews@un.org, *Women's Empowerment key to achieving UN goals*, 3 October 2007.

5 It is important to stress in this regard that conscientious objection is a right of an individual, *i.e.* natural person, and not of the state itself or other institutions (hospitals, clinics or other health centers). The delivery of reproductive health services such as induced

for lawful health services on the basis of conscientious objection under certain circumstances effectively inhibits the access to these services. This would be the case if, for example, the objecting practitioner does not immediately refer the patient to other non-objecting medical practitioners who will perform the requested services. Often there are mechanisms established by the medical profession aimed at considerations about the legitimacy of the objection. Thus, even an existing legal right to abortion might in reality be of lesser significance for women if reproductive health services including abortion services are not made available/accessible.[6] Currently in many national jurisdictions legal provisions permitting abortion are disconnected from the issue of accessibility of health services for women "whose circumstances are within the grounds permitted for terminating a pregnancy" (Rahman, Katzive and Henshaw 1998, p. 57). Since the human right to health comprises reproductive health, which is closely linked to safe abortion and abortion services, a short review of the emergence and development of these key concepts will be undertaken in part 3. In the view of some legal scholars the concept of "reproductive health" constitutes a challenge to religious authorities because its origins are of a secular character "requiring implementation by pragmatic legal rules that measure the validity of such laws by their practical consequences" (Cook, Dickens and Fathalla 2003, p. 98).

This author has chosen the topic mainly because this is a legal area in which we currently may witness some very interesting and relevant developments, especially with regard to the jurisprudence of human rights bodies/courts on the universal as well as on the regional and domestic level (part 5), in addition to the adoption of high level consensus documents (see for example Council of Europe 2008) and debates in the legal doctrine.[7] Another objective of the essay will be therefore to examine whether there exist consistent jurisprudential and other in-

---

abortion may in other words conflict with the practitioner's ethics/religious faith, "or the practitioner's sense of the best interests of the patients themselves or of social order" (Cook, Dickens and Fathalla 2003, p. 62). Significantly, a great number of domestic jurisdictions such as the British Abortion Act from 1967 exclude refusal on grounds of conscience of "treatment which is necessary to safe the live or to prevent grave permanent injury to the physical or mental health of a pregnant woman." See Dickens and Cook (2000, p. 3).

6 The UN Committee on Economic, Social and Cultural Rights has elaborated on the meaning of these two terms in the context of health services in its General Comment No. 14 of 11 August 2000 (UN Doc. E/C.12/2000/4, § 12). Thus, availability implies that functioning public health – care facilities, goods and services have to be available in sufficient quantity within the State party to the Covenant. Accessibility on the other hand comprises four overlapping dimensions: non-discrimination, physical accessibility, economic accessibility (affordability) and information accessibility. See also RFSU (2004b, pp. 36-37).

7 The most recent essay which according to its author "expresses the author's concern over the increasing estrangement between a new voluntaristic doctrine of human rights and the most basic precepts of ethical reason" is Cornides (2008, pp. 107-134).

terpretative statements[8] with regard to reproductive rights, i.e. whether the various international bodies expose a coherent standpoint as to the scope of the same state obligations and thereby reduce the risk of unnecessary fragmentation of law. The European Court of Human Rights demonstrated recently in the Grand Chamber decision in the *D.H. v Czech Republic* case its recognition of the interconnectedness of universal and regional human rights regimes.[9]

Besides the doctrine of "margin of appreciation", which often is applied by international treaty bodies, many provisions in international law of significance for women's rights make them subject to national jurisdiction. The intention of this essay is therefore to give also a few illustrative examples of current trends of relevance for the subject matter within domestic jurisdictions as the most contentious subject matter related to reproductive health on the national level continues to be the abortion issue and the question of how to resolve situations of competing interests. Seeing that the provisions dealing with the right to life include ethical and moral dimensions, states do not have uniform legislation and practices. In other words, there is a lack of consensus on the issue of the beginning of life[10] and therefore induced abortion continues to be a source of debate and controversy regarding the morality and legality of this practice, including access to health services for such purposes.

2. Gender Equality and Empowerment of Women – A Justification for Reproductive Rights[11]

Since time immemorial the human being has striven to protect this private sphere from interference, i.e. being in charge of one's own fertility and reproduction. These aspirations have been gradually transformed into rights and obligations,[12] embodied and protected by customary, religious, and later in legal

8 In the *D.H. and Others v the Czech Republic* case the ECtHR made, for example, use of the GC of the HRC in its argumentation. ECtHR, Appl. No.57325/00, Judgment of 13 November 2007.

9 ECtHR, Appl. No. 57325/00, Judgment of 13 November 2007.

10 For a recent and interesting discussion as to whether in cases of *in vitro* fertilization the woman can change her mind right up to the moment when the fertilized ovum is transferred see ECJ (Grand Chamber), *Sabine Mayr v. Bäckerei und Konditorei Gerhard Flöckner OHG*, Case C-506/06, Judgment 26 February 2008.

11 Ruth Dixon-Mueller distinguishes in this regard at least three types of reproductive rights: "1. the freedom to decide how many children to have and when (or whether) to have them; 2. the right to have the information and means to regulate one's fertility; 3. the right to control one's own body" (Dixon-Mueller 1993, p. 12).

12 The most frequently cited examples of state's obligations within this legal topic include the duty to ensure that men and women have equal access to a full range of contraceptive choices and reproductive health services as well as guaranteeing access to information about sexual and reproductive health.

rules on the national as well as on the international level. Thus, the contemporary international human rights system is founded on a number of legally binding international treaties as well as soft law instruments which reflect fundamental values by making use of principles of ethics and social justice (i.e. "ensuring equitable access for all persons to goods and services that fulfill basic human needs" (Dixon-Mueller 1993, p. 186)). For example, provisions relating to equality and prohibition of specific forms of discrimination represent a prominent feature of international human rights instruments. The preamble (§ 4) of the European Convention on Human Rights refers to fundamental freedoms as a "foundation of justice and peace." Interestingly, Pope Benedict XIV said during his recent speech to the UN General Assembly that human rights were becoming the common language and the ethical substratum of international relations. The merit of the Universal Declaration of Human Rights was that it enabled different cultures, juridical expressions and institutional models to converge around a fundamental nucleus of values, and hence of rights (see UN 2008).

The right to make decisions about procreation is a basic human right because it is essential to the contemporary concept of the free individual, and if a right is arguably necessary to the freedom of an individual, i.e. to have power to direct his/her own life, it is to be considered fundamental. In other words, it is indispensable to secure women's reproductive rights in the diversity of fertility related situations which women must cope with[13] because the ability to decide such matters is the first step in enabling women to exercise other choices (Eriksson 2000, pp. 166-167 and pp. 307-308). Thus, decision-making autonomy is founded on the idea that women are fully capable of making decisions for themselves (see Council of Europe 2008, § 6; see also Lauglo and Møgedal 1999, p. 3).

Moreover, one may also argue from an equality perspective that denying women access to reproductive health services, including abortion, is discriminatory since women are disproportionately affected by such practices, i.e. they disadvantage women over men with regard to health issues (Center for Reproductive Rights 2005, p. 31; Council of Europe 2008, § 2).[14] In addition, the CEDAW Committee has taken the position that "(i)t is discriminatory for a State party to refuse to provide legally for the performance of certain reproductive health services for women"[15] (see also Banda 2008, p. 6). Reproductive rights are, therefore, *sine qua non* for the attainment of any genuine/de facto equality between men and women, a principle which is at the very heart of international human rights law and represents a prominent aim for many international organizations.

---

13 Some women are unable to conceive, others are unable to avoid pregnancy and/or have too many pregnancies to be able to restrict the size of their family.

14 *D v Ireland* ECtHR, Appl. No. 26499/02.

15 CEDAW (Committee on the Elimination of Discrimination against Women), GR No. 24, Women and Health, UN Doc. A/54/38, 1999, § 11

The UN Deputy Secretary-General, Asha-Rose Migiro, emphasized in a speech delivered to participants in the International Women Leaders Global Security Summit on 16 November 2007, that when women are fully empowered and engaged, all of society benefits.[16]

The UN Committee on Economic, Social and Cultural Rights has, among others, highlighted the relationship between substantial/de facto equality and some aspects of reproductive rights in its GC No 16 from 2005. The Committee stated with regard to the implementation of Article 3 of the Covenant (equality between men and women) seen in conjunction to Article 12 (the right to health) that member states are required at a minimum to remove "legal and other obstacles that prevent men and women from accessing and benefiting from health care on a basis of equality. This includes, *inter alia*, the removal of legal restrictions on reproductive health provisions."[17]

Having the aforesaid in mind, human rights lawyers (Human Rights Watch 2006b) and scholars have argued that one of the conditions for the achievement of equality between men and women, which is also one of the main objects and purposes of most human rights treaties, presupposes the right to have access to safe abortion services (Eriksson 2000, pp. 315-316; see also RFSU 2004b, pp.16-18 and p. 24).

However, at present it is solely the 2003 Protocol on the Rights of Women in Africa, supplementing the African Charter on Human Rights and Peoples' Rights, which constitutes the first international law treaty comprising a far-reaching and comprehensive definition of reproductive rights (Article 14) and which explicitly protects a woman's right "to medical abortion in cases of sexual assault, rape, incest, and where the continued pregnancy endangers the mental and physical health of the mother or the life of the mother or the fetus" (Article 14, § 2 (c)). Importantly, article 5(b) contains a prohibition of female genital mutilation (FGM).[18] The protocol is of great significance not only because of its actual word-

---

16 UNnews7@secint00.un.org. The Catholic Church has stated on the other hand that "the work of women in the home is the basis for the happiness of the whole human race" (The Guardian, 1999, at 24). The Holy See is known for frequently invoking the natural law paradigm in its defense of the traditional family and the women's position within it. The concept of female autonomy and reproductive choice as part of human rights is therefore incompatible with traditional Roman Catholic anthropology. See Gerle (2003, p. 98 and p. 103).

17 UN Doc. E/C.12/2005/4, 11 August 2005, § 29.

18 The Protocol is in force since 25 November 2005 and as of April 2008, there are 21 ratifications and 43 signatures out of 53 Member States of the African Union, www.achpr.org.

ing but also because it is illustrative of the inclusive character of the notion "reproductive rights"[19] – that is, it comprises the term "reproductive health."

3. The Evolution of Key Concepts and their Interconnectedness

3.1 The Notion "Reproductive Health" – A Significant Constituent of the Right to Health

According to a recent milestone decision of the Constitutional Court in Colombia in 2006

"The right to health, which includes the right to reproductive health and family planning, has been interpreted by international bodies on the basis of international treaties, including CEDAW, to include the duty of all states to offer a wide range of high quality and accessible health services, which must include sexual and reproductive health services" (Cook 2006, p. 28).

However, the notion "reproductive health" gained considerable attention in legal doctrine primarily during the 1980s and 1990s where it has been considered to incorporate "a clear feminist and human rights focus for its full realization", including among other things "education and counseling on sexuality, contraception, abortion; safe early abortion etc.", i.e., including access to abortion services (Dixon-Mueller 1993, pp. 204 and 207).

Reproductive health first became a new subject of regulation in the field of international human rights law during the mid 1990s, and the conceptual association between reproductive rights and reproductive health has evolved relatively recently. Thus, public international law has traditionally not been responsive to the realities of women's lives. For example, reproductive health aspects have been absent from the definition of the major components of the right to health in international human rights instruments.

Nevertheless, this lack of consideration of women's health needs has been remedied through interpretations of subsequent documents, i.e. when concepts used in a treaty are open or evolving, norms of international law subsequent to the treaty to be interpreted may be taken into account. Human rights treaties, especially, contain many vaguely defined concepts and should not be considered static but adaptable to emerging norms in international law. Evolved interpretation ensures the effective application of a treaty in terms of its object and purpose.[20] Thus, the 1994 Cairo and the 1995 Beijing UN final documents and their

19 The UN's rapporteur on violence against women emphasized that the articulation of women's sexual and reproductive rights is the final frontier for the women's movement. UN Doc. E/CN.4/2003/75, Executive summary.

20 UN Doc. A/CN.4/L.702, 18 July 2006, Fragmentation of International Law, p. 16.

follow up arrangements, which explicitly recognize women's reproductive rights and their integral nature to the broader framework of human rights, have largely contributed to an expanded understanding of the relevant concepts contained in earlier human rights treaties.[21]

The term "reproductive health" as such was set out and affirmed for the first time in Chapter VII, § 7.2 of the 1994 Cairo Programme of Action and thereby indicated a shift in the international community from demographic concerns to concerns about meeting individuals' needs for reproductive health information and services. Paragraph 7.2 of the ICPD Programme of Action defines reproductive health in the following manner:

> Reproductive health is a state of complete physical, mental and social well being and not merely the absence of disease or infirmity, in all matters relating to the reproductive system and its functions and processes. Reproductive health therefore implies that people are able to have a satisfying and safe sex life and that they have the capability to reproduce and the freedom to decide if, when and how often to do so (UNFPA 1994).

Implicit in this definition is the need for individuals to have the capability of reproducing (prevention and appropriate treatment of infertility) and the freedom to decide if, when, and how often to do so. That would, moreover, include prevention or remedy of, an unwanted or mistimed pregnancy. That is, comprehensive health care must also comprise access to safe abortion services (Bergmann 2004, p. 11). More importantly § 7.3 states that "Bearing in mind the above definition, reproductive rights embrace certain human rights that are already recognized in national laws, international human rights documents and other relevant United Nations consensus documents." In other words, reproductive rights intersect with several types of human rights and connect provisions of the major human rights treaties.

Since the Cairo Conference, the concept "reproductive health" has been repeated and re-utilized in several regional and global documents including interpretations of legally binding norms. Notwithstanding that the 1994 Cairo Programme of Action and the 1995 Beijing Declaration[22] are not legally binding in contemporary interna-

---

21 The ICPD's Programme of Action was agreed to by 179 states and the Beijing Declaration and Platform of Action were agreed to by 189 states. In addition, mention should be made of that the subsequently adopted documents dealing with the five-year review of the 1994 ICPD Programme in 1999 (ICPD + 5) and Beijing +5 (2000) reflect renewed commitment by the vast majority of states to the provisions on reproductive rights. See Ylva Bergman (2004, p. 5). The proposal put forward by the delegation of the Holy See during the ICPD + 5 to replace the phrase "respect for women's rights" with "respect for women's status" did not gain support. See Center for Reproductive Rights (2000, p. 6).

22 The definition of reproductive health in § 94 says *e.g.* that: "Reproductive health therefore implies that people are able to have satisfying and safe sex life and that they have the capability to reproduce and the freedom to decide if, when and how often to do so. Implicit in this last condition are the rights of men and women to be informed and to

tional law, except for the text reflecting customary law, they do bear great authority since they have been endorsed by the vast majority of governments in the international community.[23] It can therefore be maintained that they embody globally accepted policy norms which may have a certain effect on the judicial/quasi judicial decision-making as supporting arguments in the treaty interpretation process.

Subsequently, in the year 2000 the UN Committee on Economic, Social and Cultural Rights defined the concept "reproductive health" in its GC No. 14 as denoting that: "women and men have the freedom to decide if and when to reproduce and the right to be informed and to have access to safe, effective, affordable and acceptable methods of family planning of their choice as well as the right of access to appropriate health-care services."[24] This statement was further clarified in § 21 by stressing that: "The realization of women's right to health requires the removal of all barriers interfering with access to health services, education and information, including the area of sexual and reproductive health." Moreover, state parties to the Covenant must ensure that third parties do not limit individuals' access to health-related information and services.

Among the more recent documents reflecting international standards, mention should be made of the recommendations on ethical issues in obstetrics and gynecology by the FIGO (The International Federation of Gynecologists and Obstetricians) Committee for the ethical aspects of human reproduction and women's health from November 2003, which clearly reflects the contemporary interpretation of the concepts under review. According to the relevant section:

> Sexual and reproductive rights of individuals are essential components of human rights. They should never be transferred, renounced, or denied for any reason based on sex, race, age, language, religion, national origin, political opinion or economic condition. This statement implies certain ethical imperatives:
>
> 1. Women and men have a right to the highest available standard of health care for all aspects of their sexual and reproductive health.

---

have access to safe, effective, affordable and acceptable methods of family planning of their choice, as well as other methods of their choice for regulation of fertility which are not against the law, and the right of access to appropriate health-care services".

23 The power of some of the relevant human rights norms has been however challenged by the interpretative declarations and reservations expressed by a few number of Governments in order to avoid conflicts with religious rules as well as domestic customary practices. The UN Special Rapporteur on Religion referred to the use of reservations as a way to "legally disenfranchise women." See UN Doc. E/CN.4/2002/73/Add.2, § 74 and Hashemi (2007, p. 194 ff). The Holy See formulated its reservation to the phrase "family planning education and services" in the Convention on the Rights of the Child to mean "only those methods of family planning which it considers morally acceptable." See UN Reservations to the Convention on the Rights of Child: Holy See, www.unhchr.ch/html.menu3/b/treaty2ref.htm.

24 ICESCR, GC No. 14, *The right to highest attainable standard of health*, UN Doc. E/C.12/2000/4, § 14.

2. Women and men have the right to make choices about whether or not to reproduce.
3. Women and men need to have access to legal, safe, effective, affordable, and acceptable methods of fertility regulation consistent with their choice (2003, p. 12).

In the view of this author the endorsement of the concept "reproductive health" in international law requires among other things a holistic and comprehensive approach to existing law, i.e. the linking of several human rights provisions. It has been suggested in this regard that the term "reproductive and sexual rights" can be divided into two categories of rights: the right to reproductive health care and the right to reproductive self-determination (Center for Reproductive Rights 2002, p. 15)[25].

3.2. Examples of Various Reproductive Health Issues

The umbrella concept of "reproductive health" has multiple facets and encompasses such areas as fertility regulation, infertility, sexual transmitted diseases including HIV infection, the prohibition of female genital mutilation (FGM). The UNFPA referred recently to FGM as a common example of gender violence directed at women's sexual or reproductive capacity since at least 130 million women have been forced to undergo female genital mutilation with 2 million more at risk each year (UNFPA 2006). In the view of the FIGO Committee regarding the ethical aspects of human reproduction, "Medically harmful mutilation of body parts associated with gender or sexual function such as female genital mutilation is ethically unacceptable" (2003, p. 12). A similar standpoint has been expressed by the CESCR in its GC No. 16 from 2005 in which it interprets Article 12 of the Covenant, requiring state parties to undertake steps towards the realization of the right of everyone to the highest attainable standard of physical and mental health, as comprising prohibition of FGM.[26]

Among other examples of seldom mentioned types of violence against girls and women related to reproductive health which infringe upon reproductive self-determination, UNFPA mentions breast-ironing, a traditional practice in some West African countries involving crushing the breasts of young girls in order to deter male attention, as well as wide-spread traumatic fistula in African women often caused by gang rapes and forced insertion of foreign objects into the rape victims leading to incontinence and ostracization.

Extending the minimum age for marriage is not only a human rights issue but its consequence includes the prevention of adolescent childbearing and it has a

---

25 The International Planned Parenthood (IPPF) approaches reproductive rights from two perspectives: rights related to self-determination and rights related to reproductive health care.

26 UN Doc. E/C.12/2005/4, 11 August 2005, § 29.

health dimension as well. Child marriage, often arranged between unwilling girls and older men in the world's poorest countries, leads not only to large school drop-out rates but also to a greater risk of being exploited and contracting sexual infections, including HIV.

The aforesaid leads us to the conclusion that while the right to marry and to found a family, the right to family planning, the right to reproductive health, the right to equality and non-discrimination, the right to information and education, to physical integrity and to private and family life, are separate human rights on their own, and they are to be found in different international instruments, all of them interact with each other in a dynamic way. For this reason and in order to avoid loss of legal security, provisions of relevance should be viewed in a holistic way. In other words, the notion "reproductive health" needs to be integrated into a wider framework which addresses women's overall health, well-being and status.

Furthermore, in order to uphold a meaningful relationship between different human rights documents, the outcome of which may strengthen coherence in the international law system, it is of utmost importance that international human rights norms are interpreted in a uniform manner. In a report from 2006, the International Law Commission emphasized the principle of harmonization: "It is generally accepted principle that when several norms bear on a single issue they should, to the extent possible, be interpreted so as to give rise to a single set of compatible obligations."[27]

There are several examples of initiatives that have been and continue to be carried out with the aim of ensuring a consistent approach to reproductive health issues.[28] In addition, there seems to be a growing recognition that priority should be given to such an interpretation of human rights treaties provisions so that they can afford the best protection and status to the individual.

4. Abortion and Women's Reproductive Health in the Context of Human Rights

4.1 The Legality of Abortion and Accessibility of Reproductive Health Services

The growing concern internationally and nationally with maternal health and the legal and social position of women in society, as reflected in contemporary international law documents, has legitimated demands for the expansion of the

27 UN Doc. A/CN.4/L.702, 18 July 2006, Fragmentation of International Law, p. 8.

28 The Glen Cove Conference in 1996 and Glen Cove + 5 Conference in 2001 dealt explicitly with the integration of reproductive health issues in the work of the UN human rights committees. See Center for Reproductive Rights (2002, p. 32).

term reproductive health to include legal and/or safe abortion services under certain circumstances.[29] There is a clear tendency in the international community to recognize the adverse effects of unsafe abortions on women's health and scholars have argued that a right to abortion could be based on a claim to preserve the woman's health (Cook 1992, p. 720; Dixon-Mueller 1993, p. 177). Thus, access to safe abortion services is considered an important element of the internationally protected right to health and a universal human right (RFSU 2004b, pp. 24-25). Despite the fact that approximately 5 million women in developing countries are forced to be on the sick list each year because of complications resulting from unsafe abortions (The Lancet 2006), anti-abortion proponents often deny that abortion is a health issue. In addition, according to very recent statistics presented in The Lancet, 68 000 deaths were caused each year by illegal abortions (2006; RFSU 2004b, p. 5). In general, illegally performed abortions are also unsafe and result often in more complications and risks to women's health.

Very recently, on 16 April 2008 the Parliamentary Assembly of the Council of Europe approved a significant resolution (No 1607) aiming to remove all barriers to safe, affordable abortion services. Paragraph § 4 contains the view that:

> "A ban on abortions does not result in fewer abortions, but mainly leads to clandestine abortions, which are more traumatic and increase maternal mortality and/or lead to abortion "tourism" which is costly and delays the timing of an abortion and results in social inequalities. The lawfulness of abortion does not have an effect on a woman's need for an abortion, but only on her access to a safe abortion."

Both the CEDAW Committee and the CRC have on many occasions linked high rates of maternal mortality to lack of access and insufficient availability of comprehensive health services, including safe abortion services (Center for Reproductive Rights 2002, pp. 106-107 and p. 111). Moreover, CEDAW referred in its General Recommendation No. 24 of 1999 to the fact that "many women are at risk of death or disability from pregnancy-related cause because they lack the funds to obtain or access to necessary services." Against this background the Committee established that it is the duty of state parties to ensure women's right to safe motherhood and emergency obstetric services.[30] More importantly § 31c of the GR urges state parties "When possible, legislation criminalizing abortion

---

29 The health impact of unsafe abortion as a major public-health concern has been emphasized in § 63(i) of the ICPD + 5 Key Actions Document (*Key Actions for the further implementation of the Programme of Action of the International Conference on Population and Development*). Only the delegations from Argentine, the Holy See and Nicaragua expressed reservations to § 63(iii) in the same document stressing that: "in circumstances where abortion is not against the law, health systems should train and equip health-service providers and should take other measures to ensure that such abortion is safe and accessible." See www.unfpa.org/icpd/icpdmain.htm.

30 UN Doc. A/54/38/Rev.1, 2 February 1999, 20th session, § 27.

should be amended, in order to withdraw punitive measures imposed on women who undergo abortion." Other international bodies, too, such as the CESCR and CAT have on several occasions (EU Network of Independent Experts on Fundamental Rights 2005, p. 19) expressed their concerns over the relationship between high rates of maternal mortality and illegal, unsafe, clandestine abortions.

There is no doubt that through the legalization of abortion the detrimental effects of the illegal abortion on the health of women and adolescent girls can be diminished. Therefore, according to current international human rights law, the right to seek the interruption of pregnancy must be recognized for cases in which the continuation of pregnancy would seriously threaten a woman's life or health (EU Network of Independent Experts on Fundamental Rights 2005, p. 19). The European Parliament adopted in February 2004 a report on population and development which, after referring to the grave consequences of illegal and unsafe abortions, called for the availability of "legal and medically safe interventions" for women in need (Astra Network 2004). The Parliamentary Assembly of the Council of Europe, through the adoption of Resolution No. 1607 on 16 April 2008, invited member states to: "decriminalise abortion within reasonable gestational limits, if they have not already done so" (2008, § 7.1).

Increased internationalization has made it possible for European citizens to seek medical treatment within its member states. There is, therefore, a strong need to seek harmonization of legislation to regulate practices across national borders.

Interestingly, the argument for an amendment of the abortion law in Sweden with regard to accessibility of abortion services to third country nationals (i.e. citizens of none EU member states) was presented in a recent governmental report:

> "There is no acceptable reason to deny the right to an abortion in Sweden to women from countries outside EU. The reproductive health of women in developing countries is a high priority in Sweden. As a Member State of the European Union (EU), Sweden must equalize national legislation with the legislation of the Community and that legislation supersedes the national legislation."[31]

The Swedish Parliament adopted the proposal for legislative changes in November 2007[32] and the new Abortion Act (SFS 2007:998) entered into force on 1 January 2008.

Today, all EU Member States provide therapeutic abortion as an exception to the prohibition of abortion (EU Network of Independent Experts on Fundamental Rights 2005, p. 17). However, it should be mentioned that Malta, Ireland and Poland have a special clause in their EU treaty agreements allowing them to

31 Swedish public inquiry report: SOU 2005:90, p. 13.

32 Government Bill, prop. 2006/07:124, Abort för utländska kvinnor och förebyggande av oönskade graviditeter.

maintain their restrictive laws on abortion with only narrow therapeutic exceptions.[33] At the same time the majority of voters (59,3 per cent) in the referendum which took place on 11 February 2007 voted in favor of changing the strict abortion law in Portugal, i.e. to legalize abortion during the first 10 weeks of pregnancy.[34] Previously, abortion was illegal except in cases of rape, serious physical deformity of the fetus or when a pregnant woman's life is in danger. In addition, there are many examples of national regulations such as the 2004 clinical guidelines by the Royal College of Obstetricians and Gynecologists in the UK for the care of women seeking abortion on physical and mental health grounds which explicitly consider induced abortion as a health-care need.[35]

Nevertheless, the international picture of abortion laws and practices shows at present many contrasts. Along with the attitudinal changes, which have led globally to the increased legalization of induced abortion,[36] we also observe a tendency towards a more restrictive approach to abortion in, for example, a few European countries with a previously liberal attitude. Opposition to abortion and reproductive rights in general are on the rise in, among others, Hungary, Lithuania and Slovakia. The accessibility of abortion services is decreasing since health care professionals are increasingly reluctant or even refuse to perform abortions on moral grounds by claiming a right to conscientious objection. Especially in Slovakia the number of hospitals refusing to perform abortions by referring to conscientious objection is steadily growing.

Apparently, it may be a disadvantage to define abortion solely as a health issue disconnected from its human rights context because medical doctors then become the arbiters of its necessity and this, in turn, curtails women's entitlement to decide on their own. This was illustrated during a hearing which took place at the EU Parliament in Brussels in October 2005 when the severe consequences of not having access to safe abortion services in countries with restrictive abortion laws, among others Poland and Portugal, were revealed. At this occasion several speakers stated that abortion is a human right stemming from the right to bodily

---

33 Abortion, Report EU, p. 5. The view of the Catholic Church that abortion is "deliberate and direct killing" is still influential in the above mentioned countries. See Danguilan (1997, pp. 154-155).

34 As a result of the referendum's outcome President Silva signed in April 2007 a bill legalizing abortion on request during the first 10 weeks of pregnancy.

35 Written Comments by the Center for Reproductive Rights Pursuant to Rule 44, § 4 of the Rules of the Court, In the European Court of Human Rights (Application No. 5410/03) between Mrs. *Tysiac* and Poland, 21 September 2005, § 18.

36 A Fact Sheet produced by the Center for Reproductive Rights shows that currently, 61 per cent of the world's population live in countries where induced abortion is permitted either for a wide range of reasons or without restriction as to reason. See The World's Abortion Laws, May 2007, www.reproductiverights.org.

integrity, and the rights to life, health, equality and freedom from gender discrimination (RFSU 2005).

4.2 Conscientious Objections in Relation to Medical Services

Cultural traditions and values as well as religious norms have often been invoked against an extensive interpretation of the right to reproductive health.[37] Nevertheless, the views among representatives of different religions are divergent.[38] Also the degree of religious influence on national laws and policies varies considerably around the world.[39] Ensuring compatibility of religious norms with human rights law has thus become one of the main controversies today.

The right to religious conscientious objection is one dimension of the right to freedom of thought, conscience and religion as a protected human right in international law (e.g. Article 9 of the European Convention, Art. 18 of the ICCPR). It comprises a protection not solely of the inner faith of the individual but also the external manifestation of it through words and acts.[40] In addition, conscientious objection clauses relate to the refusal by individuals or entities to provide or cover certain health services based on religious or moral objection.[41] I have chosen to more specifically touch upon the question of religious conscientious objection since the practice of conscientious objection has the potential to seriously impact the availability of providers for reproductive health services, especially induced abortion, creating inconsistencies with international standards. In 1997 the CEDAW Committee noted in its concluding observation with regard to Italy's periodic report that the high incidents of conscientious objection

---

37 The Holy See, a few Latin American and Muslim states oppose for example the use of the term "reproductive health" since in their view it could include abortion. RFSU (2004a, p. 22).

38 Notably, to date all attempts to include language on conscientious objection to abortion for health care practitioners in international consensus documents have been unsuccessful. RFSU (2004a, p. 23).

39 Currently, there is a debate about aspects of morality including abortion within most religions. Whereas Jewish perspectives on abortion place woman's well-being as a central consideration, many national legal systems and policies which were strongly influenced by Catholicism and Islam limit the application of human rights in this area. It is, however, not atypical that Islamic schools of jurisprudence comprise different interpretations of the provisions of primary sources of Islamic law in particular verses of the Koran. See Center for Reproductive Rights (2005); Eriksson (2000, p. 185 and p. 282, footnote 486). See also RFSU (2004b, pp.16-18 and p. 24).

40 HRC, GC No. 22 of 1993, ECtHR Judgment in the *Kokkinadis v. Greece* case from 25 May 1993, Ser. A-260 § 31.

41 ECtHR, *D v. Ireland*, Written Comments by Center for Reproductive Rights, 14 April 2005, § 28.

among medical doctors and hospital personnel constitutes a major reason why women lack access to abortion services.[42]

The right to religious conscientious objection may conflict with other human rights protected by international law, and it is therefore of outmost importance that a satisfactory balance be struck between the different spheres of interests. Such a situation arises when a woman's right to lawful abortion is rendered ineffective in practice if medical doctors who refuse to perform abortion services invoke their right to conscientious objection, and there are no effective means to ensure alternative availability and accessibility of legal health services. This dilemma for the human rights movement is a challenge uncovered by, among others, Mr. Kofi Annan, the previous UN Secretary-General in his 2005 report "In larger freedom."[43]

Clauses on conscientious objection can be found in domestic abortion laws, public health laws and constitutions as well as in bilateral agreements. While many of the governments who have concluded concordats with the Vatican have agreed upon the inclusion of a provision on religious conscientious objection only with regard to exemption from armed military service, others do not refer to this issue at all. However, one of the agreements between Malta and the Vatican contains a clause relating to religious conscientious objection having the effect that Maltese legislation is generally accommodating to the prescriptions of the Roman Catholic faith, i.e. abortion is considered as a criminal offence.

Recently a draft treaty between the Slovak Republic and the Holy See on the Right to Objection of Conscience included in Article 4 (f) a reference to the right to exercise objection of conscience with regard to the performance of certain acts in the area of health care, in particular acts related to abortion.[44] Bearing in mind that approximately 70 per cent of the population in Slovakia is catholic, the EU Network of Independent Experts on Fundamental Rights considered the content of the text under discussion as constituting a potential threat to women's right to have access to certain medical services without any discrimination and thus being contrary to the international obligations, including the ICCPR, the ICESCR and CEDAW, of the Slovak Republic (EU Network of Independent Experts on Fundamental Rights 2005, p. 31). Furthermore, since restrictions imposed on the access to certain medical services, including in particular abortion which disproportionately affects women, they may be regarded as a

---

42 ECtHR, *T. v. Poland*, Written Comments by Center for Reproductive Rights, 21 September 2005, § 34.

43 His words are as follows: "When it comes to laws on the books, no generation has inherited the riches that we have. We are blessed with what amounts to an international bill of human rights. But without implementation, our declarations ring hollow. Without action, our promises are meaningless" (UN Doc. A/59/2005, § 129).

44 The reference regards the draft treaty version of May 2005, EU Network (2006, p. 34).

violation of states' obligations under Council Directive 2004/113/EC of 13 December 2004 implementing the principle of equal treatment between men and women in the access to and supply of goods and services (EU Network of Independent Experts on Fundamental Rights 2005, p. 32). As a result of the Networks' report which highlighted the potential effects of the intrusion of religion into politics, the Slovak government did not ratify the treaty with the Vatican.

The EU Network on Fundamental Rights, moreover, emphasized in its Opinion No. 4 on the right to conscientious objection and the conclusion by EU Member States of concordats with the Holy See of 14 December 2005 that:

> whether the right to religious conscientious objection is recognized explicitly in a concordat, or whether it is derived from the guarantee of freedom of religion stipulated in international human rights instruments, in the national Constitution or in specific legislation, this right should be regulated in order to ensure that, in circumstances where abortion is legal, no woman shall be deprived from having effective access to the medical service of abortion. In the view of the Network, this implies that the State concerned must ensure, first, that an effective remedy should be open to challenge any refusal to provide abortion; second, that an obligation will be imposed on the health care practitioner exercising his or her right to religious conscientious objection to refer the woman seeking abortion to another qualified health care practitioner who will agree to perform the abortion; third, that another qualified health care practitioner will be indeed available, including in rural areas or in areas which are geographically remote from the centre. Such a regulation should thus accommodate the right to religious conscientious objection, which is derived from the freedom of religion, while ensuring that the exercise of this right will not lead to others either being deprived of access to certain services in principle available to all in the State concerned, or being treated in a discriminatory fashion (EU Network of Independent Experts on Fundamental Rights 2005, p. 20).

The issue of conscientious objection relating to medical services has been dealt with also by the HRC during its review of periodic country reports. Upon the examination of the Polish report under the ICCPR in 2004 the Committee expressed in its Concluding Observations its "deep concern about the restrictive abortion laws in Poland, which may incite women to seek unsafe, illegal abortions, with attendant risks to their life and health" as well as the unavailability of abortion in practice even when the law permits it, in cases when medical practitioners refuse to carry out abortions on the basis of a conscientious objection clause.[45] Furthermore, according to the Ministry of Health in Poland the above mentioned difficulties arise out of so-called moral factors, that is the Polish peoples' religiosity, as well as political factors, i.e. the strong influence of conservative parties with anti-abortion policies promulgated by the Catholic Church and the conscientious objection clause (EU Network of Independent Experts on

---

45 UN Doc. ICCPR/CO/82/Pol, § 8.

Fundamental Rights 2005, p. 18). Against this background the HR Committee recommended that the Polish Government liberalize its legislation and practice on abortion.

Finally, CEDAW has taken the position in its General Recommendation No. 24 of 1999, which is an important contribution to interpreting the right to reproductive health, that: "It is discriminatory for a State Party to refuse to provide legally for the performance of certain reproductive health services for women. (I)f health service providers refuse to perform such services based on conscientious objection, measures should be introduced to ensure that women are referred to alternative health providers."[46]

5. Jurisprudence with Implications for Women's Reproductive Rights

Of significance for the issue under review is whether there are any decisions or statements by international courts or quasi judicial treaty monitoring bodies which may cast some light as to the content of the term reproductive rights and services.

One may without difficulty establish that to date very few cases pertaining to reproductive health and reproductive rights have been adjudicated internationally. One reason is the requirement that a complaint/communication is brought by or on behalf of a victim. The vast majority of international courts and monitoring bodies cannot initiate a legal procedure by themselves. Yet, another reason for scanty international jurisprudence seems to be the reluctance of international organs to elaborate upon the legal status of the fetus and the human rights of pregnant women.

5.1 Relevant Jurisprudence of UN's Treaty Bodies

In November 2005 the HRC dealt with a communication submitted by a 17-year old Peruvian girl (Karen Hamán) who was pregnant with a fatally impaired fetus (*anencephalic foetus*) and the gynecologist in charge had diagnosed that if the pregnancy continued it would clearly pose a risk to her life and health. Therefore, he recommended termination of the pregnancy. In other words, the circumstances in the case satisfied the conditions for a lawful abortion in Peru, which is permissible to save the girl's/woman's life or to protect her health. Notwithstanding this recommendation, the applicant's request for an abortion

46 CEDAW (Committee on the Elimination of Discrimination against Women), GR No. 24, Women and Health, UN Doc. A/54/38, 1999, § 11

was denied with the consequence that the baby died as expected just a few days after the birth.[47]

The HRC came to the conclusion in its final views that the victim's right to freedom from inhuman and degrading treatment was violated (Art. 7) since the applicant suffered from emotional distress and depression (i.e. moral suffering requiring psychiatric treatment) as a result of the denial of access to a therapeutic abortion. Most importantly, the Committee ruled that Article 2 of the Covenant was violated due to the absence of effective remedies against the refusal by the director of the public hospital to provide for the requested abortion (§ 6.2). The HRC emphasized furthermore that the denial by the public authorities of Peru of access to a therapeutic abortion to which the applicant was legally entitled endangered not only her life but also caused serious harm to her mental health, i.e. "mental suffering" (§ 6.3). The Committee ruled in addition that the protection under Article 7 is particularly important in the case of minors. The decision in the *Karen* case is innovative and it has significant implications for women's reproductive rights, since the issue of abortion was viewed in the context of women's self-determination and in a human rights context.

Apart from the case-law one may establish in the light of the HRC's GC No. 28 and the Concluding Observations on the country reports that there is an emerging consensus that, in cases of too restrictive abortion regulations, i.e. when abortion has been made criminal in all circumstances or only with too narrow exceptions, the practice of illegal abortions performed in unsafe conditions may threaten the right to life under Article 6 ICCPR (EU Network of Independent Experts on Fundamental Rights 2005, p. 17; see also Cook, Dickens and Fathalla 2003, p. 172).

5.2 Relevant Case-Law at the Regional Level

5.2.1 The Council of Europe

Despite the fact that the European Court of Human Rights has not yet arrived at the conclusion that the European Convention contains a right to seek abortion, it recognized in its inadmissibility decision in the Boso v. Italy case the need to take into account, in the regulation of abortion, the rights of the pregnant woman "as she is the person primarily concerned by the pregnancy and its continuation or termination."[48] The Court emphasized that Article 2 of the European Convention strikes "a fair balance between, on the one hand, the need to ensure protection of the fetus and, on the other, the women's interests. Having regard to the conditions required for the termination of pregnancy and to particular circumstances of the case, the European Court does not find that the respondent State has

47 *Karen Noelia Llontoy Huamán v. Peru*, Communication No. 1153/2003, 17 November 2005, ICCPR/C/85/D/1153/2003(2005).

48 *Boso v. Italy*, Appl. No. 50490/99, ECtHR, Judgment of 5 September 2002.

gone beyond its discretion in such a sensitive area" (§ 2).[49] In consequence, the Court rejected the application by the prospective father challenging Italy's abortion law for precluding consideration of the putative father's interests, i.e. invoking a violation of his right to found a family under the European Convention.

According to the prevailing views in the legal doctrine the full protection of the right to life under Article 2 of the European Convention begins only with the birth of the child. In support of this standpoint references have been made to the *travaux préparatoires* of Article 2, the practice of Member States of the Council of Europe legalizing abortion and the arguments of the European Commission, in among other things the *Brügemann and Scheuten v Germany* case of 12 July 1977 (EU Network of Independent Experts on Fundamental Rights 2006, p. 33).

The *Vo v France* case[50] is one of the very few specific cases originated in the European system in which the Court had to deal with the issue of whether a fetus has a right to life under Article 2 of the Convention. However, the Grand Chamber declined to decide on whether the fetus is to be considered as a person under that provision, and thereby protected. Instead, the Court referred in § 40 and § 82 of its judgment to the diversity of views on the point at which life begins, and by accentuating the significant variations it underlined that states have therefore a considerable discretion in the matter, i.e. it applied the margin of appreciation doctrine. Furthermore, the majority of judges took the position that "it may be regarded as common ground between States that the embryo/fetus belongs to the human race. The potentiality of that being and its capacity to become a person ... requires protection in the name of human dignity, without making it "a person" with the "right to life" for the purposes of Article 2" (§ 84). The European Court found it neither desirable, nor even possible to answer in the abstract the question of whether a fetus constitutes a person in the case at hand. Rather than deciding on the applicability of Article 2 in such situations, the Court deferred to the domestic legislator in view of an absent European consensus and in order to avoid a controversial ruling that might influence the diversity of European legal cultures. Nevertheless, five judges took the position in a separate opinion that Article 2 of the European Convention cannot be applied in pre-natal situations.[51] Most of the views expressed in the doctrine regret the Court's decision to avoid a clear statement and thereby "ensuring continuing confusion for future cases" (Plomer 2005, p. 171; Goldman 2005, pp. 277 ff.).[52]

---

49 *Boso v. Italy*, Appl. No. 50490/99.

50 Appl. No. 53924/00, ECtHR, Judgment of 8 July 2004.

51 Ibid., p. 44.

52 On 4 December 2007 the Slovak Constitutional Court blocked an attempt to outlaw abortion by referring, among other things, to the *Vo v France* case. Plús/12.01. conformity of Act No.73/1986 Coll. on artificial interruption of pregnancy as amended by Act No. 419/1991 Coll. with the Constitution. See www.reproductiverights.org.

Still, the Court's position, that if the unborn does have a 'right' to 'life' it is implicitly limited by the mother's rights and interests, is significant since it draws attention to the human rights aspects of women's reproductive rights.

Recently, on 20 March 2007, the European Court delivered its landmark judgment in the *Alicija Tysiac v Poland*[53] case. In this particular case Mrs. Tysiac accused the Polish authorities of violating the applicant's rights under Articles 3, 8, 13 and 14 of the European Convention due to the lack of an effective means of appeal against the decision of a medical doctor who refused to perform a lawful abortion justified on health reasons, with the consequence that the applicant became disabled through loss of her eyesight. The Court (six votes to one) arrived at the conclusion that the facts of the case had given rise to a breach of Article 8 of the Convention "since interruption of pregnancy touches upon the sphere of private life" (§ 106) and that "Once the legislator decides to allow abortion, it must not structure its legal framework in a way which would limit real possibilities to obtain it" (§ 156). Most importantly, the Court attached great relevance to the applicants' fears and that the pregnant woman's views should be considered in applicable procedures (§ 117). Moreover, the time factor was considered as being of critical importance: "The procedures in place should therefore ensure that such decisions are timely so as to limit or prevent damage to a woman's health which might be occasioned by a late abortion" (§ 118). Thus, the Polish authorities failed to comply with their positive obligations to safeguard the applicant's right to respect for her private life in the context of the controversy, i.e. disagreement between a pregnant women and the medical practitioner or between the doctors themselves, as to whether she was entitled to a therapeutic abortion (§ 128). Interestingly, Judge Borrego interpreted this paragraph in his dissenting opinion in the following manner: "I consider that the Court's decision in the instant case favors "abortion on demand"" and subsequently he took the position that "I respectfully consider that it is not the task of the Court to make such statements."[54] The *Tysiac* judgment has been commented in the literature as "an attempt to promulgate a full-fledged 'Right to Abortion' – not openly, but through the backdoor" (Cornides 2008, p. 126).[55]

---

53 ECtHR (4:th sec), Application No. 5410/03, Judgment (final) of 24 September 2007.

54 ECtHR, supra, p. 41. The Polish Government's appeal against the Court's Judgment was rejected by its Grand Chamber on 25 September 2007.

55 The same author expressed furthermore concern about: "The decadence into which human rights have fallen is attributable to an increasing estrangement between modern human rights talk and the perennial insights of moral philosophy, including classical (graeco-roman) and Christian thought as well as the philosophy of the era of Enlightenment" (Cornides 2008, p. 128).

With regard to the issue of conscientious objection the ECtHR explored its limits in the *Pichon and Sajous v France* case.[56] The Court found that employees such as pharmacists cannot give precedence to their religious beliefs and impose them on others by, e.g. objecting to ensure women's access to reproductive services, including refusal to sell contraceptive pills.

The European Court ruled in the 1992 case, *Open Door Counseling and Dublin Well Woman v Ireland,* that while it is within the realm of a state to protect public morals this right is not unlimited and it does not include restraints on receiving and giving information on how to obtain abortion in England.[57]

5.2.2 The Organization of American States (OAS)

There are some noteworthy developments within the inter-American human rights system as well. On 31 of October 2006 the Inter-American Commission on Human Rights released its very first statement on the abortion issue in the *Yasmina Bojorge* case declaring that the ban on abortion in Nicaragua is contrary to international law and threatens women's human rights.[58]

Moreover, in the case *Paulina Del Carmen Ramirez Jacinto v Mexico* the Government of Mexico agreed on 8 March 2006 that it had violated the rights of a 14 year old girl who became pregnant as the result of a rape in 1999 by denying her access to safe and legal abortion services (IAComHR 2007; see also Zampas 2007, p. 4). The Mexican law (Art. 136 of the Baja California Criminal Code) does not outlaw abortion for rape victims. Although the girl received permission to obtain a legal abortion, the public-sector hospital in Mexicali convinced her mother through misleading information (Lamas and Bisell 2000, p. 23) to decline the abortion. In addition, the State Attorney General took her and her mother to a Roman Catholic priest in order to dissuade Paulina from exercising her right to a legal abortion. This case is a step forward in that it was established that by denying access to legal and safe abortion services the girl was denied the right to decide over her body and reproduction. Subsequently, in April 2007,

---

56 ECtHR, Appl. No 49853/99, Judgment of 4 October 2001.

57 ECtHR, Judgment of 29 October 1992.

58 Yasmina 18 years old and five months pregnant girl died on 1 November 2006 after she had first sought emergency medical care at a hospital in Managua for painful uterine contractions, i.e. the symptoms of miscarriage. The doctors refused to provide emergency care because of the abortion laws' strict penalties. See for more information www.reprorights.se.

In November 2006 the National Assembly in Nicaragua enacted a blanket ban on abortion and thereby criminalizing relevant health services even when a woman's life is at risk. In August 2007 Human Rights Watch presented to the Supreme Court of Justice an analysis of international human rights law on abortion within the context of Nicaragua arguing, among other things, that to deny legal access to life- or health-saving abortion services contravenes international human rights standards. See HRW (2006a).

abortion was decriminalized by the Legislative Assembly for any reason during the first 12 weeks of gestation in the Federal District (Mexico City).

5.3 A Few Examples of Domestic Jurisprudence

The domestic courts in most countries have shown a cautious approach towards issues of relevance for reproductive rights and health. For example, the US Supreme Court chose not to explicitly rule on either the significant constitutional questions at issue in the case of *Ayotte v Planned Parenthood of Northern New England* from 18 January 2006. It restated, however, its precedent that abortion restrictions must contain an exception to protect women's health. During the mid-term elections in the US (7 November 2006), abortion was on the ballot in three states. In South Dakota, a ban amounting to outright criminalization of the procedure was defeated. The ban allowed for no exceptions if a woman was raped or was a victim of incest. In California and Oregon, the public voted down efforts to mandate parental involvement in abortion for teenagers.

Much celebrated have been the recent legal developments in Colombia, previously one of the most restrictive jurisdictions in the world with regard to abortion and access to reproductive health services. On 10 May 2006 the Constitutional Court in Colombia ruled in a remarkable 600 page decision that the prohibition of abortion where the life and health (physical and mental) of the woman are at risk may violate Colombia's obligations under international law.[59] Furthermore, in the view of the Constitutional Court abortion should not be considered a crime when pregnancy is a result of rape or incest or when grave fetal malformations make life outside the uterus unviable.

Concluding Reflections

In 2003 prominent legal scholars made the following observation: "The initial evolution, from addressing reproductive and sexual health issues through law on crime and punishment to applying the law on health and welfare, is incomplete internationally, and the further evolution to employ human rights law remains at its earliest stage" (Cook, Dickens and Fathalla 2003, p. 106). The current review highlighting the post-Cairo developments verifies that the interrelationship between human rights and reproductive rights has been ascertained in international law and more importantly that reproductive rights including the right to reproductive health have been widely recognized as a precondition for women's en-

---

59 "The total prohibition of abortion in all cases is a blatantly disproportionate measure as it infringes upon the rights of the pregnant woman, protected by the Constitution of 1991 as well as by the international human rights treaties that are part of the Constitutional Bundle" (Roa 2006, p. 61).

joyment of other human rights and gender equality (see Council of Europe 2008, § 7). Thus, the core value of gender equality constitutes a vehicle justifying decriminalization of abortion within reasonable gestational limits and thereby constituting a firm foundation for guaranteeing women's effective exercise of their right to access safe and legal abortion services. This essay has identified some remarkable advances in this regard.

The most recent developments within international jurisprudence to which this author has referred suggest that while the right to religious conscientious objection is accepted within the realm of freedom of expression provisions, it should not be exercised in a way depriving any individual from the possibility of exercising her rights as guaranteed under the relevant domestic legislation and that states have a duty to ensure effective access to reproductive health services as lawfully provided under the applicable legislation, including abortion. Moreover, the services must be provided in a timely manner which requires a sufficient number of trained providers. This is but one example of the increasing conceptual clarity of states obligations through international case-law.

The jurisprudential insight in the *Tysiac* case with regard to access to reproductive services, i.e. that there is a need for practical and sensitive procedures to preserve the abortion option was further developed and articulated very recently. In § 7.2 of the Council of Europe Parliamentary Assembly's Resolution No. 1607 states are invited to "guarantee women's effective exercise of their right to access to a safe and legal abortion" and that restrictions as to the effective access to safe, affordable, acceptable and appropriate abortion services "have discriminatory effects" (§ 2).

Notwithstanding the above mentioned progressive trends, a few issues related to the right to reproductive health continue to display tensions and difficulties in reconciling religion and law. Mr. Cornides has, for example, pointed out that: "abortion as a fundamental right would clearly be incompatible with the moral precepts of practically all of the world's major religious traditions" (Cornides 2008, p. 108). Despite the fact that most of the international human rights instruments are products of balancing competing universal claims and value systems, the reservations which have been made by the Holy See to consensual documents and treaties testify to the existing tension between religious dogma and international law. The 2004 Arab Charter on Human Rights refers moreover to Shari' a law as the framework of the interpretation of its provisions. However, when a law is invoked which has been viewed as created or given by God, contradiction to secular legislation initiated by governments will undoubtedly emerge.

Furthermore, the European Court of Human Rights has emphasized in the *D v Ireland* case[60] that issues such as abortion require a complex and sensitive ba-

---

[60] ECtHR, Application No. 26499/02, Judgment of 27 June 2006. The application was declared inadmissible on formal grounds, i.e. due to non- exhaustion of domestic remedies.

lancing of rights and "a delicate analysis of country-specific values and morals" (§ 90). It seems therefore that in sensitive matters the ECtHR like other international bodies often avoids difficult ethical and moral aspects in its decisions, and time and again reveals an unwillingness to impose obligations upon states party to the conventions. Thus, they prefer to rely upon domestic legislation as guidance. It is, therefore, not surprising that this essay shows that Europe has not yet a cohesive and consistent policy with regard to reproductive health and reproductive rights. On the other hand, a significant attempt at harmonization was made very recently through the adoption of the Parliamentary Assembly's resolution No. 1607 of 16 April 2008 on access to safe and legal abortion in Europe.

This review of the jurisprudential and other interpretative statements emanating from different international human rights bodies proves that they thus far have not revealed differing or contradictory views on the scope of state obligations, although some international bodies have taken the opportunity to deliver important decisions with the potential to enhance the legal protection of women's reproductive health. This trend has not been welcomed in all quarters. Critics of the *Tysiac* judgment see, for example, problems with regard to the current institutional role of the European Court of Human Rights in that it is "assuming the role of supreme law-maker" and especially "the selection and training of its Judges, and their philosophical backgrounds" has been attacked. These voices urge reforms "if it (the Court) wants to retain the respect and confidence of citizens" (Cornides 2008, pp. 128 and 129).

Reality shows, however, that there is an increased reference to treaty jurisprudence in domestic litigation "which leads to better human rights protection at the national level" (OHCHR 2008). The road-map marked by the recent international case-law will undoubtedly be a significant guide to national judiciaries and legislators. The Committee of Ministers of the Council of Europe has, for example, urged member states in its Recommendation (Rec(2004)5 from 12 May 2004) to "ensure that there are appropriate and effective mechanisms for systematically verifying the compatibility of draft laws with the Convention in the light of the case-law of the Court." This is also valid for already existing legislation (Council of Europe, 2004)[61] as well as for the expectations within other conventional systems. Particularly significant in this regard is the 2006 decision by the Colombian Constitutional Court which confirms the impact and the power of international human rights law and its potential to inspire progressive changes.

---

61 In addition, some Governments have amended domestic legislation discriminating on the basis of gender or sex in response to the CEDAW's recommendations. See OHCHR (2008).

References

E.R.R.C.	European Roma Rights Centre
HRW	Human Rights Watch
FIGO	The International Federation of Gynecologists and Obstetricians
IAComHR	Inter-American Commission of Human Rights
OHCHR	Office of the High Commissioner for Human Rights
OMCT	Organisation Mondial Contre la Torture-Europe
RFSU	Swedish Association for Sexuality Education
UNFPA	United Nations Fund for Population Activities

Astra Network. 2004. *Sexual and Reproductive Health and Rights in the European Union (EU)*. June 2004. Available at: http://www.astra.org.pl/eu_report.htm [accessed 10 August 2008].

Banda, Fareda. 2008. *Project on a Mechanism to Address Laws that Discriminate against Women*. Geneva: UN OHCHR.

Bergmann, Ylva, ed. 2004. *Breaking Through*. Stockholm: RFSU.

Cahn, Claude. 2004. "Challenging Coercive Sterilisations of Romani Women in the Czech Republic." *Roma Rights Quarterly* No 3. Budapest: European Roma Rights Centre, pp. 103-112.

Center for Reproductive Rights. 2005. *Amicus Curiae.* 18 May. Available at: www.reproductiverights.org [accessed 14 August 2008]

– 2002. *Bringing Rights to Bear*. Available at: www.reproductiverights.org/pub_bo_tmb.html [accessed 14 August 2008].

– 2005. Religious Voices Worldwide Support Choice: Pro-choice Perspectives in Five World Religions, Briefing Paper. Available at: www.reproductiverights.org/pdf/pub_bp_tk_religious.pdf [accessed 14 August 2008].

– 2000. *The Holy See at the United Nations: An Obstacle to Women's Reproductive Health and Rights*. Available at: www.reproductiverights.org/pdf/pub_bp_holyseeattheun.pdf [accessed 14 August 2008]

Cook, Rebecca J. 2006. *Foreword, Case C-355/2006, Excerpts of the Constitutional Court's Ruling that Liberalized Abortion in Colombia*. Available at: www.womenslinkworldwide.org/pdf_pubs/pub_c3552006.pdf [accessed 10 August 2008]

– 1992. "International Protection of Women's Reproductive Rights." *University Journal of International Law and Politics* Vol. 24. New York: New York University School of Law.

Cook, Rebecca J., Bernard Dickens and Mahmoud Fathalla. 2003. *Reproductive Health and Human Rights*. Oxford: Clarendon Press.

Cornides, Jakob. 2008. "Human Rights Pitted Against Man." *The International Journal of Human Rights* Vol. 12, No. 1. London, Routledge Publisher, pp. 107-134.

Council of Europe. 2008. Parliamentary Assembly Resolution No. 1607 on access to safe and legal abortion in Europe. Approved on 16 April. Strasbourg: Council of Europe.

– 2004. Recommendation on the verification of the compatibility of draft laws, existing laws and administrative practice with the standards laid down in the European Convention on Human Rights. Available at: https://wcd.coe.int/ViewDoc.jsp?id=743297 [accessed 17 August 2008].

Danguilan, Marileen J. 1997. *Women in Brackets: A Chronicle of Vatican Power and Control*. New York: Women Ink, International Women's Tribune Centre.

Dickens, Bernard and Rebecca Cook. 2000. "The scope and limits of conscientious objection." *International Journal of Gynecology & Obstetrics* Volume 71, Issue 1, 19 October, pp. 71-77.

Dixon-Mueller, Ruth. 1993. Population Policy & Women's Rights, Transforming Reproductive Choice. Westport: Praeger Publishers.

Eriksson, Maja Kirilova. 2000. Reproductive Freedom in the Context of International Human Rights and Humanitarian Law. The Hague: Martinus Nijhoff Publishers.

E.R.R.C. 2004. Coercive Sterilisations in the Czech Republic. 16 September. Available at: www.errc.org [accessed 10 August 2008]

EU Network of Independent Experts on Fundamental Rights. 2006. *Commentary of the Charter of Fundamental Rights of the European Union, M. Nowak*, Article 2 Right to life. pp. 30-36, Brussels. Available at: http://ec.europ.eu/justice_home/doc_centre/rights/charter/docs/network_commentary_final%20_180706.pdf [accessed 17 August 2008].

– 2005. *Opinion No. 4*. 14 December. Available at: http://ec.europa.eu/justice_home/cfr_cdf/doc/avis/2005_4_en.pdf [accessed 17 August 2008].

FIGO. 2003. *The Ethical Aspects of Human Reproduction and Women's Health*. London: FIGO Publisher. Available at: www.figo.org [accessed 12 August 2008]

Gerlė, Elisabeth. 2003. "Participatory Democracy and Human Rights for Women in Globalization-New Possibilities and Challenges." In D. Amnéus and G. Gunner, eds. *Mänskliga rättigheter- från forskningens frontlinjer* Nr 7. Uppsala: Studia Theologia Holmiensia, Justus Publisher, pp. 103-115.

Goldman, Tanya. 2005. "Vo v France and the Fetal Rights: The Decision not to Decide." *Harvard Human Rights Journal* Vol. 18, Spring, pp. 277-282, Boston.

Guardian, The. 1999. *Rome's Hard Road for Women*. 23 October, at 24. London: The Guardian.

Hashemi, Kamran. 2007. Religious Legal Traditions, Muslim States and the Convention on the Rights of the Child: An Essay on the Relevant UN Documentation, 29 Human Rights Quarterly, pp. 194-227, Johns Hopkins University Press.

HRW. 2006a. *Amicus Curiae Brief on Abortion – Related Provisions of Law 603 of 2006 (Penal Code).* Available at: http://hrw.org/pub/amicusbriefs/nicaragua0807web.pdf [accessed 10 August 2008].

– 2006b. *Women's rights and abortion.* Available at: www.hrw.org/women/abortion.html [accessed 12 August 2008].

IAComHR. 2007. *Report No. 21/07, Petition 161-02 (friendly settlement).* 9 March. Available at: www.cidh.org/annualrep/2007eng/Mexico161.02eng.htm [accessed 17 August 2008].

Lauglo, Marilyn and Sigrun Møgedal. 1999. *Reproductive choice*, a Background Document, EG 4: Strasbourg, Council of Europe.

Lamas, Marta and Sharon Bisell. 2000. "Abortion and politics in Mexico: Context is all." *Reproductive Health Matters* Vol. 8, pp. 10-23. London.

Lancet, The. 2006. Sexual and Reproductive Health for All. 9 December.

OHCHR, 2008. *News and Events, CEDAW now in Geneva.* 14 January. Available at: www.ohchr.org/EN/NewsEvents/Pages/Cedaw.aspx [accessed 10 August 2008].

OMCT. 2004. Interpretation of the Definition of Torture or Cruel, Inhuman or Degrading Treatment or Punishment in the Light of European and International Case Law. 30 October. Geneva: OMCT Publisher. Available at: www.omct.org [accessed 12 August 2008].

Plomer, Aurora. 2005. "A Fetal Right to Life? The case of Vo v France." *Human Rights Law Review.* Oxford: Oxford University Press, pp. 168-174.

Rahman, Anika, Laura Katzive and Stanley Henshaw. 1998. "A Global Review of Laws on Induced Abortion, 1985-1997." *International Family Planning Perspectives* Vol. 24, pp. 56-64. New York, Guttmacher Institute.

RFSU. 2005. Abortion, Making it a right for all women in the EU. Stockholm: RFSU.

– 2004a. *Breaking Through*, Stockholm: RFSU.

– 2004b. Respect Choice, Safe Abortion a Prerequisite for Safe Motherhood, Stockholm: RFSU.

Roa, Mónica. 2006. *C-355/2006: Excerpts of the Constitutional Court's Ruling That Liberalized Abortion in Colombia.* Available at: www.womenslinkworldwide.org/pub_c3552006.html [accessed 14 August 2008].

UN. 2008. General Assembly 62nd Session, 18 April, GA/10705.

UNFPA. 2006. *16 Days of Activism to End Violence against Women.* 24 November. Available at: www.unfpa.org [accessed 10 August 2008].

– 1994. *Programme of Action.* Available at: www.unfpa.org/publications/detail.cfm?ID=275 [accessed 17 August 2008].

Zampas, Christina. 2007. "Safe and Legal Abortion is a Woman's Human Right." *Human Rights Letters* Issue 1. Stockholm: Swedish NGO Foundation for Human Rights.

Chapter 3

Governing China's Population – The State Planning of Unplanned Persons

Susan Greenhalgh

At the heart of China's renowned population control program lies a modernist category that cries out for analytic and political attention: the planned/unplanned birth. At the dawn of the 21st century, China is full of images of the poster child of the nation's future: invariably an urban child, it is the planned progeny, the well educated, well dressed, healthy "quality" child who is playing and laughing as it graces the cities' pleasure spots. Elsewhere are cultural images of the unplanned child who is not supposed to exist. Usually the offspring of rural migrants in the cities, it is the uneducated, ragged, unhealthy child who is crying or fighting, disrupting social order, and generally polluting the cities' margins. These two images are never seen together but they belong side by side, for the creation of the planned child – the marker of modernity, the savior of the nation – has entailed the simultaneous creation of the unplanned child – the sign of backwardness, the obstacle that keeps China from attaining its rightful place on the world stage. Official and scholarly neglect of the unplanned child – its numbers, its socioeconomic plight, its subjectivity – adds to the importance of attending to it.

State-created, bureaucratically-elaborated social categories participate in the construction not only of cultural images, but also of social reality. Inspired by Foucault's writings on social normalization and government rationality in modern society (Foucault 1975; 1978; 1979; 1991), the anthropology of modernity has traced the modernist discourses and governmental technologies through which such normalizing categories are formed and made effective (classic studies are Rabinow 1989; Ferguson 1990; Horn 1994; Escobar 1995; Gupta 1998; on classification, Bowker and Starr 1999). In the post-World War II era, the dominant domain of such modernist discourses and technologies in third world countries such as China is "development". (Here and below, I use quotation marks to highlight the discursive construction of terms.) This work suggests that "development" is not merely a rise in economic productivity; it is also a field of power, with its own imagined futures, modernist discourses, governmental institutions and practices, and social effects. "Development" is also a form of government rationality, a logic of state whose object is the population and whose aim is normalization of society in the name of optimizing the health, welfare, and usefulness of the population (on governmental reasoning and technologies generally, Gordon 1991; Rose 1999; 2007; Dean 1999). Ethnographic research suggests that the discourses and apparatuses of "development" are highly *productive* – but rarely in the ways the planners intend (especially Ferguson 1990; Holston 1989; 1999). Once bureaucratically embedded in society, the discursive and material practices of "development" have far-ranging, often unanticipated, effects on the distribution of material goods, the allocation of social power, and the subjectivities of human beings.

Like the discourses of modernity generally, the discourses of "development" break reality down into discrete sectors – agriculture, industry, public health, urban planning, and so forth. One sector that has been relatively neglected by critics of modernity is "population". The highly naturalized character of "population" (Horn 1994) has discouraged inquiry into the bio-political dynamics and sociopolitical effects of governmental projects of population management, despite their ubiquity in modern life. In the last ten years, however, the governance of "population", especially at the microlevel of individual bodies, organs, and genes, has gained growing attention. Science studies and governmentality studies work on such topics as biological citizenship, biovalue, and genetic engineering, as well as discursive approaches to the transnational governance of third world populations (Greene 1999; Halfon 2006), are all part of this new interest in the politics of life itself. This work makes clear that "population" is much more than an aggregate of human being exhibiting vital rates (fertility, mortality, and so on). Like "development", "population" operates as a huge field of power, with its own imaginaries, discourses, institutional apparatuses, political technologies, and social effects.

"Population" and Modern Power: Classifying Life, Producing the Political

The notion of governmentality – a combination of government and rationality – gives us purchase on the mentalities, techniques, and effects of "population" (Foucault 1991; Rose 1999; Dean 1999). Focusing on more or less rationalized projects to shape conduct according to specific norms so as to achieve particular ends, such approaches allow us to link questions of governance of whole populations to questions of individual identity, and to see the historicity and contingency of the political world we take for granted. This work highlights the fundamental role of knowledge (or systematic thought) and its classificatory schemes in the making of the political. It enables us to see how governmental rationalities (plans, problematizations, visions, know-hows) become constitutive of government itself, defining such things as its object, its strategic rationale and aims, and the categories into which "life" is sorted for purposes of administration and optimization.

This emphasis on classificatory schemes for life directs our attention to the *social categories* embedded in governmental technologies for population surveillance, management, and restriction. Such technologies include the census, the survey, and the family planning program. Though seemingly neutral, and purportedly even beneficent, the categories embedded in state projects for population counting and control ("over/underpopulated", "high/low fertility", and so forth) are designed to effect direct interventions in the domain of the social. Once built into population projects, such categories are likely to be politically and culturally productive, redistributing resources and social power, transforming existing subjectivities and social groupings, and perhaps even creating new forms of personhood.[1]

The efficacy of "population" categories emerges with particular force in socialist countries, whose states enjoy exceptional power to reshape social life through their extensive control over the resources and institutions of society (see, for example, Kligman 1998). Although socialism has been proclaimed dead, throughout the postsocialist world, but especially in late socialist and market socialist regimes still dominated by communist parties, substantial chunks of socialist discourse and practice remain to shape the transitions to the "posts" (Stark and Bruszt 1998; Burawoy and Verdery 1999). The classifying activities of both classical and late socialist states are especially interesting because they are rooted in a Marxian variant of the discourses on development. Though constructed as their binary opposite, Marxian discourses of development share with capitalist discourses dreams of "progress" and "modernity" through "development" (Kornai 1992, pp. 49-62; Scott 1998, pp. 193-222). Marxian discourses, however, give greater emphasis to social and development "planning" by the state. At least theoretically, "socialist modernity" is a comprehensively planned modernity, organized and executed by the state. The developmental projects of socialist states are also intriguing because the categories of analysis and intervention employed in them are often created not from the professional discourses of (bourgeois) economics, demography, and the other human sciences, but from the ideological discourses of Marxian theory, which inflect the scientific framings of social issues. The use of Marxian categories provides a different way of "doing development", whose larger effects remain insufficiently understood even after transitions to market forms of socialism and away from formally socialist regimes altogether.

The social productivity of population categories emerges with special clarity in China, home to the world's largest national population and largest still-ruling communist party. Despite the monumental significance of China's fertility control efforts – which, official estimates suggest, have "averted" over 400 million births since the early 1970s, with profound effects at every level of the social

---

1 Research on the colonial census has highlighted the unexpected productivity of census categories in creating new group identities and new group politics, politics that, in some places, ended up not just undermining their creators' goals, but also subverting colonial rule itself (Cohn 1987; Anderson 1991; Appadurai 1996; on contemporary censuses and identities, Kertzer and Arel 2002; Szreter, Sholkamy, and Dharmalingam 2004). On the governmental functions of the family planning program in the construction of modern subjects, see esp. Ali 2002; Chatterjee and Riley 2001.

system – the categories structuring reproduction have attracted much less interest than those organizing the government of other domains of Chinese life (class, residence, ethnicity, and gender, for example). The literature on China's population work emphasizes the demographics and politics, and leaves the Marxian ideological and discursive structure of China's approach largely unexamined (major studies include Banister 1987; Tien 1973; 1991; Scharping 2003; White 2006). Some anthropological work has examined state and popular categorizing practices ("excessively populous", "population quality"), but it has not yet linked the discursive terms to the concrete bureaucratic practices, political dynamics, or sociodemographic effects of China's gargantuan birth planning project..

This article is part of a larger project that systematically analyzes the official discourses of population, how they were made and turned into political action, how they have changed over time, and with what effects. In *Just One Child: Science and Policy in Deng's China* (2008) I analyze the scientific and official construction of China's population problem during the early reform period, 1978-80. I show how the population problem was framed as a "crisis of modernization", a framing that demanded a drastic solution – the immediate institution of a one-child-for-all rule – regardless of the social and human costs. In *Governing China's Population: From Leninist to Neoliberal Biopolitics*, political scientist Edwin A. Winckler and I (2005; hereafter, *GCP*) trace the "governmentalization" of population from 1949 to 2004, showing how the management of population quantity and "quality" first became a domain of state practice, and then gradually shifted from state to market and society. *Governing China's Population* shows how the crisis-crackdown formulation of the population issue got embedded in bureaucratic practice, and the consequences for China's society, state, and position in the world.

This chapter continues the inquiry, focusing on one of the least well known and most troubling dimensions of China's population program. Its point of departure is the Chinese term "birth planning" (*jihua shengyu*), the central construct and categorical norm in the official state discourse on population. This essay tracks the process by which the birth project, designed to create a modern, planned population, produced not only a large group of "planned persons", but also a huge outcast group of unmodern, "unplanned persons" who will surely complicate China's modernization. This underground population is almost never officially acknowledged, and therefore remains little studied in China and virtually unknown beyond China's borders.[2] The anthropology of the state has illuminated the production of graded forms of personhood in contemporary society (Maurer 1997; Ong 1999). China's unplanned persons provide a striking example of such stratified citizenship.

2 Of course, some concerned scholars, journalists, and officials have addressed the issue, but this attention has been sporadic. Chinese colleagues share my belief that this underground population has not been the focus of any major research effort.

"Unplanned persons" is the term I have coined to draw attention to these people's ironic origins in state planning and their awkward status in what, not so long ago, was a theoretically planned society. The Chinese term for them, the "black population" (*hei renkou*) or "black persons, black households"(*heiren heihu*), underscores instead their illegitimate status as persons outside the household registration system. (In the late 1990s, the state expunged the term "black population" from the official lexicon, replacing it with "unregistered population." The former term stubbornly persists in popular culture, however).

I contend that this unexpected effect of China's population control project stemmed only in part from factors emphasized by other ethnographers: the workings of social structures unacknowledged in the discourse and overly totalizing assumptions of state planners (especially Ferguson 1990; Holston 1989). This contradictory effect of state birth planning was also an inevitable consequence of the way modernity itself is constituted out of binary discourses based on assumed differences between "the West and the Rest" At the heart of modernity's making lie the twin processes of social categorization and social normalization. States and other modernizing agents create modernist discourses that establish categorical norms – socially desirable, "modern" ways of being – and deviations. They then introduce bureaucratic plans, practices, and programs structured to shape society to the norm. In this moment of bureaucratic actualization, however, modernizing agencies inadvertently create the underside of modernity even as they attempt to fabricate modernity alone. Although these contradictory features of the construction of modernity are quite general, China throws them into sharp relief because of the exceptional power of the Chinese state and because of that state's ambition to create Chinese modernity at the fastest possible speed – regardless of the human costs.

To make analytic sense of this inadvertent process of political subject-making, I employ the copious notion of the political offered by the literature on governmentality. "The governmental" takes as its object a scheme, policy, or program and renders it politically meaningful by elaborating its underlying political ambitions and rationale, the techniques and technologies by which it is deployed, and it effects on human subjects and subjectivities (especially Rose 1998; Dean 1999). These aspects of what I call the life cycle of a governmental project unfold historically and often over a long stretch of time. Accordingly, my narrative will be arranged in rough chronological order, and it will span the decades since the founding of the People's Republic, from the era of high socialism under Mao Zedong (1949-76) to the years of reform or late socialism inaugurated by Deng Xiaoping (1978-present). From its birth in socialist dreams and Marxist-Maoist ideology, I follow the discursive figure "birth planning" through its theoretical elaboration, bureaucratic embodiment, and programmatic implementation, to trace its social effects on subjectivities and the distribution of economic resources and social power. By drawing on what Chinese officials, academics, and cadres told me in sometimes lengthy discussions conducted over more than 20 years, during 10 of which I was deeply involved in scholarly collaborations and policy debates in China's population field, as well as readings of their various writings, this chapter charts the construction of the unplanned Chinese person in hopes of drawing scholarly attention to the existence of this new kind of personhood, and, more generally, to the unsuspected efficacy of "population" as a domain of modern power.

Socialist Dreams and the Anti-Malthusian Roots of "Birth Planning"

China's birth planning venture was based on a beautiful dream. Fashioned in the early years of the People's Republic, it was a dream of transforming a poor, backward, agrarian nation into a prosperous, modern, industrialized power in a short period of time. China's dream differed from most in its socialist character. Under the leadership of the Chinese Communist Party (CCP), and guided by its Marxist-Leninist-Maoist understanding of historical development, the Chinese state would undertake comprehensive state planning, subjecting everything under the sun to the coordinated control of social engineers in the state (Lardy 1978; Howe and Walker 1989). State planning would enable China to accelerate its industrialization and modernization, "catch up" with the West, and achieve its rightful place of wealth and power in the world within the imaginable future.

China's dream of accelerated modernization entailed the planning not only of production, but also of reproduction. Because of China's commitment to socialism, its formulation of the population problem had to be, above all, *not*-capitalist. As good Marxists, Chinese theorists had to avoid Malthus's universal formulation of excess population as a problem of resource shortage. Instead, they had to see China's population problem as relative, or specific to its mode of production.

At mid-century, though, no Marxian formulation of the population problems of a poor, crowded "semifeudal, semicolonial" country such as China yet existed. Over the first decade of CCP rule, China's leaders worked out a distinctive Marxist-Leninist-Maoist formulation of China's population problems. In 1956-57, in the context of a nationwide campaign to promote comprehensive socialist planning, Mao introduced the novel concept of (state) "birth planning" (White 1994; Zhang 1998, pp. 29-32). Mao's construction cleverly avoided the Marx-Malthus conflict: by framing China's population problem in the Marxian language of anarchy in the "production" of human beings, he could construe unregulated human reproduction as anti-socialist, contrary to the fundamental interests of the Chinese state. This formulation of the problem allowed him to reframe the solution as one of socialist planning. In a stroke Mao had redefined the planning of births as an irrefutable task of the socialist state – and placed a weighty modernist binary, anarchic/planned childbearing or the unplanned/planned birth, at the heart of China's approach to population control.

Mao's ambivalence about the benefits of China's huge population, coupled with the tumultuous political campaigns of the 1950s and 1960s, kept the state planning of births largely off the policy agenda. Yet through a complicated political process that involved the persecution of those with other ideas and the declaration of population as "forbidden territory" (Tien 1973), the birth planning construct survived the Great Leap Forward and Cultural Revolution to become not only the sole legitimate approach to population control but also an essential task of China's government. In the mid-1970s the anarchy/plan formula was made the centerpiece of an elaborate conceptual apparatus, explored just below, that has guided thinking about population in China to this day. The significance of the birth planning formulation cannot be overstated. In the more familiar Western liberal notion of "family planning", births are planned in a voluntary way by the couple on the basis of their individual circumstances as they themselves perceive them. The role of the state is largely limited to the provision of education and contraception. In the Chinese notion of birth planning, births are planned by the state on the basis of the collective good, as determined ultimately by a small number of top party leaders.

During the revolutionary decades of the 1950s and 1960s, birth planning became the official formulation, the only way the population question could be spoken about in public discourse. Some controls on demographic discussion were lifted in the mid- to late 1970s, when population was removed from the list of "forbidden zones" and the field of population science was recreated to serve a new project of state-directed population control. Yet new restraints on demographic discourse were effectively imposed in 1978, when birth planning was made a constitutional obligation, and again in 1982, when the planning of births was declared a "basic state policy", off limits to criticism on fundamentals. To be sure, the climate for debate is more open today than it has been at any time since the mid-1950s. Since the mid-1990s the birth control program has been embracing a "quality-of-care" agenda inspired by the 1994 Cairo International Conference on Population and Development (Zhang, Gu, and Xie 1999; *GCP*, ch. 4-5).[3] Yet despite the flowering of new discourses on reproductive health, population remains a sensitive and somewhat risky subject to this day, to be discussed only within frameworks set by the state.

Theoretical Elaborations: Establishing the Rationale for, Method of, and Agent in Charge of Birth Planning

Mao died in 1976, but the concept of birth planning he had authored did not die with him. In 1978 a new leadership coalition took over, with Deng Xiaoping as

[3] The Cairo Conference fundamentally shifted the means and ends of international population policy from concern with demographic targets to concern for women's reproductive and sexual health, choice, and rights.

its head. Determined to overcome decades of sluggish economic growth and low living standards, the Deng regime rewrote the script for China's future, placing the development of market socialism and the transformation of China into a modern nation within decades at the top. Of course, China was to remain socialist and the Communist Party was to remain at the helm. But the Chinese people were to get an appealing new goal toward which to work: achieving a "comfortable standard of living" (*xiaokang shuiping*) by the year 2000. Since economic goals were expressed as per capita targets, population control – drastic population control – was to be a key item on the new agenda.

Between mid-1978 and late 1980, a bold new strategy for restricting population growth was dreamed up, tested out, and then announced to the broad masses of the Chinese people through an unusual "Open Letter" calling for all couples to limit themselves to one child (for the politics, see Greenhalgh 2008). Between the mid-1970s and early 1980s, discursive elements from many sources were drawn together and elaborated into a complex conceptual apparatus that served to legitimize and later guide the enforcement of the one-child policy. This discourse established the basic rationale, goals, and methods of birth planning under reform socialism. Although the Marxist ideology in which the population discourse is framed has lost its dominant position in reform-era Chinese politics, ideology retains a critical role in shaping policy options and choices (Misra 1998; Zhang 1996). As David Kelly has argued, "Orthodox Marxism continues to provide and propagate a discursive field, setting up the ways in which social and political reality is categorized, and thus the ways in which political problems are resolved" (Kelly 1991, pp. 21). The continued salience of Marxian constructs is clearly evident in the population domain. Although problems encountered in the enforcement of birth planning forced modification of concrete methods and targets, and the larger discursive framings in which population control practice is set have been modified to fit changing ideological orthodoxies established by successive Party Congresses ("primary stage of socialism", "socialist market economy", and so on), the political ideas about the proper rationale and means of birth planning that were worked out in the late 1970s remain intact to this day.

The most fundamental notions underlying the birth planning formulation were Marx's materialist vision of society and the associated idea of historical movement of society through successive modes of production.[4] In that vision, population was considered part of the economic base, to be planned and manipulated like steel, grain, or any other commodity. China's population theorists in the 1970s drew on Engels's notion of the "two-fold character of production" to explain why, in a developing socialist country, the production of human beings should be

4 The arguments developed in this section are based on reading of official birth planning documents and speeches by top party and government leaders, as well as Chinese works on population theory.

treated like the production of material commodities, subject to overall coordination by planners in the state. In an important article published in the *People's Daily* in 1979, top population official Chen Muhua not only made the control of population growth through birth planning central to China's definition of its national purpose and identity, she also removed it from the trivial arena of individual decisions, placing it squarely in the "serious" realm of China's historical evolution toward economic modernization and communist utopia (Chen 1979, p. 2).

The primary method by which births were to be planned was "propaganda and education" (*xuanchuan jiaoyu*). Viewing history as progress from "feudal" to "socialist", "backward" to "advanced", "traditional" to "modern", the discourse framed the project as one of political education designed to transform the old into the new, thereby propelling China into the next stage of historical development. Like "development" discourse generally, the birth planning discourse divided the world into modernist binaries, precisely in order to erode them. Although the population as an aggregate was treated as part of the material base of society, individual couples' views about childbearing were seen as organic components of the superstructure (Liu et al. in Tien 1980). As matters of thought or ideology, these notions were subject to political transformation.

The major ideological obstacles to the spread of the single-child family were remnants of "feudal" culture, in particular, the ideas that many children bring much happiness (*duozi duofu*) and that males are more valuable than females (*zhongnan qingnu*). Despite China's socialist political economy, such feudal ideas were said to linger, especially in the countryside, because of the deep influence of centuries of Confucian and Mencian thought (Hua 1985, pp. 21). Indeed, the feudal values of the peasantry were seen as being reinforced by the introduction of the household responsibility system in agriculture. This modern-binaristic (old/new) formulation of the problem was significant for a number of reasons. By labeling the preferences for several children and for sons "old-fashioned" and "feudal" in origin, the discourse rendered unthinkable the possibility that contemporary sociocultural and political-economic forces might have inadvertently reproduced them. And by tagging the ideas of the peasants "feudal" and in need of transformation into "socialist", the population discourse turned the rural masses into the primary objects of intervention and control.

The answer to the question of who should be in charge of this task drew on Lenin's views of a vanguard party which, through thorough training in Marxian thought, represented the leading edge of society. Top party leaders would be in charge of important policy decisions, while rank-and-file party members and party-affiliated "mass organizations" at all levels of society would "take the lead" in carrying it out. Working with party cadres, government officials at each administrative level were to ensure policy implementation and fulfillment of the population plan.

The party was portrayed as not only all-knowing in its understanding of the reproductive desires of the masses, but also all-powerful in its ability eventually to change their childbearing ideas and accomplish the goals set by the top leadership. In the words of the 1980 Open Letter, "The goal can be attained provided we make concerted efforts" (CC 1985, pp. 28). The solution to poor planning performance was always for cadres to redouble their efforts, to work harder to achieve the "struggle targets" established by the political center. Common to master plans for development generally (Scott 1998), the planners' assumptions – that they could bend political reality to their will – were wildly overambitious. This can-do attitude, this failure to imagine failure, was to have unintended consequences when party rhetoric met up with social reality.

Bureaucratic Inscription: From Marxian Construct to Social Category, Planning Target, and Policy Goal

To be useful, the Marxist-theoretic construct of birth planning had to be converted into a social category and inscribed in the bureaucratic apparatus guiding economic and social planning, the primary obligation of the socialist state. To facilitate birth planning work, a multi-tiered birth planning bureaucracy was tentatively established in the early 1960s, solidly reestablished in the early 1970s, and then firmly institutionalized in the early 1980s, with the creation of the inter-ministerial State Birth Planning Commission (SBPC) (later renamed the National Population and Family Planning Commission). The first step in the process of bureaucratic inscription was to integrate population goals into the economic plan by establishing long- and short-term targets for total population size and the natural growth rate of the population. As the chaos of the Cultural Revolution subsided, population planning quickly became reality. In 1971 a population target was incorporated into the Fourth Five-Year Plan (1970-74) and in 1975 national targets for the Fifth Five-Year Plan (1975-79) were translated into local targets and handed down to grassroots leaders throughout the country. From 1975 local reproductive practice became a regular, integral feature of the centrally organized, target-driven process of economic planning. With this, babies and thus persons became planned products of the socialist state (cf. White 2006).

A few years later, shorter-term planning targets were linked up to longer-term reform goals for century's end, when the first stage of socialist modernization was to be completed. In 1980 the first long-term population size goal was announced: China would keep its population within 1.2 billion by 2000 (CC 1985). As that goal began to look unreachable, the long-term target was cautiously raised. In the mid-1980s the year 2000 goal was changed to "about 1.2 billion", and around 1990 it was raised to under 1.3 billion, where it remained until the turn of the century. These planning targets were crucially important, for they were to become the focal point, the raison d'être for a whole series of practices introduced in the name of planning births and population growth.

Ensuring that plan targets were met required the construction of measures of plan performance that could be created and regularly updated at every level of the administrative system. To facilitate birth planning work, the State Birth Planning Commission and its subordinate units at each level also collected indices of planned births; late marriage and late childbearing; and the proportion of first, second, and higher-order (called "multiple") births in all births. Most important for our purposes is the planned birth rate (*jihua shengyulu*): the number of births conforming to the local birth targets during the period divided by the total number of births during the period (Wang 1991, p. 74).

Because it was based on a binary construction, the index of planned births implied the existence of its opposite, unplanned births. Yet unplanned births received less formal bureaucratic expression. While planned birth rates were proudly publicized as evidence of cadres' achievements, rates of unplanned births were less often made public. Where unplanned births were bureaucratically noted, that notice often took punitive form, as, for example, in provincial birth planning regulations, which stipulated fines, mandatory birth control surgery, and other punishments for those with unplanned pregnancies and births (see, for example, Greenhalgh 1990). Unplanned births, also known as "excess" or "above-quota" births (*chaosheng*), were also the objects of critical scrutiny in articles published in Chinese birth planning journals. In these articles, roughly 100 of which I reviewed for this essay, unplanned pregnancies and births were without exception designated "problems" that needed to be "prevented" so as to "raise the low quality" of birth planning work[5] (e.g., Chen 1991; Han 1991; Gao and Shen 1993). Designated illegal and punishable, childbearing outside the plan became an underground activity which could survive only by escaping the network of control. The bureaucratic results were monumental problems of oversight and measurement for birth cadres. Politically dangerous and virtually unsurveillable, unplanned births entered a grey zone of uncountability or, better yet, "inaccurability", in the bureaucratic apparatus. (Unplanned births could be counted, but not with any accuracy.) The unplanned birth became a danger-fraught category, the dark, unenumerated underside of the bright planned birth rate all communist cadres were supposed to raise.

Embodying the totalizing aspirations of the planners, population policy broke reproduction down into its component parts (marriage, childbearing, contraception, and so forth) and then established detailed and precise regulations so that every aspect of reproduction could be planned and controlled in a comprehen-

5 This discussion is based on an analysis of Chinese articles on "unplanned" and "excess" childbearing published between the mid-1980s and late 1990s. Of the approximately 100 articles reviewed, 16 were read closely.

sive, meticulous way. The complex regulations would then be translated into simple slogans for wide dissemination through the party's propaganda machine. Under the one-child policy announced in 1979-80, the official slogan became "late marriage, late childbearing, few births, quality births" (*wanhun, wanyu, shaosheng, yousheng*). The norm for number of children became: "Encourage one child, strictly limit second children, resolutely prohibit third and higher-order children." Such demands neglected the social structures and cultural values fostering desires for two or three children and at least one son in the countryside. Those overlooked beliefs and social practices, discussed just below, would come to plague the planners when the plans and policies were transformed into concrete political practice.

Policy Implementation: Peasant Resistance and the Proliferation of Unplanned Births

These general reproductive guidelines were established at the political center and then turned into concrete policy regulations at the provincial level. Beginning in the late 1970s, China's roughly 30 provincial-level units issued birth planning regulations and assumed responsibility for enforcing them.[6] The major task for local birth officials in urban neighborhoods and rural villages was to ensure the planning of births within their areas – in bureaucratic terms, to achieve high rates of planned births so that the population plan target was fulfilled. Each year officials at the grassroots were given a numerical quota of births that fell within the state plan. All births in excess of that number were by definition unplanned.

To achieve high planned birth rates, local officials were instructed to rely primarily on "propaganda and education." With the introduction of the one-child policy in 1979-80, they were to supplement educational means with economic rewards and penalties and, when those failed, administrative measures. Legal means were gradually introduced as well, as birth rules were incorporated into laws on social matters such as marriage, adoption, and women's rights; (Palmer 1995), and, in 2001, into a national population and birth planning law (*GCP*, pp. 158-160). In the cities, cadre control over the means of urban subsistence (jobs, housing, education, health care, rations, and so on), combined with the high costs of raising children, made it relatively easy to reach high rates of planned births (Milwertz 1997; Rofel 1999). The situation in the countryside was more complex. My own

6 This section on policy enforcement is based on wide reading of the Chinese birth planning literature, as well as two periods of field research in China, involving village fieldwork and interviews with cadres at all levels of the administrative system. For accounts of the politics of policy enforcement in the villages studied, see Greenhalgh 1993, 1994 and Greenhalgh and Li 1995.

village field research suggested that in the 1970s, when rural society was still organized in socialist collectives, cadre control over work, income, and other necessities of life made birth planning work manageable (for a countrywide account see Chen and Kols 1982). That changed with the introduction of rural economic and political reforms in the late 1970s and early 1980s. The dismantling of rural collectives brought declines in cadre power, shifts of resources into the hands of ordinary peasants, and growing peasant desires for more children, especially sons. Those desires, however, were not so much "feudal remnants", as reflections of the multiple needs children fulfilled in rural China's still-familistic culture and socioeconomy: labor, old-age support, family continuity, lineage power, and just plain love and affection (see, for example, Croll, Davin, and Kane 1985; Peng and Dai 1992; Zhu and Peng 1996; for a summary, see *GCP*, ch. 7). Increasingly, economic incentives available for policy enforcement disappeared and administrative measures failed to work.

Despite efforts to achieve the full planning of births, in the countryside there was massive resistance to a policy that was profoundly out of touch with rural sociocultural reality. Widespread opposition to the one-child rule led to big gaps in enforcement and, in turn, large numbers of unplanned births. Local cadres often colluded with peasant resisters because of unwillingness or simply inability to enforce the state's strict limits on fertility. As the tactics of resistance multiplied, the numbers and types of unplanned births – and hence children – grew. Chinese-language articles hint at the existence of a huge underground culture of escape from the birth planning network, complete with a richly nuanced vocabulary of illegitimacy: "dark births" (*ansheng*), "struggle births" (*qiangsheng*), "supplementary births" (*busheng*), "next births" (*mingsheng*), "bought births" (*maisheng*), and so on (see especially Han 1991). A few illustrative examples of these evasive strategies should suffice to make the point (for more, see Wasserstrom 1984; Chu 1991; White 2006).

One common form of resistance was to conceal a pregnancy from local officials, have the baby in a distant hospital, and then either hide it at home or place it with relatives elsewhere to care for for a few months or years. A second group of resisters came to be known as "excess-birth guerrillas" (*chaosheng youji dui*) for their practice of fleeing their home areas and moving elsewhere, often to locations along provincial borders or the peripheries of large cities, to have children. Those moving to cities became part of the 100-million-plus "floating population." A third group of evaders married and had children before reaching the legal ages (under the 1980 Marriage Law) of 20 for women and 22 for men. Those children were by definition "illegal." At birth, all of these (and many other) types of unplanned offspring were "black children", for they were "off the books" and thus ineligible for state benefits. What happened to these children? Discussions with Chinese population specialists suggest that a very small minority may have met an early death through infanticide or neglect. More ended up abandoned and, for the lucky few, adopted. The majority were probably raised by their birth parents, either as legitimate offspring whose parents succeeded in removing their "black" status by somehow acquiring registration for them, or as unregistered "black children", those I've called "unplanned persons".

If the bureaucratic categories "planned" and "unplanned" created two kinds of births, policy implementation measures attached material benefits and sanctions to the two identities. Planned single children received "one-child certificates" entitling them to preferential treatment in schooling, health care, and a host of other domains. Unplanned children, virtually all second or higher-order offspring, were denied these advantages, while their parents were subject to steep fines, loss of state-sector jobs, expulsion from the party, and many other punitive measures. As illegitimate persons, unplanned children were ineligible for inclusion in the household register, and thus for participation in a wide range of benefits (described below). As these measures were imposed on people's lives, the planned and unplanned person were transformed from mere categorical positions into concrete identities and lives, with differing levels of material well-being and life prospects.

Unfortunately, the absence of reliable statistics makes it impossible to calculate either how many unplanned births have taken place or how many of those unplanned infants have remained outside the register to become unplanned persons. Indeed, because of extensive underreporting of births – itself a form of revenge against the sharp limits on childbearing – birth statistics in China are in frightful disarray. Figures published by the SBPC suggest that the proportion of births that are unplanned fell from 32 percent in the early 1980s to 7 percent in the late 1990s (SBPC, Various years). The numbers are even smaller in the 2000s. Chinese demographers believe that, due to underreporting and other forms of statistical doctoring, the number of births counted in official surveys was understated by as much as 20 to 25 percent in the late 1980s and 30 to 35 percent in the 1990s (IF,11/23/99; IF,3/24/00). Unreported births are virtually all unplanned births. A rough order-of-magnitude estimate suggests that, between 1979, when the one-child policy was introduced, and 1997, a total of 180 million unplanned births may have taken place (for the details, see Greenhalgh 2004). Assuming all those infants lived, that works out to 14.6 percent of China's 1997 population of 1.236 billion. How many unplanned infants remained outside the register to become unplanned persons? Given their illegal and stigmatized status, it is not surprising that this population is largely uncounted – *and uncountable*. But even if a small proportion of those estimated 180 million unplanned infants failed to obtain official registration, the absolute numbers of unplanned persons would be very large.[7]

---

7 This is a conservative estimate because it is based on official records of unplanned births. Calculating authorities have no way to know how many other births occurred that were never brought to their attention.

The gap between the planners' intentions and the program's outcomes was so large in part because of the overly optimistic political assumptions built into the birth planning discourse. (Another major factor, discussed above, was the introduction of marketizing economic reforms, which weakened the apparatus of planning and policy enforcement.) What the assumption of an all-knowledgeable and persuasive party did not anticipate was the huge number of determined resisters whose interests could not be made to conform to those of the party and who would not accept the party's version of correct thinking no matter what. Another problematic assumption was that the male-oriented, familistic reproductive culture that encouraged more births was "feudal", a holdover from the old society. Although I do not have space to elaborate here, what the discourse labeled "backward" was as much a product of reform-era social and economic policy as a remnant of the past. A final, more general problem was the totalistic assumption of the planners that society could be made to bend to their will. By failing to make theoretical, bureaucratic, and/or political provisions for some degree of failure, party theoreticians and state planners ended up creating a new set of problems – and a new type of "unplanned person" – that they found difficult publicly to acknowledge, let alone address.

When Unplanned Infants Become Unplanned Persons: Human Consequences, Anthropological Concerns

The huge number of unplanned births in China is not only a planning problem or a political problem, though those are serious enough. It is also a human problem. What do we know about these costs and who bears them? Unfortunately, not much.

Given the strong son preference in rural China, and the gendered nature of contraception, abortion, and post-natal child management practices, there can be no doubt that the vast majority of these unplanned children are girls (see, for example, Johnson 1993; Zeng et al. 1993; Yuan and Skinner 2000). Whatever its gender, the unplanned infant is at greater risk of abandonment, a fate that may result in death, institutionalization in a state-run orphanage or, for the fortunate ones, adoption (see especially Johnson, Huang, and Wang 1998). The infant who is "loaned out" to relatives in another village for the first months or years of her life is deprived of her mother's milk and daily care, as well as her status as full member of her natal household.[8] If she survives – and most probably do – the unplanned infant may grow into an "unplanned person". Yet that person is legally and socially a nonperson. Ineligible for household registration, she has no right to schooling, health care, state-sector employment, and a host of other state services and benefits (Fan and Huang 1989). Of course, all do not suffer equally.

8 Unplanned infants in the villages are likely to be deprived of access to state-organized inoculations against infectious diseases, for these shots are administered by medical personnel who are responsible for birth planning (Jing 2002).

New forms of social and economic mobility emerging in China's marketizing and globalizing economy have enabled some to bypass the state's provisioning system. Some unplanned persons are now obtaining these services from the market – though at higher cost and lower quality than if they had been provided by official sources (Eckholm 1999). But we have no idea how many are getting services in other ways. Available statistics would seem to suggest that most of the unplanned persons are probably peasants living in the rural areas or peasant migrants in the cities.[9] For those in the countryside, the household register appears to be a less important mediator of state services such as education and health care than it was in the past (e.g., Zhang 1999), although inclusion in the register appears necessary for participation in land distributions. In addition, registration for the unplanned child may be bought or otherwise negotiated with sympathetic local officials (e.g., Wang 1989; Fan and Huang 1989). In the cities, however, registration continues to provide access to the full range of state services and welfare benefits. The result is that unregistered persons, in particular, rural members of the "floating population", enjoy much less than full citizenship rights (Solinger 1999; Eckholm 1999; Zhang 2001a; 2001b; 2001c).

Beyond the welfare consequences of being unplanned is the more fundamental problem of subjectivity, or sense of self. In the absence of ethnographic research, we can only surmise that being an illegitimate person, someone who was not supposed to be born and has no formal rights, has a profound impact on one's sense of who one is. Informally circulated stories of unregistered young adults suggest that, compounding the problem of lack of rights in society is the guilt such a person feels toward her parents and family for the financial and political hardships that bringing her into the world and raising her imposed on them. One can only imagine that, given the way she has been treated, the unplanned daughter feels unwanted, unimportant relative to her siblings, and a burden to her family. For such persons, creating a positive sense of personhood is likely to be difficult.

Notwithstanding the size of this population and the severity of the problems they face, little is known about this dark underside of China's planned program of population modernization.[10] With its triumphal rhetoric of planning and progress,

---

9 In 1990, for example, Shanghai and the relatively urbanized province of Zhejiang claimed planned birth rates above 95 percent, whereas the rural provinces of Fujian and Jiangxi reported rates of around 60 percent (SBPC 1991).

10 Constrained to follow state priorities, Chinese social scientists so far have pain little attention to this group, though they are certainly aware of it and its plight. In China, most social research is conducted by scholars employed in state-run organizations, whether universities or social science academies. In general, research topics are assigned to research units by central-level agencies, with financing attached to specific projects. Lack of funding makes it difficult to work on topics that fall outside the purview of state concern. Chinese population specialists I have spoken to described unplanned childbearing and the black population as highly sensitive subjects, ones they are reluctant to pursue without explicit political support (IF,9/15/99).

the official discourse on birth planning works to erase the subjectivities of the unplanned persons and deflect attention away from the problems they face. The discourse is matched by an official attitude that appears neglectful at best, punitive at worst. The attitude conveyed by the Birth Planning Commission is that unplanned persons are a result not of overly totalistic planning assumptions or overly optimistic political assumptions; they are a result of citizens failing to heed the clearly stated law that all births must be planned. Parental punishment is deserved – and meted out. Yet innocent children and young people are also punished by being deprived of essential social support. When these illegitimate young people do not cause obvious social problems, the response of state agencies appears to be to ignore them. Where they cause problems – crime, social disorder, urban blight, and so forth – the approach is more punitive (Eckholm 1999; Solinger 1999; Zhang 2001a; 2001b).

The case of a 12-year-old girl known as Xiaomin, which came to light when she turned to crime, highlights the troubles these "outlaws by birth" can encounter – and also create (Ni 2000). The third daughter of a rural Sichuan family, Xiaomin was informally adopted by a Chengdu couple who were not told that her birth parents were still alive (under which circumstances adoption is illegal). Xiaomin's happy life came to an end at age 8, when her adoptive mother died. Her father remarried. After her baby brother was born, her stepmother began actively discriminating against her. Hungry and physically abused, Xiaomin turned to snatching money and stealing food to fill her belly. At age 9 Xiaomin learned from a neighbor that she was adopted. She found a cooperative judge, who legally dissolved the adoptive relationship and sent her back to her biological parents in a mountain village. But her birth parents turned out to be dirt-poor farmers. A city girl, Xiaomin refused to do the arduous farm work her sisters were required to do. She repeatedly ran away, stole money, and engaged in other behaviors that violated village norms. At her wit's end, and legally responsible for the child-"criminal" until she reaches age 14, her mother chained the errant child to a wall. Xiaomin wants to return to Chengdu and live on the streets. But she worries about her future: "What can I do when I grow up?" she laments, "I don't have a primary education so I can't even clean toilets." When reporters visit, she asks them to take this message back to her city parents: "Daddy, Mommy, I want to go home. Please take me back."

The birth planning program was established to modernize the population, but it has had the perverse effect of creating a substantial, albeit unenumerated, class of unplanned, distinctly "unmodern" persons.[11] In the worst-case scenario, this group includes precisely the types of persons the birth planning program sought

11 They may be enumerated as members of the school population, work force, and so on, but they are not classified as "unplanned" or "black" persons.

to eliminate: "backward", poorly educated individuals who are a "drain" on the socioeconomy and a saboteur of present and future modernization. (Just as informal economies throughout the world often serve as growth points, however, the black population may actually enhance China's economic growth by providing cheap, unskilled labor and by taking the kinds of jobs official citizens shun.) In the best-case scenario, the life chances of the unplanned must surely be dimmer than those of the planned person who is showered with state support. Although their outsiders' status gives them opportunities to develop alternative modes of living, and to resist official definitions of proper personhood that may be confining, overall their marginal status must be seen as more liability than opportunity.

Since China achieved fertility levels of around two children per couple in 1992-93, the SBPC has introduced important changes in the birth control program (*GCP*, ch. 4 and 5). Although the birth planning construction remains the official one and China regularly reaffirms its commitment to population planning and the one-child policy (most recently, with the January 2007 Decision on Population and Birth Planning), with China's incorporation into transnational social policy networks, the meaning of "birth planning" is being redefined in practice (as, indeed, is the meaning of "society", "state", and "party"!). At the macrolevel, the planning process is moving from a more mandatory to a more indicative style of target setting. At the microlevel, some of the micromanagerial practices surrounding childbearing are gradually falling away. For example, in some places the practice of passing quotas down to the grassroots level is dropping away; in others newlyweds no longer need apply for permission to have a first child.

For students of modernity, this piece of Chinese political history is of interest because it generated a new kind of person, a new sort of subjectivity, whose bearers face troubling existential dilemmas (as well as some intriguing opportunities). Although the Western discourse on China's birth control program, especially that portrayed by the media, tends to exoticize and demonize China's "totalitarian" and "coercive" population program, I have stressed the parallels between the discourses and practices of China's "socialist" form of development planning and the "capitalist" forms of development planning pursued in much of the third world. I have argued that the unplanned Chinese person is the product not just of the Marxist-Leninist-Maoist ideology of "birth planning" and an extraordinarily, if now more selectively, strong socialist state, but also of the discourse of "development" and "modernity", an identity of "national backwardness", and a dream of "catching up" with the global leaders that China shares with third world states around the world.

At a broader level, the Chinese material suggests the productivity, even inventiveness, of "population" – as figure of discourse, source of social categories, and form of bureaucratic state practice. Like the larger "development" discourse of which it is a part, "population control" discourse has the power to create new classifications of social life, new types of personhood, and new forms of social and political exclusion that may subvert the goals of the state planners, even as the persons, exclusions, and subversions remain hidden from official view. In *History of Sexuality*, Foucault (1978) identified two poles around which modern biopower clusters: the disciplines of the individual body and the regulations of the population, or social body. Anthropologists have devoted great attention to the former, but much less to the latter. With its gargantuan population and fearsome birth planning program, China offers some of the world's most striking support for Foucault's observations on the social power of "population" discourse and practice. But that power operates everywhere that "population control" is on the agenda of state development planners. A new chapter in the anthropology of modernity is waiting to be written.

References

CC	Central Committee of the Communist Party
CC&SC	Central Committee of the Communist Party and State Council
IF	Interview file
SBPC	State Birth Planning Commission

Ali, Kamran Asdar. 2002. *Planning the Family in Egypt: New Bodies, New Selves.* Austin: University of Texas Press.

Anderson, Benedict. 1991. *Imagined Communities: Reflections on the Origins and Spread of Nationalism.* Rev. Edition. London: Verso.

Appadurai, Arjun. 1996. "Number in the Colonial Imagination." In Arjun Appadurai, ed. *Modernity at Large: Cultural Dimensions of Globalization*, pp.114-35. Minneapolis: University of Minnesota Press.

Banister, Judith. 1987. *China's Changing Population.* Stanford: Stanford University Press.

Bowker, Geoffrey C. and Susan Leigh Star. 1999. *Sorting Things Out: Classification and Its Consequences.* Cambridge: MIT Press.

Burawoy, Michael and Katherine Verdery, eds. 1999. *Uncertain Transition: Ethnographies of Change in the Postsocialist World.* Lanham, MD: Rowman and Littlefield.

CC. 1985. Open Letter from the Central Committee to All Communist Party and Communist Youth League Members on the Question of Controlling China's Population Growth (in Chinese). In *Zhongguo Renkou Nianjian (1985) (Population Yearbook of China, 1985)*, Population Yearbook of China Editorial Committee, ed. pp. 27-29. Beijing: Zhongguo Shehui Kexue Chubanshe.

Chatterjee, Nilanjana and Nancy E. Riley. 2001. Planning an Indian Modernity: The Gendered Politics of Fertility Control. *Signs: Journal of Women in Culture and Society* 26(3), pp. 811-846.

Chen Muhua. 1979. To Realize the Four Modernizations, It Is Necessary to Control Population Increase in a Planned Way (in Chinese). *Renmin Ribao (People's Daily)*, 11 August, p. 2. Available in English in *Population and Development Review* 5(4), pp. 723-730.

Chen Pi-chao and Adrienne Kols. 1982. Population and Birth Planning in the People's Republic of China. *Population Reports*, series J, no. 25, pp. J577-618.

Chen Youdao. 1991. Strategic Thinking on Shutting Off Multiple Births in the Rural Areas (in Chinese). *Renkou Yanjiu (Population Research)* 6, pp. 54-56.

Chu Hsiao-yang. 1991. Procreation, The Chinese People – Running Toward Paradise, Part I. *Chiushih Nientai (The Nineties)* 3, pp. 81-89. In JPRS-CAR-91-030 (30 May), pp. 78-86.

Cohn, Bernard S. 1987. The Census, Social Structure and Objectification in South Asia. In Bernard S. Cohn, ed. *An Anthropologist Among the Historians and Other Essays*, pp. 224-54. Delhi: Oxford University Press.

Croll, Elisabeth, Delia Davin, and Penny Kane, eds. 1985. *China's One-Child Family Policy*. New York: St. Martin's.

Dean, Mitchell. 1999. *Governmentality: Power and Rule in Modern Society*. London: Sage.

Eckholm, Erik. 1999. For China's Rural Migrants, An Education Wall. *New York Times*, 23 December, pp. 1, 8.

Escobar, Arturo. 1995. *Encountering Development: The Making and Unmaking of the Third World*. Princeton: Princeton University Press.

Fan Xiangguo and Huang Yuan. 1989. China's 'Black Population' (in Chinese). *Xin Guancha (New Observer)* 4, pp. 28-32.

Ferguson, James. 1990. *The Anti-Politics Machine: "Development", Depoliticization and Bureaucratic Power in Lesotho*. Cambridge: Cambridge University Press.

Foucault, Michel. 1975. *The Birth of the Clinic: An Archaeology of Medical Perception*. New York: Vintage.

– 1978. *The History of Sexuality: An Introduction, Volume 1*. New York: Random House.

– 1979. *Discipline and Punish: The Birth of the Prison*. New York: Vintage.

– 1991. "Governmentality." In Graham Burchell, Colin Gordon, and Peter Miller, eds. *The Foucault Effect: Studies in Governmentality*, pp. 87-104. London: Harvester.

Gao Changwu and Shen Jialiang. 1993. Preliminary Analysis of the Causes of Unplanned Births in the Rural Areas and Countermeasures (in Chinese). *Renkou Lilun yu Shijian (Population Theory and Practice)* 3, pp. 40-42.

Gordon, Colin. 1991. "Governmental Rationality: An Introduction." In Graham Burchell, Colin Gordon, and Peter Miller, eds. *The Foucault Effect: Studies in Governmentality*, pp. 87-104. Chicago: University of Chicago Press.

Greene, Ronald Walter. 1999. *Malthusian Worlds: U.S. Leadership and the Governing of the Population Crisis*. Boulder: Westview.

Greenhalgh, Susan 1990 The Evolution of the One-Child Policy in Shaanxi, 1979-88. China Quarterly 122 (June):191-229.

– 1993. "The Peasantization of the One-Child Policy in Shaanxi." In Deborah Davis and Stevan Harrell, eds. *Chinese Families in the Post-Mao Era*, pp. 219-50. Berkeley: University of California Press.

– 1994. "Controlling Births and Bodies in Village China." American Ethnologist 21(1), pp. 3-30.

– 2004. "Making Up China's 'Black Population.'" In *Anthropological and Historical Studies in Critical Demography,* pp. 148-172. Simon Szreter, Hania Sholkamy, and A. Dharmalingam, eds. Oxford: Oxford University Press.

– 2008. *Just One Child: Science and Policy in Deng's China*. Berkeley: University of California Press.

Greenhalgh, Susan and Jiali Li. 1995. "Engendering Reproductive Policy and Practice in Peasant China: For a Feminist Demography of Reproduction." *Signs: Journal of Women in Culture and Society* 20(3), pp. 601-641.

Greenhalgh, Susan and Edwin A. Winckler. 2005. *Governing China's Population: From Leninist to Neoliberal Biopolitics*. Stanford: Stanford University Press.

Gupta, Akhil. 1998. *Postcolonial Developments: Agriculture in the Making of Modern India*. Durham: Duke University Press.

Halfon, Saul. 2006. *The Cairo Consensus: Demographic Surveys, Women's Empowerment, and Regime Change in Population Policy*. Ithaca, NY: Cornell University Press.

Han Changsen. 1991. "In Our Country's Birth Planning Work, the Key is Excess Births, the Problem Resides in the Villages" (in Chinese). *Renkou Xuekan (Population Journal)* 91(4), pp. 15-18.

Holston, James. 1989. *The Modernist City: An Anthropological Critique of Brasilia*. Chicago: University of Chicago Press.

– 1999. Spaces of Insurgent Citizenship. In James Holston, ed. *Cities and Citizenship*, pp. 155-73. Durham: Duke University Press.

Horn, David G. 1994. *Social Bodies: Science, Reproduction, and Italian Modernity*. Princeton: Princeton University Press.

Howe, Christopher and Kenneth R. Walker. 1989. *The Foundations of the Chinese Planned Economy: A Documentary Survey, 1953-65*. London: MacMillan.

Hua Guofeng. 1985. "With Party Secretaries in Command, All Party Members [Should] Join the Effort to Do a Better Job in Birth Planning" (in Chinese). In *Zhongguo Renkou Nianjian (1985) (Population Yearbook of China, 1985)*. Population Yearbook of China Editorial Committee, ed. pp. 20-22. Beijing: Zhongguo Shehui Kexue Chubanshe. Orig. publ. in *Renmin Ribao*, 8 July 1978.

IF, 9/15/99. 1999. Discussion with Chinese demographer, 15 September, Cairo.

IF, 11/23/99. 1999. Interview with Chinese birth planning official, 23 November, Beijing.

IF, 3/24/00. 2000. Discussion with Chinese demographer, 24 March, Los Angeles.

Jing Jun. 2002. Personal communication, 23 February.

Johnson, Kay. 1993. Chinese Orphanages: Saving China's Abandoned Girls. *Australian Journal of Chinese Affairs* 30, pp. 61-87.

Johnson, Kay, Huang Banghan, and Wang Liyao. 1998. Infant Abandonment and Adoption in China. *Population and Development Review* 24(3), pp. 469-510.

Kelly, David. 1991. "Chinese Marxism Since Tiananmen: Between Evaporation and Dismemberment." In David S.G. Goodman and Gerald Segal, eds. *China in the Nineties: Crisis Management and Beyond*, pp. 19-34. Oxford: Oxford University Press.

Kertzer, David I. and Dominique Arel, eds. 2002. *Census and Identity: The Politics of Race, Ethnicity, and Language in National Censuses*. Cambridge: Cambridge University Press.

Kligman, Gail. 1998. *The Politics of Duplicity: Controlling Reproduction in Ceausescu's Romania*. Berkeley: University of California Press.

Kornai, Janos. 1992. *The Socialist System: The Political Economy of Communism*. Princeton: Princeton University Press.

Lardy, Nicholas R., ed. 1978. *Chinese Economic Planning: Translations from Chi-hua Ching-chi*. White Plains: M.E. Sharpe.

Maurer, Bill. 1997. *Recharting the Caribbean: Land, Law, and Citizenship in the British Virgin Islands*. Ann Arbor: University of Michigan Press.

Milwertz, Cecilia Nathansen. 1997. *Accepting Population Control: Urban Chinese Women and the One-Child Family Policy*. Surrey, England: Curzon.

Misra, Kalpana. 1998. *From Post-Maoism to Post-Marxism: The Erosion of Official Ideology in Deng's China*. New York: Routledge.

Ni Ching-ching. 2000. Two Families – but No Place to Call Home. *Los Angeles Times*, 29 March, pp. A1, 10.

Ong, Aihwa. 1999. *Flexible Citizenship: The Cultural Logics of Transnationality*. Durham, N.C.: Duke University Press.

Palmer, Michael. 1995. "The Re-emergence of Family Law in Post-Mao China: Marriage, Divorce and Reproduction." *China Quarterly* 141, pp. 110-134.

Rabinow, Paul. 1989. *French Modern: Norms and Forms of the Social Environment*. Chicago: University of Chicago Press.

Rofel, Lisa. 1999. *Other Modernities: Gendered Yearnings in China After Socialism*. Berkeley: University of California Press.

Rose, Nikolas. 1999. *Powers of Freedom: Reframing Political Thought*. Cambridge: Cambridge University Press.

– 2007. *The Politics of Life Itself*. Princeton: Princeton University Press.

SBPC (State Birth Planning Commission). Various years. *Zhongguo Jihua Shengyu Nianjian (Birth Planning Yearbook of China)*. Beijing: State Birth Planning Commission.

Scharping, Thomas. 2003. *Birth Control in China, 1949-2000: Population Policy and Demographic Development*. London: Curzon.

Scott, James C. 1998. *Seeing Like a State: How Certain Schemes to Improve the Human Condition Have Failed.* New Haven: Yale University Press.

Solinger, Dorothy J. 1999. *Contesting Citizenship in Urban China: Peasant Migrants, the State, and the Logic of the Market*. Berkeley: University of California Press.

Stark, David and Laszlo Bruszt, eds. 1998. *Postsocialist Pathways: Transforming Politics and Property in East Central Europe*. Cambridge: Cambridge University Press.

Szreter, Simon, Hania Sholkamy, and A. Dharmalingam, eds. 2004. *Categories and Contexts: Anthropological and Historical Studies in Critical Demography*. Oxford: Oxford University Press.

Tien, H. Yuan. 1973. *China's Population Struggle: Demographic Decisions of the People's Republic, 1949-1969*. Columbus: Ohio State University Press.

– 1991. *China's Strategic Demographic Initiative*. New York: Praeger.

Tien, H. Yuan, ed. 1980. *Population Theory in China*. White Plains, NY: ME Sharpe.

Wang Hong. 1991. "Population Planning in China." In Wang Jiye and Terence H. Hull, eds. *Population and Development Planning in China*, pp. 68-87. Sydney: Allen & Unwin.

Wang Xizhan. 1989. "Analysis of a Survey of 100 Rural 'Unplannned Birth Households'." *Renkou Yu Jingji (Population and Economy)* 4, pp. 36-37.

Wasserstrom, Jeffrey. 1984. "Resistance to the One-Child Family." *Modern China* 10, pp. 345-74.

White, Tyrene. 1994. "The Origins of China's Birth Planning Policy." In Christina K. Gilmartin, Gail Hershatter, Lisa Rofel, and Tyrene White, eds. *Engendering China: Women, Culture, and the State*, pp. 250-78. Cambridge: Harvard University Press.

– 2006. *China's Longest Campaign: Birth Planning in the People's Republic, 1949-2005*. Ithaca, NY: Cornell University Press.

Yuan Jianhua and G. William Skinner. 2000. "Shaping the Gender Configuration of Offspring Sets: The Spatial Patterning of Reproductive Strategizing in Contemporary China." Paper presented at Annual Meeting of the Association for Asian Studies, 9-12 March, San Diego.

Zeng Yi, Tu Ping, Gu Baochang, Xu Yi, Li Bohua, and Li Yongping. 1993. "Causes and Implications of the Recent Increase in the Reported Sex Ratio at Birth in China." *Population and Development Review* 19(2), pp. 283-302.

Zhang Erli, Gu Baochang, and Xie Zhenming, eds. 1999.*Guojia Jihua Shengyu Weiyuanhui Diyipi Youzhi Fuwu Shidian Xianqu (1995-1998) Pinggu Baogao Ji (Evaluations of the First Set of Quality of Care Pilot Projects Conducted by the State Birth Planning Commission, 1995-1998)*. Beijing: Zhongguo Renkou Chubanshe.

Zhang Li. 2001a. "Migration and Privatization of Space and Power in Late Socialist China." *American Ethnologist* 28(1), pp. 179-205.

– 2001b. "Contesting Crime, Order, and Migrant Spaces in Beijing." In Nancy N. Chen, Constance D. Clark, Suzanne Z. Gottschang, and Lyn Jeffery, eds. *China Urban: Ethnographies of Contemporary Culture*, pp. 201-227. Durham: Duke University Press.

– 2001c. *Strangers in the City: Reconfigurations of Space, Power, and Social Networks Within China's Floating Population*. Stanford: Stanford University Press.

Zhang Weiguo. 1999. "Implementation of State Family Planning Programmes in a Northern Chinese Village." *China Quarterly* 157 (March), pp. 202-230.

Zhang Weiqing, ed. 1998. *Zhongguo Jihua Shengyu Gailun (Summary of Birth Planning in China)*. Beijing: China Population Press.

Zhang Wei-wei. 1996. *Ideology and Economic Reform Under Deng Xiaoping, 1978-1993*. London: Kegan Paul International.

Zhu Chuzhu and Peng Xizhe, eds. 1996. *Funu Canyu de Xingcheng (The Path of Women's Labor Participation)*. Beijing: Higher Education Press.

Chapter 4

Reproduction at the Margins

–

Reproduction, Migration and Legitimacy in the New Europe

Caroline H. Bledsoe

Introduction

Contemporary Europe has witnessed some of the most remarkable population trends in history. The one that has dominated demographic attention has been a drop in fertility to levels well below replacement. Drawing nearly as much attention has been a loosening of marital bonds, producing what Lesthaeghe and van de Kaa (1986) termed the "second demographic transition": increasing rates of nonmarital union and divorce, with concomitant increases in rates of child residence in households with a single parent or in households that include a step-parent.[1] Another recent trend, however, has just begun to attract substantial demographic notice, though of late it has taken center stage in the popular media: the rise in immigration to the European Union from the developing world.[2] If there have been few demographic studies of immigrants, compared to the other two trends, even less is known about immigrants' fertility. There have been debates on whether developing country populations will bring their youthful age pyramids to help support Europe's subfertile, aging "rectangular" populations. But the frame of reference is still "native" Europe (see, however, works like Andersson and Scott 2004). How do immigrants from non-E.U. countries, especially those in marginal circumstances, envision their own reproductive life trajectories across the vast, ambiguous political boundaries whose seismic shifts can threaten their security?

In developing countries, families look to children for help with upkeep of the farm and the house, and support in times of unemployment, sickness, and political insecurity. They seek assistance from children regardless of whether they live a nearby village or in Paris or New York. How and under what circumstances one bears a child has a strong impact on the rest of the family. A key point to em-

---

1 For an overview of some regional patterns in family dynamics in Nordic, Western, and Southern European countries, see Surkyn and Lesthaeghe (2004). For similar behavior in the U.S., see Goode (1993); Bumpass, Raley, and Sweet (1995); Goldscheider et al. (2000).

2 Van Amersfoort (1999) accuses European demographic scholarship of having an "ostrich" mentality, ignoring the immigration that is unfolding all around, though in the 1990s European population literature had begun to ask about the contributions vs. costs of international migrants for residents and citizens. See van de Kaa (1993); Massey, ed. (1998); Blum (2002); and work by Lesthaeghe and colleagues (e.g., 2000).

phasize about reproduction, however, is that in an increasingly "connected" world, children offer new pathways for family mobility and security, particularly for immigrants at the margins of political legitimacy. In this, the term "reproduction" is misleading; adults *never* fully reproduce themselves. Children are born in different times, and often places, than their parents, and they have different kin configurations. They may also have different nationalities. Through connection to a child, adults potentially gain more attributes than their own.

I review a range of anthropological and demographic works and compile several case studies to address some theoretical and empirical issues of reproduction among immigrants in Europe. I focus on immigrants of more marginal status because doing so captures some unexplored facets of the value of children in this era of rapid globalization. It may shed explanatory light on quantitative fertility trends among immigrants and longstanding citizens alike. My previous work in Africa found that a woman's need to bear children for a worthy husband and his family to solidify her wifely legitimacy makes reproduction a political matter.[3] I now consider the legitimacy that bearing a child might entail as a link to a specific nation or state for an immigrant family. Most of my examples focus on circumstances of time and place of children's births. There is enormous variation on such things, of course, and the political ground shifts constantly. All this is hardly reason to discount the effort; rather, it is part of the story.

Challenges in Studying Immigrant Populations in the New Europe

Taking on any one topic in the demography of contemporary Europe is no small challenge. The European Union now has 27 member countries, a group with extraordinarily dissimilar histories and, despite efforts at "harmonization", policies governing citizenship, work, and welfare. Until the collapse of the Soviet Union in the early 1990's and its centralized control over much of central and eastern Europe, even Germany belonged to two poles of the political divide whose differences were so vast that, if plotted geographically, might have represented opposite sides of the globe. As well there is a panoply of E.U. economic and political organizations and agreements – the Economic and Monetary Union, the European Free Trade Agreement, the Club of Rome, the Treaty of Amsterdam, and so on. Wealthy countries tend to be most selective about the pieces they want to sign. Norway, with its oil riches, has seen little reason to become a full E.U. member, although it did sign the Schengen Agreement governing free passage of legitimately documented persons. Countries such as Turkey, however, have been held at arm's length. What is more, the definition of the E.U. changes almost weekly

3 Das (1995) describes a stark example from India; see also the collection in which it was published (Ginsburg and Rapp, eds., 1995). For more demographic questions, see Greenhalgh (1995); Kertzer and Fricke, eds. (1997).

as new cultural units, political boundaries, and institutions emerge, and as the rules governing access to entry, work, and citizenship are rewritten.

The question of belonging under situations of movement takes on particular importance as the power and geographical holdings of the European Union expand. Certainly the history of the U.S. could not be told without recognizing the tens of thousands of European immigrants who came every year, as late as the 1950s. Until recently, however, the subject was highly understudied in the demography of Europe. One reason has been the incomplete nature of quantitative data sources. Many European nations continue to resist collecting information on questions like religion or ethnicity, given the stark memories of Nazi Europe. Another reason stems from disagreement over who, exactly, an immigrant is. Each country has different criteria for granting or withholding citizenship or rights to live or work. Variants may include rights of "blood" descent from an appropriately recognized parent or ancestor, versus rights of "soil": citizenship by birth or naturalization. Some people settle permanently; others come for brief stints – to attend a funeral; to visit kin; or to earn money for marriage, a plot of land, school fees, or a relative's surgery.[4] And in states that reckon citizenship by descent, many groups find it difficult to disentangle themselves from the label of "immigrant" or "foreigner", regardless of how many generations have elapsed. Some have speculated that the label "immigrant" may become a perpetual category, a kind of social class in which families can become locked (de Genova 2002; Neveu 2000). Finally, while many immigrants arrive in quite straightforward ways, as part of family reunification packages or having desired skills that earn them immediate rights to residence, others immigrants lead intentionally invisible lives. Shading toward the "less legal" are people who obtained permits for seasonal work but overstayed their legal welcome, frequently with the collusion of their employers. More extreme acts of desperation have been reflected in the cases of young men racing through the Eurotunnel, clinging to the undersides of railroad cars, enduring treks across the Sahara, or negotiating the treacherous Straits of Gibraltar. For young women, there are grim crossings and voyages as well as victims of international smugglers. As for children, hundreds have been sent by their families from war-ravaged Somalia by one-way air tickets to the U.K., with no one to meet them and no traceable identity (*The Scotsman* 2003). In sum, the welcome that some migrants receive should not be allowed to overshadow the plights of many others hidden beneath the formal institutional horizon of visibility.[5] And whereas all social identities are multiple and fluid, immigrants face particularly

4 On family arrangements associated with these often-precarious structures, see Sargent and Cordell (2003). For youth schooling and employment concern, see Schiff (2003).

5 Such dilemma are depicted in the burgeoning genre of films that document the plight of undocumented immigrants across the world, who cannot seek legal or medical help without risking deportation.

precarious rights to housing, residence, and work. Under these conditions, it should not be surprising that trying to pin down the identities of people who are trying equally hard to obfuscate them is next to impossible.

Understanding this unprecedented upsurge in movements for such overlapping, ambiguous categories demands not simply calculating numbers of people. It also demands a combined social, cultural and legal lens. As my 1982-93 Sierra Leone study of child fosterage (1990) revealed, the assumption that the people are subject solely to policies on health, education, and employment in their places of origin is untenable.[6] Just as everyone who lives within a country's territorial boundary is not necessarily a countable citizen, people living outside a nation's boundaries may figure centrally in the lives of those within. What do matter a great deal in the E.U. are definitions of legitimacy and belonging that guide its member states. Among the most important points of reference were the 1985 Schengen Agreement, which eased border controls and mandated free passage across national borders for citizens of the signatory states. E.U. mandates such as these also, however, set the conditions of marginality for those who could not qualify as legitimate citizens or residents. Indeed, subsequent agreements such as the 1997 Amsterdam Treaty have placed even tighter checks at external border control, narrowed allowances for asylum and immigration, and bolstered the policing system through a vast shared information system, including photos and fingerprints. Seeking to narrow the definitions of state-defined legitimacy, some European countries reduce childhood to a biological condition, deploying sophisticated medical technologies to exclude those who do not appear to be young enough, or challenging claims to parenthood by demanding DNA tests.[7] They also reduce parent-child relations to economics, demanding evidence of adequate parental income and accommodation as a condition for reunification. The state may even redefine the temporal boundaries of childhood, and judge those left in the category on their political loyalties. Citing difficulties in integrating older children, the EU Court of Justice recently reaffirmed states' rights to conduct mandatory "integration tests" for all children 12 and over.[8] Families themselves, of course, come to use the same categories as state do. Where states use the vocabulary of biology, humanitarianism, integration, and childhood to rationalize their immigration policies, however, families use it to select for migration members whose attributes will best qualify, or can be construed, for en-

6 See also the British Transnational Communities Programme, available at http://www.transcomm.ox.ac.uk [accessed 20 June 2008].

7 Moore, Molly, "French Plan to Screen DNA of Visa-Seekers Draws Anger", Washington Post Foreign Service, 21 September 2007. Available at http://www.washingtonpost.com/wp-dyn/content/article/2007/09/20/AR2007092002620.html, p. A14 [accessed 20 June 2008].

8 "Family reunification." Europa: Activities of the European Union, Summaries of Legislation. Available at http://europa.eu/scadplus/leg/en/lvb/l33118.htm [accessed 20 June 2008].

try in a particular destination country (Bledsoe and Sow, in press). In policy discussions, concerns about legitimacy are increasingly subsumed under discussions of universal human rights (e.g., Goodale and Merry 2007), and the resulting norms produce categories that states can use to exclude as much as to include. When special rights become attached to certain family positions, especially on people in positions marked as dependent and vulnerable, a migration premium will inevitably be placed on those individuals whose attributes might qualify. The very forms of family integrity that human rights doctrine aims to safeguard thus become the lines on which individuals may be excluded or exploited, not just by governments but families themselves.

To map out some promising directions for efforts to think about reproduction and migration in the same frame, this paper examines case studies through the lenses of anthropological writings. It rests on three caveats. First, while describing quantitative levels and trends in either immigration or fertility is beyond the present focus on social dynamics, though I return briefly to the implications for understanding fertility numbers at the end. Second, beyond the scope as well is any attempt to decide whether migration is overall a bonus or a detriment to the societies that either send or receive migrants. Of interest, rather, is how people at the margins of state-defined legitimacy try to structure their reproductive lives within the shifting boundaries and policies of the E.U. Looking at these situations helps to shed light on the value of children arising from patterns of globalization, whether we consider reproduction among immigrants or among longstanding citizens. Finally, although I touch on cases that have drawn international attention, most focus less on the sensationalistic reports of immigrant dilemmas that capture public attention – perilous entries, brothels, sweat shops, refugee camps – than on routine adaptations to life at the margins.

Why Anthropology?

A discipline that has built its business on studying remote, exotic locales might seem an unlikely vehicle for studying immigration and fertility in contemporary Europe.[9] But anthropology's classic emphasis on culture and meaning as well as legitimacy and social agency,[10] together with its newer interests in globalism

9 For several examples of European anthropology, see Kenny and Kertzer (1983); Esposito (1989); Delaney (1991); Bellier and Wilson, eds. (2000); Goody (2000).

10 In recent years, there has been a surge of new kinship studies (e.g., Franklin and McKinnon, eds., 2001; Parkin and Stone, eds., 2004; and a massive study of kinship and security in Europe led by Patrick Heady: "Kinship and social security", *Max Planck Institute for Social Anthropology*, available at http://www.eth.mpg.de/kass/ [accessed 20 June 2008]). There are also many works on the politics of citizenship and reproduction: e.g., Kahn (2000); Kanaaneh (2002); and, on transnational generational relations, Cole and Durham, eds. (2006).

and citizenship, suggest promising synergies. There is a rich tradition of ethnography on Europe and its long experience with population movement for commerce, marriage, war, and the spread of religious and secular instruction.[11] Anthropologists have described patterns wherein children were sent out when a family's land holdings were threatened by too many heirs, for service, to religious orders, or to learn a trade. But ethnographies of the past were dominated by descriptions of isolated, traditional peasants. It was largely with the work of scholars such as Eric Wolf (1982), Raymond Smith (1956), Edward Said (1978), and Immanuel Wallerstein (1974) that key attention was drawn to the role of larger state and international schemes in peasant life,[12] and to the economic and psychological cost that the migration of young people to cities might entail. In northern Portugal, Brettell (1986, 1995) has reported on the impact of two and a half centuries of emigration on the lives of village family members who leave and who remain behind. Pierre Bourdieu's study of rural France, *Bal des Célebataires* (2002b) depicted the plight of aging peasant bachelors when young women left for the city, finding it unappealing to marry men whose future was shackled to a small plot of inherited land. And in a controversial work from rural Western Ireland, Scheper-Hughes (*Saints, Scholars, and Schizophrenics*, 1979) pointed to outmigration as the chief cause of mental illness among last-born males in the wake of government efforts to force small farmers off the land. Caught in the squeeze as their impoverished country struggled for viability in the larger European Economic Community scheme, Scheper-Hughes argues, rural Irish families raised girls and older sons with a recognition that they would likely emigrate. At the same time, they tried to ensure a successor for the farm by instilling the last-born son with an extreme sense of incompetence. Whether these "leftover" sons became blatantly schizophrenic or eccentric "saints", they remained bound pathologically close to home and land.

In the space of little more than a generation, of course, Western Europe has been transformed utterly, no longer producing people for export but becoming a magnet, whether for immigrants fleeing from a repressive regime or simply seeking a better life in a distant land. With fertility so low and E.U. economies thriving, it is the cultural dynamics of Europe as a new importing epicenter of persons, together with the new rule structures that are arising to govern these movements, that is so engrossing.

---

11 The case of Africa bears parallels. Contrary to images of the subcontinent as a series of isolated collectivities frozen in time and place, African peoples have long moved along historic routes to visit kin, trade, acquire training, and seek religious and medical advice. With colonial efforts to train professionals, travel routes were opened up to Europe as well.

12 For Eastern Europe, see Gal and Kligman (2000); Verdery (1995). For the Mediterranean, see Kenny and Kertzer, eds. (1983); on Italy specifically, see Silverman (1975); Esposito (1989); Kertzer and Hogan (1989); Kertzer and Brettell (1987); on Greece, see Friedl (1962).

Culturally Defined Legitimacy

For investigating reproduction in the margins of this vacillating mix of countries, policies, and people, a concept that has drawn longstanding interest in the social sciences is legitimacy. Legitimacy that falls short of ideal standards has long preoccupied political philosophers, literary critics, historians, and sociologists. But the concept gained particular currency in anthropology, where it has been applied to vast domains of research, whether on ethnicity, nationality, or economic exchange. Applied to the family, the relevant questions have been: who is a legitimate member of a family and how is this legitimacy acquired?

Anthropologist Mary Douglas (1966) argued that humans are profoundly uncomfortable with mingling elements of established categories, so they mark the boundaries between important categories with fears of pollution or contamination. Her observation finds apt examples in concerns about the legitimacy of a properly sanctioned marriage between suitable partners and the proper timing of the arrival of their offspring (e.g., Launay 1995). In most European societies of the past, but also many contemporary ones, births that occurred before marriage were regarded as transgressions of appropriate cultural boundaries: uncomfortable breaches of established temporal boundaries that defined marital categories. Indeed, nowhere in the anthropological, sociological, or historical canon have the cultural emphases on legitimacy and the social strategies they set in motion, whether to avoid accusations of illegitimacy or to use them against rivals, been more visible than in what has sometimes been called the "honor/shame" cultural complex of Mediterranean/Southern Europe (Péristiany 1966; Gilmore 1987). In these areas, where familial reputation rested on the sexual virtue of young women, the most damning evidence of a woman's immorality was the pre-marital appearance of a child, especially if there was no credible husband candidate in sight. In extreme cases, families could lose everything by a female member's immorality: claims to land, livestock, appropriate marriage partners, money, jewels, titles. To ensure that the sexual relations that produced a child occurred within the bounds of an honorable union, people calculated retrospectively a highly specific temporal sequence: a sanctioned conjugal union followed by a pregnancy (Laslett 1980). Given the enormous economic and symbolic payload that rested on this delicately timed sequence of events – not only the legitimacy of children, but the honor of men, the shame of women, and, among royalty, entire political states[13] – it should hardly be surprising that men and female elders tried to safeguard female virtue, by threat or force, if necessary.

13 Where Western society has seen legitimacy as a matter of timing, a birth that occurs within the temporal bounds of a legal union, many African societies see a child's legitimacy as a function of paternal recognition and support. If the conjugal process is proceeding smoothly, a premarital birth may be a cause for celebration: a reflection of a young woman's fertility that paves the way toward a legitimate marriage.

Movement and Legitimacy in the New Global Order

Until the 1970s, anthropologists' interests in legitimacy were confined to status in small kinship units. Questions centered on births: when children were born relative to the timing of a marriage, who they were born to, and what links they forged between households. Starting in the 1970s, however, scholars across the humanities and social sciences began to take in a bigger picture. Pursuing themes of hybrid identities and displacement in a postcolonial world, they began to explore permutations of legitimacy in the era of what has come to be called globalism, which sees the most farflung corners of the world as now interlinked and interdependent through the movement of people, objects, information, and wealth.[14] With information, business, money, and educational offerings now flowing across national boundaries, American phone companies outsource services to India and Pakistan where operators adopt American names and feign American accents in exchange for wages far lower than what American operators would accept. Mauretanian currency traders, cell phones in hand, stand alongside Senegalese cloth sellers in rural Gambian markets, checking the daily prices of the euro, the dollar, and the pound. And while diseases travel readily on jet planes, body parts speed through time and geography, detached from their original owners and sold to buyers seeking transplant surgery.[15] Scrambling to keep pace with these extraordinary changes, academic journals, books, symposia, fellowships, and prize competitions are springing up, their subject matter replete with everything from tourist art to the political economy of ethnic resistance. Whatever individual anthropologists think of the concept of globalism itself, attaching an after-the-fact chapter on "social change" to a book about a "traditional" society no longer suffices.

If social science scholarship is increasingly about citizenship and about movements of people, information, and money in an unstable world, it is also about the dynamics of marginalization in the global peripheries. Integral to this scholarship is the conviction that social classes now span international locations, and that life at the bottom of social order is often one that is led in the international margins: a life increasingly dominated by new industries of border regulators, whether geographical, political, or familial.[16] While jet-setting "dot.comers"

---

14 Examples include Benedict Anderson (1983); Gardner (1995); Hannerz (1996); Carter (1997); Bridget Anderson (2000); Sassen (1998); Hansen (2000); Haugerud et al., eds. (2000); Inda and Rosaldo, eds. (2002); Bellier and Wilson, eds. (2000); and Yanagisako (2002).

15 Such observations have led ethnographers to advocate multi-sited ethnography (Marcus 1995; Gupta and Ferguson, eds. 1997; Greenhouse et al. eds. 2002; and Ong 2002).

16 Examples include the DNA testing industry ("Immigration DNA testing", DNA Testing Service. Available at http://www.dnatestingcentre.com/Immigration.htm [accessed 20 June 2008]), as well as the United States Department of Homeland Security, available at http://www.dhs.gov/index.shtm [accessed 20 June 2008].

from Bangalore, India move in social circles with their roommates from Oxford and with Hollywood royalty, the village tradesmen with whom they grew up become increasingly vulnerable to global forces that set their prices and reduce their political communities to "ethnic enclaves." Writing of Britain, Anderson (2000) reports that while immigrant women, from places like Poland, Russia, Africa, and the Caribbean, fill the domestic "caring gap" in British society, taking care of the old, the disabled, and the very young, many must leave their own children in their own countries with relatives or friends, and with little financial support.

Agency, Legitimacy, and Immigrant Dynamics

Many of the examples in globalism studies strike a bleak note. So one final development, appearing in the 1970s, is important to insert: variously termed "processualist", "strategic", "interactionist", "constructionist", and so on. Individuals became recognized as agents capable of sizing up situations and carrying out actions, if not always to maximal economic utility then with intention (e.g., Comaroff and Roberts 1981; Bourdieu 2002a). Social life became seen as contestations over meaning, wherein people did not mechanically follow the cultural rules their societies appear to lay down but attempt to press claims on the basis of their construals.

One of the most often cited applications of these approaches has been ethnicity and national identity. Whereas ethnic groups previously were regarded as distinct isolates with static customs that demanded compliance, anthropologists have come alive to the idea that ethnic characteristics are fluid and that people may try to claim allegiance to groups that offer the most situational advantage (Barth 1969). Some quite contemporary examples, however, come from the migration literature. Many undocumented Congolese traders who cannot obtain visas in France, for example, and yet who must do business there have borrowed the papers of someone with a legitimate French visa or obtained the passport of someone from a country whose former colonial master still allowed travel to Europe. Until a few years ago, for example, a Congolese individual could borrow an Angolan passport to apply for a visa to Portugal, Belgium, Spain, or Italy; from these countries, he or she was free, under the Schengen Agreement, to travel by train to the destination country without becoming subject to border controls (MacGaffey and Bazenguissa-Ganga 2000, p. 98).

Aihwa Ong's (2002) analysis of what she calls "flexible citizenship" offers another example. Although citizenship has been conventionally conceptualized as based on political rights and participation within a sovereign state, Ong documents attempts by elite Chinese entrepreneurial managers, technocrats, and business professionals to exploit shifting national rules of affiliation for investment, work, and relocation in a vast international diaspora. "[T]he convergence of Chinese family forms with flexible strategies of capital accumulation enables them to bypass or exploit citizenship rules – whatever the case may be – as they relocate capital and/or family members overseas" (2002, p. 174). Establishing their business across national and continental boundaries, these entrepreneurs seek out emerging "loopholes" in various national laws, using their multiple potential identities to catch the allowable corners of policies in ways that were unforeseen by lawmakers. In turn, of course, states respond by readjusting their policies. Thus, as Ong observes, "To understand the tactical practices of this diasporan managerial class, we must locate them within and one step ahead of the various regimes of truth and power to which they, as traveling persons, are subject ..." (2002, p. 174). In this example, individuals who can move fluidly manage to cobble together elements of multiple systems, selectively activating characteristics that give them advantages in a distant system, in ways unanticipated by those who create the rules governing belonging. In a continuous dialectic, international managerial elites who stay ahead of rules that govern their far-flung international business diaspora effectively change the rules of the entire system.

A striking example of attempting to use identity shifting and geographical mobility to situational advantage in recent years has been that of "asylum shopping." In this practice, individuals seeking political asylum apply, often on the internet, to multiple countries, sought to match (or construe) their own characteristics with the criteria of risk that a particular destination country will accept.[17] Although E.U. countries have been trying to "harmonize" their criteria to prevent such actions, would-be settlers still look for ways to establish new identities or select facets of old ones that might qualify them for asylum in one or another country. As border controls have tightened and better ways are found to check identities, ever-more circuitous means of travel are devised.[18]

To be sure, individuals who engage in these activities do not have law-breaking as their motive. But would-e immigrants are no different from anyone else, as they to construe meanings in ways that favor their interests. Creating policies inevitably creates the potential for counter actions, whether we call them "unintended consequences"[19] or something else. As states respond, expanding the rules that will allow them to impose restrictions, the results will inevitably have create yet more ambiguous meanings that people at the margins in turn may try to press.[20]

---

17 E.g., "EU 'asylum shopping list' stalled", The Parliament: politics, policy and people. www.eupolitix.com/EN/News/200605/0427410f-8d2b-46f8-ac0b-0b3fa1877b42. htm

18 Massey (1996:3) stresses that migrants often know the system better than the authorities because their lives are built on maneuvering around its rules.

19 A study by Hoem et al. (2001) describes a 1990 Austrian policy that sought to improve economic gender imbalances by assuring women they could re-enter the work force after a birth. The result, however, was that couples with two children who had been ambivalent about having more were prompted to move on to a third child.

20 See David Cay Johnston's description of a New York accountant for the "super-rich" ("The loophole artist", *New York Times Magazine*, Dec 21, 2003:18-22).

Anthropological studies, then, increasingly attune to changes in social vulnerabilities as national context shifts. Whether one is doing business for giant corporations or seeking safe haven from political upheaval back home, mobility is the key to security in this new world. Of course, the lines dividing "them" and "us" were blurred long ago as colonial governments, missionaries, and traders reached so pervasively into our field sites, and as we saw that the new ease of communications and travel was bringing our subjects to our doorsteps, whether as co-workers, fellow citizens, or family members. In any case, places like the U.S., London, and Paris now pass as uncontested ethnographic locales.

Reproduction and Legitimacy in the Margins of the New Europe

As in the classic works on Europe, questions about reproduction continue to focus on the margins of legitimacy: rights to citizenship, to land and the goods produced on it, etc. But unlike previous emphases on legitimacy within a family headed by properly married European parents, questions today have shifted to wider territorial scales: to legitimacy across countries and world regions. If, then, children never replicate their parents, how might their "difference" broker family efforts to gain security in the new global dynamics of marginality and legitimacy? Below I examine a few case studies involving national logics that define legitimacy, and some of the responses they generate. Most examples turn on what has become a politically charged event – an immigrant child's birth – but others concern children's movement.

"Anchor babies" in the United States

I begin with a comparative example from my own country: the phenomenon of the children who have come to be labeled "anchor babies" ("A different kind of Border Cross", *Chicago Tribune*, April 30, 2003). This term refers to children who, by virtue of their birth on U.S. soil, become the means by which their families stake a future claim on legal U.S. residence.

The right to citizenship by virtue of birth on U.S. soil is inscribed in constitutional law, giving a child all the privileges and responsibilities that citizenship now entails: voting rights when he/she turns 18, the age of legal majority, vulnerability to the draft; and access to public jobs, welfare, and university scholarships. Another such right is family reunification, by which a child-citizen, upon reaching age 18, may petition to bring particular family members (parents, spouse, children, and unmarried siblings) into the country as legal residents. With citizenship in the U.S. at such a global premium, geographical contiguity to a much poorer country gives rise to quite predictable reproductive responses. Every year, a number of pregnant Mexican women try to reach the U.S. to give birth. Some do so by undertaking dangerous crossings that parallel those in Europe: trekking across deserts, entering cargo containers, and even crossing dangerous rivers. To me, however, the most striking cases are those of wealthy Mexican women who cross the border in the most routine manner, not just once but multiple times, for prenatal checks with the physician who they have engaged to deliver them. This they do by using three-day temporary visas available to individuals who can demonstrate financial stability and a residence close to the border. For one such three day visa, they schedule an induced labor or a caesarean birth. After obtaining the child's birth certificate, they return to Mexico. Eighteen years later, the now-grown U.S. citizen can apply for reunification for the rest of the family in the U.S. In effect, a non-U.S. citizen, through the highly strategic use of just one birth, can eventually transform an entire family into individuals with permanent legitimacy.

Not surprisingly, this effort to take advantage of U.S. law is beginning to arouse resentment from many in the mainstream citizenry, especially those in the border states, who object that these "anchor" children will swell population growth and take unfair advantage of "real" citizens' benefits. On the other hand, no one seems to consider banning American patients from crossing the Mexican border to obtain health care. Indeed, American physicians may refer their patients to the other side, where they know that more affordable care is available (Homedes et al. 1994). And American doctors and hospitals on the U.S. side use this idiosyncratic combination of laws and geography to their own advantage, openly advertising their services to affluent Mexican patients. In any case, the ease with which affluent Mexican women cross the border to give birth to U.S. citizens should not be allowed to obscure the risk to which thousands of impoverished women from the south are exposed when they try to stake a claim of future security in the U.S.

"Naturalizing" Ancestors in Goa

Many countries grant citizenship to the descendants of their citizens from the past. The case of the tiny state of Goa, a former Portuguese colony on the western coast in India, shows how convoluted the strategies can become, especially when incentives shift so sharply.[21] Under an old Portuguese law, Goans are eligible for Portuguese citizenship, and hence for full rights E.U. citizenship, if they can document their descent from someone born in the state before 1961, when the Indian army seized control of the territory from Portugal. Portugal at first fought the move and assisted in a number of legal cases of Goans who did not wish to be called Indians or "foreigners", though it eventually agreed to cede

21 See "Indians' Entrée to Europe is a Portuguese Passport", *Chicago Tribune*, June 8, 2003; and "Portuguese nationality law, in the historical context of the relations between Portugal and India", available at http://www.geocities.com/paulocd/PortNatLaw.htm [accessed 20 June 2008]; and "Reponse to several inaccurate articles published in the Goan Press – January and February 2004", available at http://www.colaco.net/1/PauloInaccurateGoaPressStories.htm, posted 3/3/04 [accessed 20 June 2008].

the territory to India. Most former Portuguese passport holders had been content to remain in Goa until 1986, when Portugal joined the E.U. Realizing the advantages to E.U. citizenship, many Goans began to seek Portuguese citizenship under this old law, even renouncing their Indian citizenship (Indian law does not allow dual citizenship) to obtain an E.U. passport.[22] Some applicants even tried to "naturalize" a pre-1961 Goan-born parent or grandparent posthumously, in the official Goan birth registries, to Portuguese citizenship. Others tried to graft onto their genealogy someone who was not an ancestor, or alter an actual ancestor's time or place of birth. Ironically, many of these naturalized dead ancestors had decisively renounced their Portuguese citizenship by burning their Portuguese passports; they have nonetheless been converted posthumously to the nationality of the hated colonial master.

As in the U.S. example of births with high political stakes, the fact that many Goans are trying to change their citizenship now that Portugal is becoming more affluent is regarded by many "native" Portuguese as the result of a mortifying oversight. But it also demonstrates that legitimacy is an ongoing status. Not even the empirical fact of a geographical birth location mechanically determines legitimate affiliation. Instead, descendants seek to redefine the meaning of birth in the past in ways that will give them legitimation in a changed political present.

Irish-Born Children and their Parent-Caretakers

Until 2004, Ireland, like the U.S., gave automatic citizenship to anyone born on its soil (*jus soli)*; it was last European countries to do so. Further, in 1990, the case of a man from Nigeria, Fajujonu, established that Irish children had the right to the "care, company and parentage" of their parents; thus, parents who were playing a clear role in their maintenance had rights to residence in Ireland. In the description by Kómoláfé (2002), Fajujonu became illegally resident in Ireland when his Irish visa expired in 1981. The High Court decided not only that his two Irish-born children had the right to stay; that he could remain in the country with them. In the assessment of Kómoláfé, this case led to a significant increase in Nigerian entries, both from Nigeria and from other European countries, by people who had been unable to travel for fear of being apprehended, and who sought, by giving birth to an Irish child, to gain free movement in the E.U.., as guaranteed by the Schengen Agreement. Kómoláfé's found that in the years following the Fajujonu case, there was a dramatic increase in Ireland of female migrants of childbearing age. Some wealthy Nigerian men, in fact, sent their pregnant wives to Ireland before they themselves came. The following quote from Kómoláfé's interview with "Mrs. C.", who had moved from Lagos

22 Citizens or residents of all Portugal's former African colonies had a temporal window to enact this conversion, but the window has now closed.

to Germany six years earlier, left little doubt about the relation between a birthing strategy in Ireland and the E.U. free passage possibility:

> I came to Ireland to have my baby and to obtain Irish residency status. I had lived in Germany for six years as an illegal immigrant. My mother died two years ago, but I was unable to go for her burial in Nigeria. I knew if I went I would not be able to come back to Europe. Where would I have begun again? It was a terrible experience. All I want is to be able to move from one area to another. This I am now enjoying.

In response to strong public reactions, however, including widespread allegations of manipulation against black women (Luibhéid 2003), the "Irish Nationality and Citizenship Act 2004",[23] following a Chinese woman's case,[24] resulted in an amendment to the Irish constitution that removed the *jus soli* qualification for citizenship altogether.

Kómoláfé's account also, however, points to a less obvious but critical fact concerning a much larger group of migrants in Ireland. In recent decades, he notes, Irish national authorities have been leading the way in trying to attract skilled immigrants. The country has been so desperate especially for doctors and nurses, that Irish hospitals have sometimes sent representatives on aggressive recruitment missions to countries like Nigeria to seek out such professionals who were trained at great local expense. Fajujonu himself was unemployed at the time of the court case. Still, it is hard to avoid noticing the temporal coincidence between a court decision that relaxed this piece of immigration policy, and a moment when Ireland, still something of a "developing country" compared to the rest of the E.U., could not afford to discourage professionals.

Congo-Paris Age Traders

Chinese entrepreneurial elites and foreign medical professionals are more likely to surmount immigration troubles than many other immigrants, who are more apt to get deported or have to settle, undocumented and vulnerable, in the less preferred nodes of international mobility circuits. The case of Congo-Paris traders "on the margins of the law" (MacGaffey and Bazenguissa-Ganga 2000) is rich in descriptions of strategies surrounding citizenship. Among the most fascinating cases are those of the Congolese who engage in trade in France by ma-

---

23 "Irish Nationality and Citizenship Act, 2004", available at http://www.irishstatutebook.ie/2004/en/act/pub/0038/print.html [accessed 20 June 2008].

24 "Judgment of the Court (sitting as a full Court), Right of residence – child with the nationality of one member state but residing in another member state – parents nationals of a non-member country – mother's right to reside in the other member state." 19 October 2004. Available at http://curia.europa.eu/jurisp/cgi-bin/gettext.pl?where=&lang=en&num=79958980C19020200&doc=T&ouvert=T&seance=ARRET [accessed 20 June 2008].

neuvering with children between the cracks of French citizenship rules for children, and the international airline industry.

Central and West Africans have reputations as traders that date back centuries (Guyer 2004). They have also routinely brought children into their businesses for training. Congo-Paris traders have improvised new facets of these longstanding patterns. One such effort, until a few years ago, hinged on the fact that, like the case of Ireland, children born in France were automatically French citizens, and a child's citizenship gave the parents rights to residence. When women traders from the Congo found that bearing a child in France gave them the freedom to travel throughout Schengen countries, and thus the means to start a transcontinental trading business. We see this assessment reflected in the testimony of an entrepreneur named Eloise. Lacking the legitimacy to travel to Europe early in her career, Eloise had to limit her trading to Central Africa. But she seized the opportunity that a pregnancy presented to build an intercontinental trading enterprise:

> [Eloise] traded between Zaire and Congo, saving up money to buy her ticket. When she became pregnant at the age of 20, she decided that that was the moment to go to France so that her child could be born there. Afterwards she did not need a visa to enter the country. She started trading between France and Congo when her baby was eight months old. In 1994, she had been travelling [sic] back and forth for three years. She bought babies' clothes, blouses, women's sandals ... and airfreighted them to Congo-Brazzaville, where she sold them to Senegalese wholesalers or to market retailers. Sometimes she goes to Amsterdam to buy jewelry ... [and resells it] in Brazzavile or Paris ... (MacGaffey and Bazenguissa-Ganga 2000, p. 99).

Equally revealing was what happened when France began to tighten the boundaries of citizenship, in the late 1980's of Jacques Le Pen and the National Front Party. With children born in France no longer able to be citizens, Congolese women traders turned to the potentials of children and airline tickets. Many Africans have sought work connected with the airline industry because of the advantages these positions can yield for shipping merchandise. With the termination of legitimacy in France from birth in France, undocumented Congolese women traders who could claim connection to the airline industry focused on the practice of giving substantial reductions in ticket prices to employees and their children under age 25. Many children who had been born under the citizenship-by-birth regime were well under 25, so some women who were connected with airline companies kept their trading businesses going by "adopting" child-citizens. These "children" (one adoptee was herself in her young twenties; the adopted children in another woman's account were her younger brothers) could then be dispatched on transnational trade. I stress, however, that adoption in the sense of a permanent legal transfer of a child, almost never occurs in Africa, though "fostering" (alternatively, "minding" or "caring for") are quite common. This possibility, if correct, would lend even stronger support to the authors' speculation that adoption was used to meet the qualifications for reduced airline ticket prices.

Polygamous Malian Men in "Pasqua" Paris

If the cessation, a few years ago, of citizenship rights on the basis of birth caused problems for Africans in France, the clamp-down on the presence of multiple wives created even more disruption. An account by Sargent and Cordell (2003) illuminates the struggles of Malian families who have had to negotiate the quandaries of reproductive life in a society that demands legal monogamy. The late 1980s brought severe restrictions on the immigration of spouses and the reunification of families. Polygamy was banned, while rights to citizenship and residence through a child's birth tightened sharply. Since the passage of the 1993 "Pasqua" ruling aimed for "zero-[illegal]-immigration", authorities have had the right to inspect the identity papers of anyone, whether at work, at train stations, or on the street. Because a man can lose his work and residence permits for having more than one wife, even supernumerary wives and their children who originally came lawfully have been marginalized. A man must in theory divorce such a wife, whether in name or in fact, or send her back to the place the French authorities call her "home", even if she no longer has a place there. One of the sharpest ironies, however, has been the impact on fertility. French policies, while pronatalist toward mainstream citizens, have tried to discourage high fertility among African immigrants. However, anecdotal evidence suggests that by exacerbating polygamous competition, policies that mandate monogamy may have led to increased fertility among some Malian women, and in dangerous ways. A wife may try to bear many closely-spaced children in hopes that the man will choose her to stay in Paris as his "official" wife by virtue of her reproductive accomplishments. The strain, both economic and health, appeared to be particularly hard on the second wife, who is less likely to be designated as the "official" wife.

"Visa Wives" in Norway

This final case, when it arose in 1997, drew international attention among activists and scholars. It involved "Nadia" (a pseudonym), an 18 year old Norwegian citizen whose Moroccan-born parents were naturalized Norwegian citizens (Wikan 2002a, 2002b). Nadia, in a phone call of distress from Morocco to a friend in Norway, claimed her parents had had her drugged, bound, and transported overland, around the Mediterranean, in a van by her own parents, who were trying to force her to marry a young Moroccan man. Neither Norway nor Morocco recognizes dual citizenship, and Morocco declares that Moroccan citizenship is irrevocable. Morocco, where the age of legal majority is 20, saw no reason to return Nadia, regardless of what she herself wanted, because she was a child. Norway, with an age of legal majority at 18, demanded the return of its adult citizen who was pleading for help. The parents seemed to have three goals. One was to keep the family feet planted firmly in both the Moroccan homeland and in Norway's welfare state, where Nadia's father, for a number of years, had been collecting social security benefits and a housing subsidy because of a heart problem. A second aim was to marry Nadia to a Moroccan man of strong Muslim background who might rid her of what the parents saw as loose Norwegian morality. Finally, they sought to secure entry to Norway for the man they had chosen for her: to make her, as Nadia charged, a piece of "merchandise". In fact, according to Wikan, in Pakistan, "... marriageable girls in Norway are called *visuni* – visas; and Norwegian-Moroccan girls are spoken of as gold-edged papers" (2002a, p. 140). Wikan's description implies that Nadia's parents would concede to bring her back only if she produced a child in Morocco, a Moroccan citizen. Her child's citizenship would commit her to firm Moroccan ties if she wanted to stay connected to her child. In fact, however, the national outcry the case generated forced Nadia's parents to allow her to return after a week, and the central drama ended in criminal court, with the Norwegian state prosecuting the parents for their deed.

Running throughout Wikan's description is the implication that children and their births (and there are two relevant children here, Nadia and her hypothetical Moroccan child) can be used to gain access to Europe and to keep ties with the country of origin. Of particular note are Wikan's provocative observations on a paradoxical side of dual citizenship for children and women: "Dual citizenship often is presented by academics as an asset, a resource – and so it is for the likes of them.... In this, as in many matters, the crucial question is, for whom is dual citizenship an advantage? Who stands to lose and who to gain? Children... may be the main losers, and girls most of all" (2002a, p. 140). Family reunification has an equally unsettling side: "... it exposes children of immigrants in Europe, not just Norway, to immense pressure to comply with arranged marriages, and in many cases to real force" (2002a, p. 140).

* * *

These case studies offer compelling glimpses of reproductive life in the margins of changing Europe. While some might see in them crass exploitation of legal loopholes, what they more starkly reflect is the reduction to categories that Westerners hold as a moral core precisely because other possibilities are drying up. Further, the stronger the state efforts to restrict immigrants, the more that risks to their children and families may be driven underground, beneath the formal national institutions that protect and support "legitimate" society members. While such cases may have cultural echoes back in the country of origin, "tradition" is a partial if not misleading explanation. Much of Africa still practices polygamy and values high fertility. What seems different is that in Africa, being an outside wife, while less desired than being an "inside" one, is not generally regarded as illegal, and pressure on a woman to produce a child every year would provoke community outrage (Bledsoe 2002). Further, people from many countries in the world still arrange marriages for their young family members. But back home, families rarely force a marriage so brutally if one or both partners are strongly opposed.

When marriage turns into a potential ticket to the E.U. through women, the consequences can reach far beyond local problems back home.

Conclusion

Who children become, the conditions under which they are born and raised, and the ties they forge – all matter intensely in an increasingly connected world. Trying to bear and raise children for a new state is no automatic solution to problems of belonging, even for those who bear a U.S. child-citizen. Asylum-seeking families with small children who are caught for months in the limbo of refugee camps may find themselves deported more readily than young, single workers (Kara Murphy, personal communication, 2003). But the possibility that children can play a different role for families in a new place than they did back home suggests that it is important to grasp people's views of the social legitimacy that children might offer in a new place.[25]

What about the implications of these findings for questions of fertility? Can they shed any light on how migrants' fertility may change in the European context, or come to resemble that of the "home" populations? Students of European demography agree that European populations place increasingly less emphasis on legitimacy in the sense of formally staged temporalities among entry into marriage, sexuality, and reproductive life. But is this generalization equally true for all those who inhabit Europe? The odd thing is that standards of reproductive legitimacy among those at the margins of Europe are increasingly stringent. State insistence on strong standards of political legitimacy comes to create ever-tougher standards of legitimacy in intimate family contexts. While those securely attached to the "core" of Western Europe increasingly lapse into what in the past would have been regarded as "illegitimacy", with few apparent penalties, the opposite is expected from marginal would-be newcomers.

Observations like these lead to a question. Are these two stories – efforts by immigrant families to gain legitimacy in a new state through their children, and the strikingly low and increasingly non-marital fertility in mainstream Western Europe – two sides of the same coin? I am persuaded that reproduction in developing countries is moving strongly into dynamic alignment with fertility in developed countries. One might even predict that to the extent that immigrants remain marginal, their fertility levels will remain disconnected from fertility levels in the country of immigration. One reason is that the bulk of their support must come from different sources from those that benefit more entrenched residents.

25 For parallel interests in "pathways to legitimacy", see the work of Annie Phizacklea and Bridget Anderson in the Transnational Communities Programme. Economic and Social Research Council, Oxford University. Available at http://www.transcomm.ox.ac.uk/wwwroot/phizacklea.htm [accessed 20 June 2008].

Another is that it is precisely the adaptations, if not distortions, that marginal immigrants must enact in the face of economic and legal pressures that will make their reproductive lives different from those in the mainstream. Indeed, the harder the legal lines are drawn by the host country, the sharper the fertility differences may become. What does seem clear is that in this rapidly globalizing era, studying the dynamics of fertility in the social and legal margins of Europe is becoming essential to understanding the dynamics of low fertility at the core. Needed as well as are reconsiderations of the appropriate units of analysis in fertility studies, including conventional notions of national population boundaries. Just as it is no longer possible, when considering the developing world, to rest on conventional notions of reproductive practices, it is impossible to draw conclusions about the most perplexing questions of fertility in Europe without keeping the developing world in view. The challenges posed by more global visions of population are opening the way for more culturally informed transnational demographic efforts.

Acknowledgements

This project has been supported by the Max Planck Institute for Demographic Research (Rostock, Germany) and the Woodrow Wilson International Center for Scholars (Washington DC). I thank Gunnar Andersson, Gerda Neyer, Keith Hart, Sophie Chevalier, and Carolyn Sargent for their insights, and the Irmgard Coninx Siftung for the opportunity to participate in the 2007 Berlin Roundtables.

References

Anderson, Benedict. 1983. *Imagined communities: reflections on the origins and spread of nationalism*. London: Verso.

Anderson, Bridget. 2000. *Doing the dirty work? The global politics of domestic labour.* London: Zed Books.

Andersson, Gunnar and Scott, Kirk. 2004. "Labour-market attachment and entry into parenthood: The experience of immigrant women in Sweden." MPIDR Working Paper 2004. Max Planck Institute for Demographic Research, Rostock.

Barth, Fredrik, ed. 1969. *Ethnic groups and boundaries: the social organization of cultural difference.* London: Allen and Unwin.

Bellier, Irene and Wilson, Thomas M., eds. 2000. *An Anthropology of the European Union: building, imagining and experiencing the new Europe*. Oxford: Berg.

– 1990. "The politics of children: fosterage and the social management of fertility among the Mende of Sierra Leone." In W.Penn Handwerker, ed. *Births and power: the politics of reproduction*. Boulder: Westview Press, pp. 81-100.

Bledsoe, Caroline. 2002. *Contingent lives: fertility, time, and aging in West Africa* (with contributions by Fatoumatta Banja). Chicago: University of Chicago Press.

Bledsoe, Caroline and Papa Sow. Forthcoming. "Family reunification ideals and the practice of transnational reproductive life among Africans in Europe." In Carole H. Browner and Carolyn F. Sargent, eds. *Reproduction, globalization and the state.* Durham: Duke University Press.

Blum, Alain. 2002. "Resistance to identity categorization in France." In David I. Kertzer and Dominique Arel, eds. *Census and Identity: The politics of race, ethnicity, and language in national censuses.* Cambridge, UK: Cambridge University Press, pp. 121- 147.

Bourdieu, Pierre. 2002a. "Pierre Bourdieu on marriage strategies." *Population and Development Review* 28 (3), pp. 549-558.

– 2002b. *Bal des célebataires: crise de la société paysanne en Béarn.* Paris: Éditions du Seuil.

Brettell, Caroline. 1986. *Men who migrate, women who wait: population and history in a Portuguese parish.* Princeton: Princeton University Press.

– 1995. *We have already cried many tears: the stories of three Portuguese migrant women.* Prospect Heights: Waveland Press.

Bumpass, Larry, et al. 1995. "The changing character of stepfamilies: Implications of cohabitation and nonmarital childbearing." *Demography* 32 (3), pp. 425-436.

Carter, Donald Martin. 1997. *States of grace: Senegalese in Italy and the new European immigration.* Minneapolis: University of Minnesota Press.

Chicago Tribune. April 30, 2003. "A different kind of border cross."

Cole, Jennifer and Deborah Durham, eds. 2006. *Generations and globalization: youth, age, and family in the new world economy.* Bloomington: Indiana University Press.

Comaroff, John L. and Simon Roberts, eds. 1981. *Rules and processes: the cultural logic of dispute in an African context.* Chicago: University of Chicago Press.

Das, Veena. 2001. "National honor and practical kinship: Unwanted women and children." In Faye Ginsburg and Rayna Rapp, eds. *Conceiving the new world order: the global politics of reproduction.* Berkeley: University of California Press, pp. 212- 233.

de Genova, Nicholas. 2002. "Migrant 'illegality' and deportability in everyday life." *Annual Review of Anthropology* (31), pp. 419-447.

Delaney, Carol Lowery. 1991. *The seed and the soil: gender and cosmology in Turkish village society.* Berkeley: University of California Press.

Douglas, Mary. 1966. *Purity and danger.* London: Routledge.

Esposito, Nicholas. 1989. *Italian family structure.* New York: Peter Lang.

Franklin, Sarah and Susan McKinnon, eds. 2001. *Relative values: reconfiguring kinship studies*. Durham: Duke University Press.

Friedl, Ernestine. 1962. *Vasilika, a village in modern Greece*. New York: Holt, Rinehart and Winston.

Gal, Susan and Gail Kligman. 2000. *The politics of gender after socialism: a comparative-historical essay*. Princeton: Princeton University Press.

Gardner, Katy. 1995. Global migrants, local lives: travel and transformation in rural Bangladesh. Oxford: Clarendon Press.

Gilmore, David D., ed. 1987. *Honor and shame and the unity of the Mediterranean*. Washington, DC: American Anthropological Association.

Ginsburg, Faye and Rayna Rapp, eds. 1995. *Conceiving the new world order: the global politics of reproduction*. Berkeley: University of California Press.

Goldscheider, Frances K., et al. 2000. "Men, parenthood, and divorce in the era of the Second Demographic Transition." In Caroline Bledsoe, Susana Lerner, and Jane I. Guyer, eds. *Fertility and the male life cycle in the era of fertility decline*. Clarendon: Oxford University Press.

Goodale, Mark and Sally Engle Merry, eds. 2007. *The practice of human rights: tracking law between the global and the local*. Cambridge, UK: Cambridge University Press.

Goode, William J. 1993. *World changes in divorce patterns*. New Haven: Yale University Press.

Goody, Jack. 2000. *The European family: An historico-anthropological essay*. Oxford: Blackwell Publishers.

Greenhalgh, Susan. 1995. "Anthropology theorizes reproduction: Integrating practice, political economic, and feminist perspectives." In Susan Greenhalgh, ed. *Situating fertility: anthropology and demographic inquiry*. Cambridge, UK: Cambridge University Press, pp. 3-28.

Greenhouse, Carol, et al., eds. 2002. *Ethnography in unstable places: everyday lives in contexts of dramatic political change*. Durham: Duke University Press.

Gupta, Akhil and James Ferguson, eds. 1997. *Anthropological locations: boundaries and grounds of a field science*. Berkeley: University of California Press.

Guyer, Jane I. 2004. *Marginal gains: monetary transactions in Atlantic Africa*. Chicago: University of Chicago Press.

Hannerz, Ulf. 1996. *Transnational connections: culture, people, places*. London: Routledge.

Hansen, Karen Tranberg. 2000. *Salaula: The world of secondhand clothing and Zambia*. Chicago: University of Chicago Press.

Haugerud, Angelique, et al., eds. 2000. *Commodities and globalization: anthropological perspectives*. Lanham: Rowman and Littlefield.

Hoem, Jan M., et al. 2001. "Autonomy or conservative adjustment: The effect of public policies and educational attainment on third births in Austria, 1975-96." *Population Studies* 55 (3), pp. 249-261.

Homedes, Nuria, et al. 1994. "Utilization of health services along the Arizona-Sonora border: the providers [sic] perspective", *Salud Pública Méx*, 36 (6), pp. 633-645, available at http://www.insp.mx/rsp/articulos/articulo.php?id=001726 (accessed 20 June 2008).

Inda, Jonathan Xavier and Renato Rosaldo, eds. 2002. *The anthropology of globalization: a reader*. Blackwell, Oxford.

Kahn, Susan. 2000. *Reproducing Jews: a cultural account of assisted conception in Israel.* Durham: Duke University Press.

Kanaaneh, Rhoda. 2002. *Birthing the nation: strategies of Palestinian women in Israel*. Berkeley: University of California Press.

Kenny, Michael, and David I. Kertzer, eds. 1983. *Urban life in Mediterranean Europe: anthropological perspectives*. Urbana: University of Illinois Press.

Kertzer, David I. and Caroline Brettell. 1987. "Advances in Italian and Iberian family history." *Journal of Family History* 12 (1), pp. 87-121.

Kertzer, David I. and Dennis P. Hogan. 1989. *Family, political economy, and demographic change: the transformation of life in Casalecchio, Italy, 1861-1921.* Madison: University of Wisconsin Press.

Kertzer, David I. and Tom Fricke, eds. 1997. *Anthropological demography: toward a new synthesis*. Chicago: University of Chicago Press.

Kómoláfé, Julius. 2002. "Searching for fortune: The geographical process of Nigerian migration to Dublin, Ireland." *Irinkerindo: a Journal of African Migration* 1 (1). Available at http://www.africamigration.com/index.html.

Laslett, Peter. 1980. "Introduction." In Peter Laslett, ed. *Bastardy and its comparative history*. Cambridge, UK: Edward Arnold, pp. 1-68.

Launay, Robert. 1995. "The power of names: Illegitimacy in a Muslim Community in Côte d'Ivoire." In Susan Greenhalgh, ed. *Situating fertility: anthropology and demographic inquiry*. Cambridge, UK: Cambridge University Press, pp. 108-129.

Lesthaeghe, Ron, ed. 2000. *Communities and generations: Turkish and Moroccan populations in Belgium*. Brussels: Vrije University Press.

Lesthaeghe, Ron and Dirk van de Kaa. 1986. "Twee demografische transities?" In Ron Lesthaeghe and Dirk van de Kaa, eds. *Groei of krimp?* Book volume of 'Mens en Maatschappij'. Deventer: Van Loghum-Slaterus, pp. 9-24.

Luibhéid, Eithne. 2003. "Globalization and sexuality: Redrawing racial and national boundaries through discourses of childbearing." In Lentin Ronit and Eithne Luibhéid, eds. *Women's movement: migrant women transforming Ireland*. Papers from a conference in Trinity College, March 2003, Dublin.

MacGaffey, Janet and Rémy Bazenguissa-Ganga. 2000. *Congo-Paris: transnational traders on the margins of the law*. London: International African Institute in association with James Currey, Oxford; Bloomington: Indiana University Press.

Marcus, George E. 1995. "Ethnography in/of the world system: The emergence of multi-sited ethnography." *Annual Review of Anthropology* (24), pp. 95-117.

Massey, Douglas S. 1996. "The false legacy of the 1965 immigration act." *World on the Move, Newsletter of the Section on International Migration* (3), pp. 2-3.

Massey, Douglas S., ed. 1998. *Worlds in motion: understanding international migration at the end of the millenium.* Oxford: Clarendon Press.

Neveu, Catherine. 2000. "European citizenship, citizens of Europe and European citizens." In Irene Bellier and Thomas M. Wilson, eds. *An anthropology of the European Unión: building, imagining and experiencing the new Europe.* Oxford: Berg, pp. 119-135.

Ong, Aiwa. 2002. "The Pacific shuttle: families, citizenship, and capital circuits." In Jonathan Xavier Inda and Rosaldo Rosaldo, eds. *The anthropology of globalization: a reader.* Oxford: Blackwell, pp. 172-197.

Parkin, Robert and Linda Stone, eds. 2004. *Kinship and family: an anthropological reader.* Oxford: Blackwell.

Péristiany, J.G., ed. 1966. *Honour and shame: the values of Mediterranean society.* London: Weidenfeld and Nicolson.

Said, Edward. 1978. *Orientalism.* New York: Random House.

Sargent, Carolyn F. and Dennis Cordell. 2003. "Polygamy, disrupted reproduction, and the state: Malian migrants in Paris, France." *Social Science and Medicine* 56 (9), pp.1961-1972.

Sassen, Saskia. 1998. *Globalization and its discontents: essays on the new mobility of people and money.* New York: The New Press.

Scheper-Hughes, Nancy. 1979. *Saints, scholars, and schizophrenics: mental illness in rural Ireland.* Berkeley: University of California Press.

Schiff, Claire. 2003. "Work, youth, and immigration in France." In Laurence Roulleau-Berger, ed., *Youth and work in the post-industrial city of North America and Europe.* London: Brill, pp. 232-346.

Scotsman, The. January 23, 2003. International Section.

Silverman, Sydel. 1975. *Three bells of civilization: the life of an Italian hill town.* New York: Columbia University Press.

Smith, Raymond Thomas. 1956. *The Negro family in British Guiana; family structure and social status in the villages.* Routledge and London: Kegan Paul.

Surkyn, Johan and Ron Lesthaeghe. 2004. "Value orientations and the second demographic transition (SDT) in Northern, Western and Southern Europe: An update." *Demographic Research* (S3), pp.45-86.

van Amersfoort, H. 1999. "The ostrich factor in Dutch demography." In Anton Kuijsten, Henk de Gans, and Henk de Feijter, eds. *The joy of demography and other disciplines*: Liber Americorum presented to Dirk van de Kaa on the occasion of his retirement as Professor of Demography at the University of Amsterdam. Amsterdam: Thela Thesis, pp. 177-183.

van de Kaa, Dirk. 1993. "European migration at the end of history." In Alain Blum and Jean-Louis Rallu, eds. *European Population. Vol. 2: Demographic Dynamics.* Montrouge: John Libbey Eurotext, pp. 77-109.

Verdery, Katherine. 1995. *National ideology under socialism*. Berkeley: University of California Press.

Wallerstein, Immanuel. 1974. *The modern world system*. New York: Academic Press.

Wikan, Unni. 2002a. "Citizenship on trial: Nadia's case." In Richard A. Shweder, Martha Minow, and Hazel Markus, eds. *Engaging cultural differences: the multicultural challenge in liberal Democracies*. New York: Russell Sage Foundation, pp. 128-143.

– 2002b. *Generous betrayal: politics of culture in the new Europe*. Chicago: University of Chicago Press.

Wolf, Eric. 1982. *Europe and the people without history*. Berkeley: University of California Press.

Yanagisako, Sylvia Junko. 2002. *Producing culture and capital: family firms in Italy*. Princeton: Princeton University Press.

Part 2

Paradoxes of Social Engineering

Chapter 5

A Population Policy Transition
–
Human Rights and Population Politics in India During the 1975–1977 Emergency and Today

Khadija R. Turay

Introduction

Population politics are relevant to human rights because they affect the well-being, integrity, and dignity of individuals. Over time, population politics have been shaped by development and research. Yet they also have always been profoundly dictated by national and international political climates. Occasionally, political climates that dictate population politics experience disruptions in the form of a state of emergency. These disruptions occur when state leadership believes that the "life" of the nation is in crisis because it is threatened by (alone or in combination) social disturbance, extraordinary political dissent, or unusual economic downfall. With the intent to preserve the integrity of a nation, a state of emergency limits civil rights and concentrates political power in the executive branch (Iyer 2000). Recently the international community has witnessed states of emergency declared in Chad and Pakistan.

The political validity and international acceptance of emergencies accompanied by a concentration of political power create a need to examine the extent to which human rights are upheld during a state of emergency. Further, it becomes important to consider how emergency rule may or may not impact a nation's population politics after it has ended. The period of emergency rule that took place in India between 1975 and 1977 provides unique insight into both of these topics. Although India declared states of emergency in 1962 and 1971, the 1975-1977 Emergency held socio-political significance because of the exceptional magnitude in which the career of the Prime Minister, the future of the historically significant Congress Party, and the country's social and economic fabric were simultaneously challenged. Additionally, this emergency was distinctive because it allowed India's ambitions for development to overshadow reproductive rights more than ever before through increased political will for family planning (Gwatkin 1979).

India's culturally diverse and large population and its emergent economy have always made it a paragon for examining relationships between human rights and political intervention in family planning. The 1975 to 1977 Emergency is of particular interest to those who study population politics because it illustrates the effects of implementing a population policy during a suspended democracy. It also depicts the effects of a population policy on human rights before India ratified the International Convention on Political and Civil Rights in 1979, as well as before the international consensus articulated in the 1994 International Conference on Population and Development Program of Action. The 1975-1977 Emergency time period is especially worthy of examination because after it ended, development ideologies and family planning efforts in India transitioned from tolerating a sterilization campaign which violated reproductive rights, to sustaining the presence of rights-based maternal and child health initiatives at the top of the national health agenda.

This text examines how a state of emergency assisted population politics in abusing human rights, and how the end of emergency rule helped catalyze a long lasting ideological transition in Indian population politics. A historical perspective of India's population politics will highlight the nuances of population policy transitions and factors important in reconciling state intervention in family planning with reproductive rights.

Part I of this text describes changes in India's political climate before and during the 1975-1977 Emergency, and the origins of the 1976 National Population Policy that spawned an unprecedented vasectomy campaign. Part II examines how the political climate of The Emergency allowed a vasectomy campaign to perpetuate reproductive rights abuses. Lastly, Part III examines the transition of India's population politics and how presently, despite national efforts and global political intervention and consensus building, efforts to support human and reproductive rights in India are continuously challenged by the underutilization of national health programs and social injustices experienced by females. It will be proposed that political intervention in family planning can be reconciled with human rights when multidisciplinary public policies are prioritized and political will creates an adequate climate for upholding reproductive rights.

Part I: The Emergence of the State of Emergency and the 1976 National Population Policy

After India became independent from Britain in 1947, controlling population growth was a political issue because of its proposed relationship to poverty and the economy. In 1971, India's population growth rate was 2.25 percent per year (Panandiker and Umashankar 1994), and campaigning on a platform of *Garibi Hatao,* or 'End Poverty', Indira Gandhi of the National Congress Party was re-elected as Prime Minister. After the election, factors that would prompt a state of emergency culminated. Indira's efforts to reduce poverty were waning as the nation faced the Bangladesh War, poor harvests, and an oil crisis. By 1974, inflation was rising and the poor were not better off than in 1971. Moreover, despite continued economic development, the population was growing faster than productivity. *Garibi Hatao* eventually began to fail, and it seemed unlikely to many that the economic situation would change fast enough to sustain the burgeoning population.

As the burden of proof fell on Indira's government for the nation's economic hardships, she began to experience political troubles as well. Raj Narain, whom she defeated in the 1971 election, charged her with conducting a corrupt campaign. Subsequently, the Supreme Court rendered a guilty verdict and prohibited Indira from holding elected office for six years. This validation of the accusations weakened public perception of Indira's ability to continue the political dynasty that began with her father, Jawaharlal Nehru, who was India's first post-independence prime minister. The verdict also concerned Congress Party members about their political viability, especially after the party had suffered significant defeats in the 1971 state elections. Some party officials even supported Indira's resignation from office for the sake of fortifying the party (Wolpert 2000).

Before and after the verdict was rendered, civil disobedience had increased nationwide. A combination of the social chaos, the failure of her signature economic policy, and the weakening of her political career motivated Indira to change the distribution of political power within India. Subsequently, in June 1975, Indira legitimized the distribution change by declaring a state of emergency on the premise that doing so would "prevent economic deterioration, political disruption, social disturbance, and general chaos" (Palmer 1977, p. 161). Indira then made numerous amendments to the Constitution to support her emergency powers. Specifically, she added an amendment that exonerated her from any criminal charges for acts during her tenure as Prime Minister. Regarding national affairs, she arrested her political opposition without trials, censored the media, barred the courts from hearing cases against The Emergency, and extended Parliamentary terms to prevent transfers of power.

Declaring a state of emergency gave Indira absolute executive powers that she used to shape the nation as she saw fit. Accordingly, heavily politicized policies that failed to serve the needs of citizens were adopted. A result of these policies was a Twenty Point Program that Indira justified in terms of bolstering development in India (Wolpert 2000). This program consisted of forgiving small debts owed by the poorest and increasing employment opportunities for women. However, the citizenry saw the program as chicanery and part of Indira's increasing authoritarianism, despite her remarks to the contrary (Park 1975; Malhotra 1989). Such negative sentiment contributed to the failure of the Twenty Point Program.

As the initiative failed, Indira positioned her son, Sanjay, to inherit the Congress Party (Malhotra 1989). As heir apparent, Sanjay was afforded political privileges during The Emergency such as permission to develop national policies. It had been proposed at the time that unplanned population growth would be detrimental to Indira's Twenty Point Program and, using Malthusian reasoning, Sanjay's policy agenda led the way with stronger support for effective control of population growth (Panandiker and Umashankar 1994).

In April 1976, with India's population increasing by approximately 12 million people per year, the Minister of Health and Family Planning announced a National Population Policy to reduce population growth and to help placate the nation's hardships. The policy statement declared how incentives would be allocated to participants in population control efforts, and established a target to reduce the nation's birth rate from 35 to 25 births per 1,000 women of reproductive age by 1984 (Frank 2001). The Policy statement also encouraged the government to support increased investment in girls' education, an increase in the minimum legal age of marriage, and expansion of basic health services.

After the announcement of the 1976 National Population Policy, efforts were undertaken to persuade political leaders that they should support and implement programs that would help achieve the Policy's goals. One of these programs was a campaign to promote widespread sterilization adoption among men. At the service level, the campaign involved increased efforts to encourage the performance of vasectomies nationwide. At the political level, it involved the central government applying pressure on states to facilitate an increase in vasectomies. The Policy did not force states to legislate compulsory sterilizations, and no state ever did. However, sterilization targets established by the emergency-fortified central government, combined with increased vigor of political will, created a climate within states equivalent to legislated compulsory sterilizations. Compounding the pressure was Indira's use of emergency authority to garner support for the campaign from state chief ministers, physicians, and the public health community (Landman 1977). Although achieving family planning and health targets was traditionally the responsibility of individual states, Sanjay also pressured regional political leaders to make states increase their efforts to curb population growth (Gwatkin 1979). Nevertheless, many states were hesitant to agree with population control pressures from the central government.

Part II: The Politics of Emergency Rule, Sterilization Campaign Implementation, and Human Rights Abuses

A state of emergency is the ultimate test of a government's commitment to human rights (McGoldrick 2004). During The Emergency India's sterilization campaign supported the dismissal of reproductive rights because its consequences were not intended to contribute to improving life quality and facilitating the protection of rights, but strictly to attaining the government's demographic goals. At the most basic level, during the 1975-1977 Emergency, the Indian government's method of managing population growth with this campaign limited the ability of citizens to realize the right to found a family as outlined in the Universal Declaration of Human Rights. More specifically, the campaign's implementation methods challenged concepts outlined in the International Covenant on Civil and Political Rights, which entered into force in 1976 and was ratified by India in 1978. This Covenant outlines civil and political freedoms such as equal rights of the sexes, and the civil and human rights that can be derogated during states of emergency.

The 1976 Population Policy did not significantly differ from the nation's incentive based population policy milieu prior to The Emergency. During both time periods sterilization was promoted (Stein 1998) and financial incentives were utilized as a form of coercion (Vicziany 1982a). However, the 1976 Policy and the climate it was declared in prioritized the idea that India's population growth concerns could not wait for increased development and female education to contribute to a drop in fertility (Cassen 1978). Therefore, during The Emergency incentives to adopt sterilization were intensified to be more attractive, while disincentives became more stringent. For example, the amount of money received for undergoing a vasectomy increased, and food rations were denied to couples with more than three children (Gwatkin 1979). The incentives and sanctions were also more influential because they were not ad hoc as they were before The Emergency, and were often accompanied by manipulation and sometimes violence. Additionally, they were being implemented by multiple government sectors, which allowed the campaign to affect all aspects of life. It was reported that in some areas sterilization certificates were necessary to obtain driver's licenses and to send children to certain schools (Cassen 1978).

It is conceivable that India was especially challenged to demonstrate a commitment to human rights during the 1976-1977 Emergency because of the political relationship between Sanjay and Indira. As Sanjay's influence over the sterilization campaign came from undefined political powers afforded to him by The Emergency. His influence was strongest in and around Delhi, which had the highest number of sterilizations in India at the time (Gawatkin 1978), and where it was reportedly not uncommon for men to be coerced into vasectomy booths to ensure that quotas were met (Stein 1998).

Throughout the 1975-1977 Emergency, Indira never publicly denounced Sanjay's policy excesses. When she received reports about abuses and deaths related to the sterilization campaign, she dismissed them as 'anti-Sanjay' propaganda (Dahr 2000). Conceivably, she also refrained from publicly denouncing Sanjay's actions to downplay that she had used emergency powers to bolster his political agenda. She specifically did this by giving the central government increased authority over implementing the National Population Policy. Indira's ability to do this reflected how a suspended democracy and centralized power enabled the politicization of family planning and the resulting dismissal of human rights. However, increased authority delegated to the central government and Sanjay pushed state governments to reach sterilization targets faster than before; for example, in Uttar Pradesh sterilizations rose from 175,000 in 1975-1976 to 837,000 in 1977 (Shah Commission 1978 in Panandiker and Umashankar 1994).

Retrospectively applying the principles of the International Covenant on Civil and Political Rights to India's 1975-1977 Emergency, it was acceptable for political leadership to limit democracy and declare an emergency. However, limitations articulated in The Covenant would not have supported the use of a suspended democracy and limited civil rights as a proxy for reproductive rights violations. Limitations on derogation provisions of The Covenant assure that during a state of emergency individuals are guaranteed inherent dignity and freedom from cruel, inhuman, or degrading treatment (United Nations Economic and Social Council 1985). Yet, as the sterilization campaign gained momentum via negative coercion during The Emergency, men throughout India believed that implementation methods of the campaign had been a violation of their self-worth and independence (Malhotra 1989).

Population politics within the context of The Emergency's diminished political checks and balances did not protect reproductive rights from coercion. Negative coercion via administrative and policy pressures was considered synonymous with the sterilization campaign. With an increased role in the population politics of India, the central government promulgated the concept that negative coercion was an acceptable way to achieve a reduction in population growth and support development.

Interpretations of the National Population Policy statement specifically contributed to reproductive rights abuses. The government vaguely defined terms such as 'force' and 'coercion,' which were often misconstrued during implementation (Cassen 1978). Such language made it unclear to the citizenry and those executing the campaign just how vigorous enforcement could be. Furthermore, junior officials who feared losing their jobs did not take reproductive rights into consideration as they narrowly interpreted the National Population Policy to meet quotas (Klieman 1981). Ultimately, for many civil servants, career advancement required supporting the government's development methodologies, which included reducing population growth (Gwatkin 1979).

In addition to misinterpretations of the National Population Policy statement, inconsistent incentives offered to those performing and receiving vasectomies encouraged dishonest reporting of quota performance, making it difficult to evaluate the campaign's effectiveness. Yet, without truly knowing how effective the campaign was, the central government pressed for states to perform more sterilizations. Eventually, misinterpretations of the Population Policy combined with strong political will from the central government proved to be deadly. Intense bureaucratic pressure led some states and vasectomy camps to falsely believe that they were more prepared for an increase in sterilization operations than they really were. As a result of rushing to meet targets, deaths sometimes occurred from unhygienic procedures (Cassen 1978).

Negative coercion and strong political will also obstructed opportunities to exercise the right to freely make informed reproductive choices. The government was able to use poverty as a tool of coercion, knowing that the poor could not refuse high incentives during times of economic hardship. They also realized that in addition to the censored media, the illiteracy correlated with poverty would limit citizen's knowledge of alternatives to sterilization (Vicziany 1982b). The campaign's ability to use poverty as a tool of coercion was blatant encouragement for officials to disregard reproductive decision making rights that would later be affirmed in the 1994 International Conference on Population and Development Program of Action. These rights are intricately related to individual dignity and include the right to decide "freely and responsibly the number, spacing and timing of their children" and to make reproductive decisions free from "coercion and violence" (United Nations Population Fund 1994, Principle 8).

Human rights were overtly violated by the way the sterilization campaign was implemented. The ascendancy of the campaign to national political importance also reduced the possibility that other policy changes would occur to promote development or placate the disorder The Emergency was supposed to end. Throughout The Emergency, this restriction of policy alternatives created an environment where the government's desire for development overshadowed the protection of reproductive rights. That Indira permitted this prioritization was an illegitimate limitation of rights for several reasons that would be specified by the Siracusa Principles in 1985, adopted by the UN to ensure that parties to The Covenant would not limit rights during an emergency beyond what is permitted by the document. These reasons include that less intrusive and restrictive means other than a sterilization campaign were available to achieve development, that a sterilization campaign was not necessary at the time to achieve development, and that the excessiveness of political will driving the campaign was conceivably unreasonable.

Part III: Consequences of the Sterilization Campaign and Transitioning Population Politics after The Emergency

The Emergency ended in 1977 when Indira realized that its political costs were greater than the benefits. That year she called for general elections, uncensored the media, and released political opposition from prison. It is speculated that regardless of potential consequences, Indira wanted to hold elections to legitimately regain her political standing as a democratic leader (Malhotra 1989). In theory, Indira should have been able to win the 1977 election, as even the political opposition believed that they had been freed from jail too late to effectively campaign (Malhotra 1989). However, she lost the election, in part because of negative sentiments related to The Emergency, and the nature of the sterilization campaign's abuses.

Overall, the election results reflected the decline of the Congress Party and disapproval of the sterilization campaign (Klieman 1981). Moreover, voters were disenchanted with Indira because of the poor responsiveness of authorities to rights violations and her insincere attempts to control Sanjay's actions. Voting patterns in states near Delhi illustrated the political repercussions Indira experienced in part because of Sanjay's excesses (Malhotra 1989; Rouyer 1987). Citizens had come to believe that efforts used to reach Population Policy goals represented "the conversion of the government's administrative resources into an engine of oppression, corruption, and fraud" (Mitra 1977, p. 298). Throughout The Emergency, with civil rights restricted and the press censored, Indian citizens had limited resources with which to express dissatisfaction with the administration. Hence, it is believed that India's 1977 election was the first in the world in which fertility behavior was a deciding factor (Cassen 1978).

If the effectiveness of the sterilization campaign is measured by the number of vasectomies performed, it was a success. The number of sterilizations reported between 1976 and 1977 was subject to falsification due to the desire to meet quotas. However, it is estimated that during that time period, an approximate 8.25 million sterilizations were performed (Gwatkin 1979). Nevertheless, from a human rights perspective, when the effectiveness of the sterilization campaign is assessed in deaths or compromised rights, the campaign was unsuccessful. Specifically, because of the unjust political coercion used to implement it (Vicziany 1982b) and the limits it put on reproductive decision making.

While the Population Policy had the potential to support human and reproductive rights, diminished political checks and balances of The Emergency allowed the Policy's implementation to become misguided and wrongfully focus efforts on individual fertility behavior rather than systematically improving development and family planning delivery. The presumption that politically coerced family planning would facilitate development proved counterproductive to more effectively allocating resources. For example, the sterilization campaign concentrated resources by using the country's health professionals to reach sterilization goals rather than provide other services (Cassen 1978). The government also allowed compensation for sterilization operations to rise to ten percent of the total health budget (Jeffery 1988).

Leadership that immediately succeeded Indira transitioned the tone of national population politics away from being primarily defined by negative coercion and targets, to being increasingly supportive of human rights, voluntary participation, and protecting health (Bhagat 2002). However, the policy transition did not come without challenges. Nationwide, negative coercion and family planning had become linked. This association made it difficult for the government to cultivate a positive public perception of birth-control methods, yet new leadership continued to denounce coerced sterilization.

The new leadership's stance was substantiated by post-Emergency efforts to increase the number of state sponsored reproductive health programs that supported reproductive rights related to decision making and access to healthcare. For example, initiatives such as the Child Survival and Safe Motherhood Program and the Reproductive and Child Health Program now provide improved obstetric care and immunization services. They have also helped reposition the focus of national population politics away from controlling population growth. The political will that motivates the development of maternal and child health programs has helped India support the concept that achieving the highest attainable standard of health is a human right. This political position is consistent with Article 12 of the United Nations Covenant on Economic, Social, and Cultural Rights.

In addition to creating programs, India has continued to revise its National Population Policy since 1976. The implementation of each policy has had a stronger focus on family planning and reducing maternal and infant deaths through improved health services. This shift has had more implications for the reproductive rights of women than men despite the legacy of the sterilization program. Shiffman et al (2006) credit the increase in the rise of maternal mortality on the Indian political agenda to among other factors, norm promotion by international organizations and defining events such as the debut of the Millennium Development Goals.

Although progress has been made on a public policy level to protect reproductive rights via protecting health, India has still not reached goals of the 2000 National Population Policy and international targets articulated by the Millennium Development Goals. Barriers to reaching these aims have included an underutilization of state sponsored reproductive, birthing, and child health services in states that repeatedly do poorly on related maternal and child health indicators (Gulati 2005). Also, India's federal system has difficulty holding states accountable for commitments to public health (Shiffman et al 2006).

The effect of support for reproductive rights at the center and state levels is a poignant one as demonstrated by events during The Emergency. International efforts such as the 1994 International Conference on Population and Development have helped increase the visibility of reproductive issues. Historically, however, sustainable results from reconciling state intervention in family planning with reproductive rights have been produced best with strong support and action from state and community leadership. Evidence of this is varied improvement in maternal and child health across Indian states since The Emergency. Whereas, some states have achieved dramatic improvements in health indicators compared to others. For example, in 1999 the infant mortality rate in the state of Kerala was approximately 16.3 per 1,000 live births; however the state of Rajasthan documented approximately 80.4 per 1,000 live births (Gulati 2005).

In addition to the aforementioned challenges, beliefs still pose a barrier to fully realizing the right to life for females in India. Beliefs such as son-preference remain prevalent and are believed to contribute to a lessened quality of healthcare and a higher mortality risk for female babies (Clark 2000). Moreover, son-preference has been linked to the estimation that at least 10 million female fetuses have been aborted in India since 1986 (Jha et al 2006) – even though there are laws against medical professionals informing parents of a fetus' sex as well as performing sex-selective abortions. As recently as April 2008, Prime Minister Manmohan Singh publicly denounced the practice of aborting female children at a national conference on saving female children. Nevertheless, evidence suggests that the government has not enforced restrictions despite national and international political support. Hence, it appears that today, at national and state levels, India is faced with reconciling population policies and politics with human rights such as freedoms of belief, as well as reproductive rights; especially with recent technological advances related to sex-determination. Simultaneously, the population politics of India must also acknowledge the extent to which population policies can affect health and entitled freedoms of citizens.

This predicament makes it important for population politics to address the status of women in Indian society. Doing so will require that attention is given not only to reproductive health services, but to allowing state interventions to address and improve gender disparities related to social and economic opportunities for women. A reduction in gender disparities has the potential to increase the probability of women playing a pivotal role in reproductive decision-making and health. Such endeavors, however, will require multidisciplinary initiatives on the part of the national government, states, communities, families, and individuals.

Conclusions

That the implementation of a population control program was politicized helped catalyze a disregard for reproductive rights that lasted throughout The Emergency period. Of all the nonderogable rights outlined in the International Covenant on Civil and Political Rights, the guarantees of dignity and freedom in reproductive decision making were violated by the sterilization campaign's theme of coercion. A historical review of India's 1975-1977 Emergency period demonstrates that political intervention in population growth can be brought into harmony with human rights if the political climate 1) does not allow the suspension of democracy to escalate unjust coercion and facilitate rights violations, 2) focuses on broad social rights and health rather than specifically on fertility control, and 3) produces and supports programs that promote informed reproductive decision making that is free from unjust coercion. One exception to these conditions is that even if circumstances are ideal, underutilized health systems, along with systematic gender inequality, pose a challenge to implementing rights-based state interventions in family planning. This challenge implies that changes in social policies are preconditions for reconciling state intervention with reproductive rights.

India's population policy transition is a unique historical event which epitomizes the concept that even if a country changes its policy course, inherent challenges may still remain. Additionally, the zeitgeist of The Emergency is telling of the astute nature of human rights agreements that have been proclaimed and adopted since that time. India has made progress in harmonizing population politics with human rights, and it is conceivable that the population policy transition in India can persist. However, in order to make this a reality, the formulation and implementation of policies must continue to utilize lessons learned from events that occurred during the 1975-1977 Emergency.

References

Bhagat, R. B. 2002. "Integration of demographic issues in sustainable development: reflections on India's population policies." *Population Geography*, 24, pp. 21-30.

Cassen, R.H. 1978. *India: population, economy, society*. New York: Holmes and Meier Publishers, Inc.

Clark, Shelley. 2000. "Son preference and sex composition of children: Evidence from India." *Demography*, 37, (1), pp. 95-108.

Dahr, P.N. 2000. *Indira Gandhi, the 'Emergency,' and Indian democracy*. New York: Oxford University Press.

Frank, Katherine. 2001. *Indira: The Life of Indira Nehru Gandhi*. London: Harper Perennial.

Gwatkin, Davidson R. 1979. "Political will and family planning: the implications of India's Emergency experience." *Population and Development Review*, 5, (1), pp. 29-59.

Gulati, S.C. 2005. Presidential address to the Indian association for the study of population 27th Annual Conference: population policies and programs since ICPD, 1994: Issues and challenges ahead. [Online]. Available at: http://www.iegindia.org/workpap/wp257.pdf (accessed 5 March 2008).

Iyer, Venkat. 2000. *States of emergency: the Indian experience*. New Delhi, India: Butterworths.

Jha, Prabhat, et al. 2006. "Low female-to-male sex ratio of children born in India: national survey of 1.1 million households." *Lancet*, 367, pp. 211-8.

Jeffery, Roger. 1988. *The politics of health in India*. Berkeley: University of California Press.

Klieman, Aaron. 1981. "Indira's India: democracy and crisis government." *Political Science Quarterly*, 96, (2), pp. 241-59.

Landman, Lynn C. 1977. "Birth control in India: the carrot and the rod?" *Family Planning Perspectives*, 9, (3), pp. 101-10.

McGoldrick, Dominic. 2004. "The interface between public emergency powers and international law." *International Journal of Constitutional Law*, 2, (2), pp. 380-429.

Malhotra, Inder. 1989. *Indira Gandhi: A personal and political biography*. Boston: Northeastern University Press.

Mitra, Asok. 1977. "National Population Policy in relation to national planning in India." *Population Development Review*, 3, (3), pp. 297-306.

Palmer, Norman D. 1977. "India in 1976: the politics of repoliticization: a survey of Asia in 1976: Part Two." *Asian Survey*, 17, (2), pp. 160-80.

Park, Richard. 1975. "Political crisis in India 1975." *Asian Survey*, 15, (11), pp. 996-1013.

Panandiker, V.A. Pai and P.K. Umashankar. 1994. "Fertility control and politics in India." *Population and Development Review*, 20 (Supplement), pp. 89-104.

Rouyer, Alwyn. 1987. "Political capacity and the decline of fertility in India." *The American Political Science Review*, 81, (2), pp. 453-70.

Shiffman, Jeremy, et al. 2006. "The state of political priority for maternal mortality reduction in Nigeria and India." [Online]. Available at: http://paa2006.princeton.edu/download.aspx?submissionId=60071 [accessed 5 March 2008].

Stein, Burton. 1998. *A history of India.* Malden, Massachusetts: Blackwell Publishers Inc.

UNFPA (United Nations Population Fund). 1994. *International Conference on Population and Development International Program of Action.* Cairo, Egypt. 5-13 September 1994. United Nations: New York.

Vicziany, Marika. 1982a. "Coercion in a soft state: the family-planning program of India Part 1: the myth of voluntarism." *Pacific Affairs*, 55, (3), pp. 373-402.

– 1982-83b. "Coercion in a soft state: the family-planning program of India: Part 2: the sources of coercion." *Pacific Affairs*, 55, (4), pp. 557-92.

Wolpert, Stanley. 2000. *A New history of India*. New York: Oxford.

Chapter 6

HIV/AIDS Prevention and Population Politics in Africa

Lisa Ann Richey

The HIV/AIDS pandemic should have forced a re-evaluation of global health interventions in Africa. After more than two decades of devastation by the disease, the impact of HIV/AIDS is starting to be taken seriously in analyses of development. Yet, there is still a need for theoretically-grounded social science research at the geographical interface of global discourse and local interpretation[1] to enable a critical rethinking of population policy in countries highly affected by HIV/AIDS. Technically speaking, a population policy is one that deals with fertility, mortality or migration of populations. But as illustrated by the chapters in this collection, population policies are also state interventions into some of the most intimate and private aspects of citizens' lives. African states are constrained from "above" due to dependence on international assistance and the fact that policy design and implementation typically draws on an acontextual blueprint of the population "problem". They are also resisted from "below" when the services they provide do not meet locally perceived needs. These needs are being reconfigured in countries highly affected by HIV/AIDS.

African population policies remain implemented through donor-funded family planning programs that promote modern contraceptives. This type of development "intervention" (Ferguson 1994) arises out of the view that overpopulation is the fundamental development obstacle in African countries (Richey 2008). However, there has been a supposed paradigm shift in the global discourse on population, substituting goals of fertility reduction with those of improving women's reproductive health. Where population control ideologies have met resistance, health enhancing ones may not. Contemporary population policies promote the use of modern contraceptives framed in the language of children's health, household economic security, and women's rights – all of which resonate with local policy recipients' priorities.

Yet, situating a new generation of integrated approaches to reproductive health within family planning and HIV/AIDS structures that have been historically separate, vertical, and donor driven is proving challenging in African countries. In many places, reproductive health is still under the heavy cloak of population-control initiatives. It will take a real shift in the implementation of population

---

1 Boone and Batsell argued that there has been remarkably little social science research on AIDS, and that political science in particular "must now race to catch up with the AIDS challenge and the political debates that it has spawned" (2001, 3).

policies at the clinic level to begin to reshape relationships, build trust, and change perceptions. This is unlikely to happen as long as donors and lenders are still focusing on fertility rates and contraceptive prevalence as indicators of success. Integrating HIV/AIDS prevention and treatment into the structures of maternal and child health is critical, especially as AIDS treatment and prevention of vertical transmission of HIV become more widespread in African clinics (see Richey 2008). However, integration remains difficult, especially because of the stigma that still surrounds the disease, even in an African country like Uganda which is renowned for its openness.

In this chapter, I examine some of the challenges that remain at the interface between population policy and HIV/AIDS prevention in Africa. I argue that the reproductive health agenda in Africa is caught between family planning programs that are based on population-control ideologies and the depth of the challenge of the HIV/AIDS pandemic. In the next section, I will examine the contemporary discourse on African exceptionalism, the global demographic convergence and the demographic impact of HIV/AIDS. The following section will explain why the global discourse is significant in the national contexts of African countries and will analyze and explore "success" in HIV/AIDS policies and population policies. These arguments draw on case studies of Tanzania and Uganda where I have conducted research on reproductive health since the early 1990s and the early 2000s. The penultimate section will look at the challenges of implementing a reproductive health agenda in Africa, and the final section will draw some tentative conclusions and links to policy.

African Exceptionalism, HIV/AIDS and Global Demographic Convergence

The contemporary demographic narrative in the context of HIV/AIDS presents a more nuanced version of the overpopulation problem in Africa. Yet, the challenges that African data present to demographic theories are usually not used to direct a rethinking of these theories in light of their inability to explain African phenomena, but are cordoned off into categories of outliers, commonly known as "African exceptionalism". For example, whether or not overpopulation is really a central problem for economic development often focuses on the capacity to meet food needs, the subject of debates since Malthus (1914) and Boserup's (1970) response. Contemporary analysis of agrarian change and population growth in a time of globalization supports the view that societies are able to produce the right institutional, economic responses to shifting demographics. However, Cuffaro (1997) argued that this optimism may not be justified in the context of very fast population growth and/or already high population densities, or in contexts of high inequality, inappropriate policies, or drought. From Cuffaro's description of the exceptions, we can expect that most societies will alter their responses to demographic change in order to thrive, but African societies will not.

The notion of a global demographic convergence is foundational to demographic transition theory.[2] In layperson's terms, demographic transition theory says that countries will progress over time from situations characterized by high mortality and high fertility to those characterized by low mortality and fertility. Today, cross-national demographic data is sometimes used to declare an end to the "population explosion"[3]. Wilson (2001) describes a "global demographic change of unprecedented magnitude", with most countries moving closer and closer together in terms of their fertility and mortality rates – becoming "demographically modern." After describing the global convergence of fertility rates with terms like "overwhelming", "substantial", and a "world that has been transformed" (Ibid., p. 165-166), Wilson makes a brief note of African exceptionalism:

> Although comprising less than a quarter of the world's population, the remaining high-fertility regions will, in any of the UN's future scenarios, provide the majority of the population growth expected for the next 50 years. It is not surprising, therefore, that addressing the reproductive health needs of these segments of the world's population remains of the highest priority for international population policy (Ibid., p. 166).

While the rest of the world is no longer a population "problem", Africa is clearly different. Here we see the same dynamics of population control that were prevalent from WWII to Cairo. Though they are numerically few, the Africans are responsible for a continuing population problem and therefore, they are to be the focus of international population policy. Placing responsibility for governing African populations in the international, as opposed to the national or local realm, suggests that African population problems are international problems – they exceed national boundaries – not problems of primary concern for national development or individual or family well-being. Also, the approach for dealing with these problems, "addressing the reproductive health needs" of Africans, is predicated upon the belief that their "needs" are contraceptive, and meeting them would bring down population growth.[4] Thus, we can reconcile the demographic "truth"

---

2 For a discussion of demographic concepts such as transition theory see Crook and Timæus 1997.

3 The world population growth rate peaked in the 1960s and then began declining. Explanations for declining growth rates vary by geographical region, but usually include some combination of social and economic advances, expanding education and employment for women, and access to family planning programs.

4 The concept of "unmet need" serves to the link the reproductive health agenda and the population control ideology. Deconstructing this problematic concept goes far beyond the scope of this paper, but in brief, "unmet need" has been used to show that governments can achieve demographic goals by simply focusing on satisfying the existing demand for fertility regulation and thus explicit targets are no longer necessary. This con-

that the rates of population growth are indeed declining, with a vision of "overpopulation" as a major development obstacle in Africa. As one author has described, "there are two parallel worlds: one world in which fertility is low and declining as economic development advances, and another world where fertility remains high and where much of the population is mired in poverty" (Ashford 2001, p. 41). This argument of African exceptionalism allows the recognition of a global consensus on the lessened peril of over-population, while maintaining the demographic imperative for interventions in Africa that will have the effect of reducing fertility, even if the stated aims are toward meeting reproductive health goals.

Cohen's (1998) analysis of national surveys on fertility transition in sub-Saharan Africa challenged the popular perception that the continent is demographically "stuck" in regimes of high fertility. He shows that a widespread decline in fertility is taking place, virtually across the board, and that there has been almost no survey after the early 1990s that indicates that fertility is increasing, and very few suggesting it to be stationary (Cohen 1998, p. 1445). "Instead, virtually all recent surveys point to rising age at marriage, rising contraceptive use, and declining fertility, particularly amongst certain well-defined subgroups" (Ibid.). Cohen's work attributes much of this success to family planning, and he notes the "large body of evidence [that] points to the need to increase the level of family planning services in Africa" (Ibid.). He concludes his description of declining African fertility with the point that "it is important to note that despite the fact that fertility is declining, the population of sub-Saharan Africa is still expected to double within the next 22-23 years" (Ibid.). Thus, the demographic momentum (Keyfitz 1977) of the population structure will continue to contribute to a population problem even when individuals change their fertility behavior. In such a meticulous examination of the demographic literature on fertility and its determinants in Africa, Cohen made not a single mention of AIDS.[9]

AIDS has called into question much of what we thought we knew about population, particularly in Africa. Nicholas Eberstadt, an American demographer, suggested: "with so much emphasis on the notion of an explosion, it is well worth contemplating the opposite, and now at least as likely, development: a 'population implosion'" (Eberstadt 2001). *The Economist* notes that because we do not understand what determines birth rates[5] in modern societies, "demographics will not only be the most important factor in the next society, it will also be the least predictable and least controllable one" (Economist 2001). There is no doubt now that AIDS will have some demographic impact on Africa.[6]

---

clusion reassured governments that "it was possible to achieve demographic goals without pursuing numbers-driven population policies" (Casterline and Sinding 2000).

5 Birth rate is the number of live births per 1,000 persons in a given year.

6 We should remember that as late as the early 1990's, most experts said that HIV/AIDS would have little or no impact on population growth.

In 2000, the UN's revision of the state of the world's population incorporated the impact of HIV/AIDS into its projections of the population of 45 countries defined as "highly affected" (Population Division 2001, p. 9). Of these 45, 35 are in Sub-Saharan Africa. By 2007, AIDS was the leading cause of death in the region, and Sub-Saharan Africa accounted for 68 percent of all adults living with HIV, 90 per cent of the world's HIV-infected children and 76 percent of all recorded AIDS deaths (United Nations 2008, p. 8). Given that Africa has been characterized as having an immense problem of overpopulation, there have been limited interpretations of the demographic impact of AIDS as a sort of "Malthusian check" on the rate of population growth. In a Washington Post article on the impact of AIDS[7] a US National Intelligence Council member is quoted as reacting to an Interagency Intelligence Memorandum on the devastating impact of the pandemic on Africa by saying "Oh, it will be good, because Africa is overpopulated anyway." Another ideologically revealing statement was made in a World Bank report of the early 1990s, saying: "If the only effect of the AIDS epidemic were to reduce the population growth rate, it would increase the growth rate of per capita income in any plausible economic model" (Over 1992, p. 1). The report itself was trying to estimate the impact of AIDS on developing country economies.

However, the view of AIDS as a Malthusian population check has also been embraced by a more popularised version of the population and environment discourse. Lester Brown, chairman of the Worldwatch institute, has apparently changed his tune from "demographic fatigue"[8] to one of "Africa is dying – it needs help!" It is interesting that someone who has spent decades calling for a reduction in African fertility levels, and who blamed over-population for the spread of AIDS, now sounds the alarm of the "tragedy of epic proportions" that will reduce life expectancy, raise mortality, lower fertility, create an excess of men over women and leave millions of orphans in its wake (Brown 2000). In a vein of demographic alarmism, similar to that which we have heard for 50 years

---

7 As reported in The Washington Post, Wed., 5 July 2000, page A 01, accessed online at www.washingtonpost.com.

8 Lester Brown and his colleagues from the Worldwatch Institute put forth the concept of "demographic fatigue" as the explanation for what they understand as a "crisis" engulfing the African continent (see Brown, Gardner and Halweil 1998). Blaming "over"-population for food shortages, deforestation and soil erosion in Africa is common among Neo-Malthusians who believe that people are "polluters" taxing the environment, whether they are involved in Western-based industrial production or African small-scale agriculture. However, the notion of "demographic fatigue" goes even further. It blames over-population for two of the most devastating events in post-colonial Africa: the epidemic of HIV/AIDS and the Rwandan genocide. By simply inserting the AIDS pandemic and genocide into the over-used and simplistic framework that locates population as the root of all evils, Brown pretends to address these issues and promote their solution –family planning – while actually ignoring all historical, anthropological, economic and political facets that led to these crises.

of African overpopulation, the problem now seems to be that fertility levels will become too low, and this will lead to problems such as a disproportionate number of men to women in African countries. I begin to suspect that the underlying themes are the same as in the past when I read Brown's conclusion that "this will leave many males either destined for a life of bachelorhood or forced to migrate to countries outside the region in search of a wife" (Ibid.). This image of Africans invading "countries outside the region" to marry plays into deep-seated racist and sexist fears embedded in a Western mindset from colonial discourse to the contemporary "west against the rest" ideologies. In the guise of concern for the most devastating disease burden ever placed on African societies, yet another call for control of African populations is issued to prevent "them" from migrating to where "we" live.

The impact of the AIDS pandemic on diverse aspects of development policymaking is becoming even more pronounced as the empirical documentation of the disease continues (following on from Heuveline 2003). Scholarship has shown that HIV itself has a direct impact on reducing fertility (Carpenter, Nakiyingi, et al. 1997; du Lou, Msellati, et al. 1999; Gregson, Zaba, et al. 1999 cited in Baylies and Bujra 2000). One of the first articles in a population journal to document the impact of HIV/AIDS on mortality showed that Zimbabwe experienced a massive rise in adult mortality risks from the mid-1980s to the mid-1990s (Feeney 2001). The piece concludes that "there is essentially no doubt that these increases in adult mortality risks are due to HIV/AIDS. Given the timing, age pattern, and magnitude of the changes, no competing explanation is remotely credible" (Ibid., p. 779). Anecdotal evidence from MCH clinics in Tanzania in 2000 and 2004 confirms increasing levels of maternal mortality and stillborn infants, which service providers attribute to AIDS. A literature review suggests that AIDS will have a significant detrimental impact on achievement of the Millennium Development Goals in highly affected countries (Hecht et al. 2006). As the impact of HIV/AIDS on African mortality is more accurately documented, these radical demographic facts must be taken seriously in any conceptualization of what any population policy should do in Africa.

Why is Global Discourse so Important to African Population Policy?

Donor Relations and Population policies in Uganda and Tanzania

Because population policy is so intensely donor-driven and donor-funded, the global discourse on population shapes the implementation of policies in aid-recipient states such as Uganda and Tanzania. The Tanzanian state's approach to population has gradually shifted to become more compatible with the priorities and understandings promoted by its donors and lenders. Historically, the Tanzanian government has maintained a strategically ambiguous stance in its declarations and approaches to population (Richey 2008). This ambiguity exists in both the document of the National Population Policy itself and in the directives promoted by the state for its implementation. In Uganda, the state has been similarly evasive in its population policy discussions, with its history of ethnic and religious cleavages used to justify governmental inattention (Kirumira 1998). The international interpretation of the problem has held considerable influence on the population program efforts in Uganda, and the politics of funding have led policy and program managers to support or develop programs that can attract quicker and better funding (Ibid., p. 188).

Both Tanzania and Uganda have family planning programs dating back to the late 1950s, yet they belatedly adopted population policies in the early 1990s, while Kenya's began a decade earlier.[9] The existence of a national population policy is a strong indicator of a nation-state's entry into the international arena of population players (Barret and Tsui 1999). Signing a national policy is a symbolic statement to the international community that a country recognizes that it has a population "problem" as defined in a particular way, and that it is a candidate for foreign assistance in the realm of family planning programs. The heavy dependence on donor funding means that internal population policies are framed according to external interpretations of the population problem (see Kirumira 1998 on Uganda and Richey 2008 on Tanzania). While there is still debate over the nature of the population "problem", the existence of a population policy suggests that a similar apparatus with goals of fertility reduction is at work in both countries.

The aspect of population policy that is, in effect, still given the most priority in both countries, is family planning. This organization of a family planning program as the main or only implementing arm of population policy related to fertility reduction is typical in population policy implementation (Jain 1998). The family planning sector is most visible because it receives the most attention and funding from international donors, the critical sources of development interventions in a time when state-funded health care is rapidly declining in both quantity and quality. Kiondo (1995) documents the ongoing "donorisation" of important social services in many areas as one of the main forms of development privitization taking place in contemporary Tanzania.[10] The donors' emphasis on family

---

9 In 1995, Uganda endorsed a National Population Policy whose goal is "to influence the future demographic trends and patterns in desirable directions in order to improve the quality of life and standards of living of the people" Government, U. (1999). The NCSD Sustainable Development Report, accessed online at www.ncsdnetwork.org/global/reports/ncsd1999/uganda/cap1.htm.. The main goal of Tanzania's 1992 Population Policy is "to extend the horizon of the country's development plans whose principal objective is to move Tanzanians away from poverty and extend their horizon of standard of living" (United Republic of Tanzania, 1992).

10 While African governments are struggling to fund basic social services, a "key goal" of both USAID and UNFPA is for recipient countries to move toward self-reliance in

planning stems from the way that population is understood as a problem in a global discourse that emphasizes reducing fertility levels as a prerequisite to development. It could be argued that African states, weakened by dependence on international aid and loans and the conditionalities accompanying its structural adjustment programs, have become even more receptive to the agenda of its international donors and lenders in tackling many development issues, including population.

Even though funding for family planning is the topic of recurring domestic debates, the US is the largest single donor in population issues channelling its assistance through USAID and UNFPA; the US has contributed an average of $437 million per year between 1995 and 2000 (USAID 2000).[11] USAID is working on population issues in more than 60 countries, and most of its assistance is concentrated in 25 countries that account for three-fourths of the population in the Third World (USAID 2000). In both Tanzania and Uganda, the reproductive health agenda of USAID is still predicated upon the centrality of the population "problem." In Tanzania, "the objective of the program is to promote changes in behavior to reduce high fertility rates, high-risk births, infant mortality, and the rising rates of HIV transmission" (USAID 2001). In Uganda, "the objective of USAID activities in the health sector is to reduce fertility, reduce maternal and child mortality, and slow the transmission of HIV/AIDS" (USAID 2001).[12] Other bilateral and multilateral donors also fund population activities in the two countries, but irrespective of the particular donor, the global discourse is often very much the same.[13]

HIV/AIDS policy success in Uganda

Uganda has been presented as the first African "success" story in the fight against HIV/AIDS. In the early 1990s, Uganda was one of the first countries to recognize AIDS as a major obstacle to development. Coordinated by a National AIDS Commission and funded by major donor agencies, the Ugandan govern-

---

terms of family planning assistance: Colombia, Mexico, Thailand and Tunisia are recognized as countries who are no longer in need of family planning assistance (USAID 2000).

11 In Tanzania, USAID planned to use 4 million dollars in fiscal year 2001 for the purchase of contraceptives, promotion of family planning and long-term and permanent family planning methods; it also planned to use $6.928 million for HIV/AIDS activities USAID (2001). Tanzania Activity Data Sheet: Congressional Budget Justification FY 2002. Washington, DC: accessed online at www.usaid.gov/country/afr/tz/621-001.html. In Uganda, AID committed 5 million dollars for its family planning work and $11,382,000 for HIV/AIDS USAID (2001). Uganda Activity Data Sheet: Congressional Budget Justification FY 2002. Washington, DC: accessed online at www.usaid.gov/country/afr/ug/617-004.html.

12 The Tanzanian program began in Fiscal Year 1995, while in Uganda, the program began in Fiscal Year 1993.

13 A detailed assessment of the various donors, programs and projects in the two countries is far beyond the scope of this paper, but can be found in Richey 2008.

ment has promoted a multi-pronged strategy to combat AIDS including public information campaigns, research, voluntary testing and counselling, safe blood transfusions, school health programs, home-based care for people living with AIDS, and a broad campaign to treat sexually transmitted infections (STIs).[14] In the early 1990s, Uganda reported the highest infection rates in the world, with an estimated 15 % of the population living with HIV/AIDS, yet by the end of 1999, the county had managed to bring down the prevalence of HIV to less than 10% (Kirumira 2001). By 2001, the country had managed to bring the prevalence down to 5 percent (Hogle 2002). The greatest declines in HIV incidence are thought to have taken place in the late 1980s and early 1990s.[15]

While the Ugandan "success" is attributed to large-scale behavioural change, Caldwell (2000) points out that analysts are assuming that behavioural change must be occurring only because this is the residual category after other changes have been excluded. There seems to be little evidence of unusually high levels of condom use by adolescents or in commercial sex relationships – the two factors that Caldwell suggests are most likely to halt the African pandemic. The "success" in Uganda is linked to the country's open policy toward the pandemic and "perhaps the most vigorous IEC [Information, Education and Communication] and program support services for HIV/AIDS prevention and control in Sub-Saharan Africa" (Kirumira 2001). Museveni's leadership on AIDS was linked to democratization and the reconstruction of local government as a means of rebuilding social cohesion in the country (De Waal 2003). When the World Bank convened two "learning events" to discuss Uganda's progress based on the premise that "optimism now exists in the fight against AIDS in sub-Saharan Africa due to the dramatic declines in HIV prevalence observed in Uganda", they placed particular importance on the country's "social cohesion" (World Bank 2001).

"Social cohesion is defined as the norms and social relations embedded in the social structures of societies that enable people to coordinate action to achieve desired goals" (World Bank 2001). In Uganda, the social cohesion hypothesis claims that information about AIDS and who is affected by it is more likely to be transferred through personal communication networks, and that there has been a high-level of government and civil society leadership to openly communicate the facts about AIDS risks and prevention to the population. Three broad

---

14 It should be noted that Tanzania also has a National AIDS Control Programme that was formalized in 1988 to monitor the progress of the epidemic. The Tanzanian program received criticism for a thinly-spread program that lacked effective top level support and while lip-service has been paid to multisectorality, in practice, AIDS has been seen as a health issue (Bujra and Baylies 2000).

15 Kirumira points out that figures on prevalence and mortality due to HIV/AIDS are inherently subject to error, and gives a fair assessment of the data limitations. Still, his conclusion is that the decline is "real" although the measurements may be imprecise (Kirumira, 2001).

"unwritten policies" are the key elements of the country's creative response to AIDS and distinguish it from the limited capacity of other states in dealing with the epidemic: leadership, diversity of approach, and openness (Parkhurst 2001). These might explain why there is little evidence of similar behavioural change in neighboring countries at similar stages of the pandemic. In sum, the current "success" in Uganda's struggle against AIDS is being read to suggest that policy does make a difference, even in changing intimate behavior, and that leadership is an important factor, or perhaps the important factor, in distinguishing Uganda's program from that in other African countries.

But if Ugandan leadership on HIV/AIDS, arguably a reproductive health issue, is so successful, then why do we not see similar levels of "success" in Uganda's family planning program? Uganda's "success" with its National Aids Control Policy has affected the global discourse on HIV/AIDS in Africa and the potential for constructive action on the part of international donors and national governments. However, AIDS policies and population policies have not been brought together under the larger rubric of "reproductive health." Instead we find competing bureaucracies at all levels of implementation. Furthermore, the realities of the HIV/AIDS epidemic on demographic processes are not being taken seriously either at the level of international conceptualisation of the population problem or at the national level of policy formulation. Uganda's "successful" AIDS policy may be contributing to a lack of "success" in its population policy.

Population policy Responses: Fertility in Tanzania and Uganda

In spite of the "success" of one area of Uganda's reproductive health policy, another area, that of fertility decline, has been less successful. Uganda is an intriguing outlier in discoveries of East African fertility transition. In the late 1960s, fertility rates were similar throughout the East African Community, ranging from 6.6 to 7.1. Today Kenya's fertility rate is 4.9, Tanzania's is 5.4, and Uganda's remains close to 7.[16] It is well-known that Kenya has experienced a precipitous decline in fertility levels throughout the 1990s and into the 2000s (Brass and Jolly 1993; Watkins 1998), and fertility has also been declining, although less dramatically, in Tanzania (Kirk 1996; Larsen 1997). However, during the same period Uganda did not experience a significant decline in its fertility levels, despite having a similar population policy and family planning program (Vavrus and Larsen 2001), and has still not done so.

Research suggests that one possible explanation for the different fertility trajectories may be local differences in contraceptive knowledge, contraceptive use patterns and ideal number of children (Vavrus and Larsen 2001). Lloyd, Kaufman, and Hewett (1999) argue that both Tanzania and Uganda have lower levels of con-

16 http://www.prb.org/

traceptive use than expected when compared to other African countries with similar levels of educational attainment. Yet, simply examining levels of use does not provide much insight about the differences between the two countries since more Ugandan women are using family planning than their Tanzanian counterparts.[17]

Perceptions about contraceptives provided by national family planning programs may be an important part of local level policy implementation. Notions of contraceptive "acceptability"[18] have been evolving as a focus on the "user perspective" in population programs has gained credibility. Nuwagaba (1997) suggested that "ignorance" about modern contraception, such as the belief that contraceptives lead to sterility, may be responsible for low levels of use in Uganda. Perceptions of contraception are shaped by individual understandings and local ideologies, but they are also responses to the policies designed to promote family planning. Both Uganda and Tanzania had already been successful at increasing levels of awareness by the mid-1990s.[19] Thus, while we know that local people have ideas about family planning methods and their meanings, we still do not have sufficient understandings about these perceptions – how they differ across traditional and modern methods, and from one method to another, and how these understandings shape decision-making and fertility outcomes, especially in a time of AIDS. Nuwagaba (1997) states that Uganda is still a pro-natal society with a heavily entrenched value for children as labor sources, although this claim is not empirically-based.

The apparent stagnation in Ugandan fertility levels actually masks increasingly unequal birth rates between rich and poor. When fertility rates were analyzed according to socioeconomic status, it was shown that fertility levels increased by nearly one child per woman for the poorest two quintiles over the past five years and decreased by around one child for the richest 40 percent (Ministry of Finance 2002). Young women, presumably the most "modern" in orientation appear to be contributing disproportionately to Uganda's high fertility levels. Vavrus and Larsen (2001) found that there is higher fertility at lower ages in Uganda than in Tanzania, while there are comparable levels of fertility at higher

---

17 During the last decade, the percent of married Tanzanian women who reported ever-use of family planning has increased from 25.6% of married women in the 1991/92 Demographic and Health Survey (DHS) to 35.6% by the 1996/97 DHS. Uganda, despite its persistently high fertility shows similar trends with 21.5% of married women reporting that they have ever used a method in the 1988 DHS and 33.9% having used a method in the 1995 survey.

18 Acceptability of any method is dependent on the relationship between a woman, her sexual partner(s), the technology itself, the service delivery environment and underlying material and symbolic values in her society (Heise, 1997).

19 Demographic and Health Surveys show that 88.5% of all married Tanzanian women know a contraceptive method (1996), while the figure is even higher – 93.4% – for Ugandan women (1995).

ages among women in the two countries. Ironically, young Ugandan women are more familiar with modern contraceptives (91% of 15-19 year-olds reporting knowledge of at least one method compared to only 66% of Tanzanian women), and they are slightly more likely to be using any method of family planning than their Tanzanian counterparts. In sum, young Ugandan women know more about modern methods, are more likely to use a method, and still produce more children than their Tanzanian counterparts.

Here is where Uganda's AIDS policy may be having an unintended negative impact on its population policy. A study of the impact of sexual behavior changes on HIV and fertility in Uganda found an increase in the age of sexual debut and a decline in nonregular partners, but that these had little impact on lowering fertility (Bessinger, Akwara and Halperin 2003). This study also confirmed that childbearing is increasing among the youngest cohort of women (ages 15-19) (Ministry of Finance 2002). Kirumira (1996) suggests that the impact of HIV/AIDS in Uganda has led women to assume a "produce or marry early" imperative. Young Ugandan women may be aware that they are likely to contract HIV/AIDS in the course of their sexual lives and thus want to begin their childbearing early so as to insure that they will be able to have children before being overcome by the disease. It may be that the awareness of HIV/AIDS created by the successful national program is having a paradoxical effect on fertility decision-making among young Ugandan women. Therefore, to understand how population policies are working, we need to know more than simply how many women are using which methods; we need to understand the paradoxical relationship that may exist between family planning usage and reproductive choices.

Challenges of Implementing a Reproductive Health Agenda in Africa

Questioning the Depth of the Paradigm Shift

What does the "post-Cairo" paradigm shift in the global population discourse mean for international donors and national policies? One aspect of this shift is illustrated in the name changes of a single family-planning organization, which was called the "Association for Voluntary Surgical Contraception" (AVSC) when I began fieldwork on Tanzania's population policy in the early 1990s. It shifted to the "Association for Voluntary Safe Contraception" by the end of the decade, and it is now called "Engender Health."[20] In Tanzania, signs along the road to Muhimbili Hospital direct visitors to the large Norwegian-funded build-

20 A letter from its president on the reasons for changing the organization's name explains: "We also found that the name "AVSC" closed rather than opened doors to new opportunities and funding" http://www.engenderhealth.org/pubs/ehnews/sp01/sp01_2.html.

ing with a green star logo for the "Reproductive and Child Health Programme" – the same building that had housed what used to be called the "National Family Planning Programme." But rhetorical priorities and material commitments from donors differ.

When I was in Tanzania in 2000 and 2004, the agenda of women's reproductive health as a replacement for narrowly-defined family planning had begun to creep into the official discourse, but it had not made many inroads in implementation. Officially, the "National Family Planning Programme" was renamed the "National Reproductive and Child Health Sector" (RCHS) (consisting of 6 programs one of which is the Family Planning Unit). The current head of the RCHS is also the director of the family planning program. When I asked her what had changed during the five years since my earlier fieldwork, her reply, "not much", tells us a lot about the impact of the post-Cairo paradigm shift on reproductive health programs in Tanzania. As for the critical reproductive health challenge that HIV/AIDS presents to the implementation of programs designed to prevent births, not disease, the last "main general finding" of the 1997 Tanzanian report states: "Integration of STI/HIV/AIDS in most of MCH/FP clinics has not been *started.*"

Challenges to Implementing the Cairo Agenda in the Context of HIV/AIDS

HIV/AIDS cannot be merely inserted into the existing family planning programs, re-named reproductive health programs. The reproductive health agenda can benefit from the lessons learned from years of trying to insert "women" into "development" though WID programs. Ultimately, the conceptualisations of the "problems" and "solutions" had to be changed, and the concept of "gender" has encouraged a rethinking of the meanings of development and the power relations that constitute who does development for whom. HIV/AIDS must bring about an analogous paradigm shift within the implementation of the reproductive health agenda – it challenges us not just to expand the scope of population policies and interventions to include tackling the disease, but to rethink the justifications of these policies, their primary actors, and their goals.

There has been much criticism of the reluctance of international donors to come forth with sufficient funding for the goals set at the Cairo Conference of 1994. By the mid-2000s, it had become clear that the global patterns of international aid funding reflected a shift in priorities away from reproductive health. As measured by 2005 data, the actual percent of donor funds for AIDS activities in developing countries was 60 percent greater than the eight percent agreed upon in Cairo (Van Dalen and Reuser 2005, p. 36). The seemingly overwhelming nature of the HIV/AIDS pandemic, coupled with reluctance on the part of recipient governments, has been blamed for the scarcity of reproductive health resources. Reproductive health goals, including but in no means limited to combating the AIDS pandemic, are not easy to quantify, measure and monitor. Thus, it is difficult to demonstrate their efficacy in Congressional audits, making them less attractive points of U.S. donor intervention. However, as advocates from very different points in the AIDS debates are arguing, in the words of demographer John C. Caldwell, "We now know enough about the social context of the epidemic, and the interventions that would probably succeed, to begin to limit the epidemic's impact without waiting for the development of vaccines or depending on antiretroviral drugs for prolonging life" (Caldwell 2000, p. 117). For Caldwell, this means trying to bring the number of people to whom each infected person transmits the disease down below one, making the epidemic die out. This can be done by reducing transmission where it is at its highest level, commercial sexual relations and premarital adolescent sexual activity. Caldwell is critical of the characterization of education as the "magic pill" against African AIDS. "Africans have been educated by AIDS programs to know that the disease is deadly and is largely spread among them by high-risk sexual activities. The epidemic cannot be defeated by more education" (Caldwell 2000, p. 126). In Botswana, anti-AIDS educational messages have become so prevalent that some rural dwellers call AIDS "the radio disease" (*The Economist* 2001).

USAID claims that "family planning programs help slow the spread of HIV/AIDS by providing information, counselling, and male and female condoms (USAID 2000). However, I would argue that HIV/AIDS cannot be defeated by the existing reproductive health policies that still focus on family planning as the solution to reproductive health problems. In the Preface to their edited book on AIDS in Africa, Baylies and Bujra (2000) contend that AIDS has added a new dimension to gender relations, as men and women see their lives in danger from "normal sexual relations." AIDS renders women a "lethal threat" both to men and to their patriarchal structures of control (Ibid., p. xiii). Therefore, gender must be at the forefront of reproductive health policies in the time of AIDS (see Dixon-Mueller and Germain 2000). However, a meaningful shift from population control to reproductive health requires far more than simply adding "gender" as a variable in the existing formulas for population and development. Baylies reminds us of the tendency to co-opt a "women's agenda" or to use "gender analysis" in instrumental ways for promoting other development or "health" agendas and she cautions against this sort of "focus on women" within AIDS initiatives (Baylies and Bujra 2000, p. 22).

Reproductive health in Uganda and Tanzania is caught between the "business of AIDS" (see Setel 1999) and the "problem" of overpopulation. Baylies and Bujra point out that AIDS work faces the same hurdles as other development interventions: "apathy, extra stress and pressure on limited resources of time or money, projects which can be hi-jacked by the already well-placed, bids for personal as well as collective improvement, corruption, abuse and manipulation of external contracts, the use of the most vulnerable to promote careers and so on" (Baylies and Bujra 2000, p. xiii). Indigenous social demographic literature is new in Uganda and Tanzania and comes primarily from the problems posed by

HIV/AIDS. Kirumira notes that even this literature in Uganda is mired in a "population crisis perspective" and is statistically-oriented, focusing on surveying and controlling women's fertility (Kirumira 1998, p. 58).

Tentative Conclusions and a Few Words on Policy

Uganda's campaign against AIDS has presented a significant challenge to the discourse on reproductive health in Africa. No longer can donors or governments claim either that AIDS is just one among many diseases that plague poor nations, or perhaps more importantly, no longer can its immensity be used as a justification for inaction. The stereotype of Africa as a socio-economic basket-case beyond the ability of public policy to grapple with the AIDS pandemic is incommensurable with a notion of the Ugandan AIDS "success" story. However, the paradox that may exist in Uganda – that its "successful" HIV/AIDS policy is contributing to a less than successful population policy – calls for further investigation. Is the national program of public education making young people aware of their likelihood of contracting the disease, so that they decide to reproduce at younger ages to insure that they are able to do so? If the ability to live long enough to reproduce is perceived by young Ugandan women to be their major reproductive health problem, what does this say about population policies and the "problems" that they are designed to address?

Baylies and Bujra (2000) suggest that the old debates about the efficacy of the "developmentalist state" may need to be reopened by the demands that AIDS presents. African states may be pushed to become more "developmentalist" by the immense scope of the HIV/AIDS pandemic, with its myriad effects at all levels of society and by the need to gain control over the plethora of players in AIDS work. However, the particular place of gender within reproductive health interventions, including but not limited to AIDS work, suggests that the state should become more "feminist" as well.

Population policies, as all kinds of policy, result from political processes. Klugman emphasizes "that policies are recognized as resulting not from logic, rationality, or what appears to be irrefutable evidence. Rather, decision makers have to be won over with processes and terms which they understand and value, but which, in and of themselves, surface women's needs and validate their demands" (Klugman 2000, p. 116). Goetz's analysis of gender equity in South Africa and Uganda suggests that women's capacity to meaningfully participate in politics and influence decision-making depends on the degree to which the state promotes and implements policies on social equality and the degree of legitimacy enjoyed by feminist social movements and politicians (Goetz 1998, p. 258). In Uganda, Tripp (2001) has argued that the women's movement is not only one of the most coordinated and active social movements within the country itself, but also one of the most effective women's movements in Africa. Yet, promoting reproductive health has not yet been taken up as a priority for this movement (see Richey 2005).

The Cairo outcome makes clear that "the manipulation of decision-making environments ... should be guided not by demographic targets or objectives but by the primacy of health, empowerment, and rights" moving both "beyond family planning" and "beyond demography" (Dixon-Mueller and Germain 2000, p. 71). The shift in demographic dynamics related to both AIDS and fertility suggests that new population "problems" will need to be solved by population policies. Discussions of reproductive health, development policies, and HIV/AIDS must not be hijacked by simple behavioralist explanations of how Africans are "different", but instead must be placed within the complex web of socio-economic realities that shape how societies experience disease. Maternowska (2006) demonstrates how controlling sexual behaviour in the context of preventing HIV or pregnancy has little meaning in a context of poverty such as Haiti where entire households are reliant on sexual transactions. The "macroeconomic rationale" for donor funding and government intervention into reproductive health issues is becoming startlingly clear, so any lack of a "sense of urgency" for these issues can be predicated only on a misunderstanding of them. Grounding these interventions in a framework of human rights brings attention to both the gender disparities and geopolitical inequalities at play (Stein 2000). Human rights should provide the foundation for a new generation of integrated policies that promote healthy sexuality, informed and consensual reproductive choices, and the development of the individual and her or his society. This means that AIDS should neither be left out of reproductive health, nor allowed to subsume all of its resources.

References

Ashford, Lori S. 2001. "New Population Policies: Advancing Women's Health and Rights." *Population Bulletin* 56(1).

Barrett, Deborah A. 1995. *Reproducing Persons as a Global Concern: The Making of an Institution.* PhD Dissertation, Dept. of Sociology, Stanford University.

Baylies, Carolyn and Janet Bujra, eds. 2000. *AIDS, Sexuality and Gender in Africa: Collective Strategies and Struggles in Tanzania and Zambia.* (Social Aspects of AIDS Series). London and New York: Routledge.

Bessinger, R.Alwara, P. and D. Halperin. 2003. "Sexual behavior, HIV and fertility trends: a comparative analysis of six countries. Phase I of the ABC study." Washington, D.C., United States Agency for International Development (USAID), 82. (USAID Cooperative Agreement No. HRN-A-00-97-00018-00).

Boone, Catherine and Jake Batsell. 2001. "Politics and AIDS in Africa: Research Agendas in Political Science and International Relations." *Africa Today.* 48 (2): pp. 3-33.

Boserup, Ester. 1970. *Women's Role in Economic Development.* New York: St. Martin's Press.

Brass, William and Carole L. Jolly. 1993. *Population Dynamics of Kenya.* Washington, DC: National Academy Press.

Brown, Lester R., Gary Gardner, and Brian Halweil. 1998. "Beyond Malthus: Sixteen Dimensions of the Population Problem." Sept. 1998, *Worldwatch* paper #143.

Bujra, Janet and Carolyn Baylies. 2000. "Responses to the AIDS Epidemic in Tanzania and Zambia." In C. Baylies and J. Bujra, eds. *AIDS, Sexuality and Gender in Africa: Collective Strategies and Struggles in Tanzania and Zambia.* London and New York: Routledge, pp. 25-59.

Caldwell, John C. 2000. "Rethinking the African AIDS Epidemic." *Population and Development Review* 26(1): pp. 117-135.

Carpenter, Lucy M. and Jessica S. Nakiyingi, et al. 1997. "Estimates of the Impact of HIV Infection on Fertility in a Rural Ugandan Population Cohort." *Health Transition Review* 7 (suppl 2): pp. 113-126.

Casterline, John B. and Steven W. Sinding. 2000. "Unmet Need for Family Planning in Developing Countries and Implications for Population Policy." *Population and Development Review* 26 (4): pp. 691-723.

Cohen, Barney. 1998. "The Emerging Fertility Transition in Sub-Saharan Africa." *World Development* 26 (8): pp. 1431–1461.

Crook, Nigel and Ian Timæus. 1997. *Principles of Population and Development with Illustrations from Asia and Africa.* Oxford: Oxford University Press.

Cuffaro, Nadia. 1997. "Population Growth and Agriculture in Poor Countries: A Review of Theoretical Issues and Empirical Evidence." *World Development* 25 (7): pp. 1151-1163.

Dixon-Mueller, Ruth and Adrienne Germain. 2000. "Reproductive Health and the Demographic Imagination." In H. B. Presser and G. Sen, eds. *Women's Empowerment and Demographic Processes: Moving Beyond Cairo.* Oxford: Oxford University Press, pp. 69-94.

De Waal, Alex. 2003. "How Will HIV/AIDS Transform African Governance?" *African Affairs* (102): pp. 1–23.

Desgrées du Lou, Annabel, Philippe Msellati, et al. 1999. "Impaired Fertility in HIV-1 Infected Pregnant Women: A Clinic-Based Survey in Abidjan, Cote d'Ivoire." *AIDS* 13: pp. 517-521.

Eberstadt, Nicolas E. 2001. "The Population Implosion." *Foreign Policy Magazine,* March/April.

Economist, The. September 23, 1999. "Too many or Too Few."

Economist, The. August 9, 2001. "The New Demographics."

Feeney, Griffith. 2001. "The Impact of HIV/AIDS on Adult Mortality in Zimbabwe." *Population and Development Review* 27 (4): pp. 771–780.

Goetz, Anne Marie. 1998. "Women in Politics and Gender Equity in Policy: South Africa and Uganda." *Review of African Political Economy* (76): pp. 241-262.

Gregson, Simon and Basia Zaba, et al. 1999. "Low Fertility in Women with HIV and the Impact of the Epidemic on Orphanhood and Early Childhood Mortality in Sub-Saharan Africa." *AIDS* 13 (supplement A): pp. 249-257.

Robert Hecht, Anita Alban, Kate Taylor, Sarah Post, Nina B. Andersen, and Ryan Schwarz. 2006. "Putting it Together: AIDS and the Millennium Development Goals." *PLoS Med* 3 (11) November 28.

Heise, Lori L. 1997. "Beyond Acceptability: Reorienting Research on Contraceptive Choice." In *Beyond Acceptability: Users' Perspectives on Contraception.* London: Reproductive Health Matters for the WHO, pp. 6-13.

Heuveline, Patrick. 2003. "HIV and Population Dynamics: A General Model and Maximum-Likelihood Standards for East Africa." *Demography* 40 (2): pp. 217-245.

Hogle, Janice A. 2002. "What Happened in Uganda? Declining HIV Prevalence, Behavior Change, and the National Response." *Project Lessons Learned Case Study.* Washington, DC: US Agency for International Development.

Jain, Anrudh Ed. 1998. *Do Population Policies Matter?: Fertility and Politics in Egypt, India, Kenya, and Mexico.* New York: The Population Council.

Keyfitz, Nathan. 1977. *Applied Mathematical Demography.* New York: Wiley-Interscience, John Wiley and Sons.

Kiondo, Andrew S. Z. 1995. "When the State Withdraws: Local Development, Politics and Liberalisation in Tanzania." In P. Gibbon, ed. *Liberalised Development in Tanzania.* Uppsala: Nordic Africa Institute, pp. 109-176.

Kirk, Dudley. 1996. "Demographic Transition Theory." *Population Studies* 50: pp. 361-387.

Kirumira, Edward K. 1996. *Familial Relationships and Population Dynamics in Uganda: A Case Study of Fertility Behavior in the Central Region.* Copenhagen: University of Copenhagen Institute of Sociology.

– 1998. "Developing a Population Policy for Uganda." In H. B. Hansen and M. Twaddle, eds. *Developing Uganda.* Oxford: James Curry, pp. 185-193.

– 2001. "HIV/AIDS Incidence and Prevalence: Reality or Myth?" Copenhagen Conference on Gender, Sexuality and HIV/AIDS: Research and Intervention in Africa.

Klugman, Barbara. 2000. "Empowering Women through the Policy Process: The Making of Health Policy in South Africa." In H. B. Presser and G. Sen, eds. *Women's Empowerment and Demographic Processes: Moving Beyond Cairo*. Oxford: Oxford University Press, pp. 95-118.

Larsen, Ulla M. 1997. "Fertility in Tanzania: Do Contraception and Sub-Fertility Matter?" *Population Studies* 51: pp. 213-220.

Lloyd, Cynthia B., C.E. Kaufman, and Paul C. Hewett. 1999. *The Spread of Primary Schooling in Sub-Saharan Africa.* New York: The Population Council.

Malthus, Thomas R. 1914. *An Essay on Population.* New York: E.P. Dutton and Co.

Maternowska, Catherine M. 2006. *Reproducing Inequities: Poverty and the Politics of Population in Haiti.* New Brunswick, NJ and London: Rutgers Univ. Press.

Nuwagaba, Augustus. 1997. "Population Crisis in Sub-Saharan Africa: Who is Responsible? An Illustrative Analysis of Population Trends in Uganda." *Eastern Africa Social Science Research Review* 13 (2): pp. 75-88.

Over, Mead. 1992. *The Macroeconomic Impact of AIDS in Sub-Saharan Africa.* Washington, DC, The World Bank: pp. 1-35.

Parkhurst Justin and Louisiana Lush. 2004. "The political environment of HIV: lessons from a comparison of Uganda and South Africa." *Social Science & Medicine.* Volume 59, Issue 9, November, pp. 1913-1924

Population Division United Nations. 2001. *World Population Prospects: The 2000 Revision Highlights.* New York: United Nations.

Richey, Lisa Ann. 2005. "Uganda: HIV/AIDS and Reproductive Health." In W. Chavkin and E. Chessler, eds. *Where Human Rights Begin; Health, Sexuality and Women in the New Millenium.* New Jersey: Rutgers University Press.

– 2008. *Population Politics and Development: From the Policies to the Clinics.* New York and London: Palgrave MacMillan.

Sanderson, William C. and Molly E. Hellmuth, et al. 2001. "Botswana's Future: Modeling Population and Sustainable Development Challenges in the Era of AIDS: Executive Summary." Laxenburg, Austria: International Institute for Applied Systems Analysis.

Sen, Gita and Srilatha Batliwala. 2000. "Empowering Women for Reproductive Rights." In Harriett B. Presser and Gita Sen, eds. *Women's Empowerment and Demographic Processes: Moving Beyond Cairo.* London and New York: Oxford University Press, pp. 15-36.

Setel, Philip W. 1999. *A Plague of Paradoxes: AIDS, Culture, and Demography in Northern Tanzania.* Chicago and London: University of Chicago Press.

Sharpless, John. 1997. "Population Science, Private Foundations, and Development Aid: The Transformation of Demographic Knowledge in the United States, 1945-1965." In F. Cooper and R. Packard, eds. *International Development and the Social Sciences.* Berekeley: University of California Press, pp. 176-200.

Sinding, Steven W. and John S. Caldwell. 1997. "Where is the International Population Movement Going? Cairo's Legacy." *Supplement to Health Transition Review* 7.

Sinding, Steven W. 2001. "Learning by Doing: Testing the Supply-Side Hypothesis at USAID." IUSSP Seminar on the Production and Dissemination of Population Knowledge, Brown University, Providence RI.

Stein, Zena A. 2000. "International Women's Health." In M. Goldman and M. Hatch, eds. *Women and Health.* San Diego: Academic Press.

Tripp, Aili Mari. 2001. "The Politics of Autonomy and Cooptation in Africa: the Case of the Ugandan Women's Movement." *The Journal of Modern African Studies* 39 (1): pp. 101-128.

Uganda, Government of. 1999. *The NCSD Sustainable Development Report.* Accessed online at www.ncsdnetwork.org/global/reports/ncsd1999/uganda/cap1.htm.

UNAIDS. 2000. "The United Nations on the Demographic Impact of the AIDS Epidemic." *Population and Development Review* 26 (3): pp. 629-633.

United Nations. 2008. *Declaration of Commitment on HIV/AIDS and Political Declaration on HIV/AIDS: midway to the Millennium Development Goals: Report of the Secretary General.* 1 April 2008, A/62/780.

USAID. 2001. "Tanzania Activity Data Sheet: Congressional Budget Justification FY 2002." Washington, DC: Online at www.usaid.gov/pubs/cbj2002/afr/tz/621-001.html [accessed Sept. 18, 2008].

– 2001. "Uganda Activity Data Sheet: Congressional Budget Justification FY 2002." Washington, DC: Online at www.usaid.gov/pubs/cbj2002/afr/ug/617-004.html [accessed Sept. 18, 2008].

– 2000. "Saving Women's Lives, Protecting Women's Health: US Global Leadership in Family Planning." Washington, DC: USAID, pp. 1-12.

United Republic of Tanzania. 1992. *The National Population Policy.* Dar es Salaam: The Planning Commission of the President's Office.

Van Dalen, Harry P. and Mieke Reuser. 2005. "Assessing the Size and Structure of Worldwide Funds for Population and AIDS Activities." The Hague: Netherlands Interdisciplinary Demographic Institute.

Vavrus, Frances and Ulla Larsen. 2003. "Girls' Education and Fertility Transitions in Tanzania and Uganda." *Economic Development and Cultural Change* 51: pp. 945-975.

Watkins, Susan. 1998. "Local Transformations in Reproductive Ideologies in a Global Context 1930–1997." Paper prepared for a Rockefeller Foundation Meeting Bellagio May 18–22, 1998.

Wilson, Chris. 2001. "On the Scale of Global Demographic Convergence 1950-2000." *Population and Development Review* 27 (1): pp. 155-171.

Chapter 7

The Positive Impact of Population Policy on Human Rights in Sub-Saharan Africa

Rachel Sullivan Robinson

Introduction

Although home to only 12 percent of the world's people, sub-Saharan Africa has the fastest growing population of any region of the planet: at the current rate of natural increase, 2.5% per year, the population will double in less than 30 years (PRB 2007). In response to this rapid growth, between 1988 and 1999 two-thirds of sub-Saharan African governments adopted national population policies designed to limit fertility and reduce population growth rates (Sullivan 2007). As documents dictating the simultaneously most personal and social of matters, these policies both exemplify and make visible the politics of population in sub-Saharan Africa at the turn of the twenty-first century. This chapter describes the experience of sub-Saharan countries with population policy during the past twenty-five years, focusing particularly on the reasons for population policy adoption and the policies' effects on human rights. From the perspective of a sociologist and a demographer, I argue that political intervention in family planning and fertility behavior has been, and can continue to be, in harmony with human rights. In particular, population policies hold particular promise for improving gender equity. I do not, however, enter the debate on whether fertility decline is a morally appropriate policy goal. I take as given that countries adopted population policies and explore the causes and effects of these policies. In addition to examining overall trends in sub-Saharan Africa, I focus on the case of Nigeria, which adopted a population policy in 1988, to further illustrate the relationships between the politics of population, population policy, and human rights.

The "human rights" I refer to in this chapter primarily encompass reproductive rights as defined by the 1994 Cairo Programme of Action.

> [Reproductive rights recognize the] basic right of all couples and individuals to decide freely and responsibly the number, spacing and timing of their children and to have the information and means to do so, and the right to attain the highest standard of sexual and reproductive health (United Nations 1994, para. 7.3).

Reproductive rights are a key component of gender rights, and this is particularly true in sub-Saharan Africa, where almost a quarter of married women report having unprotected sex despite not wanting any more children (Sedgh et al. 2007).

Broadly speaking, the positive impact of population policies has derived from their symbolic, strategic, and practical sides. Symbolically, these policies sent a message to citizens that the government was concerned with reproductive health, thus emphasizing that reproductive health was a topic worthy of thought and attention. Strategically, they provided reproductive health and rights language that could be used by individuals, advocacy groups, and in the courts. Practically, they served as a means to raise money from donors for contraceptive supplies and provided governments with the opportunity to assess the demography of their countries. Specifically, population policy in sub-Saharan Africa has had four main positive effects on human rights: 1) increased opportunity to address unequal gender rights, 2) increased potential to solve poverty-related problems, 3) increased capacity to carry out reproductive decisions, and 4) improved survival of women and children. The first two positive effects were achieved through the language of the policies and the policy planning process itself, while the last two positive effects were achieved through greater availability of contraception. Notably absent in the sub-Saharan African case is *any* evidence of the incentives and quotas associated with population policy implementation in China (Li 1995) and India (Vicziany 1982) that led to flagrant human rights abuses.

This chapter explores the process of population policy adoption across sub-Saharan Africa generally, while drawing on detailed information from fieldwork from the specific case of Nigeria. Its goal is to provide background on population politics in sub-Saharan Africa while speaking to the broader themes of the book, specifically the relationship between population politics and human rights. I start by offering some theoretical perspectives on how to conceptualize population policies, then describe the process of population policy adoption across all countries and in Nigeria. I conclude the chapter by describing the positive impacts of population policies on human rights.

Theoretical Perspectives

Population policies, and their interaction with human rights, are but one way to study the politics of population. The size, composition, distribution, and reproduction of populations can increase and decrease the power of social actors ranging from governments to elders to individual women and men. For this reason, issues related to fertility, migration, and mortality easily and rapidly become political. Although population policies can address any or all of these three areas, they tend to focus on fertility, itself a politicized topic because of its relationship to sex and gender. Regardless of focus, the politics of population are ascribed at multiple points in processes of population policy. In this chapter, I focus on the interaction of population politics and human rights when countries decided to adopt population policies, and in terms of the policies' impacts.

I treat population policies as part of governmentality, the collection of practices, institutions, analyses, and tactics described by Foucault that "allow" the exercise of political power over a population (Foucault 1991, p. 102). Foucault developed the concept of governmentality by tracing the shift in the source of sovereignty from power over a territory to power over a population that occurred between the 16th and 18th centuries in Europe. The goal of governmentality is the welfare of the population, the ultimate source of the government's power, and the means through which the government controls the population are expressions of governmentality. One aspect of this control is physical (via the police), while the other is via disciplinary practices. When states structure individuals' lives via educational, medical, penal, and military institutions and discourses, they transform populations into objects of care, and in so doing solidify their sovereign power (Foucault 1988; 1991). From this perspective, states adopt population policies to "govern" their populations, meaning to manage and regulate them in the name of strengthening the state. Population policy is yet another way to make the population an object of care, and in so doing, enhance and consolidate the state's power.

Ginsburg and Rapp (1991) and Greenhalgh (2003) have used Foucault in a similar manner to understand the relationship between population management and state power. Other scholars have identified the role of population policy in governance without explicitly referencing Foucault. Speaking generally, Eberstadt (1994, p. 30) noted that, "The adoption of comprehensive population policy marks an eventful change in the conception of the role of government in civic life", while Newland (2001) described how Indonesia used its family planning program as a means to restructure the relationship between citizens and the state. In examining fertility-limiting policies in Asia during the 1960s, Ness and Ando (1984) found that, among other factors, strong nationalist movements facilitated the promulgation of such policies. These cases show how population policy exemplifies the dual nature of all acts of governance: management of the population and strengthening of the state.

Population policy is thus fundamentally about population *politics* in two senses. In the first sense, population policy is "political" in the contentious meaning of the word: it instigates a discussion about the appropriate composition and size of populations, which quickly trickles down to the individual behaviors required to bring about that ideal population. In the second sense, population policy is "political" in the governance meaning of the word: it is intimately linked to the process of regulation, control and formation of the population. The politics of population understood in both senses have ramifications for human rights. Specifically, marginalized groups, as less desirable members of society, will always be at risk of exploitation, and all groups may be at risk, depending on the degree to which the government respects individual rights in implementing the policy.

Population Policy Adoption in Sub-Saharan Africa

The term "population policy" can refer to policies targeting any area of demographic behavior. The population policies I discuss in this chapter focus primarily on reducing the number of children born per woman, and in so doing, reducing the population's growth rate. In addition to this central concern, most sub-Saharan African population policies have a number of other commonalities. First, they all state that improving the quality of life of the people is the policy's primary goal. Second, they generally link well-being to a variety of issues, including health, education, employment, mortality, and migration. Third, and particularly relevant to this analysis, most policies describe the need to improve women's status as an explicit goal, and/or as a means to reduce fertility and induce economic development.

Population policy in sub-Saharan Africa is a recent phenomenon, as is shown in Figure 1. The first two countries to adopt population policies were Kenya in 1967 and Ghana in 1969 (Chimbwete et al. 2005; Locoh and Makdessi 1996). No other country in sub-Saharan Africa adopted a policy until 1988, when Liberia, Nigeria, and Senegal did so, beginning a trend that carried through until 1999 (Sullivan 2007). By 1999, 32 countries had adopted population policies, leaving only 15 countries out of 47 without such policies. Many of the remaining countries without policies can best be described as having experienced significant conflict over the period in question (e.g., Angola, Burundi, Congo, Democratic Republic of the Congo, Eritrea, Somalia, and Sudan), and it is not surprising that governments in crisis would not adopt policies, population or otherwise (ibid.).

But what causes the spatial and temporal diversity of population policy seen in Figure 1? When thinking about the timing of policy adoption, it is most productive to break it down into two periods separated by the 1994 United Nations International Conference on Population and Development (ICPD) held in Cairo. Policy adoption processes following the ICPD should differ from those that concluded prior to the conference because the ICPD's Programme of Action, signed by 179 countries, *promoted* population policies.

> Population-related goals and policies are integral parts of cultural, economic and social development, the principal aim of which is to improve the quality of life of all people (United Nations 1994, Principle 5).
>
> To achieve sustainable development and a higher quality of life for all people, States should reduce and eliminate unsustainable patterns of production and consumption and promote appropriate policies, including population-related policies, in order to meet the needs of current generations without compromising the ability of future generations to meet their own needs (Ibid., Principle 6).

These explicit statements, in addition to the Programme of Action's overall message that government-managed policies and programs can bring about desirable social change, indicate that countries that did not already have a population policy in 1994 would have felt pressured to adopt such a policy after that date.

Countries adopted population policies for a variety of reasons: to improve quality of life, as part of processes of governmentality, because of pressure from outside organizations (cf. Hartmann 1995 and Liagin 1996, but also Sullivan 2007 for a different perspective), and because of the influence of global norms (cf. Barrett 1995; Barrett and Frank 1999). Charismatic leaders have also played a role in policy adoption in some places, including Nigeria. Although all of these explanations matter, I focus on the quality of life and governmentality explanations because of their relationship to human rights and the politics of population. In the discussion of these two explanations below, I draw on three sources of evidence: the text of the policies themselves, the results of a statistical analysis comparing all countries in sub-Saharan Africa, and interviews with population experts in Nigeria (for a complete discussion of the statistical analysis and fieldwork see Sullivan 2007). I conducted these interviews in Abuja in 2006 with experts from the population field: those working for government ministries, bilateral organizations, multilateral organizations, local and foreign non-governmental organizations, and foundations.

Quality of Life

Quality of life is fundamentally about the availability of sufficient resources for all people. As such, one of the primary explanations for population policy adoption is a perceived imbalance of population and resources. This explanation is pervasive in the literature explaining population policy adoption in sub-Saharan Africa (cf. Lacey 1990; Nassim and Sai 1990), and there exists support for it in the policy texts, in the cross-country analysis, and in my interviews with Nigerian policy experts.

The text of many population policies explicitly states that the purpose of the policy is to improve the quality of life. For example, the first goal of Nigeria's population policy is "to improve the standards of living and the quality of life of the people" (Federal Republic of Nigeria 1988, para. 4.1.1), while Cameroon's policy says that "the goal of the national population policy of Cameroon is to improve the quality of life of the population, within the limit of available resources, in accordance with human dignity and fundamental human rights" (Republic of Cameroon 1993 III.B). In the absence of general references to improving quality of life, population policies list the specific areas targeted for improvement by the policy, such as health, education, and employment, all of which clearly impact overall quality of life.

Demographic and economic factors, as components of quality of life, also influenced policy adoption, based on the results from the statistical analysis. Indeed, countries that adopted policies before the 1994 Cairo Conference had larger populations with higher fertility rates and lower economic growth than those that adopted policies later (after 1994) or not at all (Sullivan 2007).

Finally, in terms of the perspective of population experts in Nigeria, many justified the policy on the grounds of an imbalance between resources and population size. Many noted in particular the economic crisis that followed the oil boom in the 1970s, while others spoke more generally about the equilibrium between resources and population.

> [If you don't] keep your population growth in line with your resources, you're likely to go down poverty lane (Ministry of Health official #1).

> The economy of the country was no longer able to cope with the huge population growth … resources were dwindling and quality of life was deteriorating so fast (National Population Commission official).

> The government realized the fact that we needed to have a population policy to make sure that we have the population that we can manage; we have a population that the economic resources can match (International NGO representative).

When pressed as to why this imbalance, which had existed for many years prior, suddenly came to matter in the 1980s, respondents referred to the charismatic Minister of Health, Professor Olikoye Ransome-Kuti. Respondents described Ransome-Kuti as an enlightened, dynamic, internationally renowned, and good man with foresight, who was "key" and "instrumental" to the population policy process.

There is thus evidence from the text of the policies, the statistical comparison of countries, and the words of Nigerian population experts that countries adopted population policies in the hopes that these policies, and their associated programs, would improve the quality of life of the people.

Governmentality

In addition to addressing the population regulation side of governance, population policies also exhibited countries' efforts to strengthen the state. Many policies speak of the "nation" in general terms, or reference the population as the most important resource in the country (cf. Federal Republic of Nigeria 1988; Gouvernement du Mali 1991). Policies are also frequently nationalistic in tone, as exemplified by Nigeria's 1988 policy, whose title is the "National Policy on Population for Development, Unity, Progress and Self-Reliance", and which was published in pamphlet form with a green and white cover mimicking Nigeria's flag (Federal Republic of Nigeria 1988). Senegal's policy refers to the obligation of the state to "protect the family and attend to its physical and moral well-being" (République du Sénégal 1988, para. 3.1.1), and Ethiopia's policy explicitly describes the population's important role in "nation building efforts" (Transitional Government of Ethiopia 1993, p. 6). Statements like this indicate that governments had motives for adopting population policies that went beyond altering the composition and structure of the population.

Based on the statistical analysis of all countries, the influence of governmentality changed over time: before Cairo, the countries that adopted policies were more difficult to govern as they were more ethnically and linguistically diverse, while following Cairo, the countries that adopted policies actually had more efficient and stable governments (i.e., with greater constraint on the executive). I interpret these findings to mean that the first countries to adopt population policies did so as an active expression of governmentality, and thus in order to consolidate their power. The later countries, on the other hand, adopted population policies as a more passive act of governmentality, because there was a regional and global impetus to do so. Population experts in Nigeria spoke of the importance of population policy for guiding citizens' reproductive behavior, an explicit reference to the governance purposes of population policy.

A variety of factors explain why sub-Saharan African governments adopted population policies during the late 1980s and throughout the 1990s, including a desire to improve people's quality of life, governmentality processes, external organizations, and charismatic leaders. Case studies of population policy adoption in other countries highlight similar factors. For example, Chimbwete et al. (2005) show that although international actors were very important to Malawi's population policy process (culminated in 1994), the concerns of the government, particularly its head, explain the timing of the policy adoption. Richey (1999; 2003) presents Tanzania's 1992 population policy as resulting from donors and lenders, who tied reductions in population growth to neoliberal economic policies. Importantly, the case studies highlight the active role played by sub-Saharan African governments in the policy adoption process. I turn next to the impact of these policies on human rights.

Effects of Population Policy on Human Rights

Although the motivations for population policy in sub-Saharan Africa have not always been strictly to improve human rights, the effects on population policy on human rights in sub-Saharan Africa can be seen in four main areas related to human rights: 1) increased opportunity to address unequal gender rights, 2) increased potential to solve poverty-related problems, 3) increased capacity to carry out reproductive decisions, and 4) improved survival of women and children. As I mentioned above, the language of the policies and the policy planning process itself produced the first two outcomes, while greater availability of contraception led to the second two positive effects. I discuss each of these factors in turn below, again drawing on the language of the policies as well as my 2006 interviews in Nigeria

Addressing Unequal Gender Rights

Population policies introduce language that women and women's groups can use to promote their rights, both within the household and at the national level, initiate a discussion of the distribution of power across sex, generation, and space, and provide a framework within which to discuss sex and contraception – taboo subjects in many traditional African societies. This discussion often takes the form of active resistance on the part of those who stand to lose from a redistribution of power, but is nonetheless an important step in the process towards gender equity.

In terms of language, even policies that predate the 1994 ICPD promote free choice in number and timing of children. For example, "A national policy must recognize that all couples and individuals have the basic right to decide freely and responsibly on the number and spacing of their children and to have information, education, and means to do so" (Federal Republic of Nigeria 1988, para. 1.5). Similarly, "All couples and all individuals have the fundamental right to freely and wisely choose the number and spacing of their children, and to access information regarding those decisions" (République du Benin 1996, para. 3.1.2). More uniquely, Sierra Leone's (1988) policy states, "Population policy should be humane and responsible, fully respecting individual freedoms and rights as well as religious beliefs and cultural values" (Republic of Sierra Leone 1988, para. I.6). Having such language in policies whose ultimate goal is to change fertility behavior is crucial to ensuring that people's rights are not restricted during the implementation process.

Respondents in Nigeria noted that the population policy raised awareness about family planning, and signaled the importance of reproductive health issues by indicating the government's commitment to them. The policy made family planning a legitimate topic of discussion, particularly in more rural areas, but even in urban areas, where culture and religion made such discussions challenging. Government support of reproductive health and family planning condoned reproductive health, a crucial step towards ensuring people's access to it.

Finally, in terms of generating debate on population issues, Nigeria's 1988 population policy caused an uproar. Some women's and Christian groups were upset because of the part of the policy that expressed an ideal number of children per woman, as opposed to per family (Osuide 1988). This implied that the policy benefitted Muslim men, who could marry up to four wives and thus have more children than Christian men. Negative reaction was also based on the policy's endorsement of contraception and planned fertility, which was offensive to religious leaders of a variety of faiths (ibid.). These negative reactions in turn made implementation of the policy challenging, but indicate the existence of an active debate about the policy and reproductive rights more generally.

These examples show that by enabling a discussion about reproductive health as well as about the relationship between individuals and the state, population policies help to begin securing a nexus of rights related to reproductive health and gender equity.

Increased Potential to Solve Poverty-Related Problems

Population policy encourages states to consider demographic variables when planning for the future. To write a population policy requires examining existing demographic data, and considering projections of related trends into the future. Although states themselves may not be able to meet the needs of the population in terms of numbers of schools, teachers, or hospitals, having an *accurate* list of needs helps states procure the desired and appropriate aid from development partners. This is a key step in correcting the imbalance of power between global and national actors. If, for example, a country can articulate exactly what it needs to provide health care to its citizens, and ensure that children are educated, it lessens the possibility that another set of objectives will be imposed by donors.

Respondents in Nigeria echoed this benefit to population policies, and emphasized that policies are important because they provide a framework that has two key implications: 1) it provides structure and coherence to a related set of programs, which are then actually implemented on the ground, and 2) it gives donors a list of tasks to consider funding.

> Policy articulates government's intent on an issue and it shows the direction government chose on an issue (Bilateral organization representative).

> You have to have a framework to do whatever you want to do for your people in a coherent way (Ministry of Information official).

> [Without a policy], people will not know how to go and help you (Ministry of Health official #1).

Respondents also felt that policies were important parts of interacting with donors, specifically because they defined target areas, but also because they helped in managing (and possibly attracting) donors. Population policy thus serves as a valuable planning exercise that allows countries to contemplate their vision for the future, and how they want to go about achieving it.

Increasing Capacity to Enact Reproductive Decisions

Just as population policies indicate to citizens that family planning is an appropriate topic of conversation, they also signal to international donors that the government is worthy of funding for population activities (Barrett and Tsui 1999). Indeed, population policy has also increased the amount of funding received for contraceptive commodities (ibid.). While funding for contraceptives from bilateral and multilateral donors comes with conditions, and may be earmarked for activities which the donors care about particularly, contraceptive availability greatly facilitates women, and men, attaining their reproductive rights. For those women and couples who want contraception, donor funding is a key component to enhanced access.

The Nigerian policy increased the amount of funding for population activities. The World Bank gave Nigeria a credit of $78.5 million for population activities (Odimegwu 1998), and USAID also gave $67 million (Liagin 1996). All but UNFPA funding stopped in the mid-1990s, however, when donors "decertified" Nigeria because of the human rights abuses associated with Sani Abacha's rule, and most of the World Bank money was never disbursed because of infighting between groups that laid claim to it (*Choices* 2000). Despite these setbacks, the funding had the potential to greatly increase contraceptive availability. These policy outcomes help explain why respondents uniformly felt that it was better for countries to have population policies than not.

Improved Survival of Women and Children

Population policy also serves to increase the focus on maternal and infant mortality, which remain high in sub-Saharan Africa, and directly reduce the likelihood of a secure existence. Across sub-Saharan Africa, the average maternal mortality ratio in 2005 was 900 deaths per 100,000 births, a figure 100 times greater than in developed regions (United Nations 2007). Infant mortality was similarly high: in sub-Saharan Africa in 2005 there were 99 deaths per 1,000 live births to children less than one year of age, compared to five per 1,000 in developed countries (ibid.). Many of these deaths were due to poor delivery conditions and infectious disease, but a portion was also due to pregnancies to women who already had large numbers of children, and to pregnancies that were closely spaced together. By helping to reduce the overall number of pregnancies, and increasing the spacing between them, family planning can reduce infant and maternal mortality (McCarthy and Maine 1992; Potter 1988; Trussell 1988).

Many sub-Saharan African countries have framed their policies as a means to reduce infant and maternal mortality through birth spacing, both as a health goal, and to reduce resistance to population policy. Policies frequently mention the dangers to maternal and infant health associated with pregnancies that are before age 18 or after age 35, that are spaced more closely than two years, or to women who have more than four children. Any improvements to maternal and infant health resulting from programs associated with population policy directly improve quality of life.

Population policies thus positively impact human rights through a variety of channels, ranging from their language to their impacts on individuals' well-being via increased contraceptive availability. Although the potential exists that such policies could be used to inhibit people's ability to exercise their reproductive rights, there is no evidence that such outcomes have occurred in sub-Saharan Africa.

Conclusion

In this chapter I outlined the experience of population policy adoption in sub-Saharan Africa. Governments adopted population policies for a variety of reasons, some of which were related to human rights (improving quality of life and the status of women), and others of which were related to the politics of population (increasing government strength). As a result of population policy, women and men in sub-Saharan Africa have legal documents that protect their reproductive rights, as well as better access to contraception.

Despite the progress in human rights achieved through population policy in sub-Saharan Africa, clearly population policy as political intervention simultaneously poses the potential for infringement on human rights. India and China are of course the most famous, and chilling, examples of this abuse because they so severely and coercively limited reproductive and family choices of individuals and couples. This type of scenario is unlikely, however, in sub-Saharan Africa for two reasons. First, the texts of population policies are in fact carefully written in the language of choice and rights, both those policies that precede the 1994 Cairo Conference, and especially those that come after. Such language provides legal protection, and also sets up a government commitment to rights. Because sub-Saharan African governments adopted population policies at a time when the family planning movement was transitioning into a reproductive health and rights movement (Hodgson and Watkins 1997), sub-Saharan African population policies were crafted more with rights in mind than those that came before. A second reason that population policy is unlikely to infringe on human rights in sub-Saharan Africa is that no government has exerted significant pressure on policy implementation. It is difficult to tell whether this outcome is due to respect for rights, insufficient political capacity and will, or cultural preferences for large families, but the outcome is the same: no coercion.

Although fertility rates have declined in most sub-Saharan African countries since the 1980s (Kirk and Pillet 1998), they remain high and populations continue to grow quickly. On average, women in sub-Saharan Africa have between five and six children in their lifetimes (PRB 2007). To the extent that global neoliberalization negatively impacts the economies of sub-Saharan Africa, the motivation for governments to lower their countries' birth rate will remain. These factors combined imply a need to ensure that the positive outcomes of population policy continue to exist, and that the global community supports efforts in African countries to realize reproductive rights. The best contributions the global community can make to positive political intervention in family planning are the following:

1. Ensure adequate contraceptive supply and help set up contraception manufacturing facilities in sub-Saharan African countries
2. Encourage the development of primary health care systems to provide health care to women, children, and men, and make contraceptive provision part of that health system
3. Eliminate the global gag rule so that US funds can be given to organizations regardless of whether they discuss abortion with their clients
4. Ensure that not all funding for population activities shifts to AIDS-related matters, particularly as this results in an emphasis on male-controlled contraceptive methods (condoms)

Although the risk exists for political intervention in reproductive matters to lead to abuses in human rights, the potential for positive impact outweigh these risks. In the case of sub-Saharan Africa, population policies have benefited the pursuit of human rights and have opened discussions that must continue in order to enpsure that these rights are fully achieved.

Figure 1: Population Policy Adoption across Time and Space in Sub-Saharan Africa

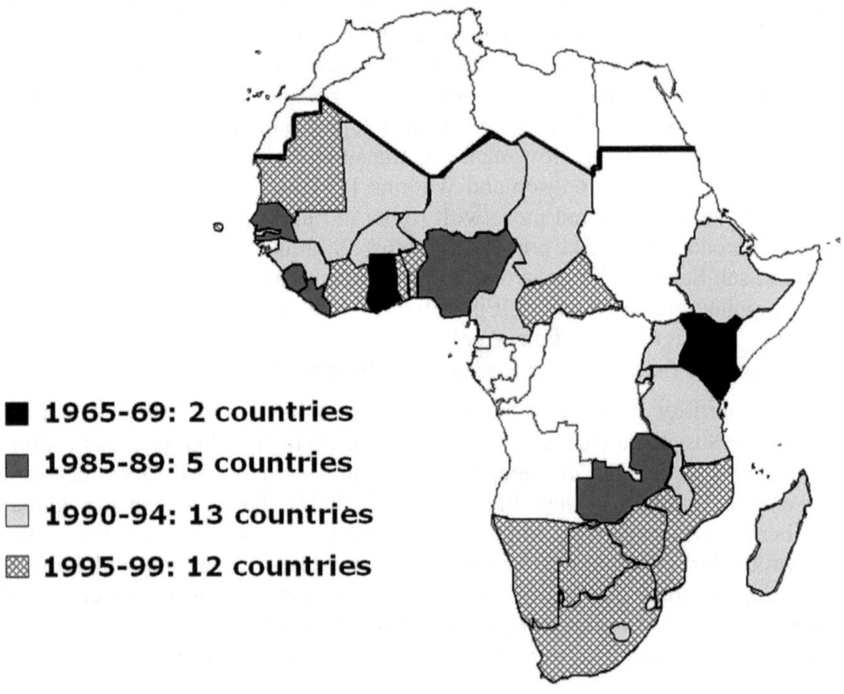

References

Barrett, Deborah A. 1995. *Reproducing persons as a global concern: the making of an institution.* Ph.D. Stanford University.

Barrett, Deborah and Amy Ong Tsui. 1999. "Policy as symbolic statement: international response to national population policies." *Social Forces* 78(1), pp. 213-234.

Barrett, Deborah and David John Frank. 1999. "Population control for national development: from world discourse to national policies." In John Boli and George M. Thomas, eds. *Constructing world culture: international nongovernmental organizations since 1875.* Stanford, CA: Stanford University Press, pp.198-221.

Chimbwete, Chiweni, Susan Cotts Watkins, and Eliya Msiyaphazi Zulu. 2005. "The evolution of population policies in Kenya and Malawi." *Population Research and Policy Review* 24(1), pp. 85-106.

Choices. 2000. "Development strategies suffer until we address population issues." *Choices* 1(4), pp. 4-9.

Eberstadt, Nicolas. 1994. "Population policy: ideology as science." *First Things* 40, pp. 30-38.

Federal Republic of Nigeria. 1988. *National policy on population for development, unity, progress and self-reliance.* Lagos, Nigeria: Federal Republic of Nigeria.

Foucault, Michel. 1988. "Political technology of individuals." In Luther H. Martin, Huck Gutman and Patrick H. Hutton, eds. *Technologies of the self: a seminar with Michel Foucault.* London: Tavistock, pp. 145-162.

– 1991. "Governmentality." In Graham Burchell, Colin Gordon, and Peter Miller, eds. *The Foucault effect: studies in governmentality.* Chicago: University of Chicago Press, pp. 87-104.

Ginsburg, Faye and Rayna Rapp. 1991. "The politics of reproduction." *Annual Review of Anthropology* 20, pp. 311-343.

Gouvernement du Mali. 1991. *Declaration de la politique nationale de population du Mali.* Bamako, Mali: Gouvernement du Mali.

Greenhalgh, Susan. 2003. "Science, modernity, and the making of China's one-child policy." *Population and Development Review* 29(2), pp. 163-196.

Hartmann, Betsy. 1995. *Reproductive rights and wrongs.* Boston, MA: South End Press.

Hodgson, David and Susan Cotts Watkins. 1997. "Feminists and neo-Malthusians: past and present alliances." *Population and Development Review* 23(3), pp. 469-523.

Kirk, Dudley and Bernard Pillet. 1998. "Fertility levels, trends, and differentials in sub-Saharan Africa in the 1980s and 1990s." *Studies in Family Planning* 29(1), pp. 1-22.

Lacey, Linda. 1990. "The new generation of African population policies." In Godfrey Roberts, ed. *Population policy: contemporary issues*. New York: Praeger, pp. 135-146.

Li, Jiali. 1995. "China's one-child policy: how and how well has it worked?" *Population and Development Review* 21(3), pp. 563-595.

Liagin, Elizabeth. 1996. *Excessive force: power, politics, and population control.* Washington, DC: Information Project for Africa, Inc.

Locoh, Therese and Yara Makdessi. 1996. *Population policies and fertility decline in sub-Saharan Africa.* Translated by Moursund, Fallon M. Paris: Centre Français sur la Population et le Développement.

McCarthy, James and Deborah Maine. 1992. "A framework for analyzing the determinants of maternal mortality." *Studies in Family Planning* 23(1), pp. 23-33.

Nassim, Janet and Fred T. Sai. 1990. "Family planning and maternal and child health in the World Bank's population, health, and nutrition program." In Helen M. Wallace and Giri Kanti, eds. *Health care for women and children in developing countries*. Oakland, CA: Third Party Press.

Ness, Gayle D. and Hirofumi Ando. 1984. *The land is shrinking: population planning in Asia.* Baltimore, MD: The Johns Hopkins University Press.

Newland, Lynda. 2001. "The development of the prosperous family: family planning in West Java." *National Women's Studies Association Journal* 13(3), pp. 22-48.

Odimegwu, Clifford. O. 1998. *An appraisal of the national population policy for development.* Research Report No.10, Ibadan, Nigeria: Development Policy Centre.

Osuide, Simeon. 1988. "The 1988 Nigerian population policy." *Habitat International* 12(4), pp. 119-123.

Population Reference Bureau (PRB). 2007. *World population data sheet.* Washington, DC: Population Reference Bureau.

Potter, Joseph E. 1988. "Does family planning reduce infant mortality?: comment." *Population and Development Review* 14 (1), pp. 179-187.

République du Benin. 1996. *Declaration de politique de population de la République du Benin.* Proto-Novo, Benin: Centre Panafricain de Prospective Sociale.

Republic of Cameroon. 1993. *Declaration de la politique nationale de population.* Yaoundé, Cameroon: Commission Nationale de Population.

Republic of Sierra Leone. 1988. *National population policy for development, progress, and welfare.* Freetown, Sierra Leone: Republic of Sierra Leone.

Républic du Sénégal. 1988. *Déclaration de la politique de la population.* Dakar, Senegal: Ministry of Planning and Cooperation, Directorate of Human Resources.

Richey, Lisa. 1999. "Family planning and the politics of population in Tanzania: international to local discourse." *The Journal of Modern African Studies* 37(3), pp. 457-487.

– 2003. "Women's reproductive health and population policy: Tanzania." *Review of African Political Economy* 96, pp. 273-292.

Sedgh, Gilda, Rubina Hussain, Akinrinola Bankole, and Susheela Singh. 2007. *Women with an unmet need for contraception in developing countries and their reasons for not using a method.* Occasional Report No. 37, New York: Guttmacher Institute.

Sullivan, Rachel. 2007. *Leveraging the global agenda for progress: population policies and non-governmental organizations in sub-Saharan Africa.* Ph.D. University of California, Berkeley.

Transitional Government of Ethiopia. 1993. *National population policy of Ethiopia.* Addis Ababa, Ethiopia: Office of the Prime Minister.

Trussell, James. 1988. "Does family planning reduce infant mortality? An exchange: comment." *Population and Development Review* 14 (1), pp. 171-178.

United Nations. 1994. *Cairo programme of action.* United Nations: New York.

– 2007. *The Millennium Development Goals Report.* United Nations: New York.

Vicziany, Marika. 1982. "Coercion in a soft state: the family planning program of India – part I: the myth of voluntarism." *Pacific Affairs* 55(3), pp. 373-402.

Chapter 8

Emancipation or Child Benefits? – New Family Policies in Germany and Europe

Steffen Kröhnert and Reiner Klingholz

Fertility Decline and Population Policy in Europe

Following the end of the Second World War, the shock over the National Socialist dictatorship and its misuse of the science of demography ran so deep in the old Federal Republic that a discussion on population policy was in effect ruled out for decades. In the decades that followed, the pronatalist policies pursued by state-socialist regimes led to a situation in which the concept of "population policy" continued to be marred by the stain of totalitarianism.[1]

Nor was there any need for a discussion on population policy in Germany up to the late 1960s. After all, the "baby boom" was still in full swing and there was little reason to doubt that, as then-German chancellor Konrad Adenauer put it, "people will always have children". In the 1970s, though, West Germany's fertility rate declined to one of the lowest figures reported worldwide. Yet even in 1979, when the West German fertility rate had already reached the low level still present until today, namely 1.4 children per woman, Chancellor Helmut Schmidt declared that it was not within the purview of the state to seek to influence fertility development.[2] There was, he stated, no legitimate reason to question a couple's individual decision whether or not to have a child. The fear of a looming authoritarian state fully obscured the fact that both government inaction and a well-intended family policy whose impacts have not been properly assessed inevitably must have a massive influence on this individual decision in Germany.

Demography has intensively researched the reasons for this decline in fertility, pointing above all, to the following circumstances:

1. The end of family-based economic activities in farming or artisanal households and the introduction of state pension systems eliminated the economic reasons to bring a large number of children into the world

1 To cite an example, in 1967 the Rumanian dictator Ceausescu banned both contraception and abortion, succeeding – for one single year – in doubling the country's birth rate. In 1976 the government of the German Democratic Republic (GDR) introduced what it called a "baby year with full pay" with a view to compensating for the GDR's constant population losses due to emigration to the West.

2 See Süddeutsche Zeitung, 3 August 1979: "Schmidt warnt vor Katastrophenstimmung wegen Geburtenrückgangs."

(Mackenroth 1953). Children could no longer serve as cheap labor in family-run businesses or farming operations and they were no longer required to provide for their parents in old age. Under the conditions of industrial society, the more certain and less costly way to gain entitlement to a pension is to take on employment eligible for social insurance, not to rear a large number of children.

2. Rising female educational levels go hand in hand with growing opportunity costs for children. The term opportunity costs refer to the cost of an alternative foregone by choosing a particular activity, in this case the decision to have children and to forego gainful employment (Becker 1960). At the same time the costs involved for raising, feeding, clothing, caring for, and educating children have continued to rise. If in the early 20th century, a 14-year-old boy could find a job in farming or industry, enabling him to contribute to his family's income, today parents often need to pay for a phase of schooling and training that may extend to twenty or more years.
3. Finally, the biographical options available to members of a modern society are far greater than those open to members of an agrarian or early industrial society (Birg 1987; Birg, Flöthmann, and Reiter 1991). If, in earlier times, marriage was often the only possible and accepted way to escape a patriarchally structured parental home or life as a servant, today young people are free to choose among a wide range of educational and training options, places to live, and forms of partnership. Under these circumstances, the decision to start a family will necessarily curtail a person's biographical freedom of choice, or it will find itself sidelined by the "competing pleasures of life."

These circumstances are plausible and verifiable when it comes to explaining declining fertility in the transition from agrarian to industrialized society. But viewed against the background of persistent attempts to discredit any active population policy in Germany, they have, in our opinion, gone unchallenged for too long. This in turn has made it possible to ignore for three decades the causes and long-term implications of extremely low fertility rates in Germany. Fertility decline was long seen as something like the hallmark of a modern society.

Two conventional explanatory approaches have served to encourage a careless treatment of the problem involved in a high percentage of childless persons and low birth rates in Germany, contributing at the same time to the lack of a plan and of an orientation for family policy:

i) The theory of the demographic-economic paradox

The assumption underlying this paradox is derived directly from the economic theory of fertility decline and may be formulated this way: "The greater the wealth, the fewer the children." Up to the 1970s a negative correlation of this kind between economic development and fertility was in fact given for all industrialized and developing countries (Coale and Watkins 1986).

For Birg, the demographic-economic paradox refers to the "proposition that there is an inverse relation between the number of children that people in the developed world and people in the growing middle-class of developing countries actually have, and the number they could afford to have in view of their constantly rising real income" (Birg 2001, p. 42). This phenomenon is explained in essence with reference to the rising opportunity costs of having children under the conditions of high female labor force participation rates[3] and levels of vocational qualification. Accordingly, there is a demographic price to pay for women's prosperity, modernity, growing labor force participation, and the increasing options available to women to shape the course of their own biographies. In Birg's eyes, the demographic decline of modern societies unfolds in keeping with a scientific logic of its own.

In fact, women's labor force participation rates rose constantly in all Western European countries (except Ireland) between the 1970s and 1980s (Klammer and Daly 2003) – a period in which all of these countries reported declines in fertility rates (Figure 1). The rise in employment levels in the EU between 1983 and 1992 – and thus also a good share of economic growth – was due nearly exclusively to an increase in the rate of women's labor force participation (Rubery, Smith, and Turner 1996). In other words, a rising women's labor force participation rate simultaneously boosted European prosperity and – at least according to the theory of the demographic-economic paradox – triggered Europe's demographic decline.

ii) The theory of value change

The second line of argument mainly sees normative grounds at the root of the fertility decline observed in modern societies. However, depending on the political standpoint involved, a "change in values" can be interpreted either as modernization or as a loss of traditional values, and it is this state of affairs that has ignited a number of controversies over population and family policy that continue to this day.

In the perspective of conservative political or religious circles, it is modern society itself that works in favor of a loss of traditional values. Capitalism, it is argued, leads to egoism, to a dissolution of gender roles and a breakdown of the institution of marriage. The only way to stem the ongoing process of demographic decline, it

---

3 The term women's labor force participation rate refers to the percentage of all women in a given age group (often between 15 and 65 years, though other age limits are also used) that are engaged in or actively seeking gainful employment. In other words, the rate includes both employed women and women registered as unemployed. By contrast, the term employment level refers only to persons actually gainfully employed, excluding unemployed persons.

is further claimed, is to return to traditional family values. As, for example, the political scientist Tilman Mayer puts it: "The population issue arises when the sum of desired individual lifestyles dissolves the given supraindividual context." He then notes: "The older people are when they marry, the more often marriages are divorced; the more urbane in character life is, the older a society grows, the more that society will need to recruit immigrants" (Mayer 1999, p. 96).

This concern is also shared in church circles. As German Cardinal Karl Lehmann put the matter (2004, p. 10), "In my opinion, the only viable approach to counteracting a further demographic decline of the population is to strengthen the family and marriage as a lifelong bond."

A thesis of the same tenor, albeit with other connotations, is advanced by liberal and more leftist-oriented opinion leaders. The latter speak not of a loss of traditional values but of a "change in values", under the motto "everyone has the right to lead his own life" cited as the reason not to have children as an expression of a new individual liberty. According to this view, the only conceivable way back to higher fertility rates would be to abandon the model of an open, liberal society. Extreme advocates of this line of argument continue to reject any and every discussion over possible avenues to raising fertility rates, asserting that in this case "children ... are regarded as the private property, or human capital, of their parents, and as such are expected to generate a payback (in the form of pensions)" (Butterwegge 2004, p. 282).

Both of these theoretical approaches, the conservative no less than the leftist-liberal, are ultimately based on similar premises: namely, that Germany's low fertility rate is a necessary consequence of a social system based on liberal or free-enterprise principles. While in the one case this view gives rise to a fundamental critique of the existing social order, in the other case it leads to indifference.[4]

In the past both lines of argument have served to obstruct an objective discussion on the possibility that fertility may well be subject to social influence. The view long prevalent in politics was that the demographic-economic paradox and the ineluctable process of value change deprive the state of the instruments it would need to influence the population's fertility. If at all, it was argued, the only way to influence fertility would be to intervene massively in people's individual liberty, and for this reason it is better not to discuss the issue at all.

This conclusion dominated the discussion in Germany up to the very recent past. The 300-page final report issued by the German Bundestag's Commission of

---

4 The title of the 2004 annual conference of the Heinrich Böll Stiftung (Greens Party) in Baden-Württemberg was: "We're growing older, there are fewer of us – So what!" The title may be seen as a succinct expression of the stance of a good number of people with a leftist orientation in politics when it comes to the issue of demographic change and low fertility rates in Germany.

Inquiry on "Demographic Change", which took ten years (1992 to 2002) to inquire into all aspects and phenomena involved in demographic change, nowhere even addresses the possibility of using political measures to raise fertility in Germany (Deutscher Bundestag 2002).

For fear of reactionary policies, Germany seems to have completely forgotten that there are a good number of democratic countries that can look back on a long history of population policy. The general public in Germany is largely unaware that France's current fertility rate of two children per women (2006) – one of Europe's highest – is due not only to the childcare facilities available there but equally to an uninterrupted 60-year history of population policy. As early as 1939 France adapted the "*Code de la famille*", Europe's first modern pronatalist population policy (Kaufmann 2003). Over the course of decades this policy has had a crucial impact on society's attitudes toward children and the choice of individuals to have children.

A Cross-European Comparison: Low Birth Rates Everywhere?

While for several decades now there have been a number of European industrial societies with similarly high levels of development, no convergence has been observed in the total fertility rates of these countries (Figure 1). Even though this is a region with comparable economic framework conditions, fertility rates range between just under 1.4 in Germany, Italy, and Spain and roughly two in Iceland[5] and Ireland – a discrepancy of 60 percent. While since the 1970s fertility in Italy has declined by nearly 50 percent, namely from 2.4 to 1.35, Sweden reports a decline of no more than 1.9 to 1.8 (Figure 1).

While all Western European countries have total fertility rates of below 2.1 children per women – the level that would be needed to guarantee a stable population development – it is the disparities in individual countries that will, in the medium to long term, entail marked impacts on national population development. The reason is that while countries with total fertility rates of 1.7 and above will, in the long term, be able to use moderate immigration to hold their populations at stable levels, the populations of countries with low fertility, including Germany,

5 Iceland was intentionally included in the study, even though it is a small nation with a population of only 300.000. In recent decades Iceland has experienced a remarkable course of economic and social development, and today it is one of the world's most prosperous and modern countries. The indicators used for the present study confirm this. Because in Iceland the transition from a traditional to a highly modern society was effected without the decline in fertility to rates far below the replacement level that has often been observed elsewhere, the development of Icelandic society must be seen as of particular interest in the present context.

Italy, or Spain, will, in the foreseeable future, shrink appreciably, with the number of deaths growing at a rate in excess of the number of births.[6]

Thus far, demographic research has been unable to demonstrate that individual pronatalist policy measures have any durable effects (Bavagos and Martin 2000). However, all this proves is that one-dimensional attempts to influence reproductive behavior – e.g. payment of birth premiums or other monetary incentives – have failed and that what is called for is a comprehensive look at the phenomenon of low fertility rates:

> "... any discussion of the impact of public policy on couples – and, more precisely, on fertility – requires a redefinition of the traditional approach to family policies. This is especially true in view of the increasingly blurred borderlines between family policy and other public policy domains such as old age, employment, gender equality, etc." (Bavagos and Martin 2000, p. 19)

We are convinced that it is in fact possible to prove that, viewed over the long term, the framework conditions in place in a given country – in particular as regards gender equality – have a sustained impact on fertility rates. In what follows, we will seek to prove, on the basis of a microanalysis and a set of demographic indicators, that it is today not modernity but traditionalism that is at the root of the low fertility rates reported specifically for Germany.

Figure 1: Fertility decline in selected European countries (1965 to 2006)

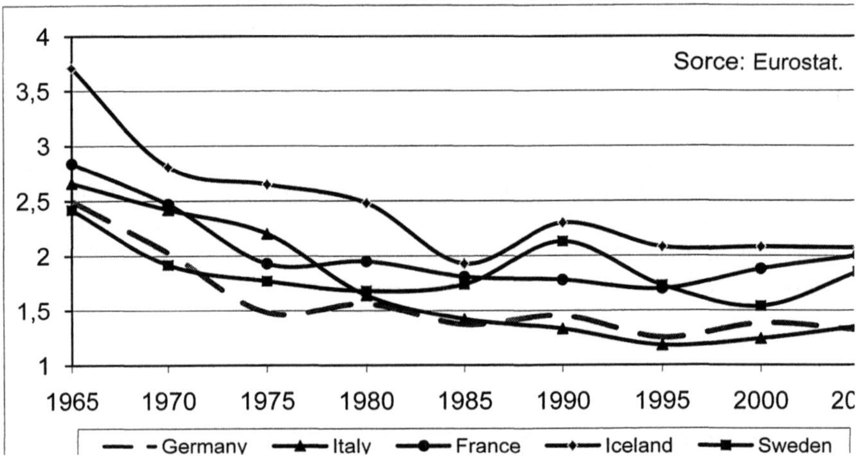

6 See the population forecasts issued by European national statistics offices, which are available via the Eurostat Online Database. While the populations of Germany, Italy, Spain, and Greece are expected to shrink appreciably by the year 2050, forecasts indicate that the populations of countries like France, the Netherlands, Iceland, and Norway will continue to grow.

Figure 2: Total fertility rate (children per woman) in Western Europe (2006)

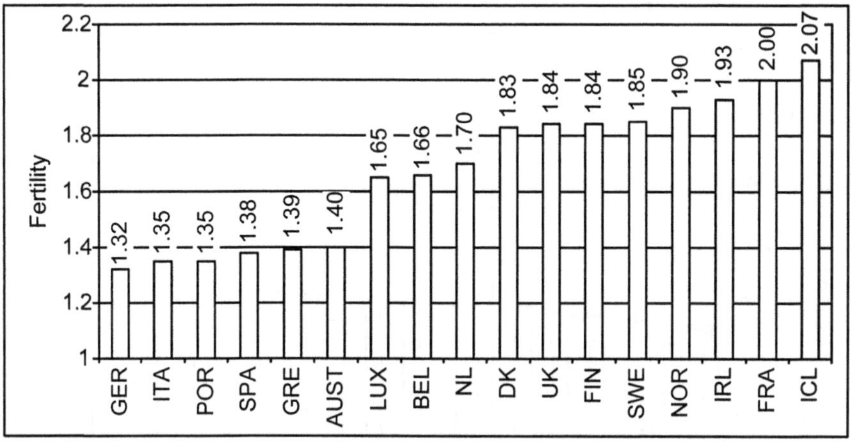

Source: Eurostat. Figures for Italy, Belgium, and Iceland: national statistics offices.

The Richer a Society, the Fewer Children it will Have? No: The Greater the Prosperity, the More Children a Society will Have

Comparative studies show that the values and attitudes that today's young people hold on family, sexuality, and children show hardly any relevant regional discrepancies (Bavagoa and Martin 2000). If, however, given similar attitudes on family and children, the actual fertility rates in Western European countries are found to diverge sharply, the reason for this discrepancy must be assumed to lie in the social conditions in the countries in question. For opportunity costs that arise in connection with starting a new family – be they economic or biographical in nature – are defined in crucial ways by the social system concerned. Surprisingly, what we find here is that starting at a certain level of social development the once inversely proportional correlation between development level and fertility rates shows a tendency to reverse (Figure 3).

Portugal, Spain, and Greece, countries that underwent modernization at a relatively late point of time and continue to be more closely attached to traditional values than northern EU countries like Norway and Sweden when it comes to economic structure, gender relations, and the role of religion in society, have appreciably lower fertility rates than those noted for countries that embarked earlier on their course of modern social and economic development and have reached more advanced levels of development. And it should be noted in this connection that Ireland and Iceland, both countries that embarked on modernization at a relatively later juncture and today have Europe's highest fertility rates, have long since surpassed Germany in terms of economic performance.

Figure 3: Gross national product (in purchase power parities (PPP) per inhabitant) and total fertility in Western Europe (2006)

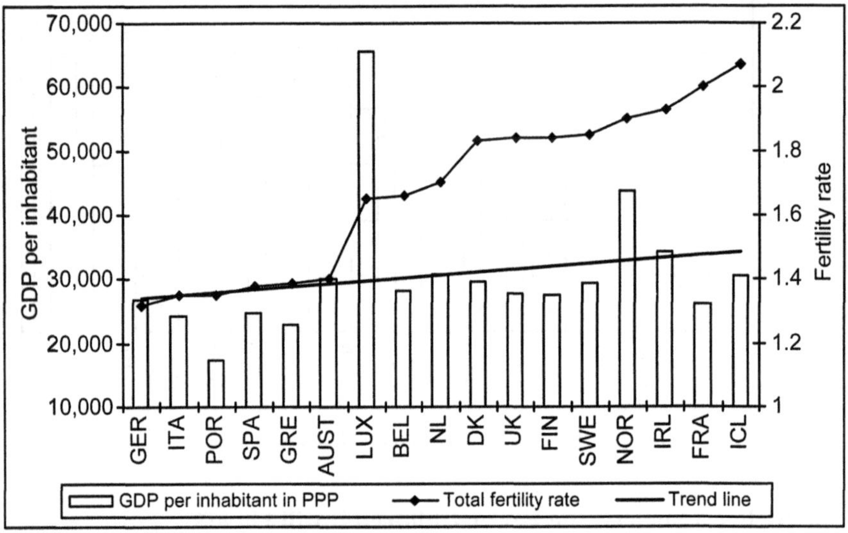

Coefficient of correlation: GDP per inhabitant / total fertility = 0.27.
Source: Eurostat, own calculations. Total fertility rate figures for Italy, Belgium, and Iceland: national statistics offices.

The More Women Stay at Home, the More Children will be Born? *No: There is No Contradiction between Working Women and Women Having Children!*

Based on Beatrice Majnoni d'Intignano (cited after Veil 2004), in Europe we can distinguish three ideal-typical phases of fertility development in connection with female labor force participation:

1. A traditional phase with high fertility rates and low levels of female labor force participation. In Germany, this era came to an end in the mid-60s and thus precedes the period in which modern contraceptives were introduced.
2. A phase with rising levels of female labor force participation and declining fertility rates. In Germany this phase occurred in the 1970s, and it still continues in southern European countries.
3. A phase resting on a modernized social system, with female labor force participation stabilized at high levels and stable fertility rates.

However, there are marked national differences in the level at which the fertility rates stabilize. While in Germany and Austria fertility rates stabilized at an early point of time at a very low level of 1.4, the corresponding figures for Scandinavia and France appear to have stabilized at higher levels, namely above 1.7 in Scandinavia and 1.9 in France (Figure 1).

A cross-European comparison shows a clear-cut correlation between female labor force participation level and total fertility rate – a fact that indicates that the more child-friendly a society is, the more likely it is that it will provide the conditions needed to reconcile children and working life. While countries like Spain, Italy, or Greece, less than 60% of whose women aged 25-59 years are employed, have Europe's lowest fertility rates, Iceland, where over 80% of women aged between 25 and 59 years have jobs, has the highest fertility rate reported for the continent, namely 2.05. But there are also deviations from the trend. Germany and Austria, for example, have low fertility rates and at the same time relatively high female labor force participation rates (Figure 4). In Germany the reason for this discrepancy is very likely to be a large share of women without children – an estimated 29% (BIB 2004), probably the highest figure worldwide. This may be seen as an indication that children represent an important obstacle to the career development of German women. In Germany many women prefer to have no children at all than to accept limitations on their career development.

Figure 4: Female labor force participation rate (25 to 59 years of age) and total fertility in Western Europe (2006)

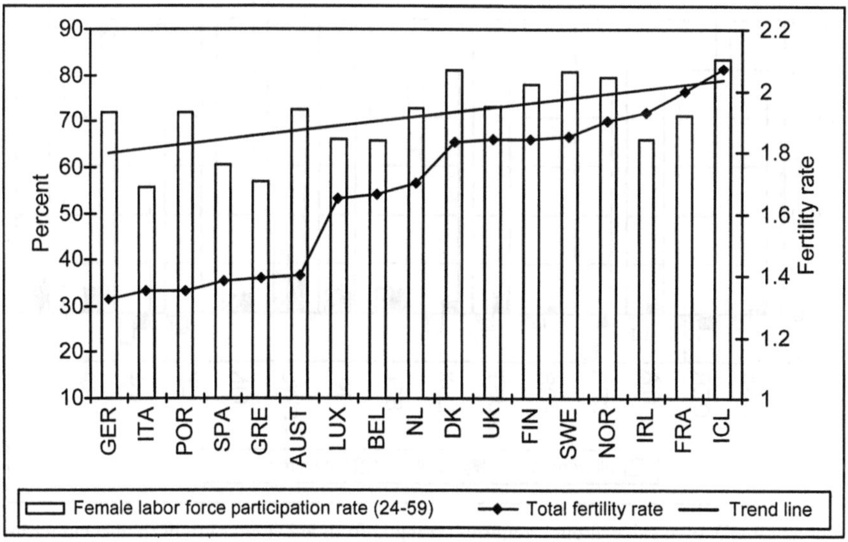

Coefficient of correlation between female labor force participation rate and total fertility rate = 0.63.

Source: Eurostat, own calculations. Total fertility rates for Italy, Belgium, and Iceland: national statistics offices.

One other good indicator of the possibilities given in Western Europe to reconcile children and job is the extent to which the female labor force participation rate changes when women have children (Figure 5). While in 2005 a total of 61 percent of German women were gainfully employed (a figure that includes the low labor force participation level reported for older women), the figure declines to 58 percent as soon as German women have their first child. And only 51.8 percent of German women continue to work when they have two children. By comparison, Sweden, Finland, and France, countries with relatively large families, report female labor force participation levels for women with one or two children that are as high as or higher than the total fertility rate. Even in Portugal, Austria, or Italy, labor force participation rates decline by no more than three to five percentage points when women have one or more children.

Figure 5: Female labor force participation levels (15-64 years of age; in percent) and deviations in these levels when women have one or two children under 15 (in percentage points)

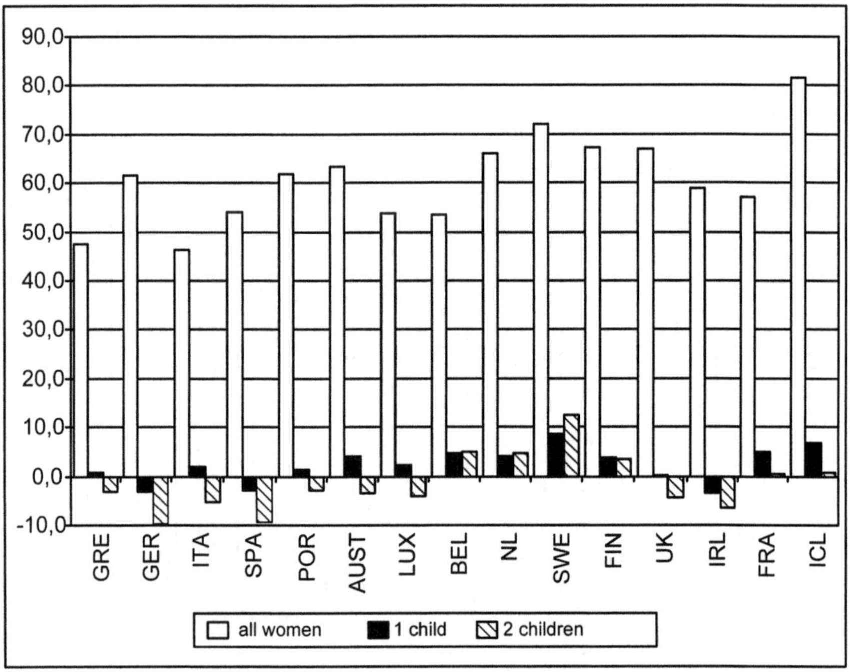

Source: OECD, own calculations; countries arranged from left (low) to right (higher) in terms their total fertility rate.

Are Childcare Facilities the Solution to the Problem of Low Fertility? *No: By Itself, Availability of Childcare Facilities for Three- to Six-Year-Olds Does Not Improve Fertility Rates*

It is an undisputed fact that childcare facilities are a condition that must be given if job and family are to be reconciled. Since 1996 parents in Germany have been legally entitled to care for their children – as a rule for half-days.[7] However, this offer is in no way sufficient, and thus far it has had no demonstrable influence on fertility rates (Hank, Kreyenfeld and Spieß 2003). Evidently, mothers are in this case forced to sharply restrict or even to abandon their employment until their child has reached the age of three. For highly qualified working women in particular, this is tantamount to a sensitive loss of career opportunities.

In fact, in Western European countries there is a clear-cur correlation between fertility rates and the percentage of children below the age of three that attend childcare facilities (Figure 6). In countries with relatively large families, like France, the figure for children under the age of three attending day-care centers is 28% (in 2004); and the figures for Sweden 40% and Denmark (62%) are even higher. As in other countries with low fertility rates, including Italy,[8] Spain, and Austria, the corresponding figure for Germany is ten percent or lower.

In Germany, women's professional ambitions continue to clash with socially mediated and internalized demands that women should care individually for their own children. The view that the fact that mothers work has negative impacts on children's development has a long tradition, and in a poll conducted in western Germany in 1996, this view was found to be endorsed by the largest number of respondents of any other European country (European Commission 1996, p. 44). For this reason many women view work and family as competing goals, and the outcome is often that women decide against starting a family of their own.

---

7 Since 1996 parents in Germany have had a legal entitlement to a place in a childcare facility (BverfG decision on § 218 StGB). The background of this decision handed down by the German Federal Constitutional Court was that legal entitlement would serve to encourage women in their decision to carry their unborn children to term. This entitlement was anchored in the German Eighth Social Security Code – SGB VII (Children and Youth Welfare Act), § 24. It covers every child from the age of three to school age, providing as a rule for half-day care. The German federal states have adopted – in part differing – implementing regulations of their own in this matter in their state acts implementing the Children and Youth Welfare Act.

8 While Italy has a high rate of care for preschool-age children, it also has a low level of coverage for children aged under three (Della Sala 2002).

Figure 6: percentage of under-three-year-olds in childcare facilities and total fertility (2004)

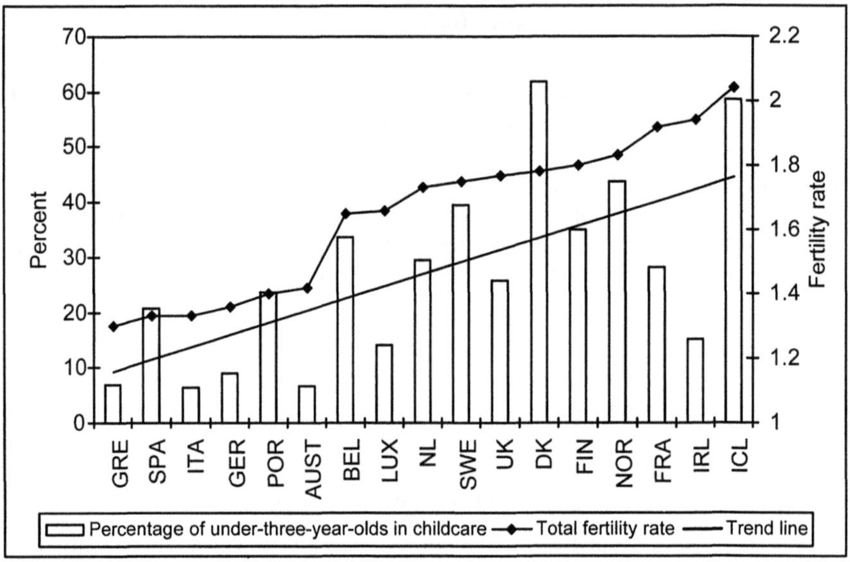

Coefficient of correlation for percentage of under-three-year-olds in childcare/ total fertility rate = 0.69.

Source: Eurostat, OECD, own calculations. Total fertility rate figures for Italy and Belgium: national statistics offices.

Does a 'Traditional' Gender-Related Division of Tasks Serve to Guarantee the Natural Reproduction of the Population?
No: There are More Children Born Where Women and Men Enjoy Equal Rights

The theory of the demographic-economic paradox would seem to indicate that fertility rates decline when women break into well-paid profession domains otherwise dominated by men. Yet reality proves exactly the opposite. The overall rate of female university graduates at first shows a weak negative correlation with the fertility rates noted for the individual countries under consideration (see Column n of the table in the annex below). But if we take as an indicator for the advancement of women into well-paid former male domains not total academic degrees per se but degrees in engineering and natural sciences, we find one particular tendency that should not be overlooked: In Germany, with its low birth rates, only 4.8 of 1000 women aged between 20 and 29 have such degrees. The corresponding figure for Sweden is 9.9, for France 12.9, per 1000 women (Figure 7).

Figure 7: Academic degrees in engineering and natural sciences per 1000 women (20 to 29 years of age) and total fertility rate (2005)

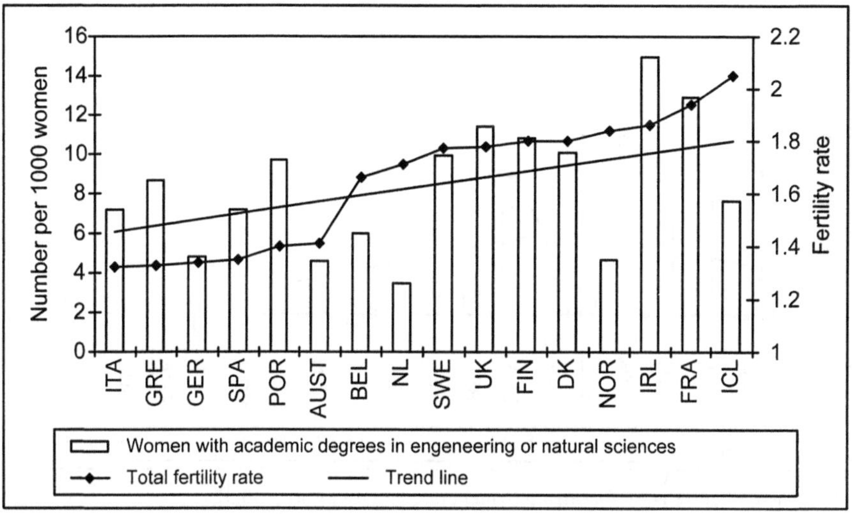

Coefficient of correlation for women with academic degree / total fertility rate = 0.40.
Source: Eurostat, own calculation. Figure for Belgium's total fertility rate: Belgian national statistics office.

The discrepancy between numerous economic indicators for men and women in a given society tells us something about how equal the terms are under which both are able to participate in social life. This goes e.g. for the discrepancy between men's and women's unemployment and labor force participation rates. It may generally be said for modern industrialized developed countries: The larger the gender disparities, the lower the fertility rates.

To cite an example, in Spain, Greece, and Italy, countries with low birth rates, labor force participation rates of 24- to 59-year old women are more than 25 percentage points lower than the rates reported for men of the same age group. In Sweden this "gender gap" amounts to only six percentage points, in Finland only to four. Germany, with a difference amounting to 11.6 percentage points, ranks roughly in the middle (see the table, annex, columns f, g, h).

Roughly the same applies for unemployment (Figure 8; table, annex, columns 1, j, k). In Spain and Greece women (aged between 25 and 49) have unemployment rates roughly twice as high as their male counterparts. In all, seven of the eight countries with the lowest fertility rates report female unemployment rates that are appreciably higher than those reported for men, whereas this is the case in only two of the nine countries with higher fertility rates (France and Denmark).

Figure 8: Discrepancy between unemployment rates (women – men, aged 25 to 49), in percentage points, and total fertility (2006)

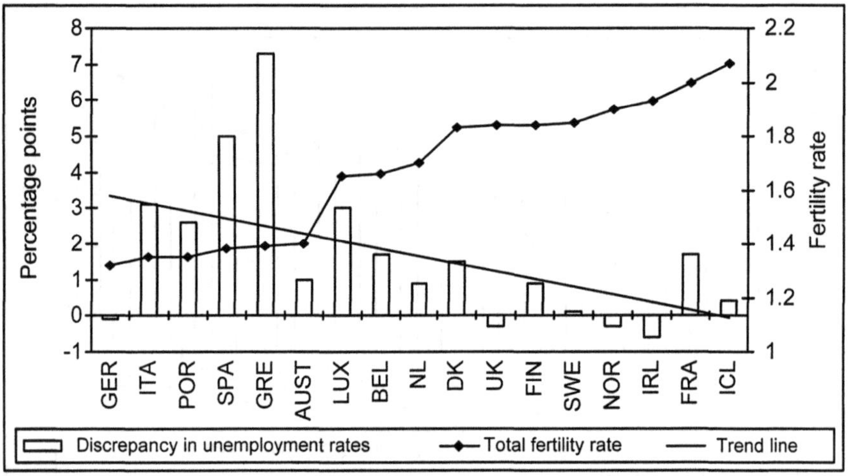

Coefficient of correlation for unemployment rate / total fertility = -0.57
Source: Eurostat, own calculations. Total fertility rates for Italy, Belgium, and Iceland: national statistics offices.

Do 'Traditional Family Structures' Lead to More Children?
No: Family Does Not Presuppose Marriage

It is often claimed that declining fertility rates are linked to a "loss of traditional values" in modern society. Where institutions like marriage and family show signs of dissolution, where women assume male roles, conservative theory claims, it is children who pay the price.

Conservative circles and religious fundamentalists are already raising their voices, warning of a looming extinction of mankind and pointing to family planning and women's rights as the cause of low fertility rates (Kröger, van Olst, and Klingholz 2004). But does this alleged correlation between traditional family structures and high fertility rates in fact exist?

There is little doubt that the binding character of the institution of marriage has lost some of its force in recent decades. Relationships between men and women have lost some of the certainty they may once have had. More and more people are deciding against marriage, and those who do marry have no guarantee that the bonds between them will hold a life long. In recent decades divorce rates have increased everywhere in Europe (BIB 2004).

But there is nothing to indicate that societies with stable marital relationships have higher birth rates. If we take the relation between divorces and marriages in a given year as a measure for the stability of marriages, we do not find a negative correlation between frequency of divorce and fertility. If we exclude Ireland, a country where divorce was illegal until 1996 and that continues to report very low divorce rates, we even find a positive trend (Fig. 9). While in 1995 the divorce figures reported for France and Norway, both countries with relatively high fertility rates, were only half as high as the figures for new marriages, the corresponding figure for Italy was no more than one fifth.[9]

The reason for the – seemingly baffling – correlation is certainly not that unstable relationships work in favor of higher fertility. Instead, divorce rates must be seen as an indicator for gender equality. Where women are in a position to lead their lives without financial dependence on their male partners, the importance of emotional ties assumes a relevance greater than that in relationships that are legally fixed and bear the marks of economic necessity. This, together with social acceptance of divorce, evidently increases the probability that marriage will be followed by divorce. But it does not lead to lower birth rates. The reason is that in societies in which men and women have equal rights in their working lives, women with children may be certain that they will be able to live in financially secure circumstance even after they have divorced.

Figure 9: Correlation between total fertility and marriage and divorce rates per 1000 inhabitants (2005)

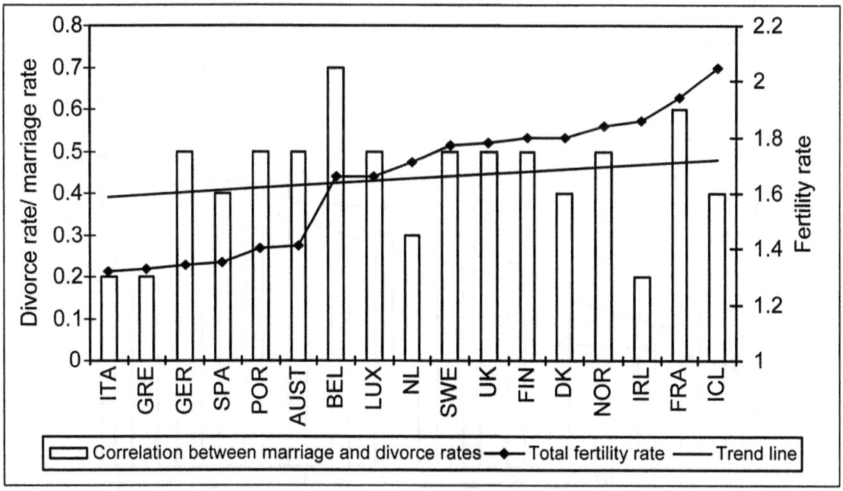

Coefficient of correlation for marriage and divorce rates / total fertility rate = 0.23.
Source: Eurostat, own calculations. Total fertility rate for Belgium: national statistics office.

9 The fact that couples in Italy often separate without any formal divorce (Wanrooij 2001) shows that divorce – which was legalized in Italy only in 1970 – continues to be highly stigmatized in Italian society.

One other piece of evidence in support of this correlation is that, generally, more children are born in countries with a higher percentage of children born out of wedlock. And all Western European countries with total fertility rates of over 1.7 have a percentage of children born out of wedlock higher than that reported for Germany. In fact the statistical correlation between fertility rate and percentage of children born to unwed mothers (0.81) is one of the most reliable of all the indicators under consideration here. Countries like Italy and Greece, in which nonmarital life partnerships and children born out of wedlock continue to be stigmatized, and are accordingly infrequent, have the lowest birth rates in all of Western Europe.

Societies with low birth rates, like Italy, Spain, Germany, or Greece, provide tax incentives to encourage people to marry, and they do their best to shore up the institution of marriage as a social norm. With unequal opportunities for women in the labor market and their practice of assigning childcare tasks for the most part to women, countries of this kind at the same time practically ensure that the parent responsible for raising children is and remains financially dependent on his or her gainfully employed partner. In view of the fact the emotional demands placed in partnerships have grown while the durability of ties has decreased, young people are increasingly reluctant to commit to "permanent" relationships. In the countries mentioned above this often means that women are forced to sacrifice their financial independence; for men it means the duty to become the family's sole breadwinner.

Figure 10: Fertility and percentage of nonmarital births in Western Europe (2006*)

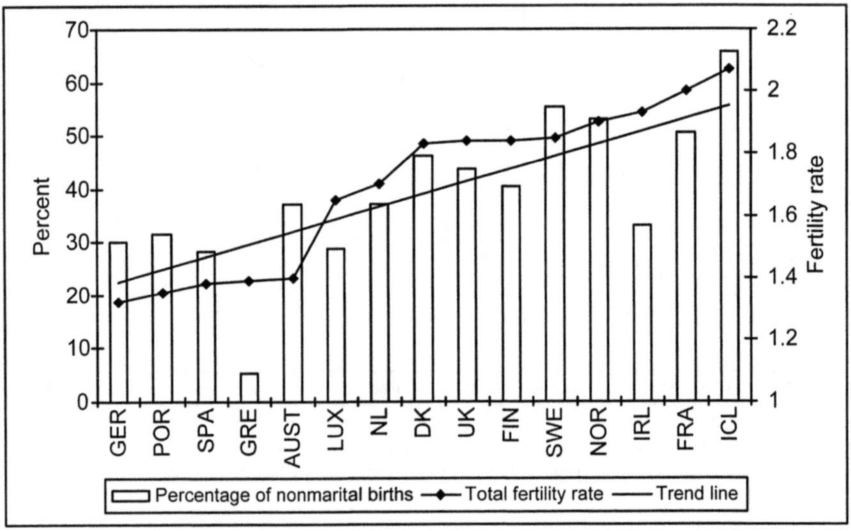

* No figures available for Belgium and Italy.
Coefficient of correlation between nonmarital births / fertility = 0.76.
Source: Eurostat, own calculations. Total fertility rate for Iceland: national statistics office.

Can Society Influence Fertility Rates?
Yes: But Child Benefits Alone Do Not Induce People to Have Children

The statistical correlation between total fertility rate and social expenditures for family and children in Europe (measured in terms of PPP per inhabitant) is relatively weak (0.31). But one problematic factor here is that social expenditure figures do not include differences in the tax burden shouldered by families with children.[10] However, a society can very well invest in family-friendliness. It just has to do so in the right way.

Germany evidently does not. German social expenditures for children and family per inhabitant are high by European comparison. And yet, Germany is a country with low birth rates. We see the reason for this discrepancy in the fact that viewed in connection with the German tax system, Germany's family-related social expenditures continue to be geared to promoting the "male breadwinner model" (Dingeldey 2002).

Nowhere else in Europe is the model "father as sole breadwinner and nonworking wife" promoted with tax breaks as high as they are in Germany (Rürup and Gruescu 2003). The model of "tax-splitting for married couples" in place in Germany serves to calculate a couple's payable taxes on the basis of the total income of both partners. In this case, the greater the income disparity between the partners is, the larger the amount of taxes saved will be. These savings reach their maximum level when one partner has no earnings at all. By setting a relatively high threshold for the point at which it is worthwhile for a couple to start earning a second income, this tax system encourages married women to withdraw from working life (Dingeldey 2002).

Today the majority of European countries have individualized tax systems – in Sweden, Finland, or Greece it makes no difference at all for tax purposes whether it is the father (or the mother) or the two parents together who earn the family income. Other countries (like France) calculate income taxes on the basis of a "tax splitting for families", with taxes declining with the number of children.

The German family support system, on the other hand, has traditionally been geared to boosting the breadwinner's earnings. The child benefits paid out in Germany are the second highest in all of Europe, second only to Luxembourg. Until the end of 2006, the legally guaranteed "parental leave period" in Germany – 36 months – was among the longest provided in all of Europe. For 24 months following the birth of a child, the state paid, in addition to child benefits,

10 The term social expenditure refers to the social benefits, including the administrative costs involved, provided to recipients (in this case, families and/or children) in cash and services (Beriè/Fink 2000). In reference to the field of family/social affairs, this as a rule means direct financial benefits (like child or childcare benefits) and expenditures for the infrastructures needed for childcare services.

earnings-linked parental benefits if one parent did not work full time. Only in 2007 did Germany adopt a 12-14-month parental leave arrangement that provides for the possibility of parental benefits amounting to roughly two thirds of a parent's last earnings, a form of parental support that has proven its worth in Scandinavian countries.

Figure 11: Fertility and social expenditures per inhabitant for family and children, in PPP (2005*)

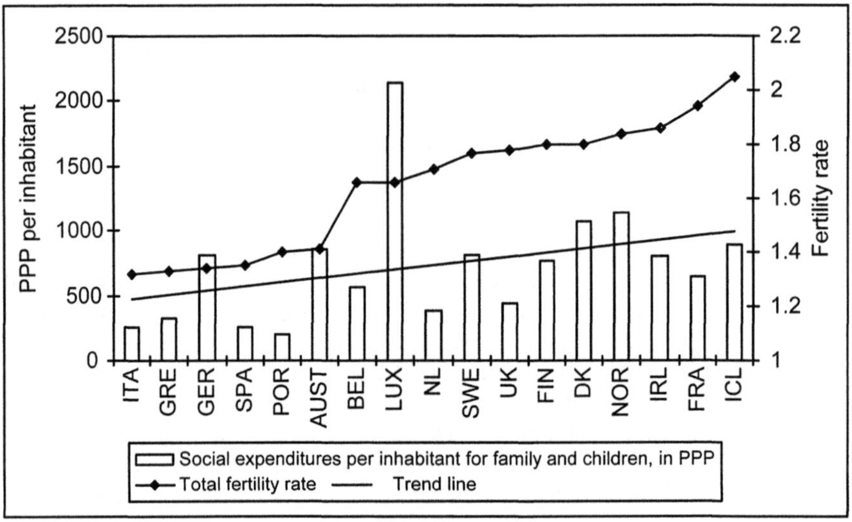

*Figure for social expenditures in Portugal from 2004.
Coefficient of correlation for total fertility rate / social expenditures for family and children = 0.37.
Source. Eurostat, own calculations. Figure for Belgium's total fertility rate: national statistics office.

Until now almost three quarters of German social expenditures for children and family (71 percent) went into pure transfer payments like child and parental benefits (Rürup and Gruescu 2003). On the other hand, countries with high birth rates invest a far greater share of their social expenditures in services designed to allow both parents to continue working. The figure for France is 45%, for Sweden 50%, and for Denmark 59% of social expenditures for family and children (Rürup and Gruescu 2003).

And it is precisely these services that appear to have positive effects on fertility rates: In the first place, women with professional qualifications are often not interested in staying home once they have had a child, since doing so would undercut the value of their qualifications. And in the second place, a tax-based "increase" in the breadwinner's earnings, including child-related benefits, is simply not sufficient to compensate for additional needs for children *and* the loss of a second income.

The outcome of this decades-long practice of German family policy is obvious: A study published by the German Federal Centre for Health Education (BZgA) in 2005 proves that, in western Germany, up to the year 2004, 90 percent of the fathers interviewed were the main source of income for their family, while it was mainly their female partners who cared for children and household.[11] Nor is there any doubt as to what happens when, under the conditions given at present, the main breadwinner "exits the picture": In Germany single parents account for the highest rate of social welfare recipients among all population groups. Over one third of all persons affected (36.4%) are reliant on social welfare (Bundesregierung 2005). The fact that both men and women are reluctant, under these conditions, to "risk" having a child is more than understandable.

The parental benefits introduced in Germany in 2007 are far better suited to meeting the need of qualified young women, or their partners, for a brief but financially secure parental leave and a rapid reentry into the working world. This is shown by the fact that in 2007 Germany's total fertility rate suddenly rose to 1.45, the highest figure reported since German reunification, as well as by the fact that more and more fathers are making use of the option of parental leave.

Conclusion

A decline in fertility to the low rates we can observe e.g. in Spain, Greece, or Germany is not the result of any ineluctable natural law. Indeed, it must instead be seen as the consequence of a development in a society in which the emancipation of women plays an important role. Today most Western European women are interested in pursuing their own vocational development and gaining economic independence, and this has become increasingly important for the most recent generation.[12] All the same, many women continue to wish to have family and children. If, however, women (and their partners) are more emancipated and more "modern" than the society they live in, their desire for children and their life planning are likely to be more than difficult to reconcile. In this case more and more people decide not to have children at all. On the other hand, societies that acknowledge and support the new role played by women tend to have relatively higher fertility rates.

The aim of the present cross-European comparison is to place the possibility that the state has to influence fertility rates in a new light: For one thing, the wide-

11 In roughly 50 percent of families in eastern Germany, the female partner contributed as much as or more than the male partner to their family's earnings.

12 In a European survey conducted in 1996, 71 percent of women between the ages of 15 and 24 years concurred when asked if, for a women, having an income of one's own was a "must". For the group of women over the age of 55 the result was 10.4 percent lower (Europäische Kommission 1996).

spread view that only authoritarian states are capable of carrying out a pronatalist policy seems evidently incorrect. For another, the social development of modern industrial nations does not inevitably lead to declining fertility rates. On the contrary, it is precisely modern societies with a high degree of gender equality that may set the stage for relatively high fertility rates.

Against the background of an evaluation of various socioeconomic and demographic indicators, we conclude that the following measures may well contribute to raising fertility rates in Germany as well as in other European societies with low birth rates:

1. The precondition necessary to reconcile the vocational development of parents with the desire to start a family is provision of childcare opportunities for children starting at the age of one as well as universal all-day care for school children. Only in this way is it possible for working parents (who wish to do so) to return to work following the birth of a child, without having to fear losing either their professional qualification or their earnings.
2. When a parent takes parental leave to care for a newborn child, it makes good sense to provide financial support for this move only for a short period of time – although the support provided should be in line with what people actually earn. The new parental benefits provided in Germany are a real step in this direction. At the same time, though, far more money should be invested in services designed to enable both parents to work. Alongside childcare facilities, these would include funding for day-care mothers or household help.
3. It would also be important to promote the responsibility of male partners to assume childcare tasks. After all, a partnership-based division of the burdens and responsibilities involved in caring for children is part and parcel of gender equality. This would include incentives designed to induce fathers to take – state-funded – temporary parental leave to do their share in caring for their children. Measures of this kind are already in place e.g. in Sweden. In fact, under the Swedish arrangement, if families are not to lose their entitlement, fathers are also required to take part of the parental leave provided for under the law. This too is a sure sign that the new family policy is on the right track.
4. The tax system should be geared to family-friendly work arrangements such as flexible working hours and provide for equal treatment of men and women when it comes to hiring and promotions. In view of a situation in which the working population will soon be shrinking and competition for young, qualified workers will be on the rise, this would make good sense, and not only in terms of family policy. This would serve to cast a family-friendly personnel policy in the light of a crucial competitive advantage.

5. Business enterprises should offer and guarantee family-friendly working conditions and working hours and provide men and women equal opportunities when it comes to hiring and promotions. In view of a situation marked by working populations expected soon to begin to contract as well as by intensified competition for young, qualified staff, it is not only in terms of family policy that this makes good sense. It is in this way that a family-friendly personnel policy may take on the aspect of a crucial competitive advantage

The correlations referred to above between socioeconomic indicators and national fertility rates are neither inescapable in terms of causality nor constantly linear in course. There is little doubt that a given country's fertility rate is also influenced by historical development, political framework conditions, cultural experience, employment-related traditions, and issues bound up with national mentalities. All the same, in our view the indicators selected as best reflecting the characteristics of the social conditions given in the countries under consideration provide a clear-cur basis for an interpretation of family-friendly conditions.

In the long run, social structures shape not only the behavior but also the norms and values of a population. In Germany the clash between what people demand of modern life and a policy that has, in essence, clung to traditional notions of the family has led to a situation in which both actual and desired birth rates are among Europe's lowest. Only when society, in unison with all policy fields, works to guarantee real gender equality in both working life and childcare, will it be possible to reconcile the desire for children with the vocational aspirations of men and women. It is more than likely that under these conditions fertility rates would once again begin to rise, even in Germany.

Appendix

The analysis has made use of the most up-to-date data available for as many countries as possible. Wherever dates from before 2006 have been used, more recent data were either not available or complete. Each of the coefficients of correlation was calculated on the basis of the total fertility rate of the year for which the socioeconomic indicator was available.

Selected socioeconomic indicators and total fertility rates in Western European countries

Column	a	b	c	d	e	f	g	h	i	j
	Total fertility rate (number of children per woman (2004)	Total fertility rate (number of children per woman (2005)	Total fertility rate (number of children per woman (2006)	Gross national product per inhabitant, in purchasing power parities (2006)	Labor force participation rate for women aged between 25 and 59 years (2006)	Labor force participation rate for men aged between 25 and 59 years (2006)	Labor force participation rate disparity (men – women, 25 to 59 years) in percentage points (2006)	Unemployment rate for women from 25 to 59 years (2006)	Unemployment rate for men from 25 to 59 years (2006)	Unemployment rate disparity (women – men), 25 to 59 years, in percentage points (2006)
Greece	1.3	1.33	1.39	23000	56.9	87.8	30.9	12.1	4.8	7.3
Spain	1.33	1.35	1.38	24700	60.5	85.9	25.4	10.3	5.3	5.0
Italy	1.33	1.32	1.35	24300	55.6	83.3	27.7	7.5	4.4	3.1
Germany	1.36	1.34	1.32	26900	71.8	83.4	11.6	9.8	9.9	-0.1
Austria	1.42	1.41	1.40	30000	72.6	87.0	14.4	4.7	3.6	1.0
Portugal	1.40	1.40	1.35	17500	71.9	84.9	13.0	8.7	6.1	2.6
Belgium	1.65	1.66	1.66	28200	65.9	81.9	16.0	8.0	6.3	1.7
Luxembourg	1.66	1.66	1.65	65700	66.0	88.7	22.7	5.6	2.6	3.0
Sweden	1.75	1.77	1.85	29300	80.9	86.9	6.0	5.2	5.1	0.1
UK	1.77	1.78	1.84	27700	73.0	86.2	13.2	3.7	4.0	-0.3
Netherlands	1.73	1.71	1.70	30700	72.8	88.8	16.0	4.3	3.4	0.9
Finland	1.80	1.80	1.84	27500	77.9	82.0	4.1	6.8	5.9	0.9
Denmark	1.78	1.80	1.83	29600	81.0	89.1	8.1	4.2	2.7	1.5
Norway	1.83	1.84	1.90	43800	79.6	87.0	7.4	2.6	2.9	-0.3
France	1.92	1.94	2.00	26100	71.4	83.7	12.3	8.3	6.6	1.7
Ireland	1.94	1.86	1.93	34200	66.0	86.9	20.9	3.4	4.0	-0.6
Iceland	2.04	2.05	2.07	30600	83.5	93.0	9.5	1.9	1.5	0.4
Correlation with total fertility rate				0.27	0.63	0.33	-0.55	-0.69	-0.43	-0.57

(continued)

Column	k	l	m	n	o	p	q	r	s	t
	Percentage of children born out of wedlock (2006)	Percentage of under-three-year-olds receiving care in childcare facilities (2004)	Female university graduates per 1000 female population between 25 and 34 years of age (2005**)	Women with degrees in engineering and natural sciences per 1000 women aged between 20 and 29 years (2005)	Divorces / marriages per 1000 inhabitants (2005)	Social expenditures for family and children in purchasing power parities per inhabitant (2005)	Total female labor force participation rate, 2005 (15 to 64 years)	Female labor force participation rate (15 to 64 years), women with one child (2005)	Female labor force participation rate (15 to 64 years), women with two children (2005)	Female labor force participation rate (15 to 64 years), women with three children (2005)
Greece	5.3	7.0	0.5	8.7	0.2	321.8	47.5	48.4	44.4	37.4
Spain	28.4	20.7	0.9	7.2	0.4	260.9	54.0	51.1	44.7	38.5
Italy	n/a	6.3	1.1	7.2	0.2	263.8	46.3	48.3	41.0	27.4
Germany	30.0	9.0	2.1	4.8	0.5	814.4	61.5	58.4	51.8	36.0
Austria	37.2	6.6	1.8	4.6	0.5	857.9	63.5	67.7	60.1	46.5
Portugal	31.6	23.5	2.9	9.7	0.5	n/a	62.0	63.5	59.2	46.1
Belgium	n/a	33.6	0.9	6.0	0.7	567.2	53.6	58.3	58.5	39.4
Luxemburg	28.8	14.0	n/a	n/a	0.5	2142.1	53.7	56.0	49.8	33.8
Sweden	55.5	39.5	2.2	9.9	0.5	807.4	72.1	80.6	84.7	75.6
UK	43.7	25.8	1.7	11.4	0.5	441.5	66.8	67.1	62.4	42.3
Netherlands	37.1	29.5	1.0	3.5	0.3	380.1	66.0	70.1	70.6	59.9
Finland	40.5	35.0	2.9	10.8	0.5	767.3	67.3	71.2	70.9	60.1
Denmark	46.4	61.7	1.1	10.1	0.4	1068.1	73.2	n/a	n/a	n/a
Norway	53.0	43.7	1.1	4.7	0.5	1132.2	72.3	n/a	n/a	n/a
France	50.5	28.0	1.0	12.9	0.6	644.4	57.1	62.2	57.6	38.1
Ireland	33.2	15.0	1.1	15.0	0.2	797.1	58.8	55.4	52.5	42.3
Iceland	65.6	58.7	0.4	7.6	0.4	894.4	81.6	n/a	n/a	n/a
Correlation with total fertility rate	0.76	0.69	-0.16	0.40	0.23	0.37				

Source: basic data: Eurostat, national statistics offices of Italy TFR 2004+2006, Belgium TFR 2004-2006, Iceland TFR 2006, Columns r,s,t: OECD (2007): Babies and Bosses. Reconciling Work and Family Life, Vol. 5

References

Bagavos, Christos and Claude Martin. 2000. *Sinkende Geburtenraten, Familienstrukturen und politische Reaktionen.* Synthesebericht. Materialsammlung, No. 10. Wien: Österreichisches Institut für Familienforschung.

Becker, Gary S. 1960. "An Economic Analysis of Fertility.", *Demographic and Economic Change in Developed Countries*. Princeton: Universities-National Bureau Conference Series (11).

Beriè, Hermannand and Ulf Fink. 2000. *Europas Sozialmodell – Die europäischen Sozialsysteme im Vergleich. Eine volkswirtschaftliche Analyse.* Berlin: WISO-Institut für Wirtschaft und Soziales GmbH.

Birg, Herwig. 1987. *A Biography Approach to Theoretical Demography.* IBS-Materialien, No. 23. Bielefeld: University of Bielefeld.

Birg, Herwig, Ernst-Jürgen Flöthmann, and Iris Reiter. 1991. *Biografische Theorie der demografischen Reproduktion*. Frankfurt am Main/ New York: Campus.

Brossè-Verbiest, Stéphanie and Norbert Wagner. 2003. "Familienpolitik in Frankreich." *KAS Auslandsinformationen* 7/03, pp. 54-75.

Bundesinstitut für Bevölkerungsforschung. 2004. *Bevölkerung. Fakten, Trends, Ursache, Erwartungen. Die wichtigsten Fragen.* Wiesbaden: Bundesinstitut für Bevölkerungsforschung/ Statistisches Bundesamt.

Bundesregierung. 2005. *Lebenslagen in Deutschland. Der 2. Armuts- und Reichtumsbericht der Bundesregierung*. Berlin: Bundesministerium für Arbeit und Soziales.

Bundeszentrale für gesundheitliche Aufklärung. 2005. *Männer leben. Eine Studie zu Lebensläufen und Familienplanung.* Köln: Bundeszentrale für gesundheitliche Aufklärung.

Butterwegge, Christoph. 2004. "Sozialreform, demografischer Wandel und Generationengerechtigkeit." *Neue Sammlung* 44 (3), pp. 259-282.

Coale, Ansley J.and Susan Watkins, eds. 1986. *The Decline of Fertility in Europe*. Princeton: Princeton University Press.

Della Sala, Vincent. 2002. "'Modernization' and Welfare-State Restructuring in Italy: The Impact on Child Care." In Sonya Michel and Rianne Mahon, eds. *Child Care Policy at the Crossroads. Gender and Welfare State Restructuring*. New York: Routledge, pp. 171-187.

Deutscher Bundestag. 2002. *Schlussbericht der Enquete-Kommission Demografischer Wandel – Herausforderungen unserer älter werdenden Gesellschaft an den Einzelnen und die Politik.* Bundestags-Drucksache 14/8800.

Dingeldey, Irene. 2002. "Das deutsche System der Ehegattenbesteuerung im europäischen Vergleich." *WSI-Mitteilungen* 3/2002.

Europäische Kommission. 1996. "Frauen und Männer in Europa: Wie steht es um die Chancengleichheit?" *Eurobarometer* 44.3.

Eurostat. 2004. *Eurostat Jahrbuch 2004*. Luxembourg: Europäische Kommission.

Eurostat Online-Datenbank, Europäischer Datenservice, Internet: www.eds-destatis.de (Data: March 2005).

Hank, Christian, Michaela Kreyenfeld, and Katharina Spieß. 2003. *Kinderbetreuung und Fertilität in Deutschland.* MPIDR-Working Paper. Rostock: Max-Planck-Institut für Demografische Forschung.

Kaufmann, Franz-Xaver. 2003. *Varianten des Wohlfahrtsstaates. Der deutsche Sozialstaat in internationalen Vergleich.* Frankfurt am Main: Suhrkamp.

Klammer, Ute and Mary Daly. 2003. "Die Beteiligung von Frauen an europäischen Arbeitsmärkten." In Ute Gerhard, Trudie Knijn, and Anja Weckwert, ed. *Erwerbstätige Mütter. Ein europäischer Vergleich.* München: Beck, pp. 193-217.

Knudsen, Knud and Kari Wærness. 2001. "National Context, Individual Characteristics and Attitudes on Mothers' Employment: A Comparative Analysis of Great Britain, Sweden and Norway." *Acta Sociologica*, 44 (1), pp. 67-79.

Kröger, Inga, Nienke van Olst, and Reiner Klingholz. 2004. *Das Ende der Aufklärung. Der internationale Widerstand gegen das Recht auf Aufklärung.* Berlin: Berlin-Institut für Bevölkerung und Entwicklung.

Kröhnert, Steffen, Nienke van Olst, and Reiner Klingholz. 2004. *Deutschland 2020 – die demografische Zukunft der Nation.* Berlin: Berlin-Institut für Bevölkerung und Entwicklung.

Lehmann, Karl. 2004. "Politische Studien-Zeitgespräch. Die Herausforderung der Katholischen Soziallehre heute." *Politische Studien* (396), pp. 9-14.

Lutz, Wolfgang and Nadja Milewski. 2004. *Als ideal angesehen Kinderzahl sinkt unter zwei. Wandel der Normen in Deutschland und Österreich. In: Demografische Forschung aus erster Hand (2).* Rostock: Max-Planck-Institut für demografische Forschung..

Mackenroth, Gerhard. 1953. *Bevölkerungslehre.* Berlin: Springer.

Mai, Ralf. 2004. "Altersselektivität und regionalpolitische Konsequenzen der Abwanderung aus Ostdeutschland." In *Städte im Umbruch. Online-Magazin für Stadtentwicklung, Stadtschrumpfung, Stadtumbau und Regenerierung.* Internet: www.schrumpfende-stadt.de

Mayer, Tilman. 1999. *Die demografische Krise. Eine integrative Theorie der Bevölkerungsentwicklung.* Frankfurt am Main: Campus.

OECD. 2002. *Employment Outlook 2002.* Paris: OECD.

Pinelli, Antonella. 1995. "Woman's Condition, Low Fertility, and Emerging Union Patterns in Europe." In Karen Oppenheim Mason and An-Margritt Jensen, eds. *Gender and Family Change in Industrialized Countries.* Oxford: Clarendon Press.

Rubery, Jill, Martin Smith, and Eloise Turner. 1996. *Bulletin on Women and Employment in the EU.* Brüssel.

Rürup, Bert and Sandra Gruescu. 2003. *Nachhaltige Familienpolitik im Interesse einer aktiven Bevölkerungsentwicklung.* Berlin: Bundesministerium für Familie, Senioren, Frauen und Jugend.

Veil, Mechthild. 2004. "Frankreich – Geburtenraten und Müttererwerbstätigkeit." *KAS-Auslandsinformationen* 1/04, pp. 1-12.

Wanrooij, Bruno P. F. 2001. "Italy." In Robert T. Francoeur, ed. *The International Encyclopedia of Sexuality*. New York: Continuum International.

Chapter 9

Departing China – Identification Papers and the Pursuit of Burial Rights in Fuzhou

Julie Y. Chu

From undocumented migrants (Chavez 1992; Coutin 2000; Mahler 1992) to the "flexible citizen" (Ong 1999), anthropologists have noted the various meanings and effects that state identification papers could have as mediators of persons and populations. Our IDs make certain claims on us. Whether we like it or not, they authorize certain origin stories about us (e.g., of "natural" birth and national territory) and in turn, can compel us along certain paths and moral careers as particular kinds of legal subjects (e.g., as "citizen", "refugee" or "alien") (cf. Kumar 2000). Identification documents, as Yngvesson and Coutin show (2006), can exert a powerful "pull" on people, inspiring some like adoptees to trace paper trails to lost "roots" while forcing others like deportees to return to places where they no longer feel at "home." At the same time, because documents are mobile and manipulable, generative as well as transposable (cf. Latour 1986; Latour and Woolgar [1979] 1986), IDs can also enable longings and belongings beyond "the national order of things" (Malkki 1995). Aihwa Ong, for instance, has noted how for Chinese tycoons holding passports from multiple countries, state identifications have become less about "attestations of citizenship, let alone of loyalty to a protective nation-state" than about one's desire and capacity for responding flexibly to the flows of global capital across various markets (1999,p. 2). Perhaps nothing captures the unpredictable means and ends of identification papers better than this post-9/11 rallying call among anti-immigrant and border security groups in the U.S.:

> "For terrorists, travel documents are as important as weapons. As an inspiration for the 2005 passage of the Real ID Act, with its promise to federalize standards for issuing identification in the U.S., this quote – plucked from the 9/11 Commission Report (National Commission Report 2004) – offers yet another reminder both of the instability of identification papers as an index of national belonging and state entitlement as well as of ID's continual importance to the state's project for having a firm grip over its national body" (Torpey 2000; Caplan and Torpey 2001).

As someone who studies transnational migration out of Fuzhou, China – a region infamous as the veritable capital of Chinese human smuggling[1] – I have

1 Peter Kwong (Kwong 1997; 2001) suggests that this distinct wave of illegal immigration from rural Fuzhou in Fujian Province began in the early 1970s, though it really picked up only after 1986 with the passage of the U.S. Immigration Reform and Control

long been familiar with these tensions between the ID's hegemonic dispositions and its indeterminate capacities as an agent of social identities and realities. That such tensions could lead to unexpected and puzzling ends was crystallized for me one April afternoon in 2001 when I encountered this tombstone in a hilly cemetery on the edge of Longyan village (figure 1). Amidst a uniform block of urn graves housing cremated remains, here was this unique monument not only to the deceased but also, it seems, to this dead man's U.S. "Green Card",[2] which is faithfully recreated here from the three-quarter portrait to the fancy U.S. seal and the bureaucratic personal data in English (i.e., "Alien Resident", name, registration number). What would inspire some people in Fuzhou to memorialize their loved one in the form of the U.S. Green Card?

Figure 1: Tombstone memorializing the "Green Card" of the dead

In a place like Longyan where over 85% of households have relatives abroad, it was no secret that *shenfen* or identification overseas was considered a great achievement among working-age adults; something that substantiated both one's

Act which offered a blanket, one-time amnesty to all previously undocumented migrants and enabled subsequent and widespread chain migration among the Fuzhounese (cf. Chin 1999; Guest 2003; Chin 2001; Kyle and Koslowski 2001). The extent of this new massive wave of emigration from Fuzhou has been documented by a number of researchers. For instance, Liang and Ye (2001) noted how by 1995, Fujian province ranked first in emigration flows out of China, sending 66,2000 people or 28% of China's total emigrant population. Paul Smith (1994) suggested that between 1991-1994, an annual 25,000 Fuzhounese entered illegally into the U.S. (cf. Kwong 2001). Other estimates suggest anywhere between 10,000 to 100,000 enter every year (Smith 1997, p. x).

2 "Green card" is the colloquial term for the identification card issued to legal permanent residents or "resident aliens" of the United States.

superior ability and one's bright prospects for living the "good life". What I would like to explore here, however, are the much less obvious claims that identification papers could make on persons at the liminal "margins of life" (Kaufman and Morgan 2005) and particularly, on the capacity of the newly departed for achieving not only a "good death" but more importantly, a "good *after*-life".

This chapter is a product of my efforts to retrace the pragmatic logics and paper trails that could link this tombstone (figure 1) to a recent epiphenomenon among the very old and frail in Longyan for seeking the Green Card through formal applications for U.S. permanent residency. As I will show, village elders, unlike their working-age counterparts, had very little interest in the entitlements to travel, labor and residence overseas that identification as a U.S. Green Card holder could offer. Instead, as a means to avoid a new local policy for mandatory cremation in China, elderly desires for the Green Card exceeded and destabilized the very domains of "persons" and their "rights" commonly associated with the mediation of state IDs – the nation (Ygnvesson and Coutin 2006), the market (Ong 1999) and life itself (Agamben 2005; 1998; Petryna 2002). My aim in the remainder of this chapter is to highlight some of the challenges raised by this Fuzhounese case over ID's claims on bodies – both of the living and especially of the dead – in relation to questions of personhood and entitlement, economy and value, and the politics of family, population and social reproduction.

The data I analyze here is based on fifteen months of ethnographic research between 2000 and 2005. For eleven of those months (September 2001-July 2002), I resided continuously in the emigrant village I call "Longyan" and conducted participant-observation, oral histories and open-ended interviews with a broad range of residents including the elderly subjects discussed in this chapter.[3] I approach the case described below as an anthropologist interested in the kinds of political agencies and social worlds made possible at the intersection of human rights and population politics. As such, my goal here is not to move from the empirical particularities of a case study to broad, positivist generalizations about human rights or population politics per se. Rather I use insights gained through my ethnographic encounters to reflect on the very limits of "human rights" and "population" as the objects of various normative claims (and counter-claims) to social order, well-being and justice. Specifically, by tracing the historical contingencies and cultural logics of this case, my aim is to trouble certain discursive and pragmatic assumptions about "the human" in human rights agendas as well as in state projects for identifying and managing the subjects of its population.

3 For the purpose of protecting subjects' confidentiality, I have disguised all identifying markers of "Longyan" and its residents from this article's text and citations with pseudonyms.

Managing the Newly Dead

Since 1956 when Chinese party leaders began promoting cremation as a "civilized" and "rational" alternative to the "superstitious" excess of traditional funeral and burial practices (Cheater 1991), illegible or unmarked graves have often cropped up in obscure corners of communities, particularly in rural areas, in quiet defiance of state campaigns for funeral reform (cf. Teather 1999, pp. 414-415). Yet aside from the ten-year period of the Cultural Revolution (1966-1976) when all popular religious practices, including death rituals, came under intense scrutiny and attack (Bruun 1996), state mandates for cremation rarely inspired sustained and uniform enforcement at the local level[4] until after 1997 – a year in which mandatory cremation gained both the force of law with the State Council's issuance of "Provisions on the Administration of Burials" as well as new symbolic weight with the exemplary death of party leader and reform-era icon Deng Xiaoping, who not only had his remains cremated and scattered across land and sea but also donated his corneas and other body parts for organ transplantation and medical research (Faison 1997). As a final reminder of the productive potentiality of bodies – even after the fact of life – for serving the nation-state and its modernizing projects, Deng Xiaoping's economized remains were meant to incite China's ongoing "population problem" (*renkou wenti*) and in turn, extend the state's existing techniques for the centralized planning and policing of bodies from the newly born to the newly dead.

As Chinese anxieties over population shifted in recent years from the social effects of excessive fertility to those of an increasingly aging population[5], the newly dead have emerged as an important object of state reform, its rising numbers prompting renewed state concern over the "problems" traditional funeral and burial practices pose for economic development. Not only did buried bodies take up land that the state claimed could be put to better uses, but as officials regularly noted, the accompanying mortuary practices – including the construction of elaborate coffins and tombs, the hiring of ritual specialists, keeping the corpse in wake for weeks, holding extravagant banquets and funeral processions, and the burning of paper money and other ritual objects – also squandered re-

4 Li and O'Brien (1996) have also noted how along with birth planning, funeral reform has been noted by local cadres as an especially hard task to enforce in contemporary rural China.

5 In 2002, the Chinese Academy of Sciences issued a report on the social problems anticipated by a sharp increase in China's aging population. The percentage of people aged 65 years and above is expected to rise from 5.5% in 1990 to 13.3% in 2025 and 23% or 114 million in 2050. What's more, the growth rate among the very old – that is, of Chinese older than 80 – is even higher than that of seniors as a whole which the report suggests will create a heavy burden on society (2002). Additionally, in Fujian province, data from the 2000 Chinese population census suggests that the population is aging even faster than the national average.

sources like money, timber and labor time, encouraged public unruliness and social disorder, and posed fire hazards and other problems of public health, pollution and environmental erosion. In contrast, cremation, officials argued, not only economized dead bodies, land use and other resources but also provided a much needed "scientific" antidote to the "feudal superstitions" and "vulgar customs" of traditional funerals and burials. Like surplus births under the "One Child" policy, the surplus bodies of the buried dead were largely seen as a problem of unruly peasants in the countryside who needed to be "civilized" by being brought under the rational planning and management of new state cremation and funeral reform administrations.

As with birth planning (*jihua shengyu*) in the Post-Mao era, this new mandatory cremation policy centrally required the mediation of paperwork to produce its legal effects on the ground. While in the past, state identification and tracking of persons ended with certification of death, under mandatory cremation the death certificate became merely the regulatory trigger for a new normative trail of paper which *ideally* would lead the dead to an official state crematorium, where they would need to obtain proof of cremation before they could be legally put to rest either through the scattering of ashes (à la Deng) or through urn burial in a state-registered cemetery specifically designed for cremated remains. This Green Card tombstone (figure 1) actually sat in one of these state-sanctioned cemeteries and as such, can be seen as a direct, if ambivalent, product of the state's new efforts for managing the dead through what I call the "work" in paperwork.

One of the most striking things about the cemetery where this tombstone rested was how many of its resident dead, including this man in the Green Card, were actually complete strangers to the people of Longyan whose village provided the land for this site. While this was partly because this state-sanctioned cemetery was meant to serve not only Longyan but the entire rural districts or *jiaoqu* surrounding Fuzhou city, there was also something decidedly unpleasant, eerie and even dangerous about this place to local villagers. This was evident by the cemetery's half-empty gravesites and scarcity of local visitors, not to mention the occasional village rumors of its bad supernatural vibes from the restless ghosts of children whose bones may have been disinterred and discarded to make room for this new site to the warnings of Mazu, goddess of the sea, who purportedly told a villager through a spirit medium that these grounds were haunted and extremely unlucky. Although I never knew whether it was in celebration or in protest that the Green Card was chosen for the tombstone of this dead stranger (figure 1), Longyan villagers certainly would have seen it as quite tragic for someone with overseas status not only to die so young but moreover, to squander the potential benefits of Green Card possession by ending up cremated and interred in this place.

For it was precisely through Green Card possession that villagers had sought to reclaim burial rights for the dead after local enforcement of mandatory cremation began in earnest in 1999. Not unlike China's birth planning policy (Greenhalgh 2003), mandatory cremation in Longyan lead to a proliferation of legal subjectivities and distinctions among the newly departed, producing not only the very legal category of the registered, "planned" dead but also its illicit and exceptional counterparts – the undocumented, "unplanned" dead secretly buried in unmarked graves and the state-exempted, cosmopolitan dead with claims to overseas status and foreign protection from China's demands on their bodies.[6] While overseas connections did not always translate into state privileges under Mao especially during the Cultural Revolution (Fitzgerald 1972), numerous scholars have noted how new Post-Mao policies promoting the rights of overseas Chinese helped revitalized certain ritual activities that had previously been dismissed and criminalized as "superstition" (*mixin*) for local populations (Feuchtwang and Wang 1991; Eng 2006; Lin 1993; Liu 1998; Thuno 2001; 1998; Dean 1993; Woon 1990; Feuchtwang 2001). This included ancestor worship and burial rites, which were often reframed as permissible "custom" among the overseas-connected in order to accommodate the yearnings of many diasporic (and wealthy) Chinese for reconnecting with China through initial visits and investments in the restoration of old graves and ancestral halls in their native homes. In his analysis of death rituals under the PRC, Martin K. Whyte even suggested that "Overseas Chinese" – that is, both returnees from abroad and those with kin overseas – have been permitted the special right "to select burial rather than cremation" ever since 1949 (1990, p. 196). Yet though I was well aware of the Post-Mao policy for courting overseas Chinese interest and investment through preferential treatment of them and their dependents (*qiaojuan*) in mainland China (Woon 1990; Wang 1985; Nyíri 2002; Barabantseva 2005; Thuno 2001), it was not until Zhu Huarong first approached me with her mother's Green Card application that I realized how such state privileges for the overseas-connected could extend beyond living relatives to their aspiring ancestors and the newly dead.

Departing China

It did not surprise me when Zhu Huarong first pulled out a crisp INS[7] envelope during her visit to my village residence one March evening in 2001. As the resi-

6 Chinese Muslims, Tibetans and other state-recognized ethnic minorities are also exempt from mandatory cremation. In fact, burial rights of ethnic minorities are reiterated in national legal provisions on the rights of minority groups and as such, can be said to be more uniformly recognized by the state than the claims of exemption among the overseas-connected, which are probably recognized by officials only at the regional or local level in rural Fuzhou.

7 Since my field research in 2000-2002, the U.S. Immigration and Naturalization Service (INS) has been completely reorganized with its functions divided between several different administrative units including ICE (Immigration and Customs Enforcement) and

dent "American" in the village – a bona fide *sidising* (Fuzhounese for U.S. citizen) among would-be U.S. migrants – I was used to having friends, acquaintances and even strangers in Longyan thrust a variety of immigration-related paperwork into my hands: form letters acknowledging applications received and pending; thick packets of forms to be completed; long checklists of additional documents to assemble; return envelopes and postcards; passport photographs and health records; photocopies of tax returns, citizenship certificates and long-distance phone bills from sponsors overseas. Mostly, people simply wanted me to translate the English text on the various immigration documents they received from overseas. Often they sought me out not as their primary translator but as someone to reread paperwork others had already explained to them, as if through these recursive acts of translation, they could better verify the "real" in their documents and in turn, assure themselves of the true status of their applications. Occasionally, like Zhu Huarong, they also hoped that I could lend them my penmanship to help fill in some basic immigration forms.

I had known Zhu Huarong for a good three months before she came by my place with a letter from the U.S. National Visa Center in tow. Nine months before we met, Zhu Huarong's nineteen year-old daughter had successfully entered the U.S. on a temporary travel visa. Though the daughter was currently flitting around the New York tri-state area as an undocumented and underemployed migrant, her emigration had largely relieved Zhu Huarong and her husband of the social expectation and mounting pressure for going abroad themselves. With a working-age child now overseas to send remittances home, the 44 year-old Zhu Huarong thought of herself as "already old" and ready for retirement in Longyan. Given that she had never mentioned any desire for going abroad, I was not surprised when Zhu Huarong told me that the INS letter she had in her hands was for another family member. Though, I would have guessed that the most likely candidate for emigration was Zhu Huarong's seventeen-year old son who was on the verge of graduating from middle school with few prospects for further education or decent employment opportunities in Fuzhou.

There were certain moments in the life cycle, such as one's coming of age and emergence as head of household, which I had come to associate with yearnings for the Green Card in Longyan. Such expectations were quickly derailed when Zhu Huarong revealed that it was actually her elderly mother who was hoping for a Green Card in this case. Zhu Huarong's mother, Chen Xiuyang, turned out to be a Green Card applicant unlike any of the working-age villagers who, up until that point, had been the main people asking me for help with their immigration paperwork. A small frail woman with a stooped back and milky eyes,

CIS (Customs and Immigration Services) – both of which are now housed under the new post-9/11 Department of Homeland Security. I refer to "INS" in this paper because this was still the extant administrative unit for U.S. immigration at the time of my research.

Chen Xiuyang first greeted me in Zhu Huarong's kitchen by enthusiastically grasping my hand with both of hers after making a painstakingly slow entrance into the room on a knobby wooden cane. Clutching my hand turned out to be not only a gesture of gratitude on Chen Xiuyang's part but also, as I quickly realized, a way for her to familiarize herself with me through touch since her eyesight was failing her in old age. Almost blind and barely mobile, this 82-year old woman could hardly be seen as the typical aspiring Fuzhounese migrant, responding to the "push-pull" of labor markets by following the flows of capital overseas. Nor was she drawn to the national mythos of "the American Dream" by aspiring for the good life abroad. In fact, Chen Xiuyang confessed that she had neither intentions for ever moving to the U.S. nor for visiting there at all since on her one and only trip to see her son in New York, she had a thoroughly isolating and terrible time. There had been nothing to do there, she complained, when her son and everyone else she knew had to go to work their long shifts at restaurants, garment factories and what not. While in the village there were always neighbors and friends she could visit, in the U.S. she found herself perpetually alone and stuck in her son's cramped apartment with the television blaring sights and sounds she could not even make out. No, America was definitely not for her, she told me with a little shrug and sad shake of the head.

Instead, Chen Xiuyang hoped that Green Card possession would enable her to reach another destination altogether by helping her to secure burial rights (and *rites*) for a smooth and prosperous transition from death to the afterlife. As I discovered when other elderly villagers showed up at my doorstep with their own Green Card applications in hand, Chen Xiuyang was not alone in her quest to circumvent mandatory cremation, which most seniors vaguely described as a sacrilegious and harmful practice which threatened the proper passage of the dead from this world to the next. As in other Chinese communities where popular religion was widespread (de Groot 1972; Rawski et al. 1988; Ahern 1973; Weller 1987; Feuchtwang 1974; Doolittle 1865), people in Longyan described the initial period after death as an uncertain and daunting journey to the gates of purgatory, a time when the spirit often lingered between worlds neither completely free of the corpse nor the entrapments of this-worldly life. As Chen Xiuyang explained, the newly dead did not even know that they were no longer among the living during the first seven days after they had expired. In fact, mourners during this initial period typically went through the motion of attempting to call the spirit back to the body as a traditional nod to the Chinese notion that "death is by no means absolute, but may, like other insensibilities, be only temporary" (de Groot, p. 29). It was only after the initial seven days and nights, Chen Xiuyang continued, when the spirit of the deceased finally crossed over a bridge between the worlds that s/he came to the realization of his/her own death.

To get to this point though, the spirit required a specific series of ritual interventions by the living to help steer the dead on the right path towards judgment in the ten courts of hell and eventually, to reincarnation and rebirth (Teiser 1993; on the structuring of hell, see Eberhard 1967; Orzech, 1994). This included providing the dead with sustenance for his/her journey through daily food offerings and moreover, protection from demons and ghosts through payments of spirit money and the ritual chanting of hired specialists. Without such human care and intervention (as was the fate of strangers with no kin), the deceased was bound to become lost in limbo between the worlds as a wandering and hungry ghost (Wolf 1978; Feuchtwang, 1974). Such an outcome was not only tragic for the dead but also hazardous to the living, who had to contend with the negative effects of the displaced, desperate and often vengeful spirits still lingering in this world.

Since the demand for sending the dead to state crematoriums disrupted the customary sequence of ritual practices for directing the newly dead to the afterlife, villagers like Chen Xiuyang feared that this policy would also convert promising ancestors into hopeless and threatening ghosts. Additionally, there was widespread fear among seniors that cremation itself would "feel like dying twice" by doing violence to bodies not quite purged of the spirit of the newly dead. On top of these concerns, rumors also circulated of state negligence and improper handling of ashes involving not only mix-ups of human remains but also the contamination of animal remains and other non-human debris with the ashes of loved ones – all of which were believed to have dislocating and disturbing effects on the spirit of the dead.

In fact, the state demand for cremation seemed so unacceptable to villagers that when this policy was first announced in Longyan, people claimed that some ailing seniors committed suicide and in the most miraculous cases, willed their own timely deaths so that they could be properly put to rest before the official launch of mandatory cremation. Chen Xiuyang's own husband had passed away just a couple days before the new policy went into effect. This was not simply luck or coincidence. Rather, as Zhu Huarong told me, her father who was already ill at the time, had deliberately expedited his own death so he could be buried instead of cremated. For those who missed this small window between the policy's announcement and its enforcement, the one alternative to wholesale defiance of the policy through secret burials of the unregistered dead was to claim exemption as a subject under the rule and protection of a foreign state. As Old Man Liu, my self-proclaimed godfather in Longyan told me, "If you have *shenfen* elsewhere, then the government can't drag you to be burned."

Green Card possession, in this sense, was highly desirable because it enabled the elderly to claim the U.S. not only as their official residence but more importantly, as an alternative point of departure for exiting not just China but the entire world of the living, so that when they passed on they could trump the Chinese state's demands for "dragging" the newly dead through state crematoriums on their way to the afterlife. As villagers like Chen Xiuyang knew, with the proper papers peasant subjects seen as part of the unproductive rural surplus of the nation could be repositioned as highly desirable overseas Chinese; subjects whose economic investments and national loyalties to China were to be encouraged through such measures as the loosening of state regulation over their ritual practices. So long as one could obtain the right *shenfen*, the same burial practices denounced as "feudal superstition" among peasant subjects could be recoded as "traditional custom" to be respected under state policies for returning overseas Chinese. In turn, even without physical relocation overseas, becoming a Green Card holder could help reconstitute the spatial-temporal order of village lives by enabling some like Chen Xiuyang to challenge the Chinese state's efforts for monopolizing the meaningful terms and expected trajectories of life, death and personhood.

The "Work" in Paperwork

Why the Green Card, in particular, became the *shenfen* of choice for the newly dead requires that we look specifically at the productive "friction" (Tsing 2005) and unexpected conjuncture of Chinese population politics, U.S. immigration agendas and Fuzhounese cosmology – all of which were brought into awkward alignment through the mediation of paperwork. Pragmatically speaking, reclaiming rights of the dead demanded villagers' attention to what Bruno Latour (1986) has described as the "power of papershuffling." For as far as village elders were concerned, avoiding cremation was a matter of pitting one ID and its paper regime against the claims of another. Just as new Chinese demands for proof of cremation aimed to produce a more economically "rational" and "quality" (*suzhi*) population in Post-Mao China, Green Card applications were also meant to incite a certain productive body as imagined through U.S. immigration policies. Although most seniors in Longyan could point to relatives overseas, only those lucky enough to have adult children with legal U.S. status could imagine becoming the state-exempted, privileged dead with the capacity to chart their own route to the afterlife. For it was only through the privileged U.S. program for family reunification[8], which gave the spouses, minor children and parents of

---

8 Spouses, minor children and parents of adult U.S. citizens are the only groups whose emigration to the U.S. and access to U.S. visas are not numerically restricted by U.S. immigration law. Additionally, 480,000 visas annually are set aside for adult children and siblings of U.S. citizens and for spouses or unmarried children of permanent residents to reunite with immediate family in the U.S. Altogether, according to the Migration Policy Institute, the U.S. family reunification program accounts for about two-thirds of permanent immigration each year. While immediate kin no doubt comprise the most privileged category for emigration to the U.S., it must be noted that immigration via family reunification has become more difficult in recent years with more restrictive U.S. laws such as the 1996 Illegal Immigration reform and Immigrant Responsibility Act (IIRIRA), which among other things reject family ties as a rationale for stay of deportation, and on the bureaucratic logistical end, with the immigration authority facing an application backlog of 3.9 million since 2001.

adult U.S. citizens priority to emigrate, that village elders could even contemplate possessing the Green Card in the first place. So although most seniors in Longyan could point to relatives overseas, only those lucky enough to have adult children with legal U.S. status could imagine becoming the state-exempted, privileged dead with the capacity to chart their own route to the afterlife.

It was not enough, however, to be the parent of an adult U.S. citizen. For one thing, no application for the Green Card could be initiated without seniors first *mobilizing* their children overseas to file a petition on their behalf as their U.S. sponsor. Nor could applications be completed without further transnational coordination with sponsors for gathering the personal data and supporting paperwork of both parties into one single application file (figure 2).

Figure 2: Form I-130 from the U.S. Green Card application demanding personal data from both sponsor and applicant

B. Information about you.	**C. Information about your relative.**
1. **Name** (Family name in CAPS) (First) (Middle)	1. **Name** (Family name in CAPS) (First) (Middle)
2. **Address** (Number and Street) (Apt.No.)	2. **Address** (Number and Street) (Apt. No.)
(Town or City) (State/Country) (Zip/Postal Code)	(Town or City) (State/Country) (Zip/Postal Code)
3. **Place of Birth** (Town or City) (State/Country)	3. **Place of Birth** (Town or City) (State/Country)
4. **Date of Birth** (mm/dd/yyyy) 5. **Gender** ☐ Male ☐ Female 6. **Marital Status** ☐ Married ☐ Single ☐ Widowed ☐ Divorced	4. **Date of Birth** (mm/dd/yyyy) 5. **Gender** ☐ Male ☐ Female 6. **Marital Status** ☐ Married ☐ Single ☐ Widowed ☐ Divorced

In fact, the very pragmatics of paperwork demanded not only proof of an active transnational connection and kinship tie between applicant and sponsor but more importantly, demonstrations of certain normative desires and capacities by both parties for reuniting as U.S. subjects. Take, for instance, a form like the "Affidavit of Support" (figure 3), which required the sponsor to prove both his/her financial means and personal willingness for keeping the applicant from becoming a state burden. Here through demands for demonstrations of social bonds via financial commitments, one can glimpse U.S. ideals and interests for producing subjects who were not only fiscally solvent but also well situated as productive members of localized, nuclear family units to be assimilated and "naturalized" within the territorial nation.

Ultimately, it was also through their engagements with paperwork that village seniors sought to resituate themselves in an alternative cosmology of value and in turn, destabilize ID's ontological and disciplinary claims on bodies within both Chinese population politics and the U.S. program for family reunification. In fact, one did not need to look further than the very mundane practices of inscription – such as the filling in of personal data on forms – to encounter the productive "friction" embedded in villagers' pursuit of Green Cards for the dead.

Figure 3: Items of Sponsor's Sworn Deposition on I-134, Affadavit of Support

b. If a United States citizen through parent(s) or marriage, give citizenship certificate number ____________

c. If United States citizenship was derived by some other method, attach a statement of explanation.

d. If a lawfully admitted permanent resident of the United States, give "A" number ____________

2. That I am ______ years of age and have resided in the United States since (date) ____________

3. That this affidavit is executed on behalf of the following person:

Name (Family Name)	(First Name)	(Middle Name)	Gender	Age

Citizen of (Country)	Marital Status	Relationship to Sponsor

Presently resides at (Street and Number)	(City)	(State)	(Country)

Name of spouse and children accompanying or following to join person:

Completing immigration forms always provided occasions in Longyan for reflecting on the past and for anticipating the future (cf. Miyazaki 2006). It was also typically a group affair that pulled together the reading, writing, interpretive and networking contributions of multiple people, despite the form's usual incitement of the single applicant as the author of the task. Even on the simplest forms, there were often a few empty spaces that defied easy inscription without some discussion, coordination and consensus with others. Chen Xiuyang, for instance, could barely get past the blanks for her surname and first name without encountering problems with the initial "Biographic Data" form of her Green Card application. In fact, we had only reached the space for date of birth when Chen Xiuyang was already stumped and had to dispatch her daughters to look for the answers by searching for her official Chinese documents around the house. As she explained to me while her daughters rummaged for her papers, she simply could not recall her official biographical details offhand because her Chinese identification documents were so full of wrong information about her. After retrieving Chen Xiuyang's various papers, Zhu Huarong and her sister tried to point out all the bits of their mother's biography that had been carelessly recorded and reproduced from one identifying document to another by Chinese bureaucrats and state agents over the years. Here was that birthday more than two months off. Here was her education level listed as high school graduate though she had never attended high school. Nobody had ever bothered to check if the information was wrong or right, Zhu Huarong shrugged. "No one ever asked me", Chen Xiuyang interjected.

Having to fill in an official yet fictive birthday on her application was one way in which Chen Xiuyang highlighted the radical alterity embedded in IDs and their paper trails. In this case, form filling provided an opportunity for Chen Xiuyang and her daughters to reflect on the gaps and tensions between various parts of the person as officially documented and as collectively remembered. In turn, it allows us to see how elderly villagers like Chen Xiuyang could come to embrace *shenfen* such as the Green Card as more than simply an ontological entitlement of "natural" subjects in the national order of things, but as an *achievement* grounded in savvy mobilization of a network of allies that not only linked adult U.S. citizens to their Chinese parents in Longyan but more importantly, the filial living to their beloved dead.

Needless to say, the Green Card application's incitement of family reunification between sponsor and applicant could hardly account for the kind of future Chen Xiuyang aspired for at the end of her bureaucratic journey through U.S. immigration control. While Chen Xiuyang certainly recognized the importance of family, particularly of her son overseas, for remaking her identification and her future as a Green Card holder, it is worth noting how little her son's actual U.S. residence had to do with Chen Xiuyang's ultimate goal for "reunification" and "resettlement", which she only hoped to achieve post-mortem after leaving this world for the next. Becoming properly situated as an ancestor in the afterlife was, after all, centrally about reconnecting the related living and the dead; it prevented the spirit of the newly departed from becoming lost and estranged from their kin as threatening and hungry ghosts. Though not a guarantee by itself, Green Card possession promised to help secure the path to such "family reunification" in the afterlife by protecting the newly departed from the dislocating effects of passing through state crematoriums in China. That the bureaucratic form could not imagine the applicant's destination beyond a U.S. address was in no ways a barrier to Chen Xiuyang's aspirations for the good afterlife as an ancestor reunited with the filial living. If anything, Chen Xiuyang's capacity to shift the terms of personhood and kinship beyond the biopolitics of life depended on the persistence of such alterity in IDs and their paper trails.

Claiming Personhood and Rights in the Afterlife?

One aim of this paper has been to offer a critical appraisal of the facticity of state identification and its usual associations with ontology and entitlement. In some ways, IDs are not unlike newspapers as a mediator of the "imagined community" of the nation (Anderson 1991 [1983]). IDs can be wielded as instruments of state control to reinscribe the limits of a nation's embrace of its population. Yet as my case shows, IDs can also move beyond the bureaucratic and policing domains of the state, be it China or the U.S., to take on differential values and effects. The Green Card, like any other state identification, can take on a social life of its own (Appadurai 1986).

Nonetheless, there is still a powerful line of thinking following Weber (1968) to Foucault (1979; 1991) to Agamben (1998; 2005) that would have us believe that bureaucratic networks of writing and documents only work to rationalize bodies as legible, biopolitical objects of "the population" to be managed in the delimited and disenchanted sphere of this-worldly life.[13] While certainly the aims of both China's mandatory cremation policy and the U.S. Green Card application conjure such fantasies of state governmentality, Fuzhounese struggles over the trajectories of IDs and bodies also demand attention to a broader and perhaps more longstanding kind of politics and politicized life – a life *after* "life itself" – that was both distinct from yet still intimately entangled with modern formations of biopower. In this case, through their maneuverings for the right paperwork to ensure the transition of persons from corporeal life to a good afterlife, elderly applicants suggested that what was at stake in IDs was not just the biopolitical subject of reproductive and economic value but also, what we might think of as the *cosmo*-political subject of karmic credit and rebirth.

At the intersection of human rights and population politics, what this Fuzhounese case best enables us to see are the epistemological and ontological limitations of "the human" as the Archimedian point for thinking about persons, their aspirational pursuits and their claims to rights. At the same time, it also shows how population management can enable other-worldly agendas beyond the life-enhancing aims of state biopolitics. As such, elderly desires for the Green Card in Longyan simultaneously highlight and disturb the conventional boundaries of modern juridical notions of "natural rights" which delimit political recognition of personhood to the zone of the living, whether that "person" is imagined as the sovereign, self-owning human being in human rights discourse or as the biopolitical citizen-subject under the care and regulation of nation-states (Asad 2003, pp. 127-158).

This, however, is not an argument for privileging some discrete "local" way of seeking political recognition against the hegemonies of state regulation and human rights practice. If anything, IDs mediation of these claims on the newly dead body in Fuzhou pointed less to the mutual opposition of Fuzhounese cosmology and state or human rights agendas than to their *interpenetration* as regimes of value. The fact that state population policies could lead to new social distinctions among the dead or that cremated remains could be memorialized through the U.S. Green Card highlighted such ongoing entanglements of bio- and cosmo-politics in the reproduction of persons and kinship ties among the Fuzhounese. Paperwork may have helped obscure the messiness of these unfinished struggles over the valuation of bodies and lives, but it did not erase such struggles altogether. If anything, the very "work" in paperwork made it possible to accommodate the divergent claims to both a secular-rational *and* a karmic order by bracketing off official complicities and village interests in the good afterlife from the legible enactments and markers of the good citizen-subject.

References

2002 China's Aging Population is Expanding Fast. *Renmin Ribao (People's Daily)*, 15 August, Available in English at http://english.peopledaily.com.cn/200208/15/eng20020815_101491.shtml (Accessed September 18, 2008)

Agamben, Giorgio. 1998. *Homo Sacer: Sovereign Power and Bare Life*. Stanford: Stanford University Press.

– 2005. *State of Exception*. Chicago: University of Chicago Press.

Ahern, Emily M. 1973. *The Cult of the Dead in a Chinese Village.*, Stanford, Calif.: Stanford University Press.

Anderson, Benedict. 1991 [1983]. *Imagined Communities: Reflections on the Origin and Spread of Nationalism*. London: Verso.

Appadurai, Arjun. 1986. *The Social Life of Things: Commodities in Cultural Perspective*. Cambridge: Cambridge University Press.

Asad, Talal. 2003. *Formations of the Secular: Christianity, Islam, Modernity*. Stanford, CA: Stanford University Press.

Barabantseva, Elena. 2005. Trans-nationalising Chineseness: Overseas Chinese Policies of the PRC's Central Government. *ASIEN* 96 (July), pp. 7-28.

Bruun, Ole. 1996. The Fengshui Resurgence in China: Conflicting Cosmologies between State and Peasantry. *The China Journal* 36 (July), pp. 47-65.

Caplan, Jane and John C. Torpey. 2001. *Documenting Individual Identity: the Development of State Practices in the Modern World*. Princeton, N.J.: Princeton University Press.

Chavez, Leo. 1992. *Shadowed Lives: Undocumented Immigrants in American Society*. Ft. Worth: Hartcourt, Brace and Jovanovich College Publishers.

Cheater, A. P. 1991. Death Ritual as Political Trickster in the People's Republic of China. *The Australian Journal of Chinese Affairs*. 26, pp. 67-97.

Chin, Ko-Lin. 1999. *Smuggled Chinese: Clandestine Immigration to the United States*. Philadelphia: Temple University Press.

– 2001. "The Social Organization of Chinese Human Smuggling." In D. Kyle and R. Koslowski, eds. *Global Human Smuggling: Comparative Perspectives*. Baltimore, MD: The John Hopkins University Press, pp. 216-235.

Coutin, Susan B. 2000. *Legalizing Moves: Salvadoran Immigrants' Struggle for U.S. Residency*. Ann Arbor: University of Michigan Press.

de Groot, J. J. M. 1972. *The Religious System of China,* Taipei: Ch'eng Wen Publishing Company.

Dean, Kenneth. 1993. *Taoist Ritual and Popular Cults of Southeast China*. Princeton, N.J.: Princeton University Press.

– 1998. *Lord of the Three in One: the Spread of a Cult in Southeast China*. Princeton, N.J.: Princeton University Press.

Doolittle, Justus. 1865. *Social Life of the Chinese: with some Account of their Religious, Governmental, Educational, and Business Customs and Opinions:*

with Special but not Exclusive Reference to Fuhchau. New York: Harper & Brothers.

Eberhard, Wolfram. 1967. *Guilt and Sin in Traditional China.* Berkeley: University of California Press.

Eng, Kuah-Pearce Khun. 2006. "The Worship of Qingshui Zushi and Religious Revivalism in South China." In C. B. Tan, ed. *Southern Fujian: Reproduction of Traditions in Post-Mao China.* Hong Kong: The Chinese University Press, pp. 121-144.

Faison, Seth. February 24, 1997. "Donation of Organs is Unusual in China." *The New York Times.*

Feuchtwang, Stephan. 1974. "Domestic and Communal Worship in Taiwan." In A. P. Wolf, ed. *Religion and Ritual in Chinese Society.* Stanford: Stanford University Press, pp. 105-130.

– 2001. *Popular Religion in China: The Imperial Metaphor.* Richmond, Surrey: Curzon Press.

Feuchtwang, Stephan and Ming-ming Wang. 1991. The Politics of Culture or a Contest of Histories: Representations of Chines Popular Religion. *Dialectical Anthropology.* 16, pp. 251-272.

Fitzgerald, Stephen. 1972. *China and the Overseas Chinese; a Study of Peking's Changing Policy, 1949-1970.* Cambridge [Eng.]: University Press.

Foucault, Michel. 1979. *Discipline and Punish: the Birth of the Prison.* New York: Vintage Books.

– 1991. "Governmentality." In G. Burchell, C. Gordon, and P. Miller, eds. *The Foucault Effect: Studies in Governmentality: with Two Lectures by and an Interview with Michel Foucault.* Chicago: University of Chicago Press, pp. 87-104.

Greenhalgh, Susan. 2003. Planned Births, Unplanned Persons: "Population" in the Making of Chinese Modernity. *American Ethnologist.* 30 (2), pp. 196-215.

Guest, Kenneth J. 2003. *God in Chinatown: Religion and Survival in New York's Evolving Immigrant Community.* New York: New York University Press.

Kaufman, Sharon R. and Lynn M. Morgan. 2005. The Anthropology of the Beginnings and Ends of Life. *The Annual Review of Anthropology.* 34, pp. 317-41.

Kumar, Amitava. 2000. *Passport Photos.* Berkeley: University of California Press.

Kwong, Peter. 1997. *Forbidden Workers: Illegal Chinese Immigrants and American Labor.* New York: The New Press.

– 2001. "Impact of Chinese Human Smuggling on the American Labor Market." In D. Kyle and R. Koslowski, eds. *Global Human Smuggling: Comparative Perspectives.* Baltimore, MD: The John Hopkins University Press, pp. 235-256.

Kyle, David and Rey Koslowski. 2001. *Global Human Smuggling: Comparative Perspectives.* Baltimore: Johns Hopkins University Press.

Latour, Bruno. 1986. Visualisation and Cognition: Thinking with Eyes and Hands. *Knowledge and Society.* 6, pp. 1-40.

Latour, Bruno and Steve Woolgar. [1979] 1986. *Laboratory Life: The Construction of Scientific Facts.,* Princeton: Princeton University Press.

Li, Lianjiang and Kevin J. O'Brien. 1996. Villagers and Popular Resistance in Contemporary China. *Modern China.* 22 (1), pp. 28-61.

Liang, Zai and Wenzhen Ye. 2001. "From Fujian to New York: Understanding the New Chinese Immigration." In D. Kyle and R. Koslowski, eds. *Global Human Smuggling: Comparative Perspectives.* Baltimore, MD: The John Hopkins University Press, pp. 187-216.

Lin, Guoping. 1993. *Fujian Popular Beliefs.* Fuzhou, China: Fujian People's Press.

Liu, Hong. 1998. Old Linkages, New Networks: The Globalization of Overseas Chinese Voluntary Associations and its Implications. *The China Quarterly.* 155 (Sept. 1998), pp. 582-609.

Mahler, Sarah. 1992. *American Dreaming: Immigrant Life on the Margins.* Princeton, NJ: Princeton University Press.

Malkki, Liisa. 1995. Refugees and Exile: From "Refugee Studies" to the National Order of Things. *Annual Review of Anthropology.* 24, pp. 495-523.

Miyazaki, Hirokazu. 2006. "Documenting the Present." In A. Riles, ed. *Documents: Artifacts of Modern Knowledge.* Ann Arbor: University of Michigan Press, pp. 206-226.

National Commission on Terrorist Attacks upon the United States. 2004. *The 9/11 Commission Report.* New York: W. W. Norton & Company.

Nyíri, Pál. 2002. "From Class Enemies to Patriots: Overseas Chinese and Emigration Policy and Discourse in the People's Republic of China." In P. Nyíri and I. R. Saveliev, eds. *Global Chinese Migration: Trends in Europe and Asia.* Aldershot, Hampshire, England; Burlington, VT: Ashgate, pp. 208-241.

Ong, Aihwa. 1999. *Flexible Citizenship: The Cultural Logics of Transnationality.* Durham, NC: Duke University Press.

Orzech, Charles D. 1994. Mechanisms of Violent Retribution in Chinese Hell Narratives. *Contagion: Journal of Violence, Mimesis, and Culture* 1 (Spring, 1994), pp. 111-126.

Petryna, Adriana. 2002. *Life exposed: Biological Citizens after Chernobyl.* Princeton, NJ: Princeton University Press.

Rawski, Evelyn Sakakida, Watson, James L. and Joint Committee on Chinese Studies (U.S.). 1988. *Death Ritual in Late Imperial and Modern China,* Berkeley: University of California Press.

Smith, Paul J. 1994. The Strategic Implications of Chinese Emigration. *Survival* 36 (2), pp. 60-77.

Smith, Paul J., ed. 1997. *Human Smuggling: Chinese Migrant Trafficking and the Challenge to America's Immigration Tradition.* Washington D.C.: The Center for Strategic and International Studies.

Teather, Elizabeth K. 1999. High-Rise Homes for the Ancestors: Cremation in Hong Kong. *Geographical Review* 89 (3), pp. 409-430.

Teiser, Stephen F. 1993. "The Growth of Purgatory." In P. Ebrey and P. N. Gregory, eds. *Religion and Society in T'ang and Sung China*. Honolulu: University of Hawaii Press, pp. 115-146.

Thuno, Mette. 2001. Reaching out and Incorporating Chinese Overseas: The Transterritorial Scope of the PRC by the end of the 20th Century. *China Quarterly.* 168 (Dec. 2001), pp. 910-929.

Torpey, John. 2000. *The Invention of the Passport: Surveillance, Citizenship and the State.* Cambridge, UK: Cambridge University Press.

Tsing, Anna. 2005. *Friction: An Ethnography of Global Connection,* Princeton: Princeton University Press.

Wang, Gungwu. 1985. External China as a New Policy Area. *Pacific Affairs* 58 (1), pp. 28-43.

Weber, Max. 1968. "Bureaucracy." In *On Charisma and Institution Building.* Chicago: Chicago University Press, pp. 66-77.

Weller, Robert P. 1987. *Unities and Diversities in Chinese Religion.* Seattle: University of Washington Press.

Wolf, Arthur P. 1978. "Gods, Ghosts, and Ancestors." In A. P. Wolf and E. M. Ahern, eds. *Studies in Chinese Society.* Stanford, Calif.: Stanford University Press, pp. 103-130.

Woon, Yuen-Fong. 1990. "International Links and Socioeconomic Development of Rural China: An Emigrant Community in Guangdong." *Modern China* 16 (2), pp. 139-172.

Yngvesson, Barbara and Susan B. Coutin. 2006. Backed by Papers: Undoing Persons, Histories, and Return. *American Ethnologist* 33 (2), pp. 177-190.

Part 3

Reproductive Politics as Religious and National Icons

Chapter 10

Population Policy in the Islamic Republic of Iran

Homa Hoodfar

Introduction

Iran, in contrast to its regional counterparts such as Turkey and Egypt, embarked rather late in concerning itself with population issues. The first official family planning policy was introduced in 1967. The inattention to family planning stemmed from a lack of appreciation of the importance of population issues rather than from any official desire for continued population growth. In fact, Iran has been experiencing a rapid population growth since the turn of the century, from 10 million inhabitants in 1900 to 33.7 million in 1976, 59.5 million in 1996 and 70.4 million in 2007.[1]

The 1967 family planning program primarily targeted the urban population and focused on women as its main recipients, even though many traditional contraceptive methods (notably coitus interruptus or condom use) are male-oriented. The program, devised under Mohammad Reza Shah Pahlavi's aegis, was followed by a number of limited improvements in women's legal status, notably the introduction of a Family Protection Law which curbed men's unilateral right to divorce at will and limited the practice of polygamy by requiring court authorization or the first wife's permission (Sansarian 1982; Aghajanian 1991b; Aghajanian 1996). More importantly, child custody following divorce was to be decided in the child's best interest rather than by traditional precedent, which denied custody (except of infants) to divorced mothers (Mir-Hosseini 1993). On the whole these modest reforms presented the most significant improvement in the legal position of women in twentieth-century Iran and aroused strong opposition (Paider 1995; Sanasarian 1982).

Both the family planning program and the reform of family and divorce laws were sharply criticized by the conservative and religious opposition, notably Ayatollah Khomeini (Algar 1981). Many religious leaders used their Friday sermons to condemn family planning as an imperialist plot to reduce the number of Muslims and subjugate Muslim countries. Although historically contraception had been permitted in Islam, following the introduction of the Shah's program many religious leaders denounced it as *haram* (religiously not permitted).[2]

---

1 Statistical Centre of Iran.

2 This is despite the fact that there had been some formal attempt by the government to have religious authorities in Qum pronounce the use of contraception permissable.

The success of the revolution in 1979 and the establishment of the Islamic Republic left the family planning program in shambles (Hoodfar 1995). The country's new leaders continued to view the program as an imperialist tool for maintaining Western dominance over the "Third World", and in particular, its Muslim populations. For a short period, there was some confusion over whether drugstores could continue to sell contraceptive pills, since some religious leaders had pronounced them un-Islamic. This situation promoted the development of a black market in contraceptives in major cities where demand remained relatively high. However, after some public debate, religious authorities conceded that there was no religious impediment to the use of contraceptives. Nonetheless, supplies continued to be erratic and prices skyrocketed.[3]The family planning board was dismantled and employees of family planning clinics were transferred to other sectors, notably school health visits.

The Approach to Development

The early years of the Islamic state were largely consumed with establishing and stabilizing the new regime by eliminating oppositional groups and consolidating the regime's ideological position on economic and social matters. This process was especially difficult as the new political leadership was composed primarily of independent religious leaders with little political experience.

The emerging consensus on development approaches differed fundamentally from that of the Shah's regime, which had essentially followed the trickle-down theory and had concentrated on the urban middle classes and developing an urban economy through oil revenues. The Shah's introduction of land reform not only markedly altered rural structures but also induced a rapid rate of urbanization (Haliday 1979; Loony 1982). In contrast, the Islamic Republic gave priority to meeting the population's most basic needs, striving to avoid alienating the poor and less privileged who constituted the Islamic regime's major constituency. Moreover, conscious that the rural population remained apprehensive about the new government,[4] the Islamic regime directed substantial effort to securing their support. These tasks were rendered particularly arduous during and after the economic and emotional hardships imposed on the nation by the Iran-Iraq war of 1981-88.

---

3 Although a considerable amount of contraceptive pills were distributed by the Ministry of Health to low-income women who requested them. Research data however indicated that high market prices encouraged women to re-sell their oral contraceptives and other medications in order to supplement their incomes. Nonetheless, this indicates that demands remained high during these years (Ladier-Fouladi 1996).

4 Due in part to the fact that together, the religious authorities owned or controlled more than one fifth of the best arable land in Iran, and had thus opposed the Shah's land reform policies (1963), which was all that the peasantry had gained during the Pahlavi era.

The Islamic government identified three major channels through which it tried to reach the less-privileged segments of society: the provision of basic foodstuffs, the availability of basic health care, and access to education. Clearly, the government could not sustain this approach for an extended period for a population growing as fast as in Iran at that time.

The expansion of Islamic education was an immediate preoccupation of the regime. The government viewed education as a vehicle for disseminating its ideology and counteracting the westernized worldview promoted by the previous regime. Thus, primary school manuals were quickly revised, and within a few months after their ascendance to power, a substantial amount of religious material was added to the curricula. With the help of volunteers and committed personnel, new schools were established in rural areas.[5] Although there was some debate about gender-specific education for boys and girls which caused critics to anticipate negative consequences for female students, the Islamic regime has been fairly active in encouraging parents to send daughters to school (Mehran 1991; UNICEF 1995). These efforts disarmed many parents who previously opposed female education on religious grounds, and they increased social pressure to educate daughters. Moreover, a successful adult literacy campaign was launched with the noteworthy effect that the classes attracted more women than men (Mehran 1991 and 1992).[6] The net result has been that the literacy rate for adult males increased from 48 percent in 1970 to 84 percent in 2000 and 88.7 percent in 2007. Female literacy climbed even faster, rising from less than 25 percent in 1970 to more than 70 percent in 2000 and to 80.3 percent in 2007[7]. However, the rapidly increasing school-age population constituted a considerable challenge to the regime's ability to continue providing, much less improving, universal basic education and made many religious leaders conscious of the problems entailed by a rapidly growing population.

Improving universal access to basic health services has been another avenue through which the regime has communicated its commitment to the poor in Iran. The government allocated a substantial segment of its budget to health issues, giving priority to basic health care and mother-and-child health centers. Moreover, the government took advantage of a professional sector that was young and committed to the goals of the revolution, encouraging them to implement an

5 During the early years of the revolution, many young men and women worked in the poorer districts as teachers or nurses for little or no pay, under the auspices of Basiaj (mobilization).

6 As Hoodfar's research (1993-1996) indicates, the flexible class hours particularly in rural areas, as well as the possibility for woman without childcare to bring their children with them to the class, has particularly encouraged many women to participate in the classes.

7 Earth Policy Institute 2001 and Statistical Centre of Iran 2008.

efficient, low-cost health system. Many of the new managers and medical personnel were themselves from smaller towns or had lived outside the major cities and were familiar with the needs of the diverse geographic areas, particularly Iran's more than 40,000 rural villages.[8] The Ministry of Health has in this way developed one of the most fascinating and cost-efficient health delivery networks in the developing world (Shadpour 1994).

The achievements have been commendable. Infant mortality, which at the peak of the oil boom in the 1970s remained higher than Egypt's despite Iran's much greater per capita income, dropped substantially, as did maternal mortality (Table 1). Life expectancy increased, despite the devastating Iran-Iraq war, which consumed a considerable amount of the Health Ministry's budget and personnel. Nonetheless, the Ministries of Education and of Health perceived the rapid population growth as an increasing pressure on the system.

Table 1: Changes in the Health Profile of Iranians

	1974	1984	1990	2006
Infant Mortality Rate	91	51	60	30
Maternal Mortality Rate	–*	140*	120	76
Life expectancy	67.5	67	64.6	71.4

* The gap between rural and urban figures is considerable. Figures for 1974 are not publicly available, but according to the Budget and Planning Organization, the MMR was 120 for urban and 370 for rural areas. Similarly in 1985, the estimates were 77 for urban and 223 for rural. These figures changed to 41 and 138 for 1988, and the gap decreased over time.

Source: Shadpour 1994 and UNFPA and Population Reference Bureau 2008

The new regime had not formulated a population program, though it had pursued a series of pro-natalist policies. Many political leaders viewed a large population as an indicator of strength and a cause for celebration. Early marriage, which the regime viewed as an important tool in its eradication of moral corruption, was encouraged as a solution to many social ills, thus the legal age for marriage was reduced from 18 to 14 for males and from 16 to 9 for females. This law, however, was later amended to require that spouses first reach the age of puberty, which is usually understood to occur at age 13 for women (Kar and Hoodfar 1996).[9] But within two weeks of Ayatollah Khomeini's return to Te-

8 Many Health Ministry employees (as well as some managers) had performed their national service in the Shah's health corps. While young urban men were sent to work in poor and distant villages with little preparation and often against their will, the program did familiarize them with the life-style and problems of the villagers. The program's success emerged after the revolution, as young professionals used their experience to create an efficient health network.

9 But marriages where the bride is only 9 are still not considered illegal.

hran, the Family Protection Law was effectively annulled (Kar and Hoodfar 1996; Mir-Hosseini 1993; Paidar 1995). Polygamous marriages, as well as temporary marriages, in which a man can concurrently marry an unlimited number of women for any length of time agreed upon in advance, were legalized and even encouraged.

Not surprisingly, the fertility level increased rapidly despite such mitigating factors as the Iran-Iraq war, substantial out-migration, and economic uncertainty. The 1986 national survey estimated that the population had reached nearly 50 million, an increase of approximately 16 million in one decade. Even more significant, 45 percent of Iran's population was now under the age of 14.[10] This had a sobering effect on many of the politically astute leaders who realized that a rapid increase in population would create a heavy burden on the limited resources of the country. In addition, the anticipated end to the Iran-Iraq war would lead to even more financial pressures as the government had to rebuild war-torn regions and was expected to fulfil promises which had been postponed during the war.

The rapid population growth and its implications for development were a cause for concern among some political leaders, the Budget and Planning Organization, the Ministries of Health and Education, and nationalists and intellectuals within and outside the government. Yet they were aware that the subject was extremely delicate as many of the present religious leaders had been among the most outspoken enemies of the Shah's population program. The challenge was how to turn about-face without undermining the regime and the credibility of the religious leaders. It was left to the experts and some astute political leaders to pave the way for the introduction of a population control policy. At this stage, a delicately planned mobilization of support was informally launched among the advocates of a new family planning program.

The Debate: Media, Experts and Religious Leaders

Population program advocates devised two broad strategies. First, they sought to generate public support for fertility control and a new family planning program. As the data from the national survey became available, experts and scholars (many of whom were affiliated with the Budget and Planning Organization or universities), initiated a public debate through newspapers and other media. Aware of the influence that public opinion had on the regime and religious leaders, they embarked on writing informative but also provocative articles for the

10 While some population growth can be explained by factors such as improved registration of births and a system of ration cards for subsidized goods, these factors alone cannot account for such a high rate of increase.

national newspapers, pointing out the cost and implications of an increasing and increasingly young population.[11] During 1987/1988 many newspapers regularly published articles about the dangers of over-population for Third World countries in general. These were followed by specific debates on issues concerning Iran's population in which the public was invited to participate (Hoodfar 1995).

Many government ministers, facing growing demand and shrinking budgets, understood the grave consequences of continued population growth for the country. They became willing agents of change and provided material for newspapers pointing out the implications of rapid population growth for their areas of responsibility, such as education, health, food supply, housing and municipal services (particularly public transport). Ordinary people also wrote to express their views, usually in support of the introduction of a family planning policy. Newspapers conducted interviews in the streets of Tehran and other cities on the question of population and family planning issues. "The goal was to make the population issue the talk of the town everywhere, in private and in public. Without considerable public pressure, it would have been impossible to bring the clergy into the population discussion", said one official.

An interesting aspect of this media debate was that individuals (members of the public as well as politicians and intellectuals) who opposed any kind of population control voiced their opinions as well.[12] Advocates of population programs, critics said, must be reminded that the goal should be development and not population reduction, which was interpreted as a misdirection of the nation's efforts. This dialogue served several purposes. Tolerance of criticism allowed the debates to take on a much more democratic form but also reminded the public and experts that population control should be but a small part of the government plan; the major focus was national development and better delivery of services. Nonetheless, by 1988 it was clear that there was substantial support for the introduction of an official family planning policy.

Noteworthy in this stage of debate is the absence of any discussion of the role of family law and women's rights. Articles did not refer to the problems of early marriage, polygamous marriages, and women's insecurity in marriage. The proponents of a new population policy understood these issues were off limits given the enormous weight all political-religious leaders had attached to the "Islamic family."

---

11 Contrary to its image in the West and among Iranian dissidents abroad as a crude dictatorial regime the Islamic Republic, particularly during the 1980's and 1990's gained much of its legitimacy through public support and was thus very sensitive of and responsive to public opinion.

12 See for instance the many interviews with Ayatollah Haj Said Muhammad Hussein Husseini-i Tehrani who also published a book (1415/1993) reiterating his opposition. See also Zan-e-Ruz no. 1416.

The second strategy was to convince top government ideologues of the importance of the population issue. Iran's clergy had been alienated from formal power structures in the twentieth century. In the years prior to the revolution they responded to their exclusion by withdrawing completely from modern science and thus had little appreciation of technical and theoretical advancements in the fields of development and social policy. Several population and development experts mentioned in interviews that there were attempts to draw the political leadership's attention to the population situation immediately after the revolution in 1979, but there was little appreciation then for the subject.

By the late 80's the situation had changed. Many ministers, experts, and policy makers held closed meetings with major religious leaders, particularly those judged to be more open, to inform them of the situation. According to several interviewees, these meetings were accompanied by facts and figures depicting the extent of the country's resources, the possibility of increased economic growth, and the high cost of very rapid population growth. While the experts provided demographic and economic information to the religious leaders, they reiterated that their responsibility was to inform the leaders on scientific questions but that on questions of ethics and social morality they looked to the clergy for guidance. This understanding, along with their common interest in the success of the Islamic government, formed the beginning of a long and successful collaboration in addressing population issues (Hoodfar 1997), and encouraged the clergy to re-examine their position from an Islamic perspective.

In a bold and unprecedented move, two newspapers (*Keyhan* and *Ettelaat)* published a series of eight articles by different officials and scholars and openly invited religious leaders to examine the ethical and religious dimensions of the population issue. While some religious authorities ignored the invitation, others including such conservatives as Ayatollah Azari, Ayatollah Qomi, Hojatolislam Yazdi, Hojatolislam Moqtadari, and Hojatolislam Bayat, agreed to participate. Regardless of their views about the role of the state in promoting family planning, all reiterated that nothing in the rules or scriptures of Islam prohibits the use of contraception and the choice to have fewer children. Furthermore, since context is an inherent part of ethical debate in Islam, all participating clergy found that they had to address the issue in the context of the social and political agenda of the Islamic Republic of Iran.

In 1988, Ayatollah Khamene'i (who later succeeded Ayatollah Khomeini to become Iran's official spiritual leader) discussed the necessity of introducing a family planning program. Shortly thereafter, the Budget and Planning Organization organized a national conference on population policy in Mashhad, the most important religious city in Iran. Following this event, a national birth control program was designed and ratified by Ayatollah Khomeini shortly before his death in 1989.

An Islamic Population Policy

Initially the program was housed by the Ministry of Health which could absorb the program's services in its expanding rural and urban health network, including family and mother–and-child centers. As the program became more complex, a High Council of Population was established that worked under the direction of the Ministry of Health but included deputy ministers from the ministries of education, labour and social affairs, culture and higher education, the Budget and Planning Organization, national broadcasting, the Civil Registration Organization, as well as Islamic guidance.

The making of the Islamic Republic's family planning program has been a prolonged and delicate process balancing various considerations. Policy makers were conscious, as other studies have pointed out, that the leadership's commitment to a family planning program, particularly in its infancy, would be essential to its success (Ibrahim 1995; Jain 1994). It was clear that religious/political leaders would not give their blessing to the program until it left no room for criticism from either religious or socio-economic points of view. The *ulama*, the group of religious leaders whose support was crucial for the program's success, aware that population programs in other Muslim countries had been criticized for poor success, unacceptable quality of services, and lack of respect for individual rights and communal ethical values, would cooperate only if such a move would not undermine the support of the public.

Considerable effort was directed to avoid the impression that the regime saw population control as a solution to its development problems, even though the population discussion remained focused on imbalances between demand (population) and supply (national resources). The family planning program has been presented as crisis management, not as an inherent part of the regime's development program. Religious leaders insisted that the intervention of an Islamic government in population growth can only be justified by social and economic reasons. Thus, once the crisis is over, the justification for such a program is annulled and the intervention of an Islamic government into family planning is to be stopped. This stance on the part of religious ideologues has created tension, since program directors are permanently forced to justify the continued existence and relevance of the campaign for the well-being of the country.

Both camps, the religious leaders and the experts, were committed to a policy that addressed family planning from the individual's and not from the state's perspective; the program should allow couples to decide how many children they desired, rather than serve as a disguised vehicle of population control. It was agreed that an Islamic family planning program should offer services and remedies to couples who experience fertility problems, as well as to those who wish to limit their family size. Thus, the treatment of infertility became a prominent component of Iran's family planning program, and despite the high cost of modern fertility technologies (including artificial insemination), the program has expanded its facilities across the country. The expansion of these facilities, while still falling short of actual demand, has been prominently discussed in the print media. Such media coverage was intended to communicate that Iran's is not a conventional population control program. At the same time, these facilities have provided new opportunities for the *ulama* to provide ethical guidance in this modern era of rapid technological advancement. [13]

The major goal of the program was carefully defined as the prevention of unwanted pregnancies to enable families to improve their physical and social health. This would occur through creating longer spaces between consecutive pregnancies; preventing transmission of genetic diseases; preventing the negative effects of frequent births on the health of mothers and their children; curing infertility; and expanding research in health and social work to facilitate more effective delivery of services.

At this stage, the improvement of the status of women within the family and society was raised explicitly as a vehicle for promoting the success of the family program (Hoodfar 1995; Malek Afzali 1992). This goal emerged out of critical literature on population programs, which encouraged policy makers to be sensitive to a wide array of criticism – including feminist concerns – directed at such programs. However, references to the improvement of the status of women have remained completely theoretical. None of the directors of the program ever addressed power imbalances within the family, despite evidence of their important implications for fertility patterns (Balchin et al 1995; Hoodfar 1996). Program directors have also not adopted policies or engaged in public discussion addressing the economic needs of women, including employment or other forms of economic security within marriage, even though these matters are constantly debated in the print media and women activists have explained the link between women's economic position and their fertility behaviour (Hoodfar 1996).

The only point on which program directors have expressed an intention to improve the status of women and thereby encourage them to limit family size, has been that of raising the legal age for marriage. Such an objective has not succeeded yet. Nonetheless, recognition of the importance of improving the status of women remains a significant change.

The program has managed to retain its democratic nature and, despite much emphasis placed on "two-child families" (often by emphasising the equal value of boys and girls), the government has insisted that the final choice belongs to par-

13 Here ethical questions were touched, raised in the West concerning fertility technologies, including surrogate mothers, artificial insemination from anonymous donors etc. The extensive debate has ensured about the limits of an Islamic ethic in these situations. To date, artificial insemination is permissible only with the husbands consent.

ents. However, in an attempt to coordinate government policies and remove pronatalist structural tendencies, in 1993 the government introduced a bill which suspended maternity privileges and child benefits for government and para-government employees having their fourth or more child. Although the bill had little practical effect because child benefits in Iran are negligible even for poor families, it was a vivid symbolic gesture that generated a flurry of criticism. Many physicians and others who generally supported the population program objected strongly to this measure, stating that such policies would punish the child rather then help reduce population growth. Although the law remains on the books, because of strong opposition its application is erratic at best.

Program directors were aware that their success hinged on building trust between service providers and clients. They adopted a policy of providing high quality products, even if these cost more and would somewhat retard the expansion of the program. It was made a priority to maintain abundant supplies of modern contraceptives such as pills, IUDs, and condoms, and to initiate a workable and cost-efficient distribution system both in cities and in rural areas.

The program managers also adopted the policy of "putting the truth on the table", as one of them put it. Side effects of different methods, particularly the pill and IUD were discussed openly in the print media and on radio and television. Women were advised to find out what was best for them, and the staff of clinics and health centres encouraged this individual approach. Women were often told that there is no such thing as a contraceptive without any side effects. The campaign emphasised that while the health network would try to provide the best information available, ultimately it would be up to the women (as most modern contraceptive methods are directed to them) to monitor their bodies and make their own decisions. In interviews with low-income women in Tehran, the author found that many women turned from private to public clinics, stating that the service they received there was as good as, and sometimes better than, in the private sector.

In advocating particular methods, program directors had to bear in mind the views of the religious authorities. According to them, safe temporary measures met Islamic standards while others (tubal ligation and vasectomy) were particularly problematic. Some of the religious leaders argued that because both tubal ligation and vasectomy would render the individuals *aghim* (sterile), they were not acceptable. Others argued that if the couple concerned already had children, such methods could not be considered *aghim*, but if they did not yet have children they should abstain from those methods. Some of the experts as well as religious groups argued that these methods (particularly vasectomy) are increasingly reversible. These debates were carried out in public as well as behind closed doors, and culminated in the informal consensus to offer these methods only to couples who have three children and/or are over 30 years of age.

Induced abortion has proved the most controversial issue in the debate. Most *ulama* agree that, under some conditions and before ensoulment, abortion is permissible.[14] It has nevertheless remained illegal in Iran, except when the pregnancy is judged to be detrimental to the mental and physical health of the mother. Aware of the controversy surrounding abortion, advocates of the program acknowledged the importance of the abortion issue but resisted being drawn into the debate by announcing that abortion was a health and not a family planning matter. This strategic move avoided a potential area of conflict with religious leaders who have argued that abortion is not an acceptable method of family planning or population control. This had two effects. On the one hand, the regime was able to distinguish its Islamic family planning from other, non-Islamic ones, and on the other hand, it prevented those opposing the program from using abortion as a platform on which to attack the program.[15]

Packaging Islamic Family Planning

Both the experts and religious authorities engaged in a campaign allowing ordinary people to see the complex web in which their very private decisions to have children affect not only their own lives but also the life of the nation. It became clear that the family planning campaign had to continue for some time. Given the Iranian context, the primary constituencies of the program were low-income and rural households. Yet these were precisely the segments of population that the technocratic elite found difficult to reach. In contrast, the religious leaders who were drawn into the population debate had the ability to use the people's idiom to communicate the program's agenda. Low-ranking religious leaders in particular played a decisive role in popularizing the family planning issue. By profession they are skilled orators who traditionally adopt a vernacular style, and they have intimate familiarity with the cultural practices of their local community. This made them indispensable to the consensus-building process, and the significance of their role was frequently recognized. Physicians and nurses explicitly or implicitly acknowledged this. A female staff member at one clinic said,

> It is not very often that I have good things to say about mullahs who have historically been responsible for much of women's misery. But in this case, credit should go to the religious authorities of the country and not just the most promi-

---

14 It is believed that the soul enters the fetus 120 days after conception. Ironically it was Ayatollah Beheshti, an important conservative ideologue of the regime, assassinated in the early years of revolution, who outlined a theological approach to abortion allowing a liberalization of abortion under the Shah in 1973.

15 While the issue of illegal abortion as one of the major causes of maternal health complications and death is recognized by the Ministry of Health, there has not been any attempt to discuss the matter publicly. Nonetheless the authorities are determined to address abortion related concerns within the general health agenda, not as a family planning issue.

> nent ones, but those working in different areas who then took the messages from the high ranking leaders and put this into the context of the daily life of the local people and communicated the debates and information to the people around them ...

The importance of their participation in supporting the program becomes more clear when we consider that they have at their disposal a network of tens of thousands of local mosques, most of which are patronized by members of the less privileged social groups in urban and rural areas.

The participation of religious leaders in the debates was also to some extent self-serving. It provided a chance to elaborate on the difference between an Islamic family planning program and one imposed by the "imperialists." Religious authorities saw it as their first and primary task to dispel the myth that the population debate originated in modern Western society. Reviewing debates on the permissibility of family planning and sponsoring research and republication of medieval Islamic works on contraception, they established that concern over population had preoccupied Muslim scholars long before it was discussed in the West.[16] This gave them a chance to celebrate Iran's Islamic heritage and to reinforce their independence from Western imperialism.

Their other concern was to justify the role of the Islamic government in promoting and sponsoring family planning. They justified the intervention as an attempt to resolve the dilemma of a government of the *mostazefin,*[17] the weak and the oppressed, by balancing its constitutional commitment to provide services to its population within the constraints of limited resources. After all, how can Iran move toward a just Islamic society and cherish its independence if it has no resources to educate its children? How can the nation be independent and champion the cause of the oppressed if it must beg for its food from the same imperialists that Iranians struggle to resist? To illustrate this they frequently gave data from other Muslim nations such as Pakistan and Bangladesh. Religious leaders concluded that the Muslim world should no longer be concerned with increasing the number of Muslims but rather with producing healthy, intelligent, well-trained, and moral Muslims who would be able to fight the oppressors of their nations and ensure the predominance of societies that are worthy of being called the *ummah* of Prophet Muhammad. While a Muslim government would not institute a draconian program like China's one-child policy, individuals were encouraged to make their family-building choices with the public interest in mind.

---

16 To this end there have been several publications sponsored by the University of Tehran and the Health Ministry.

17 The term mostazefin referred to the poorest segment of Iranian society under the Shah. In his rhetoric against the Shah, Ayatollah Khomeyni referred to this segment and promised that it would not be forgotten under a new Islamic regime. Mostazefin became a political and social notion to consolidate the power of the religious regime.

Maintaining a Pubic Interest in Population Issues

A key to keeping the population debate alive for many years was expanding the pool of people interested in participating in the discussion and not closing it up to a small group of experts and officials. Another aspect was keeping the media interested in providing a fresh look at the issues.

Population programs are inherently multidimensional and cut across many government organizations, from education to housing, from health to transport. The directors of the program, primarily physicians, were aware of this interconnection and tried to involve not only the religious leaders but also as many government agencies as possible. Their ultimate goal was that all government agencies should see the population program as theirs, or at the very least compatible with their goals. Creating such coordination, however, has not been easy, particularly since there are very few precedents for this kind of cooperative initiative within Iranian public sector culture before or after the revolution.

Government agencies were made aware of the implications of rapid population growth for their area of responsibility. Ministers and other high officials were invited to the first population conference in Mashhad and asked to present a paper outlining the major cost of rapid population increase from their ministry's vantage point. These papers and speeches later formed the basis of many articles and interviews printed in national newspapers. And again, the positive role of radio and television, which had the ability to reach the less-educated population, was highly appreciated.

Hoodfar, in her field contacts between 1992 and 1995, observed that family planning officials frequently and without prompting explained that population control, even if the program is housed in the Health Ministry, is a broad national issue whose implementation cuts across many organizations. Many noted that the program's success owes much to a shared responsibility by the different organizations. Such an attitude contributed greatly in building a team spirit that is not always characteristic of government institutions.

In the process of educating the public, officials also educated each other about the consequences of population growth; the process allowed members of each ministry to see their own reasons for actively participating in the promotion of the program. Moreover these debates, articles, briefs, and informative radio and television programs also provided knowledge and information for religious leaders and local mullahs who were generally new to the subject.[18]

---

18 It is clear from the published work of religious leaders on the population question that their sources of information are either newspaper articles or the documents produced by different ministries which aimed to demonstrate the implications of population growth for their achievements. See for example Hojatolismal Sadeghi Ardestani, Zan-e Ruz, 1329.

These accounts of successes should not imply that there was no tension in the process, particularly among radio and television directors who felt that, because of the government media monopoly, television and radio stations should reflect a broad spectrum of opinions on the population question. For members of the media, this situation represented their loss of autonomy as an important entity within the structure of the government.[19] Occasionally these tensions would find their way to the public arena.

Outreach Initiatives

Given the youthful population of Iran, the Ministry of Education has a particular interest in the family planning program and has cooperated closely with program directors. One of the major common interests of the two ministries is to enhance young peoples' understanding of the implications of population growth. The Ministry of Education has reworked its social science program to incorporate population issues, as well as the importance of smaller family size for Iran at this point in its history. In addition to this initiative, since a considerable number of women marry very young, at the end of their secondary education girls receive information about family planning, the cost of which is covered by the program.

After the initial phase of organizing the family planning network, program directors turned their attention to providing reliable information to their major target, the low-income population of the urban centres.[20] The campaign organized lunch-break talks which addressed family planning issues. Informative material on contraceptives and general health issues and vaccinations written in a simple but engaging manner, sometimes in the form of question and answer, was published in widely distributed workers' newsletters. Beautifully designed posters with clear messages were distributed among the public, and larger banners were hung in major squares and along the main roads. Special information videos and kits were prepared for young couples. The kits are now distributed through the offices of marriage registrars. Since young couples are expected to have blood tests before their marriage is registered, the Ministry of Health has used this opportunity to show the material at the blood analysis labs. Men and women view the videos in separate areas. The Ministry of Health is hoping to expand these opportunities to rural areas.

---

19 In effect, the Minister of Radio and Television is appointed under the direct approval of Iran's spiritual leader, and is thus effectively outside the president's jurisdiction.

20 A considerable number of these urban people are first and second generation rural-urban migrants.

Female Volunteer Community Health Workers

Despite the existence of a greater number of health facilities in urban than in rural areas, clinics and health centers have experienced difficulties in penetrating densely populated low-income and newly urbanized neighbourhoods. For this reason and because of scarce financial resources, the Ministry of Health created an organization of Volunteer Women Health Workers who act as intermediaries between clinics and their neighbourhoods.[21] These volunteers are usually married women in their reproductive years with several children who are recruited from their communities. They are expected to be sociable, to have some primary education, leadership qualities, and contacts in their immediate neighbourhoods.[22] They receive basic training through weekly sessions and become familiar with the kind of services they are expected to perform, as well as receive information about basic facilities and services which they will pass on to their neighbours. Information sessions are participatory and all women take part in discussions. A guide serves to facilitate and direct the sessions, building on pre-existing knowledge (both traditional and modern). The volunteers thereby gain confidence and health information at the same time. Health volunteers cover post-natal care, vaccinations, and family planning, and are also expected to convey the needs of the community to the clinic.

Each volunteer keeps records of approximately fifty households in her immediate neighbourhood. The women are not paid, but they do receive an information kit along with a membership card and a bag that carries the logo of the Ministry of Health. This organization has been unexpectedly successful, and the volunteer women have welcomed the opportunity to play a public role (Hoodfar 1998 and 2001). The volunteers gain respect and increase their network within the community. The organization started with a pilot project of only 200 women in 1991; by 1996 the organization included 20,000 women who worked with 600 health centers in the major cities of Iran (Table 2). By 1999 the statistics have put the figure at 41,000 volunteers who cover some 12 million low-income households country-wide (Malak Afzali 1999). Although family planning is not receiving as much attention by the government of Ahmadinajad, many of whom did not fully support the program initially, the Volunteer program continues to enjoy considerable expansion and popularity among women in the low –income neighbourhood. The early success of this initiative has attracted funding from major international organizations such as UNICEF and the World Bank, despite initial doubt about the project (Bulatao and Richardson 1994).

---

21 Although the government refers to the organization as "non-governmental", it was conceived and founded by the Ministry of Health. See Hoodfar 1998.

22 Potential volunteers are identified during the annual door-to-door fertility surveys. These women are later invited by their local community clinic to join the volunteer group and receive basic training.

Table 2: Number of Volunteers and Population Covered

Year	Population Covered	Number of Volunteers	Number of Participating Urban Health Centers
1994	1,500,000	5700	150
1995	4,218,000	13,400	417
1996	6,000,000	20,000	600
2007	15,825,043	98,688	2755

Source: Malak Afzali and Askari-Nasab 1997; Malak Afzali 1999; and the Ministry of Health, Office of Family and School Health (Office of Health Education-public participation sector) 2007.

Improving Management of Rural Services:

Much of the success of family planning in Iran has been due to the improvement and expansion of rural heath services (Shadpour 1994). By 1997 the services covered 85 percent of rural areas through the extensive network of rural health houses. Rural services have expanded by recruiting and training local staff, familiar with local cultural values. In the result the use of modern contraceptives in rural areas is almost equivalent to that in urban centres.. Beside the establishment of health houses in the villages two other initiatives have contributed to this success.

One was the introduction of family planning mobile teams. Each includes a highly trained physician who attends patients but also performs procedures such as tubal ligation, vasectomy, and provides injectables. An integral part of the teams are medical students. While they serve as competent assistants, the underlying intention is to introduce these mostly urban middle-class youth, most of them women, to the economic and cultural diversity of the nation.

A second initiative has been the training of thousands of local midwives who continue to be the major birth attendants in rural areas. They were also introduced to modern contraceptives and encouraged to participate in the family planning program. This program however has not been as successful, because the birth attendants increasingly are seeking employment elsewhere as the number of births, their source of income, has rapidly declined since 1990. Moreover, many women now prefer the hospital for delivery. .

Conclusion

There is a common assumption that religion, Islam in particular, is a major barrier to family planning and fertility control (Obermeyer 1995). In marked contrast, the Islamic Republic of Iran has demonstrated an adaptability and resilience to changing social and economic realities by pragmatically revising ideological positions. The directors of the family planning program generally admit that the most significant achievement of the program has been the creation of an understanding and appreciation of population issues among the general public, particularly in low-income rural and urban areas. There is little dispute that much of the credit for this fundamental social achievement goes to the religious and political leaders who changed their position on population issues and proceeded to mobilize thousands of local low-ranking clerics to gain support for the program. In fact, this particular aspect of the program makes it fundamentally different from the family planning policy introduced by the Shah's regime, and different as well from most other programs in counterpart countries. It is also clear that its success in Iran has greatly depended on the existence of a workable basic health network in cities and rural areas.

By the conventional criteria for family planning programs, one can easily evaluate Iran's as one of the most successful. The program has achieved a high level of contraceptive use (Table 3), a considerable decline in population growth (Table 4), as well as a decline in overall fertility (Table 5).

Table 3: Prevalence of Contraceptive Method, 1996 (1375)

Contraceptive method	Urban %	Rural %	Global %
Pill	19.0	25.8	21.9
I.U.D.	11.0	4.7	8.3
Condom	6.6	4.3	5.6
Norplant	1.2	4.2	2.5
Tubal ligation	14.4	15.7	15.0
Vasectomy	2.2	0.8	1.6
Coitus interruptus	24.2	9.6	18.0
Other traditional methods	2.1	5.0	3.3
Non-fertile	6.3	8.1	7.0
Pregnant	5.6	7.5	6.4
No fertility regulation	7.6	14.3	10.4
Total	100.2*	100.0	100.0

* Percentages do not total 100 because of rounding. Source: Reproductive Information, Health Survey Research Project, 1996, p. 24.

Table 4: Annual Rate of Population Growth in Iran[23]

Year	Population (millions)	Annual rate of growth (%)
1966	25.7	3.1
1976	33.7	2.7
1986	49.4	3.4*
1996	60.1	1.5
2003	70.4	1.1

Sources: 1966-1976 United Nations Demographic Yearbooks (United Nations, New York), 1986-1996, Iran's Centre for Statistical Information. *This figure excludes a net influx of approximately 2 million refugees from Afghanistan; the overall rate of population growth for this year is 3.8 per cent. *Country Profiles for Population and Reproductive Health, Policy Developments and Indicators 2005 (for numbers 2003)*

Table 5: Total Fertility Rate in Iran

Year	1955	1960	1970	1980	1990	2000	2005	2015 (prognosis)
Total Fertility Rate (average number of children)	7.00	7.00	6.80	6.50	5.60	2.50	2.30	2.06

Source: UN Common Database

However, given the fact that those under 18 still make up roughly 40 percent of Iran's total population, the government must continue to monitor population growth in a systematic manner for at least several decades since the process of balancing the population pyramid is much slower than reducing the fertility and population growth rates. Unfortunately, directors of the family planning boards and many experts feel that after great initial success both the government and the Ministry of Health are placing less emphasis on family planning, and they worry that this trend may modify the program's future rate of success. The change of emphasis may be a consequence of seeing the family planning program as a crisis measure, rather than part of a long-term population policy based on the country's resources and economic, political and ideological goals.

Furthermore, as Iran is approaching a fertility rate of replacement and below replacement levels, voices – including that of Mahmoud Ahmadinejad – can be heard arguing that the emphasis on two children per woman is not enough to sustain the economic and political strength of the country. Efforts are being

23 There has been much controversy over the 1986 population figure. Initially, the Centre for Statistical Information had made a higher population estimate which was later reassessed and the present figure was officially announced.

made by the government to use family law and family planning to promote a conservative family agenda, including restoring the unilateral right to divorce and revising those few rights that were gained by women during the past decade. But high urbanisation rates, a tremendous increase in educational achievements, especially among young women, who make up more than half of university students, and the experience of almost two decades of a successful family planning program, make it more than questionable whether the trend can be reversed.

References

Aghajanian, Akbar. 1996. "The Status of Women and Female Children in Iran: An Update from the 1986 Census." In Mahnaz Afkhami and Erika Friedl, eds. *The Eye of the Storm: Women in Post-Revolutionary Iran*. London: I.B. Tauris.

– 1991a. "Population Change in Iran: 1966-86: A Stalled Demographic Transition?" *Population and Development Review*. 17: pp. 703-715.

– 1991b. "Socioeconomic Modernization, Status of Women and Fertility Decline in Iran." In G. Gaburro and D.L. Poston, eds. *Essays on Population Economics*. Milan: CEDAM.

Aghajanian, Akbar and Amir H. Mehryar. 1999. "Fertility Transition in the Islamic Republic of Iran: 1976-1996." *Asia-Pacific Population Journal* Vol.14, No.1: pp. 21-42.

Algar, Hamid. 1981. *Islam and Revolution: Writings and Declarations of Imam Khomeini*. Berkeley: Mizan Press.

Amirahmadi, Hushang. 1990. *Revolution and Economic Transition, the Iranian Experience.* New York: State University of New York Press.

Asadpour, Samad. 1994. *Barnameh-hai jamiet ve tanzim-e khanevadeh* (Family Planning Programs). Tehran: Ministry of Health and UNICEF.

Balchin, Cassandra; Khawar Mumtaz; and Farida Shaheed. 1995. *The Woman Not the Womb: Population Control vs. Women's Reproductive Rights*. Grabels, France: Women Living Under Muslim Laws.

Banks, J.A. 1968. "Historical Sociology and the Study of the Population." *Daedalus* Spring: pp. 397-414.

Bulatao, Rodolfo and Gail Richardson. 1994. *Fertility and Family Planning in Iran.* World Bank, New York.

Haliday, Fred. 1979. *Iran: Dictatorship and Development*. London: Penguin Books.

Hoodfar, Homa. 1995. "Population Policy and Gender Equity in Post-Revolutionary Iran." In Carla Makhlouf Obermeyer, ed. *Family, Gender, and Population in the Middle East: Policy in Context*. Cairo: The American University in Cairo Press.

– 1996. "Bargaining With Fundamentalism: Women and the Politics of Population Control in Iran." *Reproductive Health Matters* 8: pp. 30-41.

– 1998. "Volunteer Health Workers in Iran as Social activists: Can "governmental non-governmental organizations" be agent of Democratisation?" *Occasional Papers* No. 10. WLUML

– 2001. "Muslim Women Mullahs as Volunteer Reproductive Health Workers." In Carla Makhlouf Obermeyer, ed. *Cultural Perspective on Reproductive Health*. New York: Oxford University Press

– (forthcoming). *Gender Equality and Population Policy in the Islamic Republic of Iran*. New York: Columbia University Press.

Huntington, Samuel. 1993. "The Clash of Civilizations." *Foreign Affairs*.

Husseini-e Tehrani, Haj Said Muhammad Hussein. 1415/1994. *Kahesh-e jameit: Zarbeh-e sahmgien bar paykar muslemin* (Reduction of Population: An Attack on the Muslims). Tehran: Dar-e ulom ve maref-e Islam.

Ibrahim, Saad Eddin. 1995. "State, Women and Civil Society: An Evaluation of Egypt's Population Policy." In Carla Makhlouf Obermeyer, ed. *Family, Gender, and Population in the Middle East: Policy in Context.* Cairo: The American University in Cairo Press.

Jain, Anrudh. 1994. "Notes for NGO Forum, Cairo." Unpublished memo. Population Council, Cairo.

Kar, Mehranguiz and Homa Hoodfar. 1996. "Personal Status Law as defined by the Islamic Republic of Iran." In *Shifting Boundaries in Marraige and Divorce in Muslim Communities.* Special Dossier, Women Living Under Muslim Laws.

Ladier-Fouladi, M. 1996. "La Transition de la Fecondite en Iran" *Population* 51, pp. 1101-1128.

Lieberman, S. 1979. "Prospects for Development and Population growth in Iran." *Population and Development Review,* pp. 293-317.

Looney, Robert. 1982. *The Economic Origin of the Iranian Revolution*. New York: Pergamon Press

Malek Afzali, Hossein. 1370/1992. *Vaziet-e salamat-e madaran va kudakan dar jumhuriyyeh islamiyyeh iran* (The Health Status of Mothers and Children in the Islamic Republic of Iran). Tehran: Ministry of Public Health, Health Education Division.

Malek Afzali, Hossein and Mandana Askari-Nasab. 1997. *Cost-Effectiveness of women Health vounteer project in a selected PHC Activities (family planning)*. Teheran University of Medical Sciences and Health Services.

Malak Afzali, Hussein. 1999. "Report on Women Volunteer Health workers Program". Association of family Planning, Islamc Republic of Iran.

Malthus, Thomas. 1783. *Essays in Population*. London.

Mehran, Golnar. 1991. "The Creation of the New Muslim Woman: Female Education in the Islamic Republic of Iran." *Convergence* 23 (November 4), pp. 42-52.

– 1992. "Social Implication of Literacy in Iran." *Comparative Education Review* 35(2): pp. 194-210.

Mir-Hosseini, Ziba. 1993. *Marriage on Trial: A Study of Islamic Family Law.* London: I.B. Tauris.

Mossavar-Rahmani, Yasmin L. 1983. "Family Planning in Post-Revolutionary Iran." In Guity Nashat, ed. *Women and Revolution in Iran*. Boulder, Colo.: Westview Press.

Musallam, B.F. 1983. *Sex and Society in Islam*. Cambridge: Cambridge University Press.

Obermeyer, Carla Makhlouf. 1995. "Reproductive Rights in the West and in the Middle East: A Cross-Cultural Perspective." In Carla Makhlouf Obermeyer, ed. *Family, Gender, and Population in the Middle East: Policy in Context.* Cairo: The American University in Cairo Press.

Omran, Abdel Rahim. 1992. *Family Planning in the Legacy of Islam*. London: Routledge.

Paidar, Parvin. 1995. *Women and the Political Process in Twentieth-Century Iran*. Cambridge: Cambridge University Press.

Said, Edward. 1994. *The Politics of Dispossession: The Struggle for Palestinian Self-Determination, 1969-1994.* New York: Vintage Books.

Sanasarian, Eliz. 1982. *The Women's Rights Movement in Iran: Mutiny, Appeasement and Repression from 1900 to Khomeini.* New York: Praeger.

Shadpour, Kamel. 1994. *The PHC Experience in Iran*. Tehran: United Nations Children's Fund.

UNICEF. 1995. "The profile of Girl child in Islamic Republic of Iran." Tehran.

Chapter 11

Bearing Children, Bearing the Revolution – Fertility, Culture, and Economy in Cuba

Elise Andaya

In 1985, a Cuban obstetrician wrote, "Sound children ensure the magnificent heredity of our revolution" (cited in Smith and Padula 1996, p. 69). Yet every year fewer children are being born on the island, placing into question the nature of the revolution that these children will inherit. In 2008, Cuba's National Office of Statistics announced that Cuba had, for the second consecutive year, experienced an absolute decrease in the population. With birth rates reaching their lowest-ever mark, demographers note that any reversal of this trend is extremely unlikely under current conditions.

The release of this report has provoked a frenzy of discussion about Cuba's possible demographic "crisis". Rhetoric around "barren states", "imploding populations", and national cultures in "crisis" is by now extremely familiar in the European context, where birth rates in many countries have arrived at unprecedented lows (Douglass 2005; Krause 2001). Yet this phenomenon is virtually unknown in the developing world, where high fertility, high infant and maternal mortality, and low life expectancies are the primary public health, economic, and demographic concerns.

Cuba is thus an unusual case: a "developing" nation with a "developed" demographic profile. Almost 50 years after the triumph of the 1959 revolution, socialist achievements in health and education, across all racial, economic, gender, and regional categories, are impressive. The campaigns of the 1960s and subsequent provision of free and universal education has achieved full literacy. According to the World Health Organization, Cuban life expectancy is 76 years for men and 80 years for women, comparing favorably with the 75 and 80 years, respectively, of life expectancy in the United States. Infant mortality has dropped precipitously from an estimated 60 per 1,000 live births in 1958 (MacDonald 1999) to 5 per 1,000 in 2006 and now surpasses the United States, which reported 6 deaths per 1,000 live births in the same year (UNICEF 2007). The chief causes of death are also those of "developed" nations: heart disease, cancer, and cerebrovascular disease. As Cubans frequently observe, "we live like the poor, but we die like the rich."

Following the demographic pattern of many economically developed nations, the total fertility rate has decreased with the social changes ushered in by the revolution, including free and universal health care and education, access to contraceptives, and changes in gender and familial expectations with women's education and incorporation into the labor force (Álvarez Vásquez 1985; Benítez 2003; Díaz-Briquets and Pérez 1982; Landstreet 1976). Indeed, Cuba's record on women is particularly striking: women comprise 40% of the total labor force, 66% of professionals, and 63.3% of university graduates (Comisión Económica 2004). Women also enjoy substantial sexual and reproductive autonomy: despite at-times limited options and interruptions in supply, contraception is widely available and Cuban abortion laws are the most liberal in Latin America and among the more liberal in the world.[1] While birth rates among the urban elite and middle-class were declining even prior to the revolution, Cuban total fertility has been below replacement (2.1 children per woman) for over 30 years (Benítez 2003). Cuba thus entered the second demographic transition – the transition to below-replacement fertility – alongside many European countries.

Yet while Cuba's low fertility is frequently attributed to processes of modernization, particularly with respect to women, Cuban families have also been significantly impacted by the island's continuing economic instability. Beginning in 1989, the precipitous collapse of the Soviet Union and the international socialist bloc transformed the global political-economic terrain. The disappearance of Cuba's primary economic and ideological ally sent the island into a tailspin. As the Cuban economy plummeted from the ranks of the "second world" to join the "third world", thousands fled the island, and the total fertility rate dropped from 1.8 to about 1.6 in the 1990s.

With Cuba's economic recovery since 2001, demographers and officials had looked forward to a parallel recuperation in fertility rates. These hopes, however, have not been borne out. Contrary to predictions, fertility rates further declined to 1.49 in 2007; they are the lowest in Latin America and equivalent to many Western European nations. This fertility decline, moreover, is fundamentally changing the structure of the population. Almost 20% of the city of Havana is over 60. Of a national population of just over 11 million, 1.82 million are senior citizens. Demographers estimate that this number will grow to about 2.9 million by 2025 and that the elderly will comprise 29% of the total population by 2030 (Cancio Isla 2008; Xinhua 2008). Socialism's "new man" (*el hombre nuevo*) is increasingly, in fact, an old man.

---

1 The intrauterine device is currently the most frequently used contraceptive method among Cuban teenagers and adults alike, despite not infrequent complaints of contraceptive failure and infection. Recently, however, the government has invested more resources into the production of Cuban-made birth control pills, although these are still little used. The only legal limitations on abortion state that it must be voluntary, take place within an appropriate timeframe (usually within 10 weeks), and must be performed in a medical clinic by a licensed practitioner.

These projections have greatly unsettled the island's demographers and policy-makers and raised concerns that below-replacement fertility, continuing out-migration, and the demands of an elderly population will threaten the reproduction of the socialist state. Predicting that Cuba will have to import a labor force within 20 years, leading demographer María Elena Benítez told me, "Those who should be working in 2025 should be being born now, and if they aren't born, who will work?" Cuba will thus face many of the social and economic challenges of more economically-developed countries with the resources of an "underdeveloped" one. In Europe and Asia, countries undergoing similar demographic shifts have tended to look to immigration – if with reservations – for solutions to both labor crises and low birth rates. Many analysts have thus pointed to the xenophobia and racism embedded in fears of demographic decline, as alarmist discourse about the low fertility of "proper" citizens co-exists with heightened restrictions on immigration and national opprobrium about the high fertility of migrants and minorities (e.g. Douglass 2005; Krause 2001). By contrast, Cuba's embattled socialist economy makes it a highly unlikely migrant destination. Acknowledging that fertility of Cubans currently on the island is the only factor to "play with" in this demographic decline, many observers fear that lack of attention to fertility will lead to a nation with "more coffins than cradles."

Yet anxieties around fertility always engage more than economic concerns. As anthropologist Rayna Rapp argues, "Reproduction lies at the heart of a culture's representations of itself; it is in large measure through imagining reproduction that individuals, families, and social groups conceive of the future toward which they aspire for themselves and the next generation" (Rapp 1999, p. 317). Below-replacement fertility is a potent metaphor for national decline, raising concerns about biological, social, and cultural reproduction and continuity (Douglass 2005; Ginsburg and Rapp 1995). In Cuba, as the population "fails" to fully reproduce itself and its youth increasingly choose lives outside the state and the island, the aging of the population is often viewed as a symbol of the anachronism of the socialist revolutionary project. Such interpretations, while seductive, can overly-simplify the complex decision-making processes of individuals and families as they engage with state policy, economic shifts, and cultural ideologies around gender, family, and nurturance of children.

As feminist scholars have argued, reproduction crosses both public and private spheres "in part because states, families, and other social actors understand themselves to have much at stake in the control of childbearing and childrearing" (Gal and Kligman 2000a, p. 17). While many socialist states explicitly sought to stimulate or discourage reproduction as part of production planning (Anagnost 1995; Gal and Kligman 2000b; Greenhalgh 1994; Greenhalgh 2003; Kligman 1998), the Cuban government has never articulated an explicit birth policy. Yet given current demographic trends, some Cuban experts have called for state attention to the issue, arguing that fertility behavior is "not functioning spontaneously" (Benítez 2003). Considering potential state interventions respectful of human rights, however, requires close analysis of the local social, economic, and cultural contexts in which fertility decisions are made.

In this chapter, I draw on interviews conducted over 16 months of fieldwork in Havana to examine women's reasons for limiting their fertility. While demographic discourse posits fertility decline and "modernization" as part of the same teleological process (Greenhalgh 1995), I argue that Cuba's case reveals the complex intersection of economic *underdevelopment* with structural and cultural shifts associated with "modernity." Women's accounts of the rewards and difficulties of childbearing and childrearing in Cuba thus highlight the usefulness of distinguishing between an "affective" and a "material" modernity (Hirsch 2003). Given the state's long-standing emphasis on female education and social uplift, Cuban women see themselves as modern actors, especially in comparison to their presumed counterparts in the "third world." This self-perception, however, is frequently at odds with the conditions of material poverty in which many live. As "modern" women living in a climate of economic hardship, therefore, they see themselves as responsibly, if at times regretfully, choosing to limit their fertility given the state's inability to fully provide the goods and services that it had once promised to its population.

Through this analysis, I hope to engage discussions around population policy and human rights in at least two arenas. First, I add a unique perspective to the small but growing ethnographic literature on the second demographic transition by offering a case study from an economically-developing country. I do not, however, specifically address policy recommendations. Frequently skeptical of grand models and universal laws, anthropologists insist on the irreducibility and specificity of local experience. Through long-term ethnographic research, they seek to shed light on the lives of actors whose intimate reproductive decision-making become demographic statistics. My research is thus presented in the firm belief that it is only through careful attention to the constraints and aspirations shaping the worlds of individuals and families that relevant and non-coercive policies can be designed.

My second goal is to intervene in the debate over human rights and the future of Cuban socialism. In the wake of Fidel Castro's resignation, international policy discussions – particularly in the U.S. – have tended to conflate calls for Cuba's transition to a parliamentary democracy with its transition to a market economy, treating them as interconnected (and interchangeable) processes under the rubric of "human rights." It is essential, however, to distinguish carefully between the two. It is certainly true that many of the advances under socialism have come at the price of total dedication to the revolution, its principles and, by extension, a frequently paternalistic and authoritarian leadership. As Raúl Castro has recently recognized, an overhaul of the state's creaking bureaucratic apparatus, the opening of spaces for public critique, and a removal of many of Cuba's restrictions (once intended to ensure equality, but now a source of discontent for many Cubans) are long overdue. Yet viewing the liberation of the market economy as a condition of democracy ignores the fact that many sectors of the population may be disenfranchised by this shift. As I describe in this chapter, the "islands of capitalism" (Peters 1997) found in the informal, tourist, and remittance economies have resulted in a vast increase in social and economic stratifications that resonate through Cuban social life.

The commitment of Cuba's socialist government to the "politics of life" has continually challenged conventional definitions of human rights. When international watch groups accuse Cuba of violating political freedoms (e.g. Human Rights Watch 1994; 1999), Fidel Castro has countered by pointing to the revolution's superb social indices as evidence of its moral legitimacy. In essence, the government has argued that political rights cannot be given primacy over social and economic rights, such as the state-supported right to food, housing, health care, and education. In the post-Soviet economy, however, as in other formerly socialist countries, the shift in economic power from the state to individual families has resulted in highly uneven benefits to the population. While the full effects of these transformations are yet to be seen, it may be women – who are responsible not only for their own well-being, but for the care of children and the elderly – that suffer most from the weakening of the state and its social supports. The potential growth of such gendered inequality is fertile ground for the discussion of both population policy and human rights.

Methodology

The data on which this chapter is based was collected over 16 months of ethnographic field research conducted in Havana from 2001-2005.[2] For 12 months from 2004-2005, I observed twice-weekly prenatal and neonatal healthcare consultations in a busy family doctor clinic located in a densely populated neighborhood of Havana.[3] The team of doctors and nurses patiently introduced me to the basic tenets of Cuban reproductive health policy and practice, and generously permitted me to accompany them on home visits, as well as on several overnight emergency shifts. My stint in the clinic also allowed me to observe and talk to women and their partners about their decision-making practices as they nurtured

2 My fieldwork in Cuba was generously funded by dissertation research grants from Fulbright-Hays and from the Wenner-Gren Foundation for Anthropological Research, and was supported by an institutional affiliation with the Juan Marinello Center for Research and Development of Cuban Culture.

3 In order to maintain the confidentiality and anonymity of all participants, I have chosen not to include potentially identifying characteristics of the clinic and neighborhood settings.

certain pregnancies to term or chose to terminate others. The data, opinions, and insights gathered through hundreds of hours of participant-observation in various clinic sites as well as in daily social life was complemented by extended semi-structured interviews, lasting between one and three hours, with 32 women and 18 men[4] of varying ages, racial identifications, and economic status about reproductive decision-making, kinship relations, and family life since the fall of the Soviet Union. All interviews were conducted in Spanish and the translations are my own.

My affiliation with the Working Group on the Family, a loose network of demographers, sociologists, philosophers, psychologists, and historians, also gave me the opportunity to discuss with Cuban scholars the successes, failures, and objectives of policies intended to change familial and reproductive behavior. My colleagues were unfailingly generous in sharing their knowledge and in allowing me to consult the considerable Cuban research on gender, reproduction, and the socialist family housed in institutional libraries. Tracing the threads outwards from pragmatic issues of reproductive decision-making and responsibility for childcare to state and individual concerns about nurturance and responsibility for citizens and families thus led me to the heart of discussions about the socialist project in the 21st century.

Cultural Values of Mothering and Family

Low fertility in economically-developed countries is often correlated with cultural shifts toward the postponement or eschewing of marriage, resulting in later childbearing (or the decision not to bear children) and consequently fewer children. In Cuba, by contrast, virtually all women become mothers, and often do so at a young age. During my research, Cubans of both sexes constantly reiterated that a woman must become a mother in order to feel "fully a woman." Motherhood is thus a highly desired and socially valorized role that is deeply intertwined with cultural ideas of gender. Succinctly capturing the cultural conflation of womanhood and motherhood, one man explained his decision to have a child with his new partner despite already having two children by other women by saying, "Who was I to tell her that she would never know what it was like to be a woman, to be a mother?" To choose not to become a mother is to cast into doubt one's "womanly" qualities that are demonstrated primarily through the nurturance and care of children.

For Cubans, the concept of family is synonymous with children, and childbearing is considered essential "*para tener su familia*" (to have one's family). While aware that some women in other countries chose to remain childless, most women with whom I spoke found such a decision unintelligible and declared

---

4 Many of the interviews with men were conducted by my research assistant, Carlos García.

adamantly that "we have a different culture, family is important to Cubans." Childless women are frequently the objects of both pity and gossip; tellingly, two of the only three women that I encountered who had not borne a child during their reproductive years found their situation too painful to be interviewed and the third agreed only because of our close personal relationship. As in many Latin American and Caribbean societies, reproduction is considered to "tie" (*amarrar*) a man to a woman and to solidify the conjugal bond. Indeed, in a context in which divorce is both common and socially accepted – 65 percent of women have divorced at least once by the time they reach 35 years of age (Benítez 2003) – the birth of a second child is frequently viewed as an effort to cement a new conjugal relationship. This prevalence of divorce, as well as a commonly-held perception of men's irresponsibility and unreliability as both husbands and fathers, arguably strengthens the importance of children in cultural concepts of family. As one woman told me, "Your children are your flesh and blood. Your parents will die, your partner may leave you or run around with others, but you will always have your children. They are your family."

Yet while motherhood is inextricably tied to cultural ideals of womanhood and family, women were also careful to stress that the biological act of parturition is not in itself sufficient. As one woman proclaimed, "Any girl can give birth, but it takes work to become a mother." It is the ongoing labor of nurturing children – and not simply giving birth to them – that is viewed as "ennobling" and as key attributes of both adulthood and femininity (Ginsburg 1989). As in other Latin American societies, the moral status enjoyed by mothers in popular culture hinges on the perception of their self-sacrifice in caring for children. During a 2005 television interview on Mother's Day, one person opined, "A mother is the one who does everything for you. You always remember her voice, her face, her advice, her embraces, the tears that she cried for you." Another explained, "A mother is the one who cares for you when you are sick or sad, who struggles for you and gives you everything. Because of her sacrifices, a mother is sacred." While bearing children is central to womanhood, it is only through the self-sacrifice entailed in caring for them that women become moral women and responsible adults in the eyes of their family and community.

The cultural value assigned to the mother-child dyad undoubtedly contributes to one of the peculiarities of Cuban fertility decline. Unlike women in Western Europe – and more akin to those in Eastern Europe – Cuban women tend to marry and bear their single child relatively young. In 1995, the average age at first marriage was 20.6 years, representing only a slight increase over the 19.5 years recorded in 1970. Women between the ages of 20 and 24 have for many years represented the most fertile cohort; in the 1980s, women between 15 and 19 years of age occupied the second place. After educational campaigns to reduce the number of teenage pregnancies (in the 1980s, about one-third of all the nation's births were to teenagers), women between the ages of 25 and 29 now represent the second most-fertile cohort (Benítez 2003).

Such reproductive patterns contrast with those of women in many economically-developed countries, where changing gender expectations, reductions in state support (in the case of many formerly socialist states), migration of women away from their natal home, and transformations in family life have all impacted reproductive decision-making. For many such women, the difficulty of combining work and childcare in the context of sparse state and/or familial assistance makes early motherhood unthinkable. The Cuban case, however, illustrates women's response to a locally specific convergence of progressive state policies and economic constraints. On the one hand, generous maternity leaves, the provision of rations that until recently covered individuals' basic needs, and the provision of childcare for working mothers (albeit insufficient, as I discuss below) helps to relieve women of some of the stress of resolving these necessities entirely in the private or familial sector. One the other, the chronic housing shortage in many urban areas means that young couples frequently continue to live with their parents. Indeed, recent Cuban household surveys reveal that the decline in number of children in the home has been accompanied by a rise in the number of grandchildren (Benítez 2003). While overcrowded living conditions are frequently a source of tension and dissent, they also provide support for working mothers as grandparents – particularly grandmothers – take up the burden of childcare and household reproduction. Arguably, then, the confluence of Cuba's pattern of youthful reproduction, economic pressures related to housing, and the socialist state's policy of early retirement (usually between the ages of 55 and 60) have provided a pool of relatively young grandparents who form essential familial supports.

While the intentional and unintentional effects of socialist policies have provided some support for working mothers, other factors such as the cultural valorization of motherhood, the state's efforts to mobilize women into the work force, and a longstanding inattention to women's domestic and reproductive needs, have also resulted in women's "triple burden" as they are urged to be mothers, workers, and revolutionaries (Gal and Kligman 2000a; Gal and Kligman 2000b; Kligman 1998; Kruks et al. 1989; La Silenciada 1996). As in other countries, socialist and otherwise, changes in gender expectations as women enter higher education and the labor force have increased the pressures on many Cuban women. Although the 1975 Family Code made an equal division of domestic labor a key principle of socialist morality, women continue to be primarily responsible for household and childcare responsibilities in addition to their professional tasks. Persistent gender stereotypes add to domestic work by representing the household as the woman's domain and men as incompetent childrearers; as one woman exclaimed in exasperation, "All men say that they're good fathers, [even though] it's the mothers that care for the children and raise them." In many households with working mothers, domestic support is provided primarily by female relatives and only secondarily by spouses. A university professor, for example, told me that her professional status depended upon her elderly mother's execution of housework and childcare duties. For many Cuban women, the work of motherhood thus extends well into old age.

Despite the socialist promise to liberate women from the domestic sphere, the state has also consistently underinvested in resources and services designed to alleviate the burdens on working mothers. With wide-spread transportation problems, food shortages, and the virtual non-existence of time-saving domestic appliances, women spend an inordinate amount of time laboring at home and in the workplace. This situation has been exacerbated by the disappearance or diminution of many state-provided services after the economic crisis of the 1990s. The critical shortage of state childcare facilities is one such example. Recent laws have barred children's entrance to state childcare until they can walk while extending paid maternity leave to one year. According to official explanations, these laws are intended to encourage breastfeeding for at least the U.N.-recommended four-month period. Popular opinion, however, holds that they are designed to relieve the chronic pressure on state childcare facilities and return the responsibility for childcare to the family – that is, to mothers.[5] Even after one year, some women – particularly homemakers whose children are the lowest priorities for placement – must continue to wait for childcare slots, thereby limiting their ability to (re)enter the work force.

While motherhood is a highly valued status that is tightly intertwined with cultural ideologies of womanhood, women thus point to the pressures of childrearing with the continuing gendered division of labor, economic constraints, and socialist policies that have both broadened and constrained women's options. As I now turn to examine, the burdens of this gendered labor have been exacerbated since the 1990s as families strive to nurture children in an era that is, for many, characterized by increased economic hardship.

Fertility and Economy

The unexpected collapse of the Soviet Union – whose favorable prices for Cuban sugar had been subsidizing the economy at billions of dollars per year – deeply undermined the state's ability to provide the cradle-to-grave nurturance promised to its population. With the disappearance of the internationalist socialist bloc, Cuba was plunged into intense and unprecedented austerity. The state implemented emergency measures envisioned only in the case of a U.S. military siege, initiating a period officially designated the "Special Period in Peace Time." Rations that once guaranteed individuals' monthly basic goods were cut

---

5 The original 2001 law was amended in 2003 to allow fathers or grandparents to be elected the primary care-giver, although as of 2005 only 17 men had requested this leave.

to provide only ten days of food. Transportation came to a standstill as oil reserves ran low, and daily rolling blackouts were so long that Cubans joked that the situation was one of *alumbrones* (intermittent light) rather than *apagones* (blackouts). Stores selling goods in Cuban pesos stood barren, and consumer goods were increasingly only available through the dollar stores that served the tourist and diplomatic markets. Average daily caloric consumption dropped 33 percent between 1989 and 1993, from over 2,800 calories per day to just over 1,800. Frequently referred to simply as "the crisis", the Special Period meant the end of many Cubans' world as they had known it.

The situation reached its nadir in 1993-94 as legislators in the U.S., urged on by many Miami-Cubans who saw the crisis as an opportunity to hasten Castro's overthrow, pushed through new restrictions on the embargo.[6] Struggling to stay afloat, the state relinquished its absolute hold on the economy, explicitly returning the responsibility for social reproduction to individual families. These dramatic changes had highly gendered consequences; it was women who overwhelmingly assumed the burden of ensuring familial survival in an economy on the brink of collapse. In 1992, a prominent feminist journalist identified this changing landscape, stating firmly,

> "The Special Period is different for women than for men … It is their effort that determine whether children have or don't have shoes; whether there is or isn't anything [to eat]; whether there are or aren't clothes to wear and soap with which to bathe" (Rodríguez Calderón 1992).

Amidst international predictions of its imminent demise, the Cuban government passed a number of new measures intended to sustain both the state and its population. With few other ready options, it opened the previously highly-restricted tourist sector and actively courted foreign investors. In 1993, individuals' possession of foreign currency was decriminalized, opening the floodgates for a flow of remittances from Cubans living overseas to their friends and family on the island (Díaz-Briquets and Pérez-López 1997; Kildegaard and Orro Fernández 1999).

The resulting dual economy – in which state workers are paid in Cuban pesos that trade at about 24 pesos to the dollar, but many consumer goods are only available in dollars[7] – has transformed Cuban society. Despite the economic re-

6 The 1992 Cuban Democracy Act and the 1996 Cuban Liberty and Solidarity Acts, popularly known as the Torricelli and the Helms-Burton Acts, respectively, after their sponsors. Among other provisions, the Torricelli Act prohibits sales to Cuba by foreign subsidiaries of American companies and forbids ships that dock in Cuba from docking in the U.S. for six months. Consequently, many countries and companies were reluctant to continue trade with Cuba or demanded higher payments from Cuba's cash-poor government.

7 In October 2004, the government officially withdrew the U.S. dollar from circulation and replaced it with the equivalent peso convertible (CUC). For ease of reference, however, I use "dollar" to refer to both CUC and U.S. dollars.

cuperation in recent years, Cuba has seen an immense growth in social and economic disparities. Class stratifications that the revolutionary government strived to eradicate have re-emerged as Cubans with access to money from outside the state sector – whether through tourism, external remittances, the informal economy, or self-employment – enjoy a far higher standard of living than those surviving only on state salaries. Prior to the fall of the Soviet bloc, for example, the differential between highest and lowest paid workers was about 5 to 1 (Evenson 2001). In 1995, however, the median monthly income of a state worker was about US$12, while a tourist taxi driver could expect to make around US$128 and a small restaurant owner potentially several thousand dollars a month (LeoGrande and Thomas 2002). The state has sought to minimize the growth of economic inequality, underwriting social and economic programs through raising taxes, implementing exchange fees for all foreign currency, and solidifying new international alliances, most recently with the government of Hugo Chávez in Venezuela. Despite these efforts, the challenges to state economic and ideological power in the wake of the Special Period are evident in contemporary life.

Changes in state and familial economies (exacerbated by the continual tightening of the U.S. embargo[8]) have particularly impacted women, who are primarily responsible for the nurturance and care of both children and the elderly. As the Cuban state and international human rights groups dispute the importance of social versus political human rights, the women I interviewed overwhelmingly identified economic stress, that in turn led to frequent marital disintegration and decisions to limit fertility, as their most pressing concern. The recurrent assertion, "*Mira, chica, yo no tenía condiciones*" (Look, girl, I didn't have the conditions) became the entry point for reproductive narratives that were densely intertwined with commentary on women's burdens as they struggled to be modern women and moral mothers in the context of Cuba's continuing economic difficulties.

The new economy has thus created inequalities in a population reared on rations, subsidized consumer goods, and values of social and economic egalitarianism. While those families with access to flows of capital from outside the state economy freely purchase goods in the dollar stores, many state workers are finding that state salaries no longer suffice for basic necessities. In 2004, for example, the average salary was about 370 pesos ($15), yet chicken thighs – enough to provide one meal for two or three people – sold at the dollar stores cost about 37.50 pesos ($1.50). Many women told me, "On our wages, if you eat, you dress in rags, and if you dress yourself, you don't eat." Comparing Cuban motherhood during and after the Soviet period, one woman declared, "I think it's always been difficult to have children, because life is hard, you have to work hard to

8 In 2004, the Bush administration approved new restrictions that limited familial support by permitting Cuban-Americans to send remittances (a maximum of $300 quarterly) only to "immediate" family and to visit only every 3 years.

give children the things that they need … But in the eighties [before the fall of the Soviet bloc] this kind of poverty didn't exist, there were more things in the stores and everything was cheaper." Another mother bitterly complained, "I don't advise anyone to have babies in today's economy. You can't! Everything is so expensive, everything is in dollars." For many women, the prospect of raising second children on already-strained household budgets is an unwelcome one.

The strains of the family life in the revolutionary period are also experienced in the tensions and strategic negotiations around housing. When I explained that I was conducting research on the Cuban family, Cubans would frequently respond, "Yes, the housing here is a real problem." For them, the difficulties of housing and the difficulties of family were virtually synonymous. While the revolution inherited a shortage of housing (particularly in Havana), the acute urban housing crisis with the virtual cessation of construction since the 1990s has forced many young couples to contemplate familial life with little possibility of obtaining their own home. Since housing cannot be commercially transacted (exchange is the only legal option), many urban dwellers live in crowded multigenerational homes or in "pigeon coops" (*palomares*) – apartments that are subdivided both vertically and horizontally as each family member begins her own family. While the oft-quoted saying, "where there's room for a bed, there's room for a cradle" underscored a popular perception that housing concerns should not prevent women from contemplating a first birth, many women concluded that more than one child would be "crazy." Since the birth of a child impacts all co-residents, concerns about space and the concomitant quality of familial relationships were significant factors in reproductive decision-making, and women reported that the opinions of co-resident family members often influenced decisions about childbearing. In this context, many women turn to abortion to limit births that they feel would put the well-being of other family members at risk.

The women I interviewed thus explicitly viewed their decision to limit their fertility as an embodied sign of their daily struggles to get by. Highlighting a widely-held sense of the state's retreat from its promises of cradle-to-grave nurturance, they tied their low fertility to a pervasive sense of social instability and economic uncertainty since the fall of the Soviet Union. At the same time, however, their reflections on their reproductive decision-making nuance economically deterministic explanations for below-replacement birthrates, and underscore the complex imbrication of economic factors with cultural ideologies of gender and nurturance. Cuban surveys demonstrate that the "ideal" family is comprised of two or three children, although women usually bear fewer (Benítez 2003). When I asked my respondents with a single child whether they would consider bearing another, most echoed one woman, who declared, "Are you crazy? In this economy? Men might like to have children but it's the women that care for them – and the man forgets about them when he leaves." It is not merely economic constraints that influence the decision to limit fertility; it is also that, given frequent divorce and cultural ideologies about gender roles, it is women who are left to care for children under at times fraught economic conditions. Indeed, as many women become "reluctant matriarchs" (Reddock 1993) in a new world characterized by attenuated state support, Cuba may join other nations in experiencing an emergent feminization of poverty.

Fertility, Modernity, and Morality

As women strive to be moral mothers in a trying economic era, socialist emphases on "rational" reproduction as a sign of modernity also influence reproductive decision-making. As I have argued, Cubans view motherhood as achieved not simply through the act of childbirth, but through adherence to a gendered script of self-sacrificing nurturance. With shifting expectations of gender roles and family relations over the course of the revolution, this nurturance – as in many countries – is evidenced through the ongoing emotional and financial investment in a few highly valued children rather than through the birth of many children (Douglass 2005; Paxson 2004; Zelizer 1985). Given the severe economic constraints that many women and their partners experience, being a modern and responsible mother frequently means opting to bear only one child.

This moral narrative around childbearing and childrearing has its foundation in long-standing international discourses that link low fertility to the achievement of modernity. Well-schooled in this discourse, Cubans too consider fertility limitation to be the hallmark of a modern woman and moral mother. Referencing Cuba's oft-deplored high abortion rate, for example, one prominent family lawyer declared, "Abortion plays a part in the low fertility rate, but [the question] is also: who are those who have abortions? Those who have enough education and culture to know that it's bad to bring a child into the world under … deficient conditions." In this evolutionary narrative, while women "in the old days" or those living in less "modern" conditions were forced to bear children for whom they could not adequately care, Cuban women today enjoy the culture and education necessary to make responsible decisions about their childbearing – that is, to choose not to continue pregnancies without adequate "conditions."

High fertility and morally-freighted concepts of modernity are thus complexly interwoven with a class discourse that has emerged with new force in the post-Soviet economy. One woman, murmuring in an aside to me as we walked down her street, claimed, "You know, the richer the people, the less they give birth. Because those with many children live very poorly, they have a lesser cultural level." In Cuba's current economic conditions, those women who bear many children are thus considered to be less responsible and less modern mothers than their less fertile counterparts – the "other" to socialist ideals of a disciplined, modern, and responsible womanhood. The mother of four explained, "I have more than two children … and so I hear people on the street saying, 'look at her, she's filled herself with children. What a way to give birth! What a way to have children for fun (*por gusto*)!" In choosing to bear more than the culturally-valued one or two children, certain women's "failure" to regulate their reproduction is often considered a sign of their lack of modernity, as well as their lack of proper maternal sentiments of nurturance in a time of economic hardship.

Conclusion: Population Policy and Human Rights

While motherhood continues to be highly valued in Cuban society, it is the care and nurturance of one or two children, rather than the birth of many, that is considered to make a woman a moral and modern mother. Women's decisions to limit their fertility thus take place in the nexus between progressive state policies that enable reproductive choices, socialist emphases on "rationality" and modernity, Cuba's continuing material poverty, and the economic, structural, and cultural difficulties of combining work and motherhood in a context of chronic shortages. Given these challenges, many women turn to Cuba's excellent medical system to prevent the birth of children for whom – for many reasons, simplified in the recurrent phrase "*no tengo condiciones*" (I don't have the conditions) – they feel they cannot provide.

While the state has historically refrained from regulating births through public policy, concerns about the economic and social costs of population aging may force it to consider potential mechanisms for stimulating fertility. Yet while the state is unlikely to approach population planning through explicit limitations on reproductive freedom, Cuba's extremely high abortion rates have also led to intermittent threats to limit access to control "abuse." Although such proposals have faced severe criticism from members of the Federation of Cuban Women, in a 2006 speech Raúl Castro linked Cuba's declining birth rate to women's "overuse" of abortion. One demographer also related an interchange with a colleague who claimed that without abortion, there would be one million more Cubans alive today. Many formerly socialist states in Eastern Europe have seen a return to a more conservative reproductive politics in the post-Soviet years, including the imposition of new restrictions on abortion (e.g. Gal 1994). Given these precedents, it is essential for feminist observers to decouple the link between abortion and fertility decline in Cuba, and to point to the complex conjuncture of factors influencing women's reproductive decision-making. Reducing availability of abortion simply infringes on women's reproductive rights and further diminishes their options.

Concerns about fertility, as I have noted, take on additional urgency in Cuba given severe imbalance between emigration and immigration. State restrictions on emigration – in defiance of international norms – have for many years aimed to control this flow. Cubans must seek permission to leave the country even temporarily, and although the previously rigid restrictions have loosened in recent years and may soon be eliminated (DPA 2008), individuals who leave or "take actions in preparation for leaving" the national territory without official permission can face up to three years in prison. These restrictions, however, are at times unevenly applied, underscoring the use of such policies as a means of population planning. While Human Rights Watch (1994, 1999) reports that dissidents are frequently denied permission to travel, less publicized are the restrictions on non-official travel for professionals, such as doctors, into whom the revolution has invested significant resources. Problems of "brain-drain" face many developing nations and merit serious state and international attention. Yet as other developing nations call for global co-operation and incentives programs to prevent the loss of professionals to developed countries (Dugger 2006), the Cuban state relies on more draconian policies to retain its trained labor force.

Age also appears to be a significant factor in the differential application of travel restrictions. According to popular experience, pensioners (whose residence in Cuba is a drain on state coffers) are far more likely to receive an exit visa than citizens of working and reproductive age. While the highly politicized nature of Cuban emigration makes its true impact on the polity and economy difficult to discern, the fact that many Cubans emigrate in their reproductive years clearly impacts Cuban population dynamics. Restrictive international migration policies could thus be understood as expressions of state disquiet about labor, population management, and the reproduction of the state. However, solutions that restrict movement and residency are highly problematic from a human rights perspective.

Much depends on the outcome of arguably the longest-running question in U.S.-Latin American politics: what will happen after the end of the Castro era? By constitutionally guaranteeing rights to education and health care, Fidel Castro had hoped to secure some of achievements of the socialist government. While the government's stance towards political freedoms is frequently problematic, the international community can only gain by financially and morally supporting efforts to provide free and accessible health and education, especially since the U.S. embargo – itself widely considered a human rights violation – substantially impacts Cuba's ability to provide for its population.[9] Given Cuba's symbolic importance in the region and its recent alliances with the Venezuelan and Bolivian socialist governments, its policy choices may pave the way for other developing nations.

Meanwhile, as I have argued, fertility trends in Cuba clearly demonstrate the disconnect between women's material and affective experiences of modernity, as they strive to be modern women in a context of continuing economic underdevelopment. Cuban analysts tend to reject the idea of the financial incentives

9 For a detailed examination of the effects of the embargo on Cuban health and medical practice, see the 1997 publication by the American Association of World Health (AAWH) based on a year-long study of Cuban medical institutions between 1995 and 1996.

adopted in several other countries, arguing that the most appropriate intervention into family life would reduce economic stress by eliminating the dual economy, increasing housing, and supporting – rather than stifling – the family-based informal sector that provides income, goods, and services on the neighborhood level. In the first months of his presidency, Raúl Castro has demonstrated his openness to such ideas. The experience of developed countries has shown, however, that the correlation between economic and demographic growth is questionable; improved economy may not stimulate fertility and bulwark the socialist state. My ground-level research, however, suggests that a harmonious "marriage" between political intervention and human rights would focus not on stimulating fertility *per se*, but on bringing about structural and economic changes that would raise Cubans' sense of familial well-being. In the end, the achievement of "well-being" may be the highest achievement of both population policy and of human rights.

References

Álvarez Vásquez, Luisa. 1985. *La fecundidad en Cuba*. Havana, Cuba: Editorial de Ciencias Sociales.

Anagnost, Ann. 1995. "A surfeit of bodies: population and the rationality of the state in post-Mao China." In F. Ginsburg and R. Rapp, eds. *Conceiving the New World Order: The Global Politics of Reproduction*. Berkeley, Los Angeles and London: University of California Press.

Benítez, María Elena. 2003. *La familia cubana en la segunda mitad del siglo XX*. La Habana, Cuba: Editorial Ciencias Sociales.

Cancio Isla, Wilfredo. 2008. "Cada vez menos cubanos en la isla." *El Nuevo Herald,* March 8.

Comisión Económica para América Latina y el Caribe, *Politica social y reformas estructurales: Cuba a principios del siglo XXI,*

Díaz-Briquets, Sergio and Lisandro Pérez. 1982. "Fertility decline in Cuba: a socioeconomic interpretation." *Population and Development Review*, 8(3), pp. 513-537.

Díaz-Briquets, Sergio and Jorge Pérez-López. 1997. "Refugee remittances: conceptual issues and the Cuban and Nicaraguan experiences." *International Migration Review*, 31(2), pp. 411–437.

Douglass, Carrie, ed. 2005. *Barren states: the population implosion in Europe*. Oxford, New York: Berg.

DPA. 2008. "Cuba considering more flexible migration rules." *DPA online,* March 19.

Dugger, Celia. 2006. "U.S. plan to lure nurses may hurt poor nations." *New York Times,* May 24, A1.

Evenson, Debra. 2001. *Workers in Cuba: unions and labor relations*. Detroit: Maurice and Jane Sugar Law Center for Economics and Social Justice.

Gal, Susan. 1994. The abortion debate in Hungary. *East European Politics and Societies*, 8(2), pp. 256-286.

Gal, Susan and Gail Kligman. 2000a. *The politics of gender after socialism: a comparative historical essay*. Princeton, New Jersey: Princeton University Press.

– 2000b. *Reproducing gender: politics, publics, and everyday life after socialism*. Princeton, N.J.: Princeton University Press.

Ginsburg, Faye and Rayna Rapp, eds. 1995. *Conceiving the new world order: the global politics of reproduction*. Berkeley, Los Angeles and London: University of California Press.

Ginsburg, Faye. 1989 Contested Lives: The Abortion Debate in an American Community. Berkeley, Los Angeles, London: University of California Press.

Greenhalgh, Susan. 1994. "Controlling births and bodies in village China." *American Ethnologist*, 21(1), pp. 3-30.

– 1995. "Anthropology theorizes reproduction: integrating practice, political economic, and feminist perspectives." In S. Greenhalgh, ed *Situating fertility: anthropology and demographic inquiry*. Cambridge, U.K.; New York: Cambridge University Press.

– 2003. "Planned births, unplanned persons." *American Ethnologist*, 30(2), p. 196-215.

Hirsch, Jennifer. 2003. *A courtship after marriage: sexuality and love in Mexican transnational families*. Berkeley: University of California Press.

Human Rights Watch. February 1994. *Stifling dissent in the midst of crisis,* New York.

– June 1999. *Cuba's repressive machinery: human rights forty years after the revolution,* New York.

Kildegaard, Arne C. and Roberto Orro Fernández. 1999. "Dollarization in Cuba and implications for the future transition." In, *Cuba in Transition: Proceedings from the Ninth Annual Meeting of the Association for the Study of the Cuban Economy*. Coral Gables, FL.

Kligman, Gail. 1998. *The politics of duplicity: controlling reproduction in Ceausescu's Romania*. Berkeley: University of California Press.

Krause, Elizabeth L. 2001. "'Empty cradles' and the quiet revolution: demographic discourse and cultural struggles of gender, race, and class in Italy." *Cultural Anthropology*, 16(4), pp. 576–609.

Kruks, Sonia, Rayna Rapp, and Marilyn Blatt Young, eds. 1989. *Promissory notes: women in the transition to socialism*. New feminist library, New York: Monthly Review Press.

La Silenciada. 1996. "Cuba: paradise gained, paradise lost – the price of integration." *Sisterhood is global: the international women's movement anthology*. New York: Feminist Press at the City University of New York.

Landstreet, Barent F. Jr. 1976. *Cuban population issues in historical and comparative perspective*. Cornell: Cornell University Press.

LeoGrande, William and Julie Thomas. 2002. "Cuba's Quest for Economic Independence." *Journal of Latin American Studies*.

MacDonald, Theodore H. 1999. *A developmental analysis of Cuba's health care system since 1959*. Lewiston, Queenston, and Lampeter: The Edwin Mellen Press.

Paxson, Heather. 2004. *Making modern mothers: ethics and family planning in urban Greece*. Berkeley, Los Angeles, and London: University of California Press.

Peters, Philip. 1997. *Islands of enterprise: Cuba's emerging small business sector,* Arlington, VA: Alexis de Tocqueville Institution.

Rapp, Rayna. 1999. *Testing women, testing the fetus: the social impact of amniocentesis in America*. New York: Routledge.

Reddock, Rhoda. 1993. "The primacy of gender in race and class." In J.E. Greene, ed *Race, class, and gender in the future of the Caribbean*. pp. 43-73. Kingston: Institute for Social and Economic Research, University of the West Indies.

Rodríguez Calderón, Mirta. 1992. "Sin tiempo para el desaliento." *Bohemia*. Vol. 84, pp. 38-42.

Smith, Lois M. and Alfred Padula. 1996. *Sex and revolution: women in socialist Cuba*. New York and Oxford: Oxford University Press.

UNICEF. *The state of the world's children 2008: child survival.*

Xinhua. 2008. "Life expectancy in Cuba approaches 80 years." *Xinhua,* May 25.

Zelizer, Viviana Rotman. 1985. *Pricing the priceless child: the changing social value of children*. New York: Basic Books.

Chapter 12

Mapping Human Rights in the Polish Abortion Debates – Reflections on the Subversion of the Democratic Polity

Magdalena Zolkos

Human Rights, Democracy and Reproduction

The high legitimacy of human rights as a moral parlance of the post-Cold War national and international politics, and the incorporation of human rights within the mainstream political thinking of today, poses a dilemma which is of particular importance for the issue of reproductive politics. If everybody speaks the language of human rights, on what grounds can one validate some of these "languages" and deny the credibility and legitimacy of others? In public debates on abortion, both the proponents and opponents of its legal prohibition or restrictive regulation often resort to human rights normativity in order to legitimize their respective positions as protective of rights of particular groups and/or individuals. Is it thus possible (and how is that to be done) to balance between these different appropriations of human rights so as to identify some of them as "inauthentic", or "flawed", or "incoherent"? And wouldn't any such attempt at differentiation run the risk of exercising an always already ideological and political view, thus becoming vulnerable to criticism of being an agent of exclusive, dogmatic and hegemonic normativity, and precluding the possibility of debate (on the abortion question but not only)? More specifically, the same dilemmas resonate strongly in any academic research done on the abortion question in regard to how one balances between the goals of *understanding* various views on reproductive politics in terms of their endorsement of human rights on the one hand, and the goals of the critical differentiation on the other.

This text has a relatively narrow geo-political and topical scope. It focuses on the question of women's reproductive rights in the context of both the restrictive abortion law and its often negligent practice in post-communist Poland. This text takes its starting point in an earlier study I completed on the conceptualizations of human rights and democracy in three discourses on the Polish abortion law: (i) national-Catholic, (ii) liberal-individual and (iii) progressive-feminist (Zolkos 2005). That study concluded that the vernacular of human rights and democracy was at the heart of the articulations of all three positions, thus demonstrating a puzzling semantic, as well as political, resilience of the notion of human rights in the Polish post-communist discourses. The discursive omnipresence of references to human rights led to the question of the possibility (and validity) of critical and/or normative differentiations between its adaptations. Wanda Nowicka, a Polish feminist activist who is one of the founders of the Federation for Women and Family Planning and has been an advisor to both the United Nations Population Fund and the World Health Organization, and who generously commented on my 2005 study, pointed out that crucial for legitimizing or de-legitimizing a given discursive appropriation of human rights in a national forum is whether and to what extent it remains consistent with the international human rights regime (meaning, in practice, the UN). While this is certainly a plausible and useful strategy of differentiation, it nevertheless runs the risk of de-problematizing and de-politicizing the international human rights regime/discourse, thus obfuscating not only its own historicity and constructedness, but also its practical-political responsiveness to and privileging of particular cultural ideology or ideologies.

As already indicated, in the Polish abortion debates both the proponents and the opponents of a restrictive reproductive law have endorsed human rights as one of their key concerns. The suggestion made here is that the importance of the interpretative negotiation between (i) the objectives of con/textual understanding of the specific discursive constellations and meanings acquired by human rights on the one hand and (ii) the objectives of their critical and/or normative differentiation is necessarily linked to the question of democracy and, more specifically, the interrelation between democracy and human rights. The significance of connecting that dual objective of understanding and critique to the nexus of democracy and human rights is that otherwise the emphasis on the faithful correspondence between the international human rights discourse and its national "translation" risks reducing human rights to apolitical claims of individual subsistence and security that transcend the boundaries of the polis and are, as it were, "granted from above." In this problematic equation human rights do indeed work as the Dworkinian "trumps", but their functioning surpasses the original authorial intent and comes to designate a strikingly rigid and one-directional relation between the state and the citizen.

This text makes an argument for linking democracy and human rights in analyzing debates on reproductive law and reproductive freedom in the post-communist (Polish) context. First, it outlines the situation establishing the 1997 abortion law in Poland. Second, it discusses the discursive logics of two adversary positions on legislating the reproductive sphere: the national-Catholic "pro-life" and the feminist "pro-choice." It argues that the feminist linkage between the institution of citizenship, political deliberation and participation on the one hand, and women's reproductive rights on the other, provides an important democratic link between human rights and democracy, which is lacking in the (very peculiar version of) natural rights narratives articulated by the "pro-life" camp. However, the point is not to dismiss the latter's claims because of their nonconformity to the mainstream international legal discourse on reproductive rights, or absence of appreciation for democratic practice, but rather to capture it as a specific human rights "language game" on its own con/textual terms. In this way it hopefully becomes possible to identify the destabilizing elements of the (allegedly) coherent and homogenous human rights discourse of the "pro-life" stance. This chapter thus argues that the denial of reproductive autonomy to Polish female citizens, which started in early 1990s and was reinforced by the governmental coalition in the period of 2005/2006-2007 of the national-conservative-populist political parties Law and Justice, Self-defense of the Republic of Poland and The League of Polish Families, cannot be reduced to a national or cultural "idiosyncrasy", or be viewed as separate from domination, subjugation and power coded in the customary gender relations. Rather, the abortion question needs to be seen as indicative of the formation of a powerful political regime, which is characterized by its fixation on social conservatism and on national-patriotic values, and which consequently undermines practices of citizenship. This regime, it is argued, throttles democratic *politics* understood as articulation, negotiation and accommodation of the diversity and plurality of experiences, points of view and subjectivities, of the members of society. It strives instead for the realization of a utopian vision of a society that is united by singular and homogenous collective morality formed under the banners of Catholic solidarism.

Polish Abortion Politics: An Overview

Shortly after the collapse of the Polish communist regime in 1989, the debate on the abortion law escalated and vehemently countered the permissiveness of the 1956 "Law on Termination of Pregnancy" (Leslie 1994, p. 457). The intention was to eradicate the "social immorality" implanted by Marxist atheism and materialism. The purpose was to signify the emergence of a radically different post-communist *moral* (and not only political) order, which would adhere to the alleged identification by the Polish society with national and Catholic values (cf. for instance the abortion bill proposal submitted to the Parliament in 1992 by the Christian-National Union) (Kulczycki 1995). However, due to the remonstrance of the liberally-minded and feminist political groups, the 1993 law nevertheless permitted abortion on medical and criminal grounds. It was embodied within the rhetoric of "national compromise", which is a highly euphemistic (and misleading) phrase considering its lack of correspondence to (and appreciation by) any of the official positions on the abortion question (Kligman and Gal 2000). Throughout the 1990s, the rhetoric of "national compromise" paved legal-discursive trajectories for the conservative Catholic position to advocate the so-called "Irish model" (more restrictive than the Polish 1993 law). For the progressive liberal and feminist groups the critique of the "national compromise" rhetoric coincided with their lobbying for the legalization of (early) abortion on socio-economic grounds, as well as for greater law-enforcement of the reproductive rights guaranteed by the law.

The extraordinary politicization of the abortion question reached its climax in 1997 when the proposal for the liberalization of the abortion law was first accepted by the Lower House of parliament, subsequently rejected by the Upper House, and then accepted again by the Lower House, and eventually challenged by the Constitutional Tribunal (Flood 2002). Just before Poland's referendum on its accession to the European Union, the social-democratic government silenced the issue of abortion liberalization, which coincided with the Catholic Church's support for enlargement. The social-democratic defeat in the 2005 elections and the strong showing of the conservative-nationalizing forces on the Polish parliamentary scene, at first relegated the abortion question to a peripheral position, meaning that the progressive position recognized the futility of striving for liberalization of the 1993 law under the given political circumstances. In October 2006, The League of Polish Families (supported by Self-defense of the Republic of Poland) started to advocate an additional restrictive revision of the 1993 law, proposing that the category of "protected unborn life" be inserted into the constitutional text. The proposal for the constitutional changes failed due to, *inter alia*, lack of support from the main coalition partner, Law and Justice.

The Polish "Pro-life" Position: Discourse and Politics

It has been characteristic of the Polish abortion debate that both the "pro-life" and the "pro-choice" positions articulated their adverse views in the language of democracy and human rights. The aim here is to develop an understanding of these positions without at the same time deciding on their validity vis-à-vis the "external yardstick" of the international human rights standards as developed under the aegis of the UN. The interpretative benefit of such a strategy is that it allows one to approach the "pro-life" and "pro-choice" claims as "language games" in their own right, and thus to capture the idiosyncratic dynamics of their embodiment of human rights with specific meanings as a con/textual (historical, ideological and relational) event.

The key discursive strategy of the national-Catholic "pro-life" position has been to monopolize the label of the *protectors* of the right to life (as a pre-political right *erga omnes*) and representatives of the "subjective experience" of the unborn fetus (Jaroszyński 1994; Słodkowska 1997; Terlikowski 2003). The extension of the rights of children to the category "unborn life" means that in the "pro-life" texts the fetus gains a quasi-civic status of a person (and with it the constitutional equality guaranteed to all state subjects). This is validated through a hierarchical positioning of the moral sphere of natural rights above the political sphere of democratic governance. Thus, the relationship between human rights and democracy projected in the "pro-life" texts is that the former provided guidance for and constraints on how the latter developed. This is captured through the concept of "moral democracy" (Okoński 2001). The "pro-life" argument has been that the vertical positioning of morality and democracy circumvents a "democratic impasse;" namely, an unavoidable tension that develops in democracy between individual liberty and the laws of social co-existence. In other words, the "democratic impasse" would be resolved by privileging one ethical discourse for the whole society (Sobański 1995).

The founding principle of "moral democracy" is that natural law (and its derivatives, natural rights) has *meta-physical connotations*. It implies legally embodied normative and unchangeable "truths", which derive from its moral (and religious) orthodoxy. In the "pro-life" texts, the presumption of natural law's immutability (in this context: the "right to life" of the fetus vis-à-vis the reproductive self-determination of women) has been phrased in terms of the "universality" of human rights (versus the alleged relativism of the pro-abortionist stance) (Tischner 2003).

In turn, the feminist "pro-choice" discourse in Poland centers on challenging the founding assumptions of the "pro-life" texts (Graff 2001; Dąbrowska-Szulc 2003; Desperak 2003). It demonstrates the repressive aspects of the allegedly democratic strategy of constructing the fetus as a state subject by arguing that, in the abortion debate, the human rights status of the fetus became counter-proportional to the human rights of women (Dunin 2001; Dunin 2004). Consequently, the seemingly innocent validation of the fetus' "subjective experience" brought about the de-subjectivization of women. In the feminist "pro-choice" texts this is depicted as correlative with the patriarchal state that thrives on the depreciative imagery of women as individuals lacking rationality and responsibility (Szczuka 2004). The "pro-choice" discourse endorses reproductive decision-making as a human right to *living* (emphasizing the quality of life and the dignity of self-determination). Also, it deliberately avoids the "natural" or "moral" rhetoric, and instead makes a conjunction between reproductive rights and citizen rights. The feminist argument in the "pro-choice" struggle for a liberalized abortion law centers on the avoidance of *dependence* through civic engagement, democratic participation and deliberation. Thus, human rights became dissociated from their teleological positioning *above* the democratic order, and were seen as a means interdependent with democracy in *keeping politics alive*. The aspect of the *mutuality* of rights and democracy was particularly pertinent: it was believed that reproductive self-determination was denied *because of* democratization flaws and that it was *because of* the prohibitive reproductive law that dependency became constitutive of women's social and domestic life.

Reproductive Human Rights and the Pursuit of Politics

This text argues that the anti-abortion rhetoric of the national-Catholic camp, while veiled as a defense of the right to life, has been primarily an exposition of a moralizing political discourse with prohibitive and coercive aspirations. Its aim to regulate reproductive liberty has exhibited three inter-related qualities of political moralizing: anti-intellectualism (in its refusal to engage with critical questioning); anti-democracy (in its leaning against the manifestation and empowerment of differing opinions); and anti-politics in general (in its aversion towards the public sphere of contestation) (cf. Brown 2001). It seems symptomatic that granting supremacy to morality over politics inspires withdrawal from the problems of the contemporary world into a preoccupation with "theological" concerns. It is thus important to understand the restrictive regulatory interventions in the reproductive sphere through the prism of their dissociation of rights and democracy. The result of such bifurcation is pejorative both from a political and from a theoretical perspective. This is because it also "blows up" human rights into abstract and intangible entities and neutralizes the radical-critical potential of human rights by re-imagining them into moral entities. It is when rights cease to function as political claims that they forfeit their transformative and emancipatory possibilities. Imagining human rights as primarily moral creates the strategies of employing them in a way which preserves and conserves the current social order instead of challenging it. Thus, human rights become "abstracted from [the] concrete and particular social contexts and, specifically, from any conception of membership of a political society" (Evans 2005).

Moreover, imagining rights as moral and superior to politics dwarfs democracy itself. The sharp dichotomy of "morality" (as a locus of rights) and "politics" (as a democratic domain) is nothing else but the Platonic opposition of truth and goodness on the one hand and force and power on the other. Consequently, the radical components of a civic and deliberative contestation, co-existence of differences, and an ever-imperfect pursuit to accommodate the whole variety of "subjective experiences" in society, are trumped by the "national values." This discourse of national values is irreconcilable with the view of reproductive self-determination as a manifestation of individual autonomy within a democratic polity. This is because facilitation of a democratic polity in the Arendtian terms of "a particular and meaningful manner of living together" (Dossa 1989) requires acknowledgment of the (moral and other) subjectivity of its participants, rather than reliance on a uniform system of "national values." Such subjectivity invokes (again, in the Arendtian mode) individual capacity for thought, consideration and judgment, rather than value conformity. The capacity for thinking as "an internal dialogue with oneself" means that "ethical action is not about applying [...] concepts like rules, values, standards", but rather challenging them in a critical and subversive manner (Meade 1996). This essay argues that the "pro-choice" discourse has the potential to allow for the discussion of abortion in ethical terms, but it is a very different conception of ethics from the hegemonic value orthodoxy of the "pro-life" position. Rather, it is a conception of ethics that avoids the sharp dichotomy of "goodness" and "power", by taking a nuanced and problematized view of moral subjectivity.

Conclusions

By way of summarizing, this essay makes three concluding points. First, it problematizes the conventional perception of the "pro-life" and "pro-choice" discourses on human rights as almost symmetrical mirror reflections. While the feminist "pro-choice" position directs strong criticism against the anti-abortion camp, it also demonstrates a great deal of carefulness not to build its discursive stance in sheer opposition to the "pro-life" position. Second, through its nuanced critique, the "pro-choice" camp is able to position its argument within a radically egalitarian vision of a democratic polity which, while it does allow for the articulation of individual ethics and judgments, remains preoccupied with the political "here and now." Third, analysis of the discursive logic of "pro-life" arguments shows that they emerge within a framework of understanding that favors value-talk and moralization above the cultivation of politics. Rather than being preoccupied with the political present, it is inadvertently future-oriented in its desire for "closure" (of the abortion issue) and for "fixing" the meaning of (reproductive) human rights.

This chapter suggests that due to the high contemporary legitimacy of human rights and the efforts to transform them from the "critique of power" into "instruments of power", the language of human rights has sometimes been adopted within abstract and all-inclusive statements, and has served to "preserve" – rather than subvert – the status quo of social and political inequalities. The heated debates on reproductive health and self-determination (in Poland but not only there), indicate the need to retrieve human rights language (and its emancipatory promise) by unwrapping it from abstract formulations and metaphysical premises. Moreover, the democratic significance of reproductive rights in post-communist contexts needs to be re-thought in a more politically challenging way. As the intriguing (and yet strategically marginalized) Polish feminist discourse suggests, there is a need to resist the temptation to imagine (reproductive) human rights in an illusionary teleological mode, i.e. as if human rights *could* and *should* ever resolve and put to rest political contestation and politicized difference.

References

Brown, Wendy. 2001. *Politics Out of History*. Princeton, N.J.: Princeton University Press.

Dąbrowska-Szulc, Ewa. 2003. "SLD-owskie obiecanki." *Zadra* 4.

Desperak, Iza. 2003. "Antykoncepcja, aborcja i … eutanazja. O upolitycznieniu praw reprodukcyjnych w Polsce." *Kwartalnik Łódź Gender* 1.

Dossa, Shiraz. 1989. The Public Realm and the Public Self. The Political Theory of Hannah Arendt. Waterloo, Ont.: Wilfrid Laurier University Press.

Dunin, Kinga. 2001. "Dwa tysiące na skrobankę." *Wysokie Obcasy*. 23 June.

– 2004. "Syndrom postantyaborcyjny." *Wysokie Obcasy*. 21 Feb.

Evans, M. 2005. "Human Rights, Moral Articulacy and Democratic Dynamism: in Defense of Normative Philosophy." In Patrick Hayden and Chamsy el-Ojeili, eds. *Confronting Globalization. Humanity, Justice and the Renewal of Politics*. New York: Palgrave Macmillan, pp.123-138.

Flood, Patrick J. 2002. "Abortion and the Right to Life in Post-Communist Eastern Europe and Russia." *East European Quarterly* 36, pp. 191-226.

Graff, Agnieszka. 2001. Świat bez kobiet. Płeć w polskim życiu publicznym. Warsaw: W.A.B.

Jaroszyński, Piotr. 1994. "Przewrotność demokracji." *Ład*. 13 Mar.

Kligman, Gail and Susan Gal. 2000. "Gendering Postsocialism: Reproduction as Politics in East Central Europe." In Sorin Anthoni and Vladimir Tismaneanu, eds. *Between Past and Future. The Revolutions of 1989 and their Aftermath*. Budapest: Central European University Press, pp. 198-215.

Kulczycki, Andrzej. 1995. "Abortion Policy in Postcommunist Europe: the Conflict in Poland." *Population and Development Review* 21, pp. 471-505.

Leslie, Brian J. 1994. "Poland, Abortion, and the Roman Catholic Church." *Boston College International and Comparative Law Review* 17, pp. 453-484.

Meade, Elizabeth. 1996. "The Commodification of Values." In May Larry and Jerome Kohn, eds. *Hannah Arendt. Twenty Years Later*. Cambridge, MA.: The MIT Press, pp. 107-126.

Okoński, Michał. 2001. "Tajemnice niewiary." *Tygodnik Powszechny*. 25 April.

Sobański, Remigiusz. 1995. "Wolność a prawo demokratycznego państwa." *Więź* 1.

Słodkowska, Inka. 1997. "Prawa nie narodzonego człowieka." *Więź* 3.

Szczuka, Kazimiera. 2004. *Milczenie owieczek*. Warsaw: W.A.B.

Terlikowski, Tomasz P. 2003. "Aborcja, Ekumenizm, Chrześcijaństwo, Religia." *Ekumeniczny Serwis Inormacyjny*. 23 Oct.

Tischner, Józef. 2003. "Dziedzictwo chrześcijańskiej Europy i jego przyszłość." *Tygodnik Powszechny*. 9 Feb.

Zolkos, Magdalena. 2005. "Human Rights and Democracy in the Polish Abortion Debates: Concepts, Discourses, Subversions." *Essex Human Rights Review* 3.1, pp. 1-21.

Chapter 13

Available Motherhood

–

Legal Technologies, 'State of Exception' and the Dekinning of 'War-Babies' in Bangladesh

Nayanika Mookherjee

> *Women needed to be protected from the emotions of motherhood so that they could return to society.*
>
> (Maleka Khan, social worker, Bangladesh Rehabilitation Program for women raped during the Bangladesh war of 1971; interviewed in 2003).[1]

The regulation and control of motherhood and the role of women as mothers have been central to various nation building projects providing legitimacy to the political interests of states in particular social and historical contexts.[2] However, are all motherhoods admissible for the nationalist project? Through an examination of the rehabilitation program for women raped during the Bangladesh war of 1971, this article attempts to examine the processes through which the motherhoods of these raped women were made available to the nation-building project of the new state of Bangladesh. The formation of Bangladesh in 1971 coincided with the rape of 200,000 Bengali women by Pakistani army personnel and their local collaborators. In its attempt to socially reinstate the raped woman after the liberation war, the newly formed state eulogized them as *birangonas* ('war-heroines') and set up Rehabilitation Programs.

The above quote by Maleka Khan, a social worker who worked in the rehabilitation program for women raped during the Bangladesh war of 1971, shows that women who had been raped needed to be "protected from the emotions of motherhood." This 'protection' was made possible by the emotional and physical dekinning of the raped women from their children: the 'war-babies' (children born as a result of their mothers being sexually violated). Introduction of exceptional laws relating to abortion and adoption in the context of the crisis of war-time rape enabled this dekinning. The Bangladeshi state, therefore, was primarily

---

1 Except for one doctor, I have not rendered the social workers and doctors cited here anonymous. This is because these social workers and doctors are well known in contemporary Bangladesh and their experiences are being documented as part of the history of rape (Akhtar 2001). Similarly, interviews of various members of International Planned Parenthood Foundation are well known and readily available in newspapers and scholarly publication in and outside Bangladesh.

2 For a theoretical discussion of motherhood see Mookherjee (2003).

concerned with containing the role of the raped women as mothers. Applied at a time when the existing legal frameworks were suspended, the introduction of these new laws led to the subsequent institutionalization of norms related to abortion, adoption and 'vagrancy' in a post-conflict situation. This article seeks to examine these legal technologies which ensured that raped women could 'return' to society and thereafter their 'legitimate' heterosexual motherhoods could be made available to the newly formed nation.

This article examines the contexts, the 'states of exception' (Agamben 1995; 2005), through which these legal technologies were introduced and how through these exceptions the norm was institutionalized. It follows Giorgio Agamben's idea (drawn from Carl Schmitt's concept) that sovereignty originates in what he calls the exception (*Ausnahme*), i.e. the capacity to suspend both laws and norms and thus create a conceptual and ethical zero-point from where the 'law' can be given. It is through the suspension and absence of the norm and the law that the exception can be produced. This production of the exception "creates and guarantees the situation that the law needs for its own validity" (Agamben 1995, p. 17) and enables the reapplication of a norm and a law. Agamben (1995, p. 1) further shows that "exceptional measures are the result of periods of political crisis" and they need to be understood in political rather than in juridical and constitutional terms. By examining the states of exception relating to abortion and adoption in the context of the crisis of war-time rape, this article shows that the state of exception not only guarantees the institutionalization of norms and laws which enable the state to regulate the reproductive capacities of women. Above all, it ensures the erasure and dekinning of some children – the 'war-babies' – a process which in turn frames the relationship between the state and the child. The state of exception through which mothers are made available also leads us to a theorisation of motherhood.

This article is based on ethnographic research in Bangladesh in 2003 including interviews with doctors, social workers, and representatives of organizations working with raped women and 'war-babies' in the Government Rehabilitation Centres. I also examine archival, government documents and press reports after the war. My analysis draws on my earlier research (Mookherjee forthcoming) which ethnographically examines the public memories of sexual violence of the Bangladesh war of 1971 and the circulation of testimonies of rape among survivors of sexual violence, their families and communities, the left-liberal civil society, different governments and state actors, press, visual and literary texts and the imaginary of the Bangladeshi nation. The narratives of women who have experienced sexual violence and were part of the rehabilitation program are not, however, the focus of this article. Rather, the article highlights the state of exception related to the legal technologies of abortion and adoption of the 'war-babies' through which the state sought to rehabilitate the 'war-heroines' and regulate their reproductive futures. The focus on doctors, social workers, and international organizations like International Planned Parenthood Federation (IPPF) working with raped women and 'war-babies' in the Government Rehabilitation Centres highlights the tactical collusion between these different actors. This is similar to Veena Das's (1995) account of the role of various organizations in the face of inter-community 'recovery' of 'abducted' Hindu and Muslim women after the Partition of India in 1947.[3] Located at the juncture of state and society, these actors show how government policies and societal reaction were ambivalent towards the raped women. This ambivalence is also bound up with emotions towards the horror of war-time rape of the women and the 'necessity' to make them available to the new nation.

The *Punorbashon* (Rehabilitation) of 'War-Heroines'

In 1947, the independence of India from British colonial rule resulted in the creation of a new homeland for the Muslims of India by carving out the eastern and north-western corners of the country, which became East and West Pakistan respectively. In the formation of Pakistan, Islam was the sole principle of nationhood unifying two widely disparate units, separated not only geographically but by sharp cultural and linguistic differences. It is important to remember that the Islam of Bengal/East Pakistan, bearing the imprint of different historical and social forces, was not the Islam of West Pakistan, as it was fused with popular beliefs and practices which represented the popular culture of Bengal. 'Orthodox' Muslims in other parts of South Asia thus interpreted the practice of Islam in Bengal as too Bengali (perceived as Hinduized), and made it the object of various reformist movements (Ahmed 1981). West Pakistani antipathy to Bengali culture was also nourished by the suspicion that though nominally Muslim, the people's 'relatively recent' conversion from low caste Hindu status made them unreliable co-religionists (Ali 1983). Reluctant to rely on religious allegiance alone, successive regimes in Pakistan embarked on a strategy of forcible cultural assimilation towards the Bengalis by targeting the Bengali language and attempting to replace it by Urdu as the only state language, so as to purge Bengali culture of its perceived Hindu elements. Over the years, various such impositions as well as West Pakistani administrative, military, civil and economic control led to the nine month long liberation war in 1971. Thereafter, East Pakistan became independent from West Pakistan and Bangladesh was formed.

---

3 Butalia (1998), Menon and Bhasin (1998) and Das (1995, pp. 55-83) have marvelously shown similar instances of inter-community sexual violence between Hindus and Muslims in the context of the violent events relating to the partition of India in 1947. They show how the abduction of women and birth of unwanted children during the partition are all dislocated from the status of being events pertaining to family and community and how they instead become events which concern the new nations, where kinship norms of purity and honour are articulated in a public discourse.

With the end of the Liberation War, Bangladesh was faced with the staggering number of 3 million dead and 200,000 women raped (out of a population of 75 million) by the Pakistani army and *Razakars* (local Bengali collaborators) in a span of nine months. The way the government of independent Bangladesh dealt with the history of rape during the war, however, was unprecedented. Instead of shrouding the issue of rape in silence (though it was framed through euphemisms of 'inhuman torture' which I address later), the newly formed Bangladeshi government eulogized the raped women as *birangonas* ('war-heroines') in their attempt to rehabilitate them and reduce social ostracism.[4] A *Punorbashon* Centre and Board were set up in 1972 and charged with the specific duties of rendering relief and rehabilitation to war-affected women. *Punorbashon* in Bengali means Rehabilitation that is, providing a new life to the raped women within idioms of 'reformation' and betterment. This rehabilitation was made possible by ensuring that the women who had become pregnant as a result of rape had access to abortion or were able to put their children up for international adoption. At the same time, the government attempted to 'marry off' the 'war-heroines' or provided them with vocational training so that they could secure jobs.

I have explored elsewhere (Mookherjee forthcoming) the varied societal reactions to the eulogization of raped women as 'war-heroines' and the responses of the raped women to the rehabilitation project. In short, by referring to the women as '*birangonas*' the state attempted to avoid possible social ostracism of the women raped by locating the violence they encountered during the war within a heroic framework. This policy also established the parental role of the state in defining the framework of citizenship for the new nation. Various women who had been raped accepted this state recognition, though they would refrain from acknowledging their violent encounter during the war in public. At the same time, various social workers argued that this label of '*birangona*' made the women visible and prone to social stigma.

The eulogizingion of raped women as 'war-heroines' and their rehabilitation were also rooted in a modernist agenda. It became a trope for the symbolic evocation of the dynamism of the new nation, which ensured its development *out* of the 'traditions and taboos of Muslim society' (National Board of Bangladesh Women's Rehabilitation Program 1974). The newly formed state became responsible for making these women available to the nation, 'returning' them and

---

4 The government designation of 'war-heroines' applied to all women who had been raped during the war, and women from all socio-economic backgrounds encountered rape. It is important to note that the history of rape has remained a topic of literary and visual media through the last thirty-five years in Bangladesh, thereby ensuring that the raped woman endured as an iconic figure.

'protecting' them from the assumed prevalence of 'Muslim'[5] traditions and taboos which might socially ostracize them and not allow them to be citizens of the new nation. It is important to note that these practices, found in the 'Muslim' country of Bangladesh in the early 1970s, were a precursor to the international legislation adopted in the 1990s regarding Forced Pregnancy during Wars (United Nations 1998) in response to the incidents of rape in Bosnia.

The reformist and modernist agenda of the Rehabilitation program, however, pathologized *birangonas* and aimed to expunge them of their ills.[6] The various euphemisms of 'inhuman torture', 'reformation' and 'returning' the *birangonas* to society highlight the ambivalence felt towards the women raped during the war. I have argued (Mookherjee forthcoming) that the rehabilitation program institutionalized cultural stereotypes and norms of subordinate femininity in Bangladesh, even though it aimed at providing a new vocabulary for social change in gender relations and citizenship for women. Kotalova (1996, p. 45) has rightly stated that 'marriage is regarded as the ultimate form of gender relatedness, adulthood and completeness in Bangladesh'. As a result, a raped woman and unwed mother might not easily be assimilated within everyday social norms. Alongside these societal ambivalences, the dekinning of the 'war-babies' became necessary so as to separate these women from their babies and make them available to the new nation. The presence of the perceived 'enemy' children was imagined to be a social stigma that would hinder the women's participation as citizens.

At the same time, if we examine these poignant, violent, war-time contexts only through frameworks of 'patriarchy', the stigma of 'unwed motherhood', the importance of 'virginal marriage' and 'judgemental societal attitudes of raped women',[7] all of which are stereotypically associated with 'South Asian' and 'Muslim societies', a large part of this complex history and how it affected the women raped would be lost. Alongside the existing discomfort about the sexually transgressed woman, it was not uncommon for family members of some 'war-heroines' (as highlighted in interviews by social workers and *birangonas*) to partake in the women's pain and to acknowledge that their ordeal had happened as a result of forceful, war-time violence. In such instances, it was important for these women to get on with their lives without being made visible as 'raped'. While feminist politics must contest the stigmatisation of raped women, it also

5 The quotes around the term 'Muslim', highlight the essentialist frameworks through which Muslim 'cultures' are examined. This is connected to the stereotype that a Muslim society is predominantly perceived as being traditional and patriarchal.

6 He idioms of rehabilitation for women prisoners in Bangladesh, like the promotion of the use of a sewing machine to earn a livelihood and the arranging of their marriages (Guhathakurta 1985, p. 83) are strikingly similar to the idioms of rehabilitation of *birangonas*.

7 One of the anonymous reviewers articulated these frameworks. Thankfully, that reminded me of the need to forefront the multiple complexities and the role of a sensitive analysis of war-time sexual violence.

needs to analyse sensitively the multiple life trajectories of the *birangonas* and their complex negotiations with the experience of this violent encounter of rape.

Behind the extensive programs of Rehabilitation lay individual *birangonas*' raw wounds, choices, and life trajectories, as evidenced in various interviews. Some women had gladly gone through abortion, relieved not to have to bear a Pakistani baby; others wanted to keep their babies but were made to undergo abortions. There were those who had endured nine months of hatred toward the pregnancy they carried, and others who had been separated from their babies due to various practical exigencies of becoming part of the 'mainstream' of life. Some women cried when their newborn children were given away while others did not even look at their babies. These varied responses of the women is highlighted in the account of a British couple (personal communication and interview) who had to first meet the mother, on the latter's insistence, before she would agree to the child's adoption. The poor, young, Muslim woman loved her baby. However, she needed to get married and decided to put her baby up for adoption. This is because of the possibility that may be in her family, the child would not be accepted because it is illegitimate. Further, it might not be included within many families as it would be perceived as the child of the enemy and rapist Pakistani father. In other instances however, 'war-babies' were absorbed within Bangladeshi families in what Bourdieu (1990) has referred to as 'practical kinship.'[8] Finally, the national practices of rehabilitation ensured that many such children were either aborted or adopted abroad. Numerous 'war-babies' who were put up for international adoption returned to Bangladesh in the 1990s as adults and fruitlessly searched for their birth mothers.

As for the women, some continued to live with their families – through the mechanisms of practical kinship and contingencies. Others married men sensitive to their violent war-time encounters. In other instances, knowledge of the rape resulted in abuse after marriage by the husband and in-laws. Some of those who were painfully ostracized by their families received government jobs and lived in various working women's hostels. *Birangonas* who were reluctant to get married instead demanded jobs from the state for their rehabilitation. Rehabilitation thereby not only created a framework of legitimacy for the parental state but also ensured that the women could make claims on the newly formed state.

In the remainder of this article, I examine the process of law-making related to abortion and adoption in Bangladesh in the context of this history of rape and

---

8 Bourdieu (1990) has defined practical kinship as distinct from official kinship which is made up of rules and rituals. "Practical kinship" refers to actual alliances resulting from the internal and external political functions of marriage. He gives instances of 'self serving lies' to which a group may give allegiance in order to conceal from itself its failure to find honourable solutions to problem cases. This has been marvellously explored by Das (1995) when exploring issues of national honour in the case of 'abductions' during the partition of India in 1947.

the rehabilitation of 'war-heroines'. The institutionalization of these laws, formulated at this juncture of crisis, and its relationship to the concerns of international fertility organisations seeking to reduce the population in Third World countries are also highlighted.

Legal Technologies of Abortion

After the war, the Relief and Rehabilitation Board, which was set up in 1972, had to tend to war-affected women on an 'emergency basis'. The 'emergency' was the problem of raped women who had become pregnant. 'Medical help' became essential for the women. This included the clinical aspect of the 'emergency programs' undertaken by the Rehabilitation Board 'for the termination of pregnancies and treatment of gynaecological disorders for the victims of the Pakistani army's physical torture' (NBBWRP 1974, p. 7), i.e. abortion, the illegality of which was temporarily suspended. 'Medical help' was organized under the auspices of International Planned Parenthood Federation (IPPF-London) and USAID. These organizations donated money, set up abortion clinics, provided medicines, and retained the services of abortion providers and gynaecologists from the US, the UK and Australia – people who not only provided safe abortions for thousands of women who had become pregnant through rape, but also trained local doctors. Notable among them were Harvey Karman, Malcolm Potts (then the medical director of IPPF), Geoffrey Davis, and Leonard Laufe, who set up 'industrial scale procedures' (Murphy unpublished ms.) of abortion. These 'Abortion' Centres[9] were set up in middle class residential areas in Dhaka. They alone terminated 95% of the pregnancies in Bangladesh occurring as a result of war-time rape. The Centres performed more than 100 abortions in the first month of their existence, and 2500 overall.[10] The availability of abortion was applauded by western feminists (Greer 1972; Brownmiller 1975) as proof of women's reproductive rights[11] and personal freedom, in contrast to the restrictions prevalent in the US.

9 Approximately 18 clinics performed medical abortions. Trumbull, "Dacca Raising the Status of Women While Aiding Rape Victims" *New York Times*, 12 May 1972, 2, as cited in Murphy (unpublished ms.)].

10 Given the chaotic post-war context, it is unsurprising that there are varied claims about the number of rapes and abortion. Dr. Geoffrey Davis, an Australian doctor, estimated (*Banglar Bani*, *Genocide Issue*, December 1972) that 200,000 women underwent abortion. He thus believed the number of raped women was 470,000, much higher than the 200,000 estimated by officials.)

11 To combat restrictions relating to the termination of pregnancy that were prevalent in the US at this time, Menstrual Extraction or ME was developed in 1971 by a California-based radical feminist self help movement. As a new *home* health care procedure, ME attempted to self-govern one's individual biology in order to avoid pregnancy [see Murphy (unpublished ms.) for a detailed account of this].

Social Workers like Hosneara, Maleka Khan and Fatema Kalam (Begum 2001, pp. 221, 238) and doctors like Dr. Lateefa Shamshuddin vividly recall the abortions and the state of the women after they were 'cured'. Abortions were done on the initiative of the Bangladeshi government but in contradiction to the Shariat Law prevalent in West Pakistan. At the time, there seemed to be no civil legislation or legal fiat regarding abortion. Dr. Geoffrey Davis found that local doctors were hesitant to carry it out, because the Koran forbids abortion. In late 1972, Menstrual Regulation (MR),[12] which is distinct from abortion (a procedure done up through between 24 and 28 weeks after conception), in terms of ensuring termination of the fetus within ninety days, was legalized. Islamic law (*Sura al Bekhara*) considers that life does not come to the fetus within that duration (personal communication, a doctor who did the abortions). Following the norms established by Islamic law, MR, as the legal form of pregnancy termination, continues to be central to Bangladesh's family planning program today. MR is not considered abortion, yet it provides cheap and safe termination of pregnancy, without circumventing the law.

The urgency with which these abortions took place attests to the utter discomfort about the raped women and their pregnancies. The semantics of abortion also expresses this discomfort. The Bengali word for abortion is *gorbhopat*, meaning the felling of the womb. Here the womb becomes a traitor because of the presence of a fetus created through rape, "an occupied territory" (Zajovic 1994, p. 36)[13] which needs to be "cleansed." Only the felling of the womb could prevent both the pollution of the nation's source of family and the undesirable proliferation of the (male) enemy's progeny. The ambiguity about the use of abortion after the war became evident to me when some doctors (known by other doctors and social workers to have helped and/or conducted abortions) initially denied that abortion had taken place, giving me instead the earlier mentioned explanation relating to Islamic law. One doctor's ambivalence is evident in her account to me, that only eight to ten women came during the war for abortion while contrarily adding that four to five abortions were daily conducted in the 'Abortion Center' in Dhanmondi, a middle class residential area in Dhaka. Abortions continued till October 1972, when MR was introduced as the acceptable legal form of termination of the fetus in Bangladesh.

---

12 According to Murphy (unpublished ms.), MR was the name given to a device in transnational family planning circles organized by USAID's Office of Population and IPPF. It was designated as "the evacuation of uterine contents from a woman who is at risk of being pregnant, before she can be declared 'obviously pregnant' by clinical examination and other diagnostic measures." [(Richard Soderstrom, 1979. "Menstrual Regulation Technology", in *Pregnancy Termination. Parfr Series on Fertility Regulation*, ed. G.I. Zatuchni, J.J. Sciarra, and J.J. Speidel . Hagerstown, MD: Harper and Row, 1979. (As cited in Murphy unpublished ms.)].

13 For debates around the abortion of women raped during Partition see Butalia (1998), Das (1995) and Menon and Bhasin (1998).

The introduction of MR as part of the national family planning program in Bangladesh circumvented the issues of legality related to abortion and yet permitted and encouraged the termination of pregnancies. Bangladesh also became an important "postcolonial 'laboratory'" (Murphy unpublished ms.) for transnational and national family planning programs and experiments which were afterwards exported to other 'Third-World' countries. Desperate for foreign aid after the war, Bangladesh turned to USAID to fund its family planning program, which constituted the US agency's largest bilateral population commitment to any one country.[14] Having assisted in the abortion of pregnancies after the war, IPPF introduced MR in 1973 and relied heavily on trained lay-women, called Female Welfare Workers or Lady Village Workers, who travelled door-to-door bringing services to homes, rather than asking women to venture to a clinic. Significantly, a large number of women raped during the war received professional training in this family planning program and worked as these Lady Village Workers, a point highlighted to me during interviews with social workers and women based in Dhaka who were raped during the war. The introduction of MR not only institutionalized the family planning program in Bangladesh but also ensured the implementation of policies which aimed to curb population growth. Feminist MR Clinics set up in Dhaka with support from the Population Council and the International Women's Health Coalition, a New York-based feminist NGO, marked the beginning of the rapid growth of NGOs and the privatization of women's health services in the 1980s (Murphy unpublished ms.). Use of this technology became the template for subsequent population control programs by means of transnational funding for reproductive health.

In the rehabilitation centres, social workers documented the personal histories of women who had been raped. These documents have, however, disappeared without a trace. Various social workers explained that, in order to ensure anonymity for the rape victims,[15] either the addresses of the women were cut out from the forms, or the documents were burnt by members of the Rehabilitation Center so as to ensure 'normality' and the smooth assimilation of the women (Akhtar 2001, p. 19). In addition, documents were lost after being given away to the *Bangla* Academy for the purpose of writing a comprehensive history. Records were also destroyed by subsequent governments after 1975, in an effort to erase evidence of rape by Pakistani armies. Further, I found no documents in the SOS Children's Village, the Women's Directorate (except NBBWRP), the

14 See Hartmann, Betsy and Hilary Standing. 1985. *Food, Saris and Sterlization: Population Control in Bangladesh*. Birmingham: Third World Publications, as cited in Murphy (unpublished ms.).

15 The 'public secrecy' (Mookherjee 2006) of the rape of women would, however, be retained in families where women continued to be members as part of the process of practical kinship, which I mentioned earlier. Anonymity, however, did not always reduce the pain of women who had been raped.

Social Work Department, and the Working Women's Hostel, all of which were established in 1972 to rehabilitate *birangonas*. The former site of the Rehabilitation Center in Eskaton was also bulldozed and a lime-green multi-storeyed building occupies its place today.

Legal Technologies of Adoption

Birangonas who were in their advanced stages of pregnancy could not abort their babies. As a result, women also gave birth to babies conceived as a result of rape. Dr. Shamshuddin described a two-tier 'cleansing' process: either the women were to abort, or they were urged to give up the babies for adoption, rather than keep them and develop emotions for them. "The women had to be made available for motherhood", she emphasized, a point reflecting Maleka Khan's views with which I started the paper that: "the women had to be protected from the emotions of motherhood so as to be returned back to society."

Some social workers recounted a total contempt on the part of the women towards their babies. Others, however, talked of women who were attached to their babies, but who realized it was necessary to give up the babies so that they could get married. Various newspaper articles, letters to the editor, state speeches, interviews with '*birangonas*', social workers and doctors indicated that the presence of the babies was thought to affect the country's social structure and perpetuate painful memories of the war. Mother Teresa set up her organisation *Shishubhaban,* a drop-in centre for women to give birth to babies (*Doinik Songbad* 17/1/72). This centre also facilitated the international adoption of many 'war-babies'. It is still located in an alleyway of Islampur in Old Dhaka, continuing in its role as an orphanage.

In contrast to the prevalent Muslim personal law and *Shariat* Law which forbids adoption, the Inter-Country Adoption Law (Habiba 1997) and The Bangladesh Abandoned Children (Special Provision) Order were passed hastily on 23rd October 1972 [16] to facilitate the adoption process. At least fifteen children had been adopted (to Toronto, Canada) prior to the passage of this law, by July 1972 (*Bangladesh Observer* 16th July 1972). Throughout 1972, children were adopted and sent to the UK, the USA, Sweden, Switzerland, Norway, Netherlands and Belgium. Various orphanages like *Khelaghor* and SOS Children's Villages Project, which was established in Dhaka at this juncture to facilitate caring for abandoned children, continue to operate up until today.[17] Under this law, people interested in adopting abandoned children applied to the Director of Social Welfare, who took the final decision on their behalf.

---

16 Reference: President's Order no 124 of 1972, later repealed by Ordinance No 5.

17 I am unable to address here the contexts within which children are dekinned and abandoned in contemporary Bangladesh.

According to Chowdhury and Shamim (1994, p. 5-6), "the Adoption Law was enacted in order to provide socio-economic protection to numerous orphans, abandoned children and so called 'war-babies'". The order legitimized the adoption of abandoned children, a practice that contradicted the prevalent Muslim personal law. The law defined abandoned children as those who were 'deserted or unclaimed or born out of wedlock' and authorized the government to appoint 'statutory guardians' – a person or authority entrusted with care and custody of the person of an abandoned child. However, no mention was made about the adoptee's right of inheritance. Inheritance under Muslim personal law in Bangladesh is primarily determined by 'blood,' which would prevent the adopted child from inheriting any property from his adoptive parents unless they specifically bequeath it to him. Apparently, the government was only interested in 'providing substitute homes for the unfortunate children' (Chowdhury and Shamim 1994, p. 6).

The Adoption Law was, however, repealed by Ordinance No 5 in 1982. The Islamicist party *Jamaat-e-Islami* then in power opposed the Law on grounds that it believed that these children were being converted to Christianity or being used for child pornography and prostitution in the Netherlands and Thailand (Personal communication, Sigma Huda, a human rights lawyer; Chowdhury and Shamim 1994, p. 6, p. 25).[18] With the 1982 repeal of the order, a nineteenth century colonial law known as the Guardian and Wards Act, 1890, was reinstated with an amendment that prohibits foreigners from being appointed guardians of minors who are citizens of Bangladesh. The aim was to ensure adoption of children by Bangladeshis instead of foreigners. The process of appointing a guardian was also deemed to be consistent with Muslim personal law, to which the child concerned belongs by birth (Chowdhury and Shamim 1994, p. 25). Henceforth, religious laws would predominate over secular laws in the case of acquiring guardianship (instead of adoption) of a child.

What is significant to note in the case of the 1972 law relating to adoption, its repeal and the implementation of the Guardian and Wards Act, is that children's place under the state was in both cases brought under the legal jurisdiction of the existent colonial Bengal Vagrancy Act, 1943. Under this act, the vagrant is defined as:

> A person not being of European extraction found asking for alms in any public place or wandering about or remaining in any public place in such condition or manner as makes it likely that such person exists by asking for alms ... (Bengal Vagrancy Act, 1943, p. 2).

18 In the mid-1970s, scandals regarding child trafficking also emerged around a Dutch adoption organisation, Terre Des Hommes. When Dr. Jack Preger tried to disclose the role of government ministers in the trafficking he was deported from Bangladesh. He now runs a street clinic in Calcutta, India. (Personal communication).

In 1972, the adoption of 'war-babies' was administered under the aegis of this Act and the Department of Vagrancy and Social Welfare. To date, this act remains in place, unmodified, and continues to be pivotal[19] to how the state regulates and controls the child in Bangladesh. Whereas the wombs of women in their first months of pregnancy could be 'cleansed' through abortion, in the case of advanced pregnancies, women's wombs could only be made clean only by making the babies, once born, unavailable to the emotions of motherhood. The womb of the Bengali woman was made accessible not only by emptying it of the baby through birth, but also by ensuring an emotional effacement. Thus, the women were kept away from their babies, the latter being further removed from Bangladesh through international adoption.

States of Exception

> The state of exception appears as the legal form of what cannot have legal form (Agamben 2005, p. 1).

That the event of abortion and adoption of the 'war-babies' after the war could only operate as a lawful form but without a legal framework highlights the state of exception through which norms and laws were suspended so as to institutionalize these very exceptions. Extra legal discourse relating to abortion and adoption emerged as a law unto itself. This is because the 'authority proves itself not to need law to create law' (Agamben 1995, p. 16). My search for any official declaration about the naming of *birangonas* (except the earlier mentioned press release in December 1971) proved fruitless. Despite the absence of any legal fiat, through frequent use in government speeches, letters to the editor and endless newspaper articles reporting on the state of the raped women and rehabilitation projects, the term *birangona* assumed the meaning of "women raped during the war" in popular parlance.

Overall, I found people quite reticent to talk about the prevalence of abortion after the war, perhaps because MR is legal and abortion is illegal in Bangladesh today. In spite of IPPF's well documented role in facilitating abortions in Bangladesh (NBBWRP 1974; Brownmiller 1975, pp. 78-86; newspaper reports), IPPF in Dhaka and London claimed ignorance and said they had no records of their role. The non-codified legality of the abortion law, people's reticence to talk about it and the destruction of records (of that of IPPF and the Rehabilitation centre) and buildings, all point to an inherent, symbolic discomfort about raped women. This

---

19 Under The Bengal Vagrancy Act, police have the authority to arrest street children who fall under rubric of 'vagrant'. Thereafter, they are kept in State run vagrant detention centres.

non-codification without a legal form was the official framework within which issues of abortion and adoption during the war could be articulated.

The practice of abortion after the war is curious, as it was never given an official legal or illegal status, but occurred due to practical necessity arising from the crisis of rape. An oft repeated comment by social workers and doctors who worked in the rehabilitation program is: "We did not know what else to do. The women had to be returned back to society." This necessity of 'returning' the women back reflects Agamben's (1995, p. 27) point: "not only is necessity not unrelated to the juridical order, it is the first and originary source of law." The passing of abortion as a law could not be ratified, as the Constitution was passed only in October 1972. Curiously, no documentation can be found on the legalisation of abortion. Its fiat seems to have been based on word of mouth, having neither a legal nor an illegal status. The war ended in mid-December 1971, and during the subsequent ten months – from January to October 1972 – the termination of any pregnancy resulting from rape was permissible. As soon as the pregnancies caused by rape during 1971 were 'cleansed', abortion was illegalized and MR, which followed the norms of Islamic law and international population control programs, was introduced, as the acceptable legal form of termination of the fetus in Bangladesh.

Necessity as the originary source of law also operated in a non-legal framework in the context of adoption of children. To social worker Maleka Khan, abortion and adoption were both necessary to "protect women from motherhood and return them to society." It is this protection which ensures that the *birangonas* could be married off and be instituted in motherhood within legitimate heterosexual alliances guaranteed under the umbrella of the new nation. The 'illegitimate' presence of the children threatened the women's availability for legal marriage alliances and motherhoods. The logistical issues of separating the children from the women and freeing the women from the children became significant. Although the prevalent Muslim personal law and *Shariat* Law forbade adoption, this law was suspended during this post-war state of exception. Instead, children born as a result of war-time rapes were immediately put up for international adoption even before it was 'legalized'.

The subsequent inclusion of child protection within the Vagrancy Act also highlights the subtext of the state-child relationship. Initially, the only means to control children born after the war and stripped of any familial setup was to place them for international adoption. By means of the geographical and emotional banishment of the children, their mothers became newly available for legitimate heterosexual motherhoods in independent Bangladesh. However, the repeal of the adoption act (ten years after the war) and the reinstitution of the Guardian and Wards Act restricted international adoption. The child-state relationship was reformulated with a renewed interest in the child, a child who had to be reinstated within Muslim personhood.

The suspension of the illegality of abortion and adoption ensured that these became the official practices guaranteeing the termination of pregnancies and the removal of 'war-babies' from Bangladesh after the war. However, the exceptional practice of abortion also made way for institutionalization of the norms of family planning, the rapid increase in the role of NGOs in addressing women's health services, and the concomitant transnationally funded population control programs centred on MR. The exception of adoption was eventually institutionalized in Bangladesh through a new state-child relationship based on the restriction of international adoption and institutionalization of children without a familial setup.

By suspending existing laws, new laws of exception can be formulated in that legal vacuum. These exceptional laws allowed the erasure of life through abortion and adoption, in the context of the national crisis of war-time rape. This shows that the state of exception here binds and, at the same time, abandons the living being to law. Here, 'law encompasses living being with its suspension' (Agamben 2005, p. 40). This allowed the state of exception to physically eliminate the 'war-babies' through abortion and adoption, as they could not be integrated into the political system and their presence stood in the way of the availability to the nation of their mothers' legitimate heterosexual motherhoods. Above all, the states of exception related to abortion and adoption and the codification of MR and the Guardian and Wards Act ensured the institutionalization of the national norm of Islamic personhood for women and children, which became pivotal to the nation-state.

Conclusion

In attempting to address which mothers are brought within the nationalist mould, the article identifies two distinctive notions of motherhood. First, the earlier comment made by Maleka Khan, the social worker who worked in the rehabilitation program of women raped during the Bangladesh war of 1971, shows that those women who were raped needed to be kept away from the emotions of motherhood by means of abortion and adoption. This view highlights the distinction between legitimate and illegitimate motherhoods and emphasizes a nationalist project that seeks to contain illegitimate motherhoods so that these same women might become available to nation-building programs as legitimate mothers. In this case, the raped women as mothers inhabit a space of illegitimate motherhood. As a result it is 'essential' to protect them from the emotions of this illegitimate motherhood so that they can re-enter society as legitimate mothers and be made available to the nation-building process. Secondly, the predominant idea of motherhood is contingent on the presence of a woman's children. In this case, however, her legitimate, heterosexual motherhood is only available to the newly formed nation after her child is removed through the abortion and adoption processes ensured by the legal technologies. Motherhood to Maleka Khan primarily seems based on the idea of the potentiality of a future, legitimate child born under the aegis of the new nation.

Drawing from Giorgio Agamben's conceptualisation of state of exception, this article has highlighted how the suspension of laws and norms relating to abortion and adoption operated as non-codified legal forms in the absence of law, as they could not exist in a codified legal form. Occurring in the context of wartime rape, the 'necessity' to free these women from the illegitimate motherhood of children born as a result of rape became a law unto itself. The political rather than the juridical system determined the exigencies of these two reproductive interventions. Following Agamben's (2005, p. 40) comment that the "law encompasses living being with its suspension", the practices of abortion and adoption bound as well as abandoned the raped women and the 'war-babies' to the law. The tactical collusion between international population control practitioners, bilateral financial aid, state and non-state actors (doctors, social workers, orphanages and international organisations) in ensuring this is palpable here.

By ensuring the purification of women through the physiological or geographical expunging of 'war-babies,' the aim of the government was to satisfy national honour and international population control by visible regulation over the women's sexual and reproductive functions. Race and gender thereby intertwine to construct the images and social practices of the 'fit' Bengali nation. Through this, the raped woman can be honourably re-membered as a producer of Bengali progeny within an acceptable marriage alliance. Introduction of abortion and adoption in a state of exception allowed the subsequent introduction of the more palatable MR and Guardian and Wards Act. The latter restricts international adoption to ensure that the children stayed within Bangladesh. Thereafter, the Bangladeshi state has sought to regulate the 'vagrant child' (read the poor, criminalized child) by institutionalizing it. The introduction of family planning, ensures the inscription of the modernist framework of the nation vis-à-vis its emphasis on Islamic personhood. This process intersects with the context of bilateral international aid relating to the population control policies instituted in Bangladesh. Further, it also introduces and provides the template for the increased role of NGOs in addressing women's health, which continues today.

Acknowledgements

Research for the project was funded by the Society for South Asian Studies (British Academy). I am particularly grateful to the various 'war-heroines' I have worked with and to Maleka Khan for sharing the complexity of their experiences related to the poignant history of rape. Various exchanges with Michelle Murphy enabled me to connect the situation in Bangladesh with an international political-economy – I am hugely thankful to her. Comments and theoretical engagement with Paolo Palladino and Mark Lacy have significantly enriched this article. The article draws from a presentation at the panel 'The State and Children's Fate: Reproduction in Traumatic Times' organized by Jessa Leinaweaver as part of the conference: "Reproductive Disruptions: Childlessness, Adoption, and Other Reproductive Complexities" held from May 19-22 2005, at the University of Michigan, Ann Arbor. My thanks to the editors at *Childhood*, three anonymous reviewers, Jessa Leinaweaver and Claudia Fonseca for getting this special issue together. Any faults here are entirely my responsibility. Thanks to Sage UK for granting permission to reprint the original article published in the Special issue, The state and children's fate: reproduction in traumatic times. *Childhood: a journal of global child research* 14[3]), August 2007, pp. 339-354.

References

Agamben, Giorgio. 1995. *Homo Sacer: Sovereign Power and Bare Life*. Translated by Daniel Heller-Roazen. Stanford: California: Stanford University Press.

– 2005. *State of Exception*. Translated by Kevin Attell. Chicago and London: University of Chicago Press.

Ahmed, Rafiuddin, ed. 2001. *Understanding the Bengali Muslims: Interpretative Essays*. Dhaka: University Press Limited.

Akhtar, Shaheen, Suraiya Begum, Hameeda Hossein, Sultana Kamal and Meghna Guhathakurta, eds. 2001. Narir Ekattor O Juddhoporoborti Koththo Kahini (Oral History Accounts of Women's Experiences During 1971 and After the War). Dhaka: Ain-O-Shalish-Kendro (ASK).

Ali, Tariq. 1983. *Can Pakistan Survive? The Death of a State*. London: Penguin Books.

Bangladesh Observer. 16 July 1972. "War Babies leave for new homes."

Banglar Bani. December 1972. Genocide Issue. Aaar kokhono gonohotta noi ("No more Genocide").

Begum, Suraiya. 2001. "Begum Hosneara: Onekdin Nikhoj Shamir Oppekhai Chilen" (Begum Hosneara: She Waited Long for her Disappeared Husband). In Shaheen Akhtar, Suraiya Begum Hameeda Hossein, Sufia Kamal and Meghna Guhathakurta, eds. *Narir Ekattor O Juddhoporoborti Koththo Kahini* (Oral History Accounts of Women's Experiences During 1971 and After the War). Dhaka: Ain-O-Shalish-Kendro (ASK), pp. 227-247.

Bengal Vagrancy Act VII of 1943. Government of East Bengal, Legislative Department.

Bourdieu, Pierre. 1992 (1990). Logic of Practice. Oxford: Polity Press.

Brownmiller, Susan. 1975. *Against Our Will: Men, Women and Rape*. London: Secker & Warburg.

Butalia, Urvashi. 1998. *The Other Side of Silence: Voices from the Partition of India*. New Delhi: Viking Penguin India.

Chowdhury, A Quamrul Ahsan and Ishrat Shamim. 1994. *Abandoned Children: Better Home, Better Future.* Dhaka: Centres for Training and Rehabilitation of Destitute Women (CTRDW), Bangladesh.

Das, Veena. 1995. *Critical Events*. Delhi: Oxford University Press.

Greer, Germaine. 1972. "The Rape of the Bengali Women." *Sunday Times*, 9th April 1972.

Guhathakurta, Meghna. 1985. "Gender Violence in Bangladesh: Role of the State." Dhaka, *Journal of Social Studies*, 30, pp. 77-90.

Habiba, Umme. 1997. '71 er Gonodhorshoner Bichar Proshonge' ("The Issue of Justice as Regards the Mass Rapes of 1971") in the Bulletin of *Ain-O-Shalish Kendra*, December 1997, pp. 2-6.

Kotalova, Jitka. 1996. *Belonging to Others: Cultural Construction of Womanhood in a Village in Bangladesh*. Dhaka: University Press Limited.

Menon, Ritu and Kamla Bhasin. 1998. *Borders and Boundaries: Women in India's Partition*. New Delhi: Kali for Women.

Mookherjee, Nayanika. Forthcoming. *Specters and Utopias: Sexual Violence, Public Memories and the Bangladesh War of 1971*. Durham: Duke University Press.

– 2006. "'Remembering to Forget': Public Secrecy and Memory of Sexual Violence in Bangladesh." *Journal of Royal Anthropological Institute* (JRAI), 12 (2), June, pp. 433-450.

– 2008. "Gendered Embodiments: Mapping the body-politic of the raped woman and the nation. Bangladesh." *Feminist Review*, Special Issue on War. Volume 88: 1, April 2008, pp. 36-53.

Murphy, Michelle. unpublished manuscript. "Travelling Technology and a Device for Not Performing Abortions." In Murphy *Seizing the Means of Reproduction*.

National Board of Bangladesh Women's Rehabilitation Program (NBBWRP). 1974. Women's Work. Dhaka: Bangladesh Co-operative Book Society Limited.

Purbodesh. 23 December 1971. Juddhe nirjatito narira birangona (Women tortured in the war are 'war-heroines').

United Nations. 1998. Rome Statute of the International Criminal Court.

Zajovic, Stasa. 1994. "Women and Ethnic Cleansing." *Women against Fundamentalism.* No 5, Volume 1. London.

Part 4

Population Politics and Minorities

Chapter 14

Discourses of Modernization and Child Allowances
–
Israeli Population Politics and their Impact on Palestinian Citizens of Israel

Steven Rousso-Schindler

In December of 2000, the Herzliya Conference on the Balance of National Strength and Security in Israel took place at the Interdisciplinary Center in Herzliya, Israel. This conference was the first of a planned annual series of conferences with the aim of producing ideas and policies that would help Israel become stronger and more secure. Many of Israel's most important Jewish political and military leaders, as well as some of Israel's intellectual leaders, were assembled to consider, in large part, the question of how to ensure a continued Jewish majority within Israel. In March 2001, a 52-page conference report called "Policy Directions" was written by the conference chairman Uzi Arad (Arad 2001) along with a number of the other participants. Among other things, the report discussed some potential policies that could be implemented in order to counteract negative Jewish demographic trends.

I personally became aware of how central the issue of demography is in Israel after I read a newspaper article in the Israeli newspaper *Haaretz* entitled, "A Very Moving Scenario" (Sheleg 2001). The article described the "Policy Directions" report and discussed the potential impact of fertility rates of Palestinian citizens of Israel on Jewish-Israelis. It stated that "the birth rate of Muslims in Israel (4.6 children per woman) is nearly double that of Israeli Jews (2.6 children per woman). Today, approximately one of every five Israeli citizens is a Muslim Arab. Within 20 years, the ratio will be one to three." The article continued, "[t]he ["Policy Directions"] document makes a number of significant recommendations, among them institution of a policy that encourages three or four children per family." Specifically, the document supported an intervention by the Israeli-state to curb the fertility rates of Palestinian citizens of Israel. This proposition surprised me as it was contrary to international law regarding reproductive rights, specifically, the right of individuals "to make decisions concerning reproduction free of discrimination [and] coercion."[1]

---

1 Programme of Action of the United Nations International Conference on Population and Development in Cairo, Egypt 1994. http://www.unfpa.org/icpd/icpd_poa.htm , "Chapter VII Reproductive Rights and Reproductive Health", 7.3. "Bearing in mind the above definition, reproductive rights embrace certain human rights that are already recognized in

After reflecting on this newspaper article, and many other articles that deal with the issue of demography, I was also struck by the regularity in which Israeli newspapers report demographic statistics that are collected by the Israeli Central Bureau of Statistics, an Israeli government agency. According to Foucault (1977, p. 99), one vital tactic of governmentality is the "science of the state" where facts such as statistics and demography are generated by the state in order to "identify problems specific to the population." Tactics of governmentality such as these are vital to the state's emergence and survival. In addition to Foucault, other scholars have discussed the various ways in which statistics have been deployed by the state (Asad 1994; Hacking 1990; Kalpagam 2000; Leibler and Breslau 2005; Porter 1986). One way the Israeli-state uses statistics is to identify the problem of the ever-worsening population dynamics between Palestinians and Jewish-Israelis. These statistics then justify policies that attempt to maintain a Jewish-Israeli population majority over the Palestinians – in Israel and in East Jerusalem as well as in the West Bank and the Gaza Strip.

In this article, I argue that the perceived negative demographic statistics have provided the impetus for the Israeli-state to implement strategies and policies aimed at both curbing the fertility rate of Palestinian citizens of Israel and increasing Jewish-Israeli fertility rates. To do this, I will first discuss how 'discourses of modernization' have been deployed against Palestinian citizens of Israel in an attempt to convince them to have fewer children. I will then discuss the Israeli-state's history of supporting plans and policies meant to both decrease the fertility rate of Palestinian citizens of Israel and increase the fertility rate of Jewish-Israelis. Finally, I will analyze the welfare cuts of 2003 enacted by the Israeli-state. These extensive welfare cuts, although targeted economically at multiple communities, also had the effect of continuing a long history of child allowance policies meant to lower fertility rates of Palestinian citizens of Israel in order to improve the demographic ratio for Jewish-Israelis. As stated above, these state-sponsored actions are not in accordance with standard international human right principles.

A Brief History of Demography in Israel

Even before the establishment of the state of Israel in 1948, the number of Jews and Palestinians that lived in historic Palestine was a serious concern for the Jewish

national laws, international human rights documents and other consensus documents. These rights rest on the recognition of the basic right of all couples and individuals to decide freely and responsibly the number, spacing and timing of their children and to have the information and means to do so, and the right to attain the highest standard of sexual and reproductive health. *It also includes their right to make decisions concerning reproduction free of discrimination, coercion* and violence, as expressed in human rights documents" (my emphasis).

elite. According to Morris (1987), on December 30, 1947 Israel's soon to be first Prime Minister David Ben-Gurion was discussing the United Nations partition plan for Palestine[2] which had been approved by Israel just four days earlier. Articulating one of his biggest concerns about the partition plan, Ben-Gurion starkly outlined the emergent Jewish State's main problem – its prospective population of 520,000 Jews and 350,000 Arabs. Including Jerusalem, the state would have a population of about one million, 40% of which would be non-Jews.

> This fact must be viewed in all its clarity and sharpness. With such a [population] composition, there cannot even be complete certainty that the government will be held by a Jewish majority ... There can be no stable and strong Jewish state so long as it has a Jewish majority of only 60% (Morris 1987, p. 28).

Ben-Gurion's concern about demography may be seen as pragmatic. If the Jews did not have an overwhelming demographic majority over the Palestinians, there could be no assurances that they would be able to maintain control of the future government or even maintain a Jewish state. Despite this potential problem, the Jewish leadership decided to officially accept the United Nation's partition plan and put off demographic concerns to the future. The Arab states surrounding Israel, who were strongly opposed to the creation of an Israeli-state, resolutely rejected the partition plan.

Immediately after the Jewish leadership formally declared the establishment of the state of Israel on May 14, 1948, the 1948 Arab-Israeli war began between Israel and Egypt, Syria, Jordan, Lebanon and Iraq. The war was won by Israel and, in addition to Palestinian land Israel had captured prior to the war, Israel succeeded in capturing even more territory than originally designated by the United Nations partition plan. After the hostilities ended, an agreement with all the countries was reached and it gave control of the West Bank (including East Jerusalem) to the Jordanians and the Gaza Strip to the Egyptians.[3] As a result, the new demographic reality was far more favorable for Israel than it would have been had Israel also retained control of East Jerusalem, the West Bank and the Gaza Strip. According to the Israeli Central Bureau of Statistics, the result was a very comfortable demographic population figure of 1,013,900 Jews to 159,100 Palestinians.[4]

The issue of demography became far more complicated after Israel took control of the West Bank and the Gaza Strip at the end of the 1967 war between Israel

---

2 This was formally known as United Nations General Assembly Resolution 181. The Resolution was aimed at dividing historic Palestine into two countries – one for "The Arab State" and the other for "The Jewish State".

3 This was the result of the 1949 Armistice Agreement between Israel and Egypt, Jordan, Lebanon and Syria.

4 Israeli Central Bureau of Statistics. "Statistical Abstract of Israel, No. 55", 2004.

and Egypt, Jordan and Syria. Taking control of the Palestinian population had potentially devastating effects on the population balance between Jews and Palestinians. In Israel proper during 1967, the ratio between Israeli-Jews and Palestinians was 2,383,600:324,443. The addition of 598,637 Palestinians living in the West Bank, 356,621 Palestinians living in the Gaza Strip and 65,857 Palestinians living in East Jerusalem (Bachi 1977) would greatly shift the demographic balance away from the Jewish-Israelis.[5] With these numbers, Israel had to carefully choose which parts of the captured lands it would annex since the Palestinians living in these areas would have to be permanently counted as part of Israel's population. The end result was that Israel decided to annex only certain parts of East Jerusalem because of its central historical role in the biblical Jewish state. The Palestinians living in East Jerusalem were immediately given "permanent resident" status and, soon thereafter, were offered Israeli citizenship. Although most of the Palestinians rejected the Israeli citizenship offer because they would be viewed as betrayers of the Palestinian cause (Davis 1997, p. 52), they have still been counted in official Israeli census figures. The Palestinians living in the West Bank and the Gaza Strip were treated very differently than those living in East Jerusalem. According to Kimmerling and Migdal (2002), the Israeli government did not want these Palestinians to get Israeli citizenship because it would endanger the demography balance (2002, p. 1137).[6] Therefore, their lands were not annexed and, as a result, the Palestinians living there are considered by the United Nations to be under Israeli occupation.[7] These people are not counted as part of Israel's population in the Israeli census.

---

5 The new demographic balance did not include Syrians who became part of Israel when the Syrian Golan Heights were annexed by Israel on December 14, 1981.

6 Palestinians in the West Bank carried Jordanian passports between 1967 and 1988 and during this time were still considered Jordanian citizens. After 1988, Palestinians from the West Bank could still use their Jordanian passports for traveling but were no longer considered citizens of Jordan. Over the next six years, Palestinians were a stateless people. In 1994, the Palestinian National Authority, created during the Oslo peace process, took responsibility for issuing identity cards and passports to Palestinians.

7 Even though the West Bank and the Gaza Strip are considered occupied territories, there is a dispute about how much of the land is legally considered occupied by Israel. United Nations Security Council Resolution 242 on November 22, 1967 called for the "withdrawal of Israeli armed forces from territories occupied in the recent conflict." The French version of this resolution, based on the original English version, includes the definite article "the" between the words "from" and "territories." The English version, which purposefully left the wording ambiguous, allows a possible reading of this law as "*some* territories" as opposed to "*the* territories."

The "Policy Directions Report" from the 2000 Herzliya Conference

Reports that contain negative demographic trends for Israel's population majority have had broad ramifications for the Israeli-state's policymaking. The "Policy Directions" report written in March 2001 has helped shape a number of the most important policy decisions in the ensuing years. Before making any specific recommendations, the report estimated that a Jewish state could no longer exist if Jewish-Israelis represented less than seventy-five percent of the total population in Israel:

> [For] those who support the preservation of Israel's character as it was when it was founded – a Jewish state for the Jewish nation – and they still constitute a majority among the Jewish population in Israel, are forced to proffer a counterstrategy that will provide an effective response to the aforementioned [demographic] trends, while recognizing that in a democratic country, the Jewish character of Israel can only be preserved if the Jewish population does not dip below approximately three-quarters of the total population … (JPS 2001, pp. 53-4).

The document then outlined a number of different strategies that the Israeli-state was trying to implement in hopes of shifting Israel's negative demographic trends in a direction that ensured a long-term Jewish-Israeli majority.

> The following are possible components of a [demographic] containment option:
> - A birthrate and development policy
> - An accelerated policy of encouraging and absorbing immigration
> - A policy of demarcating the future borders of the country that will take into consideration the preservation of the Jewish majority
> - A position on the issue of [Palestinian] refugees enabling, maximally, their return to Palestinian Authority territories [instead of Israel]
> - Adopting a policy of distribution of the Jewish population in Israel in a manner that will guarantee a Jewish majority in the various regions of the country … (ibid).

The remainder of this article will analyze how the first strategy proposed above – trying to create a demographic containment option built around developing a birthrate and development policy – has been enacted both historically and more contemporarily by the Israeli-state.

One of the key factors in population growth is the rate of reproduction in a given community. Since the population of Palestinian citizens of Israel has had a significantly higher level of births than Jewish-Israelis, the Israeli-state has produced strategies and policies for which the goal is to curb the Palestinian citizens of Israel rates of reproduction. The two strategies deployed by the Israeli-state I will discuss below are 1) promoting 'discourses of modernization' in the form of family-planning to discourage Palestinian families from having large families (Kanaaneh, 2002), and 2) supporting initiatives and policies that would exclude Palestinian citizens of Israel from benefiting from child allowances in the same way Jewish-Israelis would benefit.

Israeli-State Attempts at Manipulating Fertility Rates: Discourses of Modernization

Deploying discourses of modernization as a way to curb the Palestinian citizens of Israel birthrate began in the 1980s when the Israeli-state attempted to convince Palestinian citizens of Israel that high rates of reproduction were 'backward' or 'primitive.'[8] Having too many children was also framed as contrary to the 'modern family' in that it does not allow people to fully realize their potential as economic subjects capable of higher levels of material acquisition. Israel tried to counteract this 'backwardness' and to 'help modernize' Palestinian citizens of Israel by constructing family planning units whose aim was to encourage the use of birth control to lower high rates of reproduction. According to Kanaaneh, in the 1980s, Israel's Ministry of Health "disproportionately focused on the 'Arab sector'" (2002, p. 37) when initiating family planning projects.

A good example of how discourses of modernization are deployed against Palestinian citizens of Israel in policy planning is presented in the 2000 Herzliya Conference's "Policy Directions" report cited above. The report stated that "[controlling the birthrate of the Palestinian population] would be in line with the explicit goal of contributing to Palestinian prosperity and easing the economic-political pressure stemming from high birthrates." (JPS 2001, pp. 53-4) By citing a need to improve their economic and political situation, the report justifies the creation of a "birthrate and planning policy" that will lower the birthrates of Palestinian citizens of Israel.

According to Kanaaneh (2002), the result of this strategy within communities of Palestinian citizens of Israel in the Galilee has been somewhat complicated. Some Palestinian families who were aware of the politics of demography refused Israel's modernization discourse and continued to have many children. Other Palestinian families who subscribed to the modernization discourse chose to have fewer children. From the perspective of maintaining a Jewish-Israeli majority, fertility statistics produced by the state showed some progress in Israel's attempt to lower the rate of Palestinian citizens of Israel birthrates. "In northern Israel [where the Galilee is located] the average birth rate for Muslim women is 3.9 (Sheleg 2004)." This number is considerably lower than the national rate for Muslim women which, as stated above, is 4.6 children. Still, the strategy of encouraging Palestinians to

---

8 This is not the first time modernization has been used to promote the interests of the Israeli-state. Israeli social scientists have recently reexamined the deployment of modernization theory in studies funded by the state during the 1950s on Jews who immigrated to Israel from Arab countries. For a discussion of this debate, see Shokeid's article "On the Sins We Did Not Commit in the Research of Oriental Jews" (Shokeid, 2001) and Deshen (1997).

'modernize' through lowering birth rates did not prove successful enough since the overall Palestinian citizens of Israel birthrate continued to be significantly higher than the Israeli-Jewish birthrate (2.6 children per Jewish woman).

Israeli-State Attempts at Manipulating Fertility Rates: Child Allowances

The continuing demographic problem was one of the reasons that led people in different sectors of the Israeli elite to convene the Herzliya Conference in 2000. The result of the conference was the emergence of an Israeli policy that would further discourage high birth rates within the Palestinian population of Israel.[9] "As for the birthrate and family planning policy in Israel proper: It is feasible to move toward the implementation of a family planning policy that will encourage three to four children per family, while canceling subsidy payments to families with many children. Of course, the outlawing of polygamy should be enforced (JPS 2001, pp. 53-4)." The proposed policy to reduce "subsidy payments to families with many children" advocated in the "Policy Directions" document would be acted upon only two years later by the Israeli-state. Before analyzing this new policy, I will contextualize the history of and motivations for child allowances in Israel. This discussion will show how almost every policy decision regarding child allowances, with the exception of the actions of 1992 described below, were intended to both increase the population of Jewish-Israelis and decrease the population of Palestinian citizens of Israel.

As noted above, Ben-Gurion was deeply concerned about demography and population dynamics and how that would impact Jewish-Israelis' ability to maintain a Jewish state. In addition to this, Ben-Gurion (1971) wrote about his specific concern with the issue of fertility in his autobiography when he wrote "one of the most vital elements in the equation of survival is the fact that the Jewish birth rate is much lower than that of our neighbors and is decreasing annually (Ben-Gurion 1971, p. 837)." This worry about low fertility rates in the Jewish-Israeli community led Ben-Gurion to introduce a cash prize award in 1949 for any woman in Israel who had a tenth child. Although originally meant to encourage Jewish-Israeli woman to have many children, the award was stopped in 1959 after it was discovered that most of the recipients were actually Arab women (Friedlander 1974; Kanaaneh 2002; Wiemer 1983).

9 Though it should not be understated the extent to which this new policy impacted some of the ultra-Orthodox Jewish communities that also have very high birth-rates. Before the birthrate argument was applied to the Palestinians, secular Jews had demographic concerns about the ultra-Orthodox Jewish communities.

At about the same time that Ben-Gurion's award was abolished in 1959, the first child allowances program was introduced in the form of income tax credits to both Jewish and Palestinian families living in Israel for children up to 14 years old (Sharon 1987, p. 204). This program "provided cash allowances to families with four or more children" (King 2001, p. 315). In 1965, this same policy was expanded to children up to age of 18 years old. Although these allowances were also provided to Palestinian families, one of the stated goals of the legislation was "to check the negative trends in demographic developments" (Doron and Kramer 1991, p. 122), or in other words to promote higher rates of Jewish-Israeli fertility. In thinking how this program was going to accomplish this, Mordechai Namir, the Inner Secretariat of the ruling Israeli MAPAI (the Hebrew acronym for Israel Workers' Party) political party said in October 1958 that "special arrangements will be made in order to exclude the Arabs" (Rosenhek 1999, p. 201) from these benefits. Although these special arrangements were not formally enacted during the first nine years of the child allowance program, it was only a matter of time before a scheme was devised that made it possible to formalize the exclusion of Palestinian citizens of Israel from these benefits (without obvious bias).

In 1967, the Israeli government created a Demographic Center that was housed in the Prime Minister's office. The goal of the center was to take demographic variables into consideration and to increase the rate of reproduction by Jewish-Israeli women (Yuval-Davis 1987, p. 61). Levi Eshkol, then prime minister of Israel, said "we have to work systematically to realize demographic policy, which is intended to create an atmosphere that will encourage childbearing, in light of the fact that it is crucial for the future of the Jewish people" (Sarig 2002). In 1968, the Israeli Ministry of Housing established "The Fund for Encouraging Fertility." This fund gave housing loans to people with family members who were veterans of the Israeli military, or the Israeli Defense Forces (IDF) (King 2001; Tzur and Davids 1984; Yuval-Davis 1989). Since very few Christian or Muslim Palestinian citizens of Israel serve in the IDF, it appeared that a blueprint was found to exclude most Palestinian citizens of Israel from acquiring these housing loan benefits. To ensure that as many Jewish-Israelis as possible were entitled to this benefit, it was vital to develop a very broad definition of what was meant by an Israeli military veteran. In the end, any person who had a parent, grandparent, brother or sister who served in the IDF was allowed to have access to this benefit (Schiff 1978). Most important, this served as a model for how a system could be in put in place to formally create discriminatory practices of providing child benefits only for Jewish-Israelis.

In March 1970, a special committee appointed by the Israeli government was assembled to determine how to best limit the ability of Palestinian citizens of Israel to access additional benefits that were going to be given for children (beyond what was already in place since 1959). An internal memo circulated by the National Insurance Institute discussed how to create a system where a "basic level of welfare will be guaranteed in the case of Jewish families. For non-Jewish families a lower level of welfare will be secured" (Rosenhek 1999, p. 205).[10] Later in 1970, the formalization of a partial exclusion of Palestinian citizens of Israel from additional cash benefits for their children was installed based on the model of providing benefits for people who had served in the military. The Veterans' Family Allowance Plan, as it was called, was expanded in 1971 to include all new Jewish immigrants regardless of whether they had any family connection to service in the Israeli military. Further, Jewish-Israelis who were not obligated to serve in the IDF – for health reasons or because there was a legal exemption – were also provided this benefit (Keren-Yaar 1974, p. 14, in Rosenhek 1999). Most of the funding for this plan came from the Jewish Agency, a semi-private organization. (King 2001, p. 315)

In July 1992, Arab Democratic Party representative in the Israeli Knesset, Abdul Wahab Darawshe, drafted a bill calling for equal child allowances regardless of whether family members had served in the Israeli military (Izenberg 1992, in King 2001). The proposal was supported by the Jewish-Israeli *HaAvoda* (the political party that was in power in the government) and *Meretz* political parties. *HaAvoda* had committed "the government to abolishing discrimination against Arab citizens in regard to child allowances" (Odenheimer 1992). This was the first and only time any major Israeli political party supported giving equal child allowances to Palestinian citizens of Israel. The bill took four years to become fully implemented because there was such strong opposition. For example, in a debate in the Israeli Knesset over one year later about the national budget, there was a discussion about equalizing child allowances for Jewish-Israelis and Palestinian citizens of Israel. In the debate, right-wing Israeli MK Rehavam Ze'evi from the Moledet political party shouted "(The proposal) is an incentive for making more Arab children. They will live off us forever. They will give birth to 70 children; they do anyway ... they will give birth to 50, 60, 70 children and we will pay them discharged soldiers' grants" (Izenberg 1993, quoted in King, 2001). The budget was eventually passed and the veteran requirement to collect the child allowances was phased out between 1994 and 1996. Still, "the state welfare support mechanisms that year pulled 56% of poor Jewish families out of poverty vs. 39% of poor Arab families. This 'differential impact is the result of differences in the levels of support provided and the depth of poverty of the recipients' (Swirski et al. 1998, p. 3, quoted in Kannaneh 2002, p. 36, footnote 14)."

In November 2000, the Halpert Law, or the Large Families Law, passed and child allowances for the fifth child and any child over that (sixth and up) were increased by 33 to 47 percent (Cohen 2007, p. 10). This law was controversial

---

10 'Child Allowances for Families,' memorandum presented to the 'Special Committee' by the NII, 1 April 1970 (NII Archives, 00-A-84/599.

before it passed because it was a great expansion of the Israeli welfare system and primarily benefited families with many children. The law was supported by ministers who represented communities with large families – ultra-Orthodox Jews and Palestinian citizens of Israel – as well as some state actors who were looking for political support from the ultra-Orthodox political parties. However, some of the gains from this law were short-lived. In June 2002, the Israeli Knesset passed an economic plan that reverted back to the old 'veteran formula' of allotting child allowances by cutting 24 percent of the allowance for children whose parents had not served in the IDF. Human rights groups were appalled by this policy and the inequity of the child allowance system. Human Rights Watch released a letter afterwards noting that

> The majority of Palestinian Arab citizens are exempt from military service. Their children will bear the brunt of the cuts. The cuts will also affect the children of Jewish ultra-orthodox parents who do not serve in the military, but they are eligible for extra subsidies, including educational supplements, not available to Palestinian Arab children. Israel distributes sums of money to all parents based on the number of their children. (HRW 2002)

The Bureau of Democracy, Human Rights, and Labor within the United States Department of State released a very similar statement some time later (USDS 2003).

By 2002, then, it was clear to non-Israeli institutions that the Israeli child allowance system was discriminatory and efforts were being made to address this problem.

Finance Minister Binyamin Netanyahu's 2003 Welfare Reform

Up until 2002, it is clear that child allowance cuts were largely directed at Palestinian citizens of Israel so as to encourage lower levels of fertility. However, in June 2003, Israeli Finance Minister Binyamin Netanyahu successfully lowered the child allowances rates as part of a broader welfare reform and this policy had a great economic impact on many sectors within Israeli society. One effect this policy had was that it reduced child allowances for every child in a family. However, if a family had three or more children the impact of the child allowance reductions became disproportionately more acute.[11] The child allowance cuts most dramatically im-

11 As of January 1999, the child allowance benefit was New Israeli Shekels (NIS) 169 for one child, NIS 338 for two, NIS 676 for three, NIS 1,359 for four, NIS 1,933 for five, and NIS 2,566 for six. The new rate of allowance after the policy change was NIS 120 for one child, NIS 240 for two, NIS 396 for three, NIS 756 for four, NIS 1,157 for five, and NIS 1,558 for six. The new allowances dramatically decreased the percentage of benefit for the third child (and any more children beyond the third child). Before January 1999, there was a hundred percent increase in benefit for the third child. The new policy reduced the benefit to just sixty-five percent.

pacted families with a lot of children since they absorbed the biggest reduction in child benefits. However, they also impacted single-mothers or poor families who relied on child allowances to stay above the official poverty line.

On the surface, it seemed that these cuts did not target one particular segment of the Israeli population. Instead, they appeared to be part of a broader welfare reform aimed at reducing state expenditures. However, it was widely assumed by Jewish-Israelis that one group was in fact being targeted by the 2003 welfare cuts: the ultra-Orthodox Jews. A lot of public resentment had been built up against ultra-Orthodox Jews for their lack of participation in Israeli society and the welfare cuts were seen as a way to remedy this problem. For example, very few ultra-Orthodox Jews volunteer to serve in the IDF and it is not obligatory for them to do so as it is for all other Jewish-Israelis. Also, until Netanyahu pushed for budget cuts for education allowances in the 2003 welfare reform, there were very generous educational allowances allotted to the ultra-Orthodox Jewish community. These were viewed by many Jewish-Israelis as an unfair drain and disproportionate use of scarce economic resources. Further, ultra Orthodox Jews were (and still are) often criticized for spending too many years studying in Jewish religious seminaries when they could otherwise be contributing in the Israeli work force. All of these factors, combined with a very high fertility rates – for example, 7.7 children per family in Beitar Illit (2006 statistics), an ultra-Orthodox community in the West Bank whose population is estimated to reach 100,000 by 2010 (Ilan 2008) – makes many Jewish-Israelis believe that the ultra-Orthodox Jews are an economic burden. This sentiment was articulated in The Jerusalem Post right before Netanyahu's welfare reform took effect. "One can sympathize with Finance Minister Binyamin Netanyahu's stated goal to encourage more haredi men to enter the work force, and understand the resentment of the secular public to what they see as the haredi world's failure to shoulder its share of the economic burden" (Rosenblum 2003). The same sentiment was also expressed quite strongly in a recent newspaper article in *Haaretz.*

> In 2002, while the Halpert Law was in effect, child benefit payments for a family of 10 children, which is fairly common in the ultra-Orthodox sector, was set at NIS 6,500 a month net, worth about NIS 9,000 gross. For the sake of comparison, the average salary is now NIS 7,800 a month gross. In other words: This was a work evasion payment … When an ultra-Orthodox yeshiva student decided to bring a child into the world, he also decided that the person with a job should pay for it. (Ilan 2008)

Regardless of the extent to which the 2003 welfare cuts were targeted at ultra-Orthodox Jews, there is no doubt that Netanyahu wanted Jewish-Israelis to believe that the provision that called for child allowances cuts were directed at the Palestinian citizens of Israel. Netanyahu spent a great deal of time trying to placate ultra-Orthodox political parties whose constituents were financially hurt by these cuts. For example, in February 2005 *Haaretz* reported on the subject of "[t]he truth about the cuts in the child allowances." The article stated "[i]t turns out that 'senior government officials' tried to persuade Shas [a political party that represents the interests of ultra-Orthodox Sephardi Jews] leaders on their way into the coalition that cutting the child allowances was not meant to hurt the ultra-Orthodox (Haredim), 'only' the Arabs" (Kadman 2005). Two years later in February 2007, still working on improving his image, Netanyahu spoke at a convention of ultra-Orthodox Jewish authorities in Gush Etzion, Israel and said that the child allowances cuts were positive because "on the national level, the unexpected result was *the demographic effect on the non-Jewish public, where there was a dramatic drop in the birth rate*" (Sela 2007, my emphasis).

I believe the 2003 welfare reform was actually a two-tiered strategy employed by Netanyahu to address two of the Israeli-state's primary internal political problems. The first tier was primarily an *economic strategy* to reduce the government's fiscal responsibility towards ultra-Orthodox Jews. The goal of this policy was to get more ultra-Orthodox Jews in the workforce and to wean them away from government benefit programs. Netanyahu all but admitted this strategy when he discussed the benefits of the 2003 welfare reform to a group of ultra-Orthodox Jews in 2007. He said that a "positive thing [that] happened" was that "[m]embers of the haredi [ultra-Orthodox] public seriously joined the workforce" (Sela 2007). The second more subtle tier was the continuation of a longstanding *demographic strategy* to create a population balance that favored Jewish Israelis over Palestinian citizens of Israel. For Netanyahu, the Palestinian citizens of Israel constituted a "demographic threat" to Jewish-Israelis and on many occasions he discussed this "threat" publically. Most notably, he ignited a controversy in Israel during the 2003 Herzliya Conference when he unabashedly stated "[i]f there is a demographic problem, and there is, it is with the Israeli Arabs" (Benn 2003).

While Netanyahu never stated publically that the 2003 welfare cuts had this two-tiered structure, I believe the following quote from *Haaretz* in January 2005 revealed the nature of his intentions.

> Senior treasury officials, some say the finance minister himself [Binyamin Netanyahu], were anonymously proud this week that the cut in child allowances not only saved a lot of money, but also, they said, caused a 3.4 percent decline in the birthrate among Israeli Arab [Palestinian citizens of Israel] citizens. (Sinai 2005)

According to this quote, the economic benefit from the 2003 welfare cuts was clear: the Israeli government "saved a lot of money" from child allowance cuts. In addition to the economic benefit, there was also a demographic benefit for Jewish-Israelis: "a 3.4 percent decline in the birthrate among Israeli Arab citizens."

Netanyahu later made statements that the 2003 welfare cuts were not intended to demographically impact ultra-Orthodox Jews (as a way to lower their fertility rates). For example, in 2007, he offered several ideas about how the economic damage done by child allowance cuts could be offset for "[Jewish-Israeli] families blessed with children." He said that the Jewish Agency[12] should assist Jewish-Israelis by providing child allowances or the Israeli-state should offer a "[n]egative income tax for a person who is working and was blessed with children" (Sela 2007).

Conclusion

The longstanding belief that the Palestinian citizens of Israel constitute a "demographic threat" to Jewish-Israelis has caused the Israeli-state to create strategies and policies that attempt to counteract this perceived threat. The biggest demographic 'advantage' Palestinian citizens of Israel have is their relatively high fertility rates in comparison to Jewish-Israelis. This is the reason why the Israeli-state has placed great effort throughout its history in trying to devise schemes that will maximize the fertility rates of Jewish-Israelis while at the same time minimize the fertility rates of Palestinian citizens of Israel.

In my opinion, Netanyahu's 2003 welfare reform, including the child allowance cuts, was a two-tiered strategy that attempted to address longstanding concerns with ultra-Orthodox Jews and Palestinian citizens of Israel. The child allowance cuts were meant to be part of a broader economic welfare reform aimed to encourage ultra-Orthodox Jews to participate more in the Israeli workforce. The fact that the 2003 welfare cuts were economically aimed at the ultra-Orthodox Jews hid the fact that it also served as a continuation of a longstanding demographic strategy to curb the fertility rates of the Palestinian citizens of Israel. This is not in accordance with human right principles which demand that people have the "right to make decisions concerning reproduction free of discrimination [and]coercion."[13]

References

Arad, Uzi. 2001. *The Balance of National Strength and Security: Policy Directions*. Written with the assistance of Amos Gilboa, Aviezer Ya'ari, and Ilan Amit. New York, N.Y.: The American Jewish Committee.

Asad, Talal. 1994. "Ethnographic Representation, Statistics and Modern Power." *Social Research*, 61 (1), pp. 55-88.

12 Before the establishment of the state of Israel, the Jewish Agency was considered the pre-state Jewish government. Presently, in addition to other roles, the Jewish Agency helps facilitate economic development in Israel.

13 Programme of Action of the United Nations International Conference on Population and Development in Cairo, Egypt 1994. http://www.unfpa.org/icpd/icpd_poa.htm , "Chapter VII Reproductive Rights and Reproductive Health", 7.3

Bacchi, Roberto. 1974. *The Population of Israel. Jerusalem*. Institute of Contemporary Jewry.

Ben-Gurion, David. 1971. *Israel: A Personal History*. Funk and Wagnalls, New York.

Benn, Aluf. 2003, December 18. "Netanyahu: Israel's Arabs are the Real Demographic Threat." *haaretz.com* [online].

Cohen, Alma, Rajeev Dehejia, and Dmitri Romanov. 2007. *Do Financial Incentive Affect Fertility?* Discussion Paper No. 605. Harvard John M. Olin Center for Law, Economics, and Business. Cambridge, MA: Harvard Law School.

Davis, Uri, et al. 1980. Israel's Water Policies. *Journal of Palestine Studies*, 9 (2), pp. 3-31.

Deshen, Shlomo. 1997. "The Situational Analysis of Religious Change Revisited." In Todd M. Endelman,ed. *Comparing Jewish Societies*, pp. 343-358. Ann Arbor: The University of Michigan Press.

Doron, Abraham and Ralph M. Kramer. 1991. *The Welfare State in Israel: The Evolution of Social Security Policy and Practice*. Westview Press, Boulder.

Foucault, Michel. 1977. *Discipline and Punish: The Birth of the Prison*. Alan Sheridan, translator. New York: Pantheon Books.

– 1991. "Governmentality." In Graham Burchell, Colin Gordon and Peter Miller, eds. *The Foucault Effect: Studies in Governmentality with Two Lectures by and an Interview with Michel Foucault,* pp. 87-104. Chicago: University of Chicago Press.

Friedlander, Dov. 1974. "Population Policy in Israel." In Bernard Berelson, ed. *Population Policy in Developed Countries*, pp. 42-97. New York: McGraw-Hill.

Friedlander, Dov and Calvin Goldscheider. 1979. *The Population of Israel*. New York: Columbia University Press.

Hacking, Ian. 1990. *The Taming of Chance*. Cambridge: Cambridge University Press.

Human Rights Watch. 2002. *Israel: Cuts in Child Allowance Discriminate Against Palestinian Arab June 7, 2002*. http://hrw.org/english/docs/2002/06/07/isrlpa4026_txt.htm

Ilan, Shahar. 2008, January 13. "Statistics Bureau Reports Sharp Decline in Haredi Birth Rates." *haaretz.com* [online].

– 2008, June 2. "Child Welfare Doesn't Benefit Society." *haaretz.com*.

IMFA (Israel Ministry of Foreign Affairs). 1998. *The National Insurance Institute and Social Services*. www.mfa.gov.il/MFA/Archive/Communiques/1998/THE%20NATIONAL%20INSURANCE%20INSTITUTE%20AND%20SOCIAL%20SERVIC.

Izenberg, Dan. 1992, July 15. "Proposed Child Allowance Bill Meant to Test Rabin's Intentions." *The Jerusalem Post* [online].

– 1993, December 23. "Tempers Boil Over in Knesset Budget Debate." *The Jerusalem Post* [online].

JPS (Journal of Palestine Studies). 2001. "The Herzliya Conference on the Balance of National Strength and Security in Israel." *Journal of Palestine Studies,* 31 (1), pp. 50-61.

Kadman, Yitzhak. 2005, February 1. "A More Effective Birth Control." *haaretz.com* [online].

Kalpagam, U. 2000. "The Colonial State and Statistical Knowledge." *History of the Human Sciences*, 13, pp. 37-55.

Kanaaneh, Rhoda Ann. 2002. *Birthing the Nation: Strategies of Palestinian Women in Israel*. Berkeley: University of California Press.

Keren-Yaar, Hana. 1974. *Large-Family Beneficiaries by Place of Residence, 1973 – Survey No. 13. Jerusalem*: National Insurance Institute (in Hebrew).

Kimmerling, Baruch and Joel S. Migdal. 2002. *Palestinians: The Making of a People (Enlarged Edition)*. New York: Free Press.

King, Leslie. 2001. "From Pronatalism to Social Welfare? Extending Family Allowances to Minority Populations in France and Israel." *European Journal of Population*, 17 (4), pp. 305-322.

Leibler, Anat and Daniel Breslau. 2005. "The Uncounted: Citizenship and Exclusion in the Israeli Census of 1948." *Ethnic and Racial Studies,* 28 (5), pp. 880-902.

Morris, Benny. 1987. *The Birth of the Palestinian Refugee Problem, 1947-1949*. Cambridge: Cambridge University Press.

Odenheimer, Alisa. 1992, December 9. "Child Allowance Reform Bill Begins in February." *The Jerusalem Post* [online].

Porter, Theodore M. 1986. *The Rise of Statistical Thinking, 1820-1900*. Princeton: Princeton University Press.

Rosenblum, Jonathan. 2003, April 11. "In Every Generation There Rises Up Against Us." *The Jerusalem Post* [online].

Rosenhek, Zeev. 1999. "The Exclusionary Logic of the Welfare State: Palestinian Citizens in the Israeli Welfare State." *International Sociology,* 14(2), pp. 195-215.

Sarig, Merav. 2002, November 1. "Birth of a Nation." *haaretz.com* [online].

Schiff, Gary. 1978. "The Politics of Population in Israel." *Forum on the Jewish People, Zionism and Israel*, 28-29, pp. 173-192.

Sela, Neta. 2007, March 3. "Netanyahu Pensions Cut – Arabs' Birth Rate Declined." *ynetnews.com* [online].

Sharon, Esther. 1987. "Children's Allowances System in Israel: 1959-1987." *Rivon L'kalkala*, 33, pp. 202-16 (in Hebrew).

Sheleg, Yair. March 23, 2001. "A Very Moving Scenario." *www.haaretz.com* [accessed Sept. 18, 2008].

– May 27, 2004. "The Demographics Point to a Binational State." *www.haaretz.com* [accessed Sept. 18, 2008].

Shokeid, Moshe. 2001. "On the Sins We Did Not Commit in the Research of Oriental Jews." *Israel Studies*, 6 (1), pp. 15-33.

Sinai, Ruth. 2005, January 27. "Arab Kids Aren't A Joy." www.*haaretz.com* [online].

Swirski, Barbara, Hatim Kanaaneh, and Amy Avgar. 1998. "Health Care in Israel." *The Israel Equality Monitor (Adva Center, Tel Aviv)*, 9, pp. 1-32.

Tzur, R. and L. Davids. 1984. "Recent population concerns and government action in Israel." *Middle East Focus*, 7 (1), pp. 14–27.

USDS (United States Department of State). 2003. Israel and the Occupied Territories. Bureau of Democracy, Human Rights, and Labor: *Country Reports on Human Rights Practices – 2002. March 31, 2003.* http://www.state.gov/g/drl/rls/hrrpt/2002/18278.htm [accessed Sept. 18, 2008].

Wiemer, Reinhard. 1983. "Zionism and the Arabs after the Establishment of the State of Israel." In Alexander Schölch, ed. *Palestinians over the Green Line,* pp. 26-63. London: Ithaca Press.

Yuval-Davis, Nira. 1982. *Israeli Women and Men: Divisions Behind the Unity.* London: Change Publications.

– 1989. "National reproduction and "the demographic race" in Israel." In Nira Yuval-Davis and Floya Anthias, eds. *Woman–Nation–State*, pp. 92-109. MacMillan, London.

Chapter 15

The Right to Reproductive Self-Determination of Indigenous Peoples under Human Rights Law

Ricardo M. Pereira

Introduction[1]

As early as the seventeenth century there were attempts by international lawyers (Francisco de Victoria's "Spanish School of International Law") to protect indigenous peoples from the massacres of the Spanish conquistadors in the Americas through legal and moral theories deriving from natural law (Reisman 1995). However, these pre-positivist conceptions of natural law could not withstand the legal positivism of the nineteenth century. Since positive international law, in its classical form, was only applicable to States, aboriginal populations were not considered subjects of international law. Thus, no international legal protection for indigenous peoples existed at that time (Lerner 1991).

The few remaining guardians of indigenous peoples in the Americas were Christian missionaries such as the Jesuits, whose efforts are viewed as a mixed blessing. They tried to protect the Indians from killing and slavery, but introduced a policy of assimilation, attempting to 'civilise' and 'discipline' them. Since vibrant indigenous cultures were actually antithetical to the missionaries' aims (Hannum 1998), not only indigenous peoples' physical existence was threatened, but also their cultural survival. Ironically, the gathering of small villages into larger Indian missions actually made it easier for slave raiders to capture larger numbers of people with less effort (Abreu 1997).

Indigenous peoples have had a tragic history of forced assimilation and deprivation of their lands in many parts of the world. While descendents of European settlers achieved political independence from the colonial powers, indigenous peoples within the former colonies remained the target of discrimination and deprivation of their lands ('internal colonialism') (Daes 2000, p. 302). As indigenous peoples did not hold title to land in a way that European legal systems recognised, it was easy to divorce them from their ancestral territories to make way for colonial landowners. Tribes were assigned to reservations on marginal land, yet history has shown that even these are rarely sacrosanct even today.

Indian treaties with European powers concerning their land rights were usually disregarded once colonies gained independence. Subsequently indigenous rights,

[1] I would like to thank Matthew Bradby and the editors of this book for their helpful comments and suggestions to earlier drafts of this paper. Any errors are mine.

unlike the rights of religious and other minorities, were not recognised as an issue of international concern (Hannum 1998). In a pivotal decision in the *Cayuga Indians* case,[2] the British-American Arbitration Panel of 1926 held that the Cayuga Nation and the Cayuga as individuals had *no* status under international law. The international legal instruments that emerged soon after WWII, such as the UN Charter and the 1948 Genocide Convention,[3] did not protect indigenous peoples from 'cultural genocide' (Nettheim 1998, p. 108).

Neither the Universal Declaration of Human Rights (UDHR), nor the 1966 Covenants,[4] the UN Covenant on Racial Discrimination,[5] the European[6] or the Inter-American Human Rights instruments,[7] refer specifically to indigenous peoples. Much to their dismay, indigenous cultures are still viewed today by some governments as an anachronistic stage in human development. However the growth of international human rights law in recent decades has challenged this view, demanding modernisation of classical international law, so as to place individuals and groups of individuals as beneficiaries of international human rights (Falk 1992).

This paper analyses one aspect of post-colonialism, the practice of sterilisation and forceful birth control programmes aimed at indigenous women in certain countries, and it challenges the legality of these practices in light of the right to self-determination under international law, in relation to which, as shall be argued in this paper, the right to 'reproductive self-determination' is a subcategory. It shall thus examine whether a right to reproductive autonomy could be derived from the right to self-determination under international law.

Specifically, the first part of the paper will discuss estimates of indigenous populations and subsequently the problem of defining indigenous peoples under international law. There will then be an analysis of the legality of forceful birth control programmes as practiced against indigenous peoples (including two case-studies). Finally, an argument will be made that the right to reproductive self-determination can be derived from the right to self-determination and the right to health under international human rights law.

---

2 Cayuga Indians (Gr. Brit.) v. United States, 6 R.I.A.A. 173 (US-Brit Arbitration Tribunal 1926) (See Reisman 1995).

3 See Article 2 of the United Nations Convention on the Prevention and Punishment of the Crime of Genocide, United Nations Treaty Collection, UN: New York, 9 December 1948.

4 See e.g. UN Covenant on Economic, Social and Cultural Rights (New York: UN, 1996), GA Res. 2200 (XXI) 21 UN GAOR Supp. (No. 16) at 52, UN Doc. A/6316.

5 UN Convention of the Elimination of All Forms of Racial Discrimination (New York: UN, 1965).

6 European Convention on Human Rights, United Nations Treaty Series, 213 (New York: UN 1959), 221.

7 See e.g. Organisation of American States, American Convention on Human Rights, Organisation of American States Treaty Series, 1 (1969) 1.

Indigenous Peoples and Population Politics

Recent estimates have shown that there are between 257 and 350 million indigenous people worldwide (Vinding 2005 cited in Stephens et al. 2005, p. 11). Almost 200 million indigenous people are from Asia (China, South Asia, the former Soviet Republic and Southeast Asia), while 28 million are from Latin America,[8] 2.7 million indigenous peoples from the United States and Canada and 0.6 million from Australia and New Zealand (Montenegro and Stephens 2006).[9] Worldwide there are approximately 100 uncontacted tribes (the latest discovered near the border of Brazil and Peru on 29 May 2008), though their demographic survival is continually threatened by repression, dispossession of their lands and disease (the so-called McNeill effect).[10]

Despite this, there has been suggestion that the indigenous population in some parts of the world is recovering. The Programme for Action of the 1994 International Conference on Population and Development (ICPD) stated that:

> In some regions of the world, indigenous people, after long periods of population loss, are experiencing steady and in some places rapid population growth resulting from declining mortality, although morbidity and mortality are generally still much higher than for other sections of the national population. In other regions, however, they are still experiencing a steady population decline as a result of contact with external diseases, loss of land and resources, ecological destruction, displacement, resettlement and disruption of their families, communities and social systems.

Latin America and the Caribbean, for example, present a picture of population recovery. Citing several authoritative studies, Montenegro and Stephens (2006, p. 1860-1861) provide the following figures:

> The estimated total population of indigenous peoples before European invasion ranged from 52.9 to 150 million ... Within 100 years, the estimated total Indigenous populations dropped ... to 11 million. [Henceforth] in the 18th Century Indigenous populations represented merely 1.6% of the total population. However, some demographic recovery seems to have taken place: in 1960, the total Indigenous population of Latin America and the Caribbean was estimated as 14.1 million; by 2003 it was more than 48.4 million.

Nevertheless they point out that even though the total indigenous population may have recovered, there are fewer distinct groups. In Brazil the total number

---

8 While indigenous peoples account to only 0.2% of the population of Brazil, Latin America's largest country, they account to 71% of the total population of Bolivia (Montenegro and Stephens 2006, p. 1860).

9 Those four countries were the only ones to vote against the UN Declaration on the Rights of Indigenous Peoples adopted by the General Assembly on 13 September 2007.

10 See http://www.survival-international.org/campaigns/uncontactedtribes [accessed on 7 August 2008].

of indigenous groups has fallen from around 1000 (in the 17th Century) to 222 at the latest estimate (Montenegro and Stephens 2006).

Population policies have tended to be top-down and based on targets,[11] disregarding the particular situation of indigenous peoples. The UN Millennium Development Goals[12] are based on big targets and big numbers at national and international levels (Stephens et al. 2006). Yet for marginalised indigenous groups, such nationwide population targets fail to take into account that indigenous tribes are often represented by small numbers. A few deaths within indigenous populations are irrelevant for the attainment of a 'national target' of mortality control, but have a significant impact upon tribes which are demographically fragile.[13]

Estimates of indigenous populations vary according to the way "indigeneity" is defined and measured. It has been suggested that the development of *self*-definition of "indigeneity" may help explain the apparent recovery in population numbers (Stephens et al. 2006). It is hence paramount that the problem of finding a definition of indigenous peoples in international law is discussed.

The Definition of Indigenous Peoples in International Law

At present there is no widely accepted definition of 'indigenous peoples' under international law. An agreed definition failed to materialise in the UN Declaration on the Rights of Indigenous Peoples (UNDIP) adopted by the General Assembly on 13 September 2007. Even though no UN definition of indigenous peoples has been adopted, UN practice has been largely guided by a working definition provided by the UN Special Rapporteur Jose R. Martinez Cobo in a 1986 report (Barsh 1986), which stated that indigenous peoples are those "*having continuity with pre-invasion and pre-colonial societies* that developed on their territories" and "consider themselves distinct from other sectors of the societies now prevailing in those territories, or parts of them" and who presently form

11 Yet at the 1994 ICPD Conference there was consensus that governments needed to "shift emphasis from a top-down imposition of 'population control' measures to community-based programs that better respond to the needs of individuals and families".

12 United Nations. United Nations Millennium Declaration: United Nations, 2000.

13 The subject of population politics has become a taboo-subject for much of the past century. The belief that technological development is able to match any deficiencies in food supplies and any increase in population numbers has challenged the Malthusian theory that population growth would eventually outstrip food supplies. Yet the recent global crisis which has arisen from the food shortages and the hiking of prices of a great number of agricultural commodities, a crisis that has been largely blamed on the increasing global demand for bio-fuels and consequent exhaustion of agricultural lands to meet this global demand, has shed some doubt over those post-Malthusian theories and has led to a recurrent debate on global population policies.

"non-dominant sectors of society" with a determination to maintain "their own cultural patterns, social institutions and legal systems."[14]

The above definition is most easily applied in the Americas and Australasia. It is less straightforward to identify pre-invasion and pre-colonial societies in Africa and Asia, where in many cases Europeans colonised lands which had already been occupied by successive waves of invaders in historical times.[15] Nomadic tribes and the indigenous peoples of Asia and Africa often found themselves at the bottom of a social and political hierarchy, below both new European and older, local masters who re-asserted themselves in the post-colonial period. Other communities found themselves drawn into the territorial boundaries of expanding states (such as the Buriyat in Russian Siberia).[16]

The International Labour Organisation (ILO) Convention 169 article 1(1)[17] and World Bank Operational Directive 4.2 contain a definition of indigenous peoples which is wider in scope, as they do not necessarily require historical continuity with pre-colonial societies (Barsh 1986). The ILO Convention mentions "tribal or semi-tribal peoples" and also applies to immigrant or nomadic communities with a non-historic presence in a State. However, this looser definition of indigenous peoples in the Convention has led some governments, notably those of Brazil and Bolivia, to advance that it only applies to "forest-dwelling" populations and not to settled rural populations (Thornberry 1991).

One of the distinguishing features between minorities in general and indigenous peoples in particular is the indigenous claim to have collective property rights to land and natural resources based on historical associations,[18] together with a specific request for some degree of autonomy and self-determination (Daes

---

14 Special Rapporteur, Jose R. Martinez Cobo, *Study of the Problem of Discrimination Against Indigenous Populations* UN Doc. E/CN.4/Sub.2/1986.

15 See the Advisory Opinion of the International Court of Justice in the Western Sahara case, 1975 ICJ Rep. 12, 33.

16 A leading work on the subject is the article by Benedict Kingsbury, 1998. Indigenous Peoples" in International Law: A Constructivist Approach to the Asian Controversy, *American Journal of International Law* vol.92, issue 3 (1998), 414-457. In the UN working group's fourth session, the USSR, India and China contended that there were no indigenous peoples in Asia, only minorities (Barsh 1986). After over 140 years of forceful assimilation, the Ainu, who are the original inhabitants of the Hokkaido island in Northern Japan, have been granted the status of "indigenous people" by the Japanese parliament on 6 June 2008, which has unanimously adopted a resolution recognising the Ainu as "indigenous people that have their own language, religion and cultural identity". Bear-worshipping minority is granted special status by Japan, *The Telegraph,* June 7, 2008.

17 Convention (No. 169) concerning Indigenous and Tribal Peoples in Independent Countries, adopted on 27 June 1989 by the General Conference of the International Labour Organisation at its seventy-sixth session.

18 The United Nations Conference on Environment and Development 1992 'Earth Summit' in Rio de Janeiro.

2000). However, it is language which has been used to define "indigeneity" in most census counts (Montenegro and Stephens 2006). Language is a paramount means of self-identification and group-identification, and in Latin America alone there are roughly 400 different indigenous languages.[19]

The definition of indigenous peoples has thus a major impact on estimates of indigenous populations. It is also very significant in any government policy of fertility control which may affect indigenous peoples.

Indigenous Peoples and Forceful Birth Control Programmes

There is arguably a need for lawful efforts at birth control, including the distribution of contraceptives and family planning, since the state has a duty to guarantee the health of the population and to ensure that resources are available to future generations, which could be undermined by uncontrolled population growth, especially as the rates of fertility tend to be higher in the poorest parts of the planet.[20] In fact, it has been suggested that reproductive health and access to family planning is a fundamental human right (Babor 1999). Even though reproductive health is not specifically mentioned in the UN Declaration on Human Rights nor any of the 1966 Covenants, it could be seen as forming part of the broader right to health as enshrined in those international agreements (Eriksson 2000). Moreover, other civil and political rights could be invoked to uphold reproductive health and freedom, in particular the right to life,[21] the prohibition against inhuman and degrading treatment[22] and the right to private and family life,[23] which could be used to secure safe abortions and childbirth, confidentiality of patients seeking reproductive health services, respect for those living with HIV/AIDS and measures to reduce violence against and trafficking of women (Cook et al. 2003).

---

19 World Bank. HRO Dissemination Notes Number 8, June 7, 1993. Human Resources Development and Operations Policy. 1993.

20 High Birth Rates Threatens to Trap Africa in Cycle of Poverty, *The Guardian,* September 1, 2006.

21 See e.g. Article 6(1) of the of the Covenant on Civil and Political Rights and Article 2 of the European Convention for the Protection of Human Rights and Fundamental Freedoms. General Comment no. 6 of the UN Human Rights Committee states that the right to life could not be interpreted in a restrictive manner (i.e. the prohibition from capital punishment) but must include a positive obligation from the State, for example, to introduce measures necessary to reduce infant mortality and to increase life expectancy.

22 Article 7 of the International Convent on Civil and Political Rights states that "No one shall be subjected to torture or to cruel, inhuman or degrading treatment or punishment. In particular, *no one shall be subjected without his free consent to medical or scientific experimentation*" (emphasis added).

23 See Article 8 of the European Convention on Human Rights, Council of Europe Treaty Series, 4 November 1950.

However, this principle is open to abuse, where for example a state, or racist practitioners within the state, may seek to control an ethnic or social class within its borders (eugenic practices). This could lead to *forceful* interventions aimed at controlling the population growth of one or more specific communities. This would offend the principle of "reproductive freedom" defined as "the individual's choice to reproduce or not to reproduce" (Hernandez 1991), which has to be recognised within the context of other civil liberties and human rights guarantees.

Indigenous peoples have been targeted by forced state-sponsored sterilisation and other coercive birth control programmes which violate their reproductive rights. A notorious state-sponsored programme led to the mass sterilisation of nearly 250,000 poor women (the majority of which were indigenous) by the Fujimori government in Peru between 1996 and 2000 (Miranda and Yamin 2004). Other well-documented examples of forceful interference with indigenous peoples' reproductive rights are the US sterilisation programmes of indigenous women in the twentieth century (Dog 1990) and the Australian government's forceful removal of aboriginal children from their families between 1900 and 1969.[24] In each case, the dominant society argued that it was acting in the national interest and for the communities' own good, though the indigenous people themselves are dissenters from this view. Other countries have tried to control childbearing through coercive programmes, notoriously China's one-child policy and the sterilisation abuses in India in the 1975 "emergency" and the subsequent re-emergence in India of provider targets and disincentive schemes (Germain 2004).

Both the 1994 International Conference on Population Development[25] and the 1995 Beijing World Conference on Women Declaration[26] have held *non-coercion* to be fundamental to population and reproductive health programmes and "*coercion in any form is unacceptable*" (Babor 1999, p. 118) Reproductive policy should "address both the socio-economic forces which contribute to high rates of fertility as well as offer comprehensive reproductive health care and informed choice for every inhabitant" (Babor 1999, p. 118), but this is antithetical to the use of force. Policies focused on birth quotas and sterilisation inevitably conflict with the basic right of women to decide how many children they will bear.

Sterilisation programmes that target one specific group in the community could amount to acts of genocide and to a violation of Article 2 of the UN 1948 Genocide Convention, which prohibits "*measures intended to prevent births within a group*" with "*intent to destroy, in whole or in part, a national, ethnical, racial*

---

24 See http://news.bbc.co.uk/1/hi/world/asia-pacific/6937222.stm [accessed on 7 August 2008].

25 See para. 7.3 of the UN Population and Development Programme of Action adopted at the International Conference on Population and Development, Cairo (New York, UN, ST/ESA/SER.A/149, 1994).

26 U.N. Doc. A/CONF.177/20 (1995).

or religious group."[27] Australia's removal of aboriginal children from their families violates Article 2 (e) of the Convention and Article 6 (e) of the Rome Statute of the International Criminal Court,[28] which prohibit "forcefully transferring children from one group to another group." However, the crime of genocide requires evidence of specific "*intent to destroy (...) a group*" which has proved difficult to establish in specific cases (Cassese 2003).

There may be a need for *limited* incentives in order to guarantee the overall effectiveness of family planning programmes, but a state sponsored practice of forceful sterilisation would most clearly contravene a state's obligations under international human rights law (Babor 1999).

Case-Study: Peru's Family Planning Programme

Between 1996 and 2000 more than 250,000 women, the overwhelming majority of whom were poor and indigenous, underwent sterilisation without a proper consent process during the implementation of Peru's family planning public health policy (Miranda and Yamin 2004). The programme was undertaken in the remote, rural areas of the Andean sierra and Peruvian Amazon region, which are heavily indigenous. It aimed at reducing the population growth rate to 1.17%, having successfully reduced fertility from 2% in 1981-1993 to 1.7% in 1993-2002 during President Alberto Fujimori's term (Miranda and Yamin 2004). However, there were still many disparities between the rates of fertility in the urban and rural areas. Even though the national total fertility rate reached 2.2 in 2000, in rural areas it remained at 4.3 (Miranda and Yamin 2004).

The Peruvian Congress legalised sterilisation for family planning shortly after Fujimori announced in his second inaugural speech in July 1995 that family planning would be a priority for his government (Miranda and Yamin 2004). The Peruvian Human Rights Ombudsman Office has played a vital role in documenting gross violations of human rights during the implementation of the programme. However, it was not until President Alejandro Toledo assumed power in 2001 that formal investigations were launched into the reproductive health programme. The findings of the two investigations were that gross violations of women's reproductive rights had taken place and were thus denounced. Further, the Ombudsman Office issued another Report in September 2002[29] which has found that, in the case of sterilisations, local health-care workers were

---

27 UN Convention on the Prevention and Prohibition of the Crime of Genocide, adopted by Resolution 260 (III) A of the U.N. General Assembly on 9 December 1948

28 The Rome Statute of the International Criminal Court, A/CONF.183/9 of 17 July 1998, which came into force on 1 July 2002.

29 Defensoria del Pueblo, Informe Defensorial No. 69. Lima: Defensoria del Pueblo, November 2002.

required to meet quotas, creating incentives for coercive and negligent behaviour (Miranda and Yamin 2004).

There was no system through which individuals could claim redress for violations of their human rights under the Peruvian law (Miranda and Yamin 2004). Given those difficulties, the regional international human rights organisations may provide an alternative forum to address claims of human rights abuses during the implementation of the programme. Thus, it is encouraging that the Inter-American Human Rights Commission found the government of Peru responsible for the forceful sterilisation and death of Mamerita Mestanza Chavez as a result of the operation.[30] It remains to be seen whether the IAHRC will play an active role in obtaining redress for other victims of Peru's notorious family planning programme.

Case-Study: Australia's Stolen Generation

Australia was colonised by the British with almost no recognition of the existing legal order (Sanders 1993). The Federal Constitution at the turn of the century stated that the federal government could not legislate for Aboriginals and they were not counted in the census. Reservations were established without any degree of autonomy, and when Aboriginal rights were first litigated in the 1972 *Milirrpum v Nabalco* case, all the substantive arguments were rejected. Even though reforms in 1975 recognised aboriginals as the actual owners of their lands, it established 'land councils' for the management of reservation lands. However, it was not until 1992 that the Australian High Court upheld in *Mabo v Queensland*[31] the aboriginal land rights of the Torres Strait Islanders, rejecting the earlier judicial notion of *terra nullius* (Sanders 1993).

The constitution of the Australian Federation of 1901, for the next 50-60 years after its formation, was based on the 'White Australia' policy which encouraged white settlement, while a 'protectorate' system was applied to indigenous peoples. This 'protectorate' system prohibited indigenous peoples from marrying and forming families without the consent the state (Weller 2007). Furthermore, responsibility for Aboriginal affairs, in effect, remained with the former colonies, which became State governments after federation (Anderson 2006).

The 1997 '*Bringing Them Home*' study found that at least 100,000 Aborigines, in particular mixed race children from white and Aboriginal parents, were taken away from their parents and placed in the care of institutions, religious missions or white foster families.[32] In a landmark ruling in August 2007, South Australia's

---

30 Case 12.191. Report no. 66/00 *Maria Mamerita Mestanza Chavez.*

31 *Mabo v Queensland* Australian Law Reports 107, 1992.

32 Bringing them Home: Report of the National Inquiry into the Separation of Aboriginal and Torres Strait Islander Children from their Families, HREOC, 1997, available online

Supreme Court awarded compensation for the first time to a 'Stolen Generation' victim.[33] Against this background, recently elected Australian Prime Minister Kevin Rudd has apologised for the tragedies faced by aboriginal families of the 'Stolen Generation', breaking with the right-wing Howard administration's disregard for this issue (Anderson 2007). It remains to be seen whether the apology will translate into monetary compensation for more victims. The apology is only a "first step by acknowledging the past and laying claim to a future that embraces all Australians"[34] and as Jenny Macklin, the Australian minister for Families, Housing, Community Services and Indigenous Affairs has reportedly put it, "We have serious inequalities between indigenous and non-indigenous Australians. The apology is symbolic, but there's a lot of hard work to be done to reverse those inequalities." Moreover, it has been suggested that aboriginal child removals still happen under Australian welfare legislation (Behrendt 2000), and maternal and infant mortality rates for indigenous women and children in Australia are still much higher than the national average (Anderson 2006).

The Right of Self-Determination in International Law

Self-determination allows peoples[35] "the right, in full freedom, to determine, when as they wish, their internal and external political status, without external political interference, and to pursue as they wish their political, economic, social and cultural development" (Rehman 2003). It only emerged as a principle of positive international law in the San Francisco Conference preceding the draft of the UN Charter, which culminated in the inclusion of the principle in both articles 1(2) and 55 of that instrument (Kirgis 1994). However, there is no definition of self-determination, of who are the "peoples" entitled to be beneficiaries of the right, in the Charter or in any other human rights instrument (Alfredsson 1993). One thing, however, is clear: self-determination in International Law is the right of 'all peoples'. If indigenous groups are 'peoples', then they are beneficiaries of self-determination.

Going against the so-called 'blue water' principle (which recognises self-determination only for those territories colonised by 'foreign' invaders), a more accurate doctrine advocates that the right of self-determination remains applicable

---

from the Reconciliation and Social Justice Library at http://www.austlii.edu.au/au/special/rsjproject/rsjlibrary/hreoc/stolen/prelim.html [accessed on 7 August 2008].

33 BBC news, The Agony of Australia's Stolen Generation [online], 9 August 2007 available at http://news.bbc.co.uk/1/hi/world/asia-pacific/6937222.stm. [accessed on 7 August 2008].

34 See CNN, Full Text of Australia's Apology to the Aborigines [online] available at http://edition.cnn.com/2008/WORLD/asiapcf/02/12/australia.text/index.html [accessed on 7 August 2008].

35 Article VIII of the Helsinki Final Act.

even after the colonial period (Lerner 1991). However, the International Court of Justice (ICJ) has only endorsed the principle of self-determination in its anti-colonialist form in its 1971 Advisory Opinion on Namibia[36] and in its 1975 Advisory Opinion on the Western Sahara case.[37] Similarly, the Inter-American Commission on Human Rights in the *Miskito* case, concerning a claim brought against the relocation of a large number of Miskito Indians on the Atlantic coast of Nicaragua during the civil war, concluded that international law does not recognise a right of secession to the indigenous Miskito populations[38] and that the Indians were not self-determination beneficiaries (Anaya 1996).

Significantly, an express reference to the right of self-determination is made in article 1 of both UN 1966 International Covenants and General Assembly Resolution 1514 (XV) 1960 and Resolution 2625 (XXV) 1970, with the latest expanding the concept of self-determination beyond colonialism, by recognising the right of secession of peoples when States do not conduct "*themselves in compliance with the principle of equal rights and self-determination of peoples*" or do not "*possess (...) a government representing the whole people belonging to the territory without distinction as to race, creed or colour.*"

Therefore in any country where the government adopts a policy of exclusion of peoples on grounds of race, creed or colour from political representation, or introduces policies that aim at the subjugation or extermination of indigenous peoples, the right of self-determination arises in its external form. Thus, the right to external self-determination (secession from the State) will depend on the degree of democratic representation of a government and the fundamental rights that are available to indigenous peoples. It is pertinent for this paper to discuss whether a right to *internal* self-determination for indigenous peoples to determine their future against the undue interference with their physical well-being could include the right to reproductive autonomy.

The Right to Internal Self-Determination

James Anaya (1996), recently appointed UN Special Rapporteur on Human Rights and Indigenous People, signals that governments have increasingly moved away from the tendency to equate the word self-determination with an *absolute right to form an independent state*, citing the example of the Australian government which, in a statement to the 1991 session of the UN Working Group

---

36 Legal Consequences for States of the Continued Presence of South Africa in Namibia (South West Africa) (1970), 1971 ICJ Rep. 16, 31.

37 Western Sahara, 1975 ICJ Rep. 12, 33.

38 Inter-American Commission on Human Rights, 1983. Report on the Situation of human Rights of a Segment of the Nicaragua Population of Miskito Origin, OAS Doc. OEA/Ser.L/V/II.62, doc. 10.

on Indigenous Populations, stated that self-determination must be considered broadly – not only the attainment of independent Statehood but also the assertion of identity, language, cultures, tradition, self-management and autonomy. Therefore, if external self-determination (secession from the State) is not, realistically, available or politically feasible, the question arises as to whether another form of self-determination can be substituted for its external application (Alfredsson 1993). The Human Rights Committee used the term 'internal self-determination' for the first time (Sanders 1993) and it is now a terminology followed by most authors referring to forms of self-government, autonomy, territorial integrity or exclusive enjoyment of the indigenous lands and resources.

The right of internal self-determination of indigenous peoples is enshrined in Article 4 of the UN Declaration on the Rights of Indigenous Peoples adopted by the G.A. on 13 September 2007:

> Indigenous peoples, in exercising their right to self-determination, have the right to autonomy or self-government in matters relating to their internal and local affairs, as well as ways and means for financing their autonomous functions.

The right to internal self-determination also applies in the context of policies of fertility control of indigenous peoples. Given the specific vulnerability of indigenous peoples in most societies and what makes them distinct as a people, the right to internal self-determination, the most prominent forms being the right to self-government and autonomy, must also include the indigenous right to reject government policies that force them to yield to birth control programmes.

Self-government is "the overarching political dimension of ongoing self-determination" (Anaya 1996, p. 99). The emergence of values such as democracy and the major notions of cultural and political pluralism have reinforced indigenous communities' claims for governmental and administrative autonomy, including a right to reproductive health and generational continuity. The idea, followed in many Western societies, that decisions should be made at the most local level possible reinforces the view that indigenous communities should be able to maintain their traditional decentralised system of governance and to decide for themselves on the fertility levels in their communities. In this respect, indigenous peoples should maintain their own institutions of autonomous governance, including their customary and written law and dispute resolution and adjudication mechanisms, which have existed not only *de facto*, but as the indigenous peoples correctly claim, also *de jure*, as enshrined in articles 6 and 7 of the ILO Convention on Indigenous Peoples n.° 169 (Anaya 1996).

From this perspective, autonomous governance is not only instrumental but, in my view, also necessary for indigenous peoples to control the development of their distinctive culture, including the use of land and resources and reproductive health, against the undue interference from disingenuous groups or government.

The Right to Health as a Human Right

The right to health was first articulated at the international level under the Constitution of the World Health Organisation (WHO) 1946 and subsequently established in several binding international human rights treaties[39] and national constitutions (Hunt 2007). The right to health contains a number of elements which could be legally enforceable under national law, for example the right to non-discrimination in relation to health facilities, goods and services.[40] Yet at the international level the right to health goes far beyond discrimination within health care provision (Hunt 2007).[41] A human rights-based approach to health indicators has been proposed in order to enable progressive realisation of the right to health to be monitored and measured.[42] It has been argued that a human rights approach to health could have several advantages for health care practitioners; for example, devising equitable policies and programmes that benefit the most disadvantaged, raising more funds, and improving the terms and conditions of those who work in the health sector (Hunt 2007).

The UN Special Rapporteur on the right to health pointed out in UN General Assembly Resolution A/59/422 of 8 October 2004[43] that there were profound disparities between the health of indigenous people and that of the non-indigenous population in many countries and communities, the corollary of which is that "indigenous people tend to die younger and generally live in poorer

---

39 E.g. Article 12 of the International Covenant on Economic, Social and Cultural Rights; Article 25.1 of the Universal Declaration on Human Rights; Article 5 (e) (iv) of the International Convention on the Elimination of All Forms of Racial Discrimination of 1965; Articles 11.1 (f) and 12 of the Convention on the Elimination of All Forms of Discrimination against Women of 1979 and Article 24 of the Convention on the Rights of the Child of 1989. The right to health is also recognised in a number of regional human rights instruments, for example in Article 11 of the European Social Charter of 1961 (as revised), Article 16 of the African Charter on Human and Peoples' Rights of 1981 and Article 10 of the Additional Protocol to the American Convention on Human Rights in the Area of Economic, Social and Cultural Rights of 1988.

40 UN Economic and Social Council. General Comment no. 14 'The Right to the Highest Attainable Standard of Health" (2000) available at http://www.unhchr.ch/tbs/doc.nsf/(symbol)/E.C.12.2000.4.En [accessed on 7 August 2008]

41 Paragraph 4 of General Comment no. 14 states the right to health "embraces a wide range of socio-economic factors that promote conditions in which people can lead a healthy life, and extends to the underlying determinants of health, such as food and nutrition, housing, access to safe and potable water and adequate sanitation, safe and healthy working conditions, and a healthy environment."

42 See Report of the Special Rapporteur to the UN Economic and Social Council on the Right of Everyone to the Enjoyment of the Highest Attainable Standard of Physical and Mental Health available at http://www2.essex.ac.uk/human_rights_centre/rth/docs/CHR%202006.pdf [accessed on 7 August 2008]

43 UN General Assembly. The right of everyone to the enjoyment of the highest attainable standard of physical and mental health A/59/422 8 October 2004.

health than other population groups." Those concerns were reiterated in the third session of the Permanent Forum on Indigenous Issues,[44] which also highlighted the need to address the right to health of indigenous women, including sexual and reproductive rights. Furthermore, the World Health Organisation (WHO) has published a number of reports specifically addressing health issues facing indigenous peoples,[45] urging states to "protect the right of Indigenous people to the enjoyment of the highest standard of health."[46]

Following 20 years of negotiation,[47] the adoption of the United Nations Declaration on the Rights of Indigenous Peoples by the General Assembly on 13 September 2007, in particular the health-related Articles 24 and 31 thereof, could further add support to indigenous peoples' claim for self-determination over their health, well-being and development. Even though the Declaration is not legally binding, it could reflect state's *opinio juris* and thus provide the basis for the establishment of customary international law (Charters 2007). The Declaration could also have some persuasive impact domestically and hence influence state practice, as seen in a decision of the New Zealand Court of Appeal which invoked the Declaration when upholding Maori interests in whale-watching tourism (Charters 2007).[48]

The Right to Reproductive Health

Family planning programmes are necessary public policy mechanisms for tracking reproductive and sexual health problems, given that they are preventive in nature. Even though not all sexual and reproductive ill health represents a violation of the right to health or other human rights, it could constitute a human rights violation when it arises, in whole or in part, from the failure of a duty-bearer or State to respect, protect, or fulfill a human rights obligation.[49]

---

44 Permanent Forum on Indigenous Issues, 3rd Session (E/2004/43-E/C.19/2004/23).

45 See e.g. World Health Organisation, *WTO Traditional Medicine Strategy* (2002) available at http://www.who.int/hhr/activities/indigenous/en/ [accessed on 7 August 2007] See also the Final Report of the Special Rapporteur Matinez Cobo to the 56th session of the Commission on Human Rights, Sub-Commission on Prevention of Discrimination and Protection of Minorities, *Study of the Problems of Discrimination of Indigenous Populations* (1983), available at http://www.un.org/esa/socdev/unpfii/documents/MCS_xi.pdf [accessed on 7 August 2008].

46 World Health Assembly Resolution 54.16 International Decade of the World's Indigenous Peoples (22 May 2001).

47 The Working Group on Indigenous Peoples started the negotiations on the Draft Declaration in the 1980s until the discussions were moved to the UN Human Rights Commission in the mid-1990s. The Declaration was adopted by the Human Rights Council in 2006 and finally adopted by the UN General Assembly in September 2007.

48 Ngai Tahu Maori Trust Boad v Director-General of Conservation [1995] 3 NZLR 553.

49 Economic and Social Council E/CN.4/2004/49, Report of Special Raporteur, 16 February 2004, par. 13.

The then Commission on Human Rights (which became the Human Rights Council in 2006) has confirmed in resolution 2003/28 that "sexual and reproductive health are integral elements of the right of everyone to the enjoyment of the highest attainable standard of physical and mental health."[50] In the same vein, principle 8 of the ICPD Programme of Action adopted in 1994 states that "everyone has the right to the enjoyment of the highest attainable standard of health" which includes the state's obligation to provide access to health care services "(...) related to reproductive health care, which includes family planning and sexual health." In 1995 the Platform for Action of the Beijing World Conference on Women adopted similar provisions on reproductive health,[51] the key difference being that the latter confirms the right of women to control their sexuality (Hunt and de Mesquita n.d.).

International law has recognised the concept of 'family planning' as a basic human right in relatively recent times. Specifically, the term was used in the 1965 UN Commission Resolution on the Status of Women, which states that "married couples should have access to all relevant educational information concerning family planning" (Eriksson 2000, p. 183) Yet as Eriksson (2000, p. 183) points out, the term was not applied in the context of human rights until the 1968 UN Conference on Human Rights, when it was stated that "parents have a basic human right to determine freely and responsibly the number and spacing of their children."[52]

The most important reference to family planning as a human right is however under the Convention on Elimination of All Forms of Discrimination against Women (CEDAW), which proclaims that women and men have an equal right to decide "freely and responsibly on the number and spacing of their children and to have means to enable them to exercise this right."[53] The significance of the reference to family planning under CEDAW stems from the fact that, unlike the aforementioned UN resolutions from the UN General Assembly, CEDAW is a legally binding international treaty (Eriksson 2000).[54] The CEDAW Committee has focused on problems which are faced by indigenous women in its obser-

50 Commission on Human Rights Resolution 2003/28, preamble and para. 6.

51 Compare Paragraphs 7.2 and 7.3 of the ICPS Programme of Action and Paragraphs 94 and 95 of the Beijing Platform for Action (A/CONF. 177/20/Rev.).

52 Article 16 of Final Act Proclamation, International Conference on Human Rights, Teheran 22 April to 13 May 1968. (Ibid) The principle was restated in other forms in subsequent General Assembly resolutions and UN conference concluding provisions, e.g. paragraphs 7.2 and 7.3 of the IPCD final document and in paragraph 95 of the Beijing Declaration.

53 Article 16 (1) (e) Convention on Elimination of All Forms of Discrimination against Women. Ibid, p. 184.

54 The Committee on the Elimination of All Forms of Discrimination Against Women has been transferred on 1 January 2008 to the Office of the High Commissioner on Human Rights in Geneva.

vations to state reports, which have included recommendations regarding sexual violence faced by indigenous women (Charters 2007).[55]

Hence the right to reproductive health, which includes the right to family planning, includes both a positive and a negative obligation from the State. The positive obligation involves the requirement that the State provide all the essential health care facilities and services for its population, while the negative obligation revolves around the State's need to abstain from interfering with individual reproductive choices through coercive population control programmes.

The Programme of Action of the ICPD conference defines under Chapter VII, par. 7.2 reproductive health as "as state of complete physical, mental and social well-being and not merely the absence of disease or infirmity, in all matters relating to the reproductive system and to its functions and processes", further affirming that the definition implies that people must "have the capability to reproduce and the freedom to decide if, when and how often to do so."[56] Hence the ICPD Programme of Action and Beijing Declaration and Platform for Action remain, alongside the CEDAW, the most influential and authoritative international documents on the right to reproductive and sexual health. Both documents have subsequently been strengthened in 1999 and 2000 five-year reviews (Cook et al. 2003).[57] Even though the subsequent Millennium Development Goals, which derive from the Millennium Declaration, do not expressly refer to sexual and reproductive health, at least three of the eight Goals – on maternal health, child health, and HIV/AIDS – are relevant to sexual and reproductive health.[58]

---

55 E.g. UN Committee on the Elimination of Discrimination Against Women, *Concluding Observations: Brazil*, UN Doc A/58/38 (7 July 2003) par. 62. In addition to recommendations to State reports, Optional Protocol to CEDAW, adopted by General Assembly resolution A/54/4 on 6 October 1999, introduces a system whereby communications detailing violations of the Convention may be submitted to the Committee.

56 Available at http://www.unfpa.org/icpd/icpd_poa.htm#ch7 [accessed on 7 August 2008]

57 UN General Assembly Report of the Ad Hoc Committee of the Whole of the Twenty-First Special Session of the General Assembly: Overall Review and Appraisal if the Implementation of the Programme of Action of the International Conference on Population and Development, A/S-21/5/Add.1 New York: UN, 2000; and Further Actions and Initiatives to Implement the Beijing Declaration and Platform for Action, A/S-23/10/Rev. 1) (New York: UN, 2000).

58 Economic and Social Council E/CN.4/2004/49, Report of Special Raporteur, 16 February 2004. Some states upholding a conservative ideology have prevented the explicit inclusion of the right to reproductive autonomy in the Millennium Development Declaration (Germain 2004).

Conclusion

The oppressiveness of post-colonial State systems has confronted indigenous peoples with the terrifying prospect of genocide – birth control and sterilisation programmes just being some of the crudest forms. From this perspective, what type of governmental system would be available to meet the indigenous claims for some degree of independence in order to rule their own communities and to enable them to decide how many children to have? It is realistic to say that governments will not respond to demands which, if realised, would threaten their existence as integral units. Therefore, the attempts to create international legally binding standards for indigenous peoples throughout the world will face difficulties, especially because, while certain indigenous groups or individuals in some parts of the world favour integration with the dominant society, there is a considerable majority of indigenous groups who favour some degree of self-government. It is unfortunate to conclude that these discrepancies and variations in the claims of the world's indigenous peoples are likely to be exploited by their opponents and may weaken their international force.

The right to reproductive freedom is a fundamental tool for indigenous peoples to decide their own reproductive strategies. Yet forceful birth control programmes are not the biggest threat facing indigenous peoples, but rather government policies that aim at assimilating them. As has been discussed, there are indications that indigenous populations are experiencing recovery in some parts of the planet. It is indigenous cultures, rather than population numbers, which are under the most threat. The following passage reflects the dilemma facing indigenous peoples:

> "How can the Indian be saved"? Claudio (Villas Boas) would retort, (…) "Animals can be saved from extinction because they are content to remain animals. But all humans recognise improvement, and desire the advantages of other man. As soon as there's a shop near here, Pripuri will load his canoe with mandioca flour and paddle up the Suya-Missu. After twenty trips he will buy an outboard motor and make his business more efficient. You will see, it will be the Indian themselves who will break the isolation of the park, who will destroy their tribal society. In this cultural sense, how can the Indian be saved from extinction?" (Claudio Villas Boas, cited in Cowell 1993, p. 192)

To conclude, the right to reproductive health must be seen as an integral part of the right to self-determination under international law, which delineates the degree of autonomy of indigenous peoples to self-government including reproductive strategies. Yet it is not indigenous health which is in most danger of deterioration, but cultures which could become extinct. The right of self-determination is thus paramount for indigenous peoples to triumph over assimilationist and other neo-colonial practices – of which forceful sterilisation is just one of the repellent examples.

References

Abreu, Capistrano. 1997. *Chapters of Brazil's Colonial History 1500-1800*. Oxford: Oxford University Press.

Alfredsson, Gudmundur. 1993. "The Right of Self-determination and Indigenous Peoples." In Christian Tomuschaut, ed. *Modern Law of Self-Determination, pp.* 42-54. London: Martinus Nijhoff.

Anaya, James. 1996. *Indigenous Peoples in International Law*. Oxford: Oxford University Press.

Anderson, Ian. 2006. "Indigenous Health in Australia, New Zealand, and the Pacific." *The Lancet* vol. 367 May 27.

– 2007. "The End of Aboriginal Self-Determination?" *Futures* 39, pp. 137-154.

Babor, Diana. 1999. "Population Growth and Reproductive Rights in International Human Rights Law." *Connecticut Journal of International Law* 14: 83.

Barsh, Russel. 1986. "Indigenous Peoples: An Emerging Object of International Law." *American Journal of International Law*, vol. 80, pp. 369-385.

Behrendt, Larissa. 2000. "Consent in a (Neo) Colonial Society: Aboriginal Women as Sexual and Legal 'Other'." *Australian Feminist Studies*, 15 (33), pp. 353-367.

Brownlie, Ian. 1999. *Principles of Public International Law*. Oxford: Oxford University Press.

Cassese, Antonio. 2003. *International Criminal Law*. Oxford: Oxford University Press.

Charters, Claire. 2007. "Indigenous Peoples and International Law and Policy." 18 *Public Law Review* 1.

Cook, Rebecca, Bernard Dickens, and Mahmoud Fathalla. 2003. *Reproductive Health and Human Rights: Integrating Medicine, Ethics and Law*. Oxford: Oxford University Press.

Cowell, Adrian. 1993. *The Tribe that Hides from Man*. London: Stein and Day Pub.

Daes, Erica-Irene A. 2000. "Protection of the World's Indigenous Peoples and Human Rights." In Janusz Symonides, e.d. *Human Rights: Concepts and Standards*. Ashgate.

Dog Crow, Mary. 1990. *Lakota Woman*. New York.

Eriksson, Maja. 2000. *Reproductive Freedom in the Context of International Human Rights and Humanitarian Law*. The Hague: Martinus Nijhoff Publishers.

Falk, Richard. 1992. "The Rights of Peoples (in Particular Indigenous Peoples)." In James Crawford, ed. *The Rights of Peoples*, pp. 18-32. USA: Oxford University Press.

Follesdal, Andreas. 2000. "Indigenous Minorities and the Shadow of Injustice Past." *International Journal on Minority and Group Rights* 7.

Germain, Adrienne. 2004. "Reproductive Health and Human Rights." *The Lancet*, vol. 363 January 3, p. 65.

Hannum, Hurst. 1998. "The protection of Indigenous Rights in the Inter-American System." In D.J. Harris and S. Livingstone, eds. *The American System of Human Rights*, pp.323-343. Oxford: Oxford University Press.

Harris, David. 1998. *Cases and Materials in International Law*. London: Sweet and Maxwell.

Hernandez, Berta. 1991. "To Bear or Not to Bear: Reproductive Freedom as an International Human Right." 17 *Brooklyn Journal of International Law* 309.

Higgins, Rosalyn. 1993. "Comments on Postmodern Tribalism and the Right to Secession." In Catherine Brolmann, Rene Lefeber, and Marjoleine Zieck, ed. *Peoples and Minorities in International Law*. Dordrecht: Martinus Nijhoff Publishers.

Hunt, Paul. 2007. "The Right to the Highest Attainable Standard of Health." *The Lancet* vol. 370 August 4, p. 369.

Hunt, Paul and Judith de Mesquita. N.D. *The Rights to Sexual and Reproductive* Health Human Rights Centre, University of Essex, available at http://www2.essex.ac.uk/human_rights_centre/rth/docs/TheRightsToSexual Health.pdf [accessed on 7 August 2008].

Kingsbury, Benedict. 1998. ""Indigenous Peoples" in International Law: A Constructivist Approach to the Asian Controversy." *American Journal of International Law* vol.92, issue 3, pp. 414-457.

Kirgis, Frederic Jr. 1994. "The Degrees of Self-Determination in the United Nations Era." *American Journal of International Law*, vol. 88, pp. 304-310.

Lerner, Nathan. 1991. "The 1989 ILO Convention on Indigenous Populations: New Standards?" In Dinstein and Tabory, eds. *The Protection of Minorities and Human Rights*, p. 213. The Hague: Martinus Nijhoff.

Michalowski, S. 2004. "Health Care Law." In Steve Peers and Angela Ward eds. *The EU Charter of Fundamental Rights. Politics, Law and Policy* Portland: Hart.

Miranda J. and A. Yamin. 2004. "Reproductive Health without Rights in Peru." *The Lancet* vol. 363 Jan 3.

Montenegro, R. and C. Stephens. 2006. "Indigenous Health in Latin America and the Caribbean." *The Lancet* vol. 367 June 3, p. 1860.

Nettheim, Garth. 1998. "'Peoples' and 'Populations': Indigenous Peoples and the Rights of Peoples." In James Crawford ed. *The Rights of Peoples*, pp.108-126. Oxford: Oxford University Press.

Rehman, Javaid. 2003. *International Human Rights Law: A Practical Approach*. Pearson Education.

Reisman, Michael. 1995. "Protecting Indigenous Rights in International Adjudication." *American Journal of International Law*, pp. 350-362.

Sanders, Douglas. 1993. "Self-Determination and Indigenous Peoples." In Christian Tomuschaut, ed. *Modern law of Self-Determination*, p. 59. London: Martinus Nijhoff.

Steiner, Henry and Philip Alston. 2000. *International Human Rights In Context: Law Politics and Morals.* Oxford: Oxford University Press.

Stephens, Carolyn, Clive Nettleton, John Porter, Ruth Willis, and Stephanie Clark. 2005. "Indigenous Peoples' Health – Why are they behind everyone, everywhere?" *The Lancet* vol. 366 July 2 p. 11.

Stephens, Carolyn, John Porter, Clive Nettleton, and Ruth Willis. 2006. "Disappearing, Displaced and Undervalued: A Call to Action for Indigenous Health Worldwide." *The Lancet* vol. 367.

Thornberry, Patrick. 1991. *International Law and the Rights of Minorities*, Oxford: Oxford University Press.

Turay, Khadija. 2007. "Population Policy Transition: Human Rights and Population Politics in India during the Emergency and at the Present Moment." Paper presented at the Workshop on Population Politics and Human Rights, Berlin 14-20 February.

Wallace, Rebecca. 2001. *International Human Rights: Text and Materials*. London: Sweet and Maxwell.

Weller, Penny. 2007. "Self-determination as Motif." Paper presented at the Workshop on Population Politics and Human Rights, Berlin 14-20 February.

Notes on the Contributors

Elise Andaya (Ph.D., anthropology, New York University) is assistant professor of anthropology at the University at Albany-State University of New York, U.S. Her research interests include reproductive politics and health care, kinship, gender, and statehood in Cuba and the Americas. She has published academic articles in *Medical Anthropology Quarterly*.

Sabine Berking (Ph.D., Russian literature, University of Leipzig) is a research associate at the Irmgard Coninx Foundation Berlin, where she organizes the Berlin Roundtables on Transnationality. Her research interests include migration studies and transitional societies in Eastern Europe as well as transcultural literature, and gender. Since 1999 she is a faculty member at the Berlin Institute for the International Education of Students (IES) where she teaches cultural studies and literature. She is co-editor (with Ingo K. Richter and Ralf Müller-Schmid) of *Building a Transnational Civil Society* and of *Risk Society and the Culture of Precaution (*both Palgrave, 2006*)*. She is a permanent contributor to the "Frankfurter Allgemeine Zeitung", where she has published numerous articles on international literature.

Caroline Bledsoe (Ph.D., anthropology, Stanford University) is Melville J. Herskovits Professor of African Studies and Professor of Anthropology at Northwestern University, in Evanston, Illinois, USA. A West Africanist, she has studied marriage, fertility and contraception, child fosterage, aging, and migration of Africans to Europe. She is the author of *Women and Marriage in Kpelle Society* (1980) and *Contingent Lives: Fertility, Time, and Aging in West Africa* (2002); and co-editor of *Fertility and the Male Life Cycle in the Era of Fertility Decline* (2000), *Critical Perspectives on Education and Fertility in the Developing World* (1999), *Nuptiality in sub-Saharan Africa: Contemporary Anthropological and Demographic Perspectives* (1994), and *The Social Dynamics of Adolescent Fertility in Sub Saharan Africa* (1993).

Julie Y. Chu (Ph.D., anthropology, New York University) is an assistant professor in the Department of Anthropology at the University of Chicago with interests in economy and value, ritual life, state governmentality, and the materiality and pragmatics of mobility and travel. She is currently finishing her book *Cosmologies of Credit: Fuzhounese Migration and the Politics of Destination* (Duke UP, forthcoming). In 2009, with research support from the National Science Foundation, she will launch a new three-year ethnographic project on shipping culture at the Port of Fuzhou in China.

Maja K. Eriksson (LL.D., University of Uppsala) is professor of Public International Law at the University of Uppsala. Her field of expertise includes international human rights, public international law, and humanitarian law and refugee law. She is the author of *Reproductive Freedom in the Context of International Human Rights and Humanitarian Law* (Martinus Njuhoff Publishers, 2000) and *Documents in Public International Law* (Norstedts Juridik AB, 2008). She has published academic articles and chapters in the *German Yearbook of International Law, Tidsskrift for Retsvitenskap, Women and International Human Rights Law, Commentary on the Charter of Fundamental Rights of the European Union.*

Susan Greenhalgh (Ph.D., sociocultural anthropology, Columbia University) is professor of anthropology at the University of California, Irvine. A noted expert on the population politics of China, she is the author of *Just One Child: Science and Policy in Deng's China* (California, 2008), co-author, with Edwin A. Winckler, of *Governing China's Population: From Leninist to Neoliberal Biopolitics* (Stanford, 2005), and author of *Under the Medical Gaze: Facts and Fictions of Chronic Pain* (California, 2001). She is also editor of *Situating Fertility: Anthropology and Demographic Inquiry* and co-editor of *Contending Approaches to the Political Economy of Taiwan.* In 2002 she won the Clifford C. Clogg award for early career achievement from the Population Association of America. Before joining the University of California, she served as senior research associate at the Population Council (New York) for ten years.

Homa Hoodfar (Ph.D., social anthropology, University of Kent at Canterbury) is professor of anthropology, Concordia University, Montreal, Canada. Her research emphases are on women, religion and politics in the Middle East and North Africa as well as Muslim women in diaspora communities. Among her publications are *Women, Religion and the Afghan education movement in Iran* (Journal of Development Studies, 2007, Vol. 43/2) and *The Muslim Veil in North America: issues and debates* (with Sajida Alvi and Sheila McDonough, Toronto: Canadian Scholars' Press, 2003).

Reiner Klingholz (Ph.D., chemistry, University of Hamburg) is director of the Berlin Institute for Population and Development. He worked as science editor for the German weekly DIE ZEIT and for GEO magazine. The main focus of the Berlin Institute is research on the background and implications of demographic change. Major Berlin Institute publications include: *Male Emergency, from the Heroes of Work to the New Underclass?* (2006); *The Demographic State of the Nation: how sustainable are Germany's Regions?* (2006); and *Europe's Demographic Future* (2008). All studies are available under www.berlin-institute.org

Steffen Kröhnert, (MA, social science, Humboldt University Berlin), is a researcher at the Berlin-Institute for Population and Development. He has conducted several studies focusing on regional population development and its economic and social effects in Germany and Europe. He is co-author of *Die demografische Lage der Nation* (DTV, Munich 2006) and *The demographic future of Europe* (DTV, forthcoming). He has published several articles in *Zeitschrift für Soziologie* and *Sozialer Fortschritt*.

Nayanika Mookherjee (Ph.D., social anthropology, School of Oriental and African Studies (SOAS), University of London) is a Lecturer in the Sociology Department at Lancaster University, UK. Her research interests include anthropology of politics, affect, memory, and human rights; violence and the body; political kinship and genetics; gender and feminist theories; transnational adoption and children; medical anthropology; diasporic communities and South Asia. Funded by the Wenner Gren Foundation for Anthropological Research, her book *Specters and Utopias: Sexual Violence, Public Memories and the Bangladesh War* is forthcoming with Duke University Press. She has published chapters in: *Journal of Royal Anthropological Institute, Space and Culture, Feminist Review, South Asia, Childhood, Economic and Political Weekly*. Her two ongoing research projects explore the relationship between affective structures and the nation; and genetic citizenship and transnational adoption through the prism of 'war-babies' in Bangladesh.

Ricardo Pereira (LL.M., international law, City University, London) is a Ph.D. Candidate at the Law Department, University of Essex, United Kingdom. His research interests include environmental law, agricultural law, international human rights law (in particular the rights of indigenous peoples) and international and comparative criminal law. He has published an article in *European Environmental Law Review*, vol. 16 (issue 10) October 2007 pp. 254-268, a chapter in *Theory and Practice of Harmonisation* (edited by M. Andenas and C. Anderson), Edward Elgar Publishing (forthcoming 2008), and presented papers at a number of national and international conferences in the area of European Union environmental criminal law.

Shalini Randeria (Ph.D., social anthropology, Free University Berlin) is professor of Social and Cultural Anthropology at the University of Zurich. She was a Rhodes Scholar at the University of Oxford, Max Weber Professor for Sociology at the University of Munich and Full Professor and Chair of the Department of Sociology and Social Anthropology at Central European University Budapest. Her research interests include globalization and governance, legal anthropology, the interplay between international institutions, subaltern states and non-state actors as well as development studies and post-colonial theory. She is co-editor of *World on the Move: Globalization, Migration and Cultural Security* (2004, with Jonathan Friedman) and *Vom Imperialismus zu Empire? Globalisierung aus nicht-westlicher Sicht: postkoloniale Perspektiven* (Suhrkamp 2007, with Andreas Eckert).

Lisa Ann Richey (Ph.D., political science, University of North Carolina at Chapel Hill) is Associate Professor of Development Studies in the Department of Society and Globalisation at Roskilde University in Denmark. She is the author of *Population Politics: From the Policies to the Clinics* (Palgrave 2008) and co-editor of *Women and Development* (Women's Studies Quarterly Special Issue 2003). Her recent articles have been published in *Feminist Review, New Political Science, Third World Quarterly* and *World Development*. Her current research focuses on 'brand aid,' therapeutic citizenship and the politics of antiretroviral treatment for HIV/AIDS in South Africa and Uganda.

Steven Rousso-Schindler (Ph.D., cultural anthropology, University of Southern California) is an assistant professor in the Department of Anthropology at California State University, Long Beach in the United States. His research interests include the Israeli-Palestinian conflict, demography, national narratives and narrative theory. He has published an academic article in *Anthropology News*.

Rachel Sullivan Robinson (Ph.D., sociology and demography, University of California, Berkeley) is an assistant professor at the School of International Service, American University, Washington, D.C. Her research interests include the politics of population, reproductive health, and HIV/AIDS in sub-Saharan Africa, as well as the determinants of birth timing in the United States. She has published academic articles in *Demography* and *Population Studies*.

Khadija Turay (MPH, Global Community Health and Development, Rollins School of Public Health at Emory University) is a doctoral student in the Department of Maternal and Child Health at The University of North Carolina at Chapel Hill. Her research interests include public health policy, child survival, and maternal health.

Magdalena Zolkos (Ph.D., political science, University of Copenhagen) is a researcher in political theory at the Centre for Citizenship and Public Policy, University of Western Sydney, Australia. Her research interests include women's rights, reproductive politics and critical feminist theory. She is a co-editor of *Defunct Federalisms: Critical Perspectives on Federal Failure* (Ashgate, 2008) and the author of *Transitional Justice and Subjective Life: Trauma Testimony as Political Theorizing* (Continuum, forthcoming 2009). She has published academic articles in *European Legacy, Journal of Contemporary European Studies* and *Studies in Social and Political Thought*.